Journeys on
Old Long Island

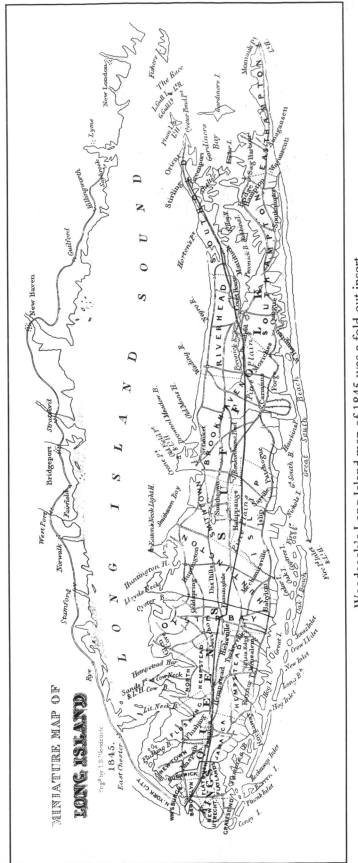

Woodcock's Long Island map of 1845 was a fold-out insert in Nathaniel S. Prime's book, *History of Long Island.*

Journeys on Old Long Island

Travelers' Accounts, Contemporary
Descriptions, and Residents' Reminiscences
1744-1893

Edited by
Natalie A. Naylor

A Long Island Studies Institute Publication
from
HOFSTRA UNIVERSITY

Empire State Books
Interlaken, New York
2002

Manufactured in the United States of America
ISBN: 1-55787-161-2
LCCN: 2002108347

Cover illustration: Coupé Rockaway Carriage, 1871. The rockaway was developed in the 1830s by a carriage maker in Jamaica and named for the nearby seaside resort. The vehicle could be driven by a coachman or the owner, and the style became very popular. This particular carriage was built by A.S. Flandrau in New York City in 1871 and could be converted to an open-air vehicle. Owned by the same family for four generations, the exterior and interior are original. Franklin Joseph of Garden City, a relative of the original owner, donated this rockaway in 1962, which is displayed in the carriage collections of the Long Island Museum of American Art, History & Carriages in Stony Brook. Photograph and permission to reproduce courtesy of the Long Island Museum. On the rockaway carriage, see also the Museum's publications, *The Carriage Collection* (1986), pp. 45-47, and *19th Century American Carriages: Their Manufacture, Decoration and Use* (1987), p. 42.

A *quality* publication by
Heart of the Lakes Publishing
Interlaken, New York 14847

Contents

Illustrations

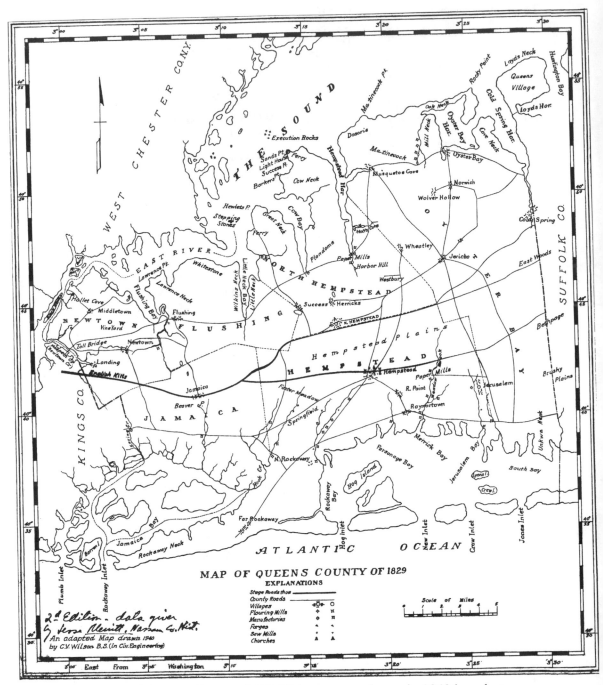

Map of Queens County, 1829. This map was drawn in 1940 based on information from the Nassau County Historian, Jesse Merritt. Lloyd Neck ("Queens Village") was part of the Town of Oyster Bay until 1881, and the Rockaway Peninsula ("Rockaway Neck") was part of the Town of Hempstead until 1898.

Introduction

Natalie A. Naylor

Accounts by travelers have been an important source for historians since they often are explicit about what residents take for granted. Among the classics in this genre are Alexis de Tocqueville's *Democracy in America* (1835) and Harriet Martineau's *Society in America* (1837). Although Long Island was not on the usual route European travelers followed on their American tours, in the colonial period it was a shortcut to Boston for some travelers (including George Washington in 1756). Moreover, it was a destination for many Anglican missionaries, Presbyterian ministers, and traveling Quaker ministers.[1] Ettie C. Hedges, librarian in the East Hampton Library, wrote "Colonial Travelers on Long Island" in 1933.[2] In this article she mentions many colonial visitors and describes the published accounts of their journeys. "Travels on Long Island" is just one of many categories Hedges identified for the library's Long Island Collection, which includes references to many accounts by travelers who visited Long Island in the nineteenth, as well as the seventeenth and eighteenth centuries. Early in my research for this book I utilized the catalog of that collection in the East Hampton Library to identify selections to include here.

The primary sources in this book are only a small sampling of what is available. They were selected to provide a variety in terms of geography and dates. Some of the accounts which are not included have only brief references to Long Island. Thus, Harriet Martineau used the example of what she observed at the "watering-place" of Rockaway as typical of the ostentatiousness and affectations of the wealthy in America.[3] Other writings may be readily available. *Picturesque America,* for example, edited by William Cullen Bryant in 1872, has vivid descriptions and engravings of eastern Long Island. Much of this material was recently reprinted in *Exploring the Past.*[4] One of the most famous visitors to Long Island, William Cobbett, an English journalist, wrote *A Year's Residence in the United States of America,* which focuses on agriculture and has been reprinted a number of times.[5]

This book had its origins in a journal kept by Laura Hawkins who had moved with her husband to Connecticut from Long Island in 1850. She came back with her sister in 1893 to visit relatives and old friends. After Hofstra University acquired the journal, I selected portions that were published in the *Long Island Forum.*[6] Some readers asked if the full journal could be publishcd. My colleague, Professor Joann P. Krieg, suggested that it be part of a larger volume, which included accounts by other travelers. In the process of preparing this publication, the scope was expanded to include some reminiscences of residents and contemporary descriptions.

This collection does not provide a comprehensive history of Long Island, but its scope is broad, and the detailed descriptions range geographically from Brooklyn and Flatbush to Orient and Montauk. The first selection is a trip in 1744 and the final one dates from 1893. The most famous traveler on Long Island was George Washington who toured in 1790. Less well known is that he had visited on two earlier occasions, as noted in my introduction to his journal entries. Not included here are writings by the earliest explorers and visitors in the seventeenth and early eighteenth centuries, some of which have been reprinted.[7] Writings from the twentieth century also can provide useful information, but they are more accessible.[8]

Some traveled on horses, others journeyed by wagon, carriage, or stagecoach. Journeys sometimes began at 5 or 6 in the morning, stopping to eat and rest the horses after several hours of riding. The main meal was usually in the middle of the day rather than the evening. Parts of the journey might be by sailboat or, in later years, steamship. By the 1840s, the railroad expedited travel, but it took many decades before all of today's branch lines were constructed. Access to Manhattan required taking a ferry until the completion of the Brooklyn Bridge in 1883. Trains terminated at the Fulton Ferry in Brooklyn or in Long Island City until the tunnel under the East River opened in 1909.

The travelers and authors are a diverse lot, ranging from President Washington and Yale President Dr. Timothy Dwight to local historians, such as Augustus Griffin and Richard M. Bayles. Elizabeth Howell Blanchard and Laura Hawkins are women who would be unknown today if their journals had not been preserved. Dr. Alexander Hamilton emigrated from Scotland, Francisco de Miranda originally came from Venezuela, and Femmetie Lefferts grew up in colonial Flatbush speaking Dutch. Travelers James Stuart and Joseph John Gurney came from across the sea (Scotland and England, respectively), while John W. Barber and Henry Howe were natives of Connecticut. Barber and Howe gathered data about Long Island for their book on New York State and preserved in their engravings depictions of some local communities in 1840. Author Charles Brockden Brown and physician and scientist Samuel L. Mitchill were well-known in their day, although Brown was just embarking on his writing career. Walt Whitman's fame has increased since he roamed his beloved Paumanok and published *Leaves of Grass* in 1855. All provide their own perspectives on Long Island and its inhabitants.

Although most of these accounts have been published, many are not readily available today. Some of the books and journals are only in specialized or larger university libraries. Even the works by Long Island historians Nathaniel Prime and Daniel Tredwell are not in all local libraries. The focus in this book is not their historical accounts of earlier periods, but their contemporary descriptions of what they themselves observed. Many of the older histories do have useful historical information. Today's readers and historians may not be as interested in their details on churches and ministers or genealogies of prominent families, but such topics do reflect the interests of their time.[9] Our hope is that this collection will make people aware, not only of the specific selections, but also the sources themselves, which often contain descriptions of other areas of Long Island. Some of the notes refer to additional information on specific topics which should also be useful. All of these first-hand, primary sources enhance our understanding of Long Island's past.

Some of the selections (e.g., those by Washington and Miranda) are included in their entirety, at least in terms of the sections dealing with Long Island. In other cases (e.g., those by Gabriel Furman, Prime, Bayles, Tredwell, Whitman, and the Long Island Rail Road), only portions are included, and readers may find equally interesting and useful information in other parts of their writings. Many of the accounts are from journals kept by the travelers. A few rely on family traditions or oral history (Griffin and Lefferts). Brown and Dwight use the literary device of a letter to describe their journeys. Reminiscences of residents include the accounts by Furman, Tredwell, and Whitman. The Rockaway poem, Barber and Howe, Bayles, and the Long Island Rail Road (LIRR) booklet provide contemporary descriptions. The guides by Mitchill and the LIRR were explicitly designed for the use of visitors and travelers.

Two of the selections deal with the Revolutionary War (Griffin and Lefferts). Their focus is not on the usual topics of the battles, Long Island's spy ring, or whaleboat warfare, but on the occupation and how the war affected individuals at home, particularly women, whose role often has been invisible in historical accounts. Rockaway, which was Long Island's first resort (or "watering place," to use contemporary terminology), is represented by Charles Brockden Brown's 1793 essay and a popular song from the 1840s. Nineteenth-century engravings depict some of the large seaside hotels, Brooklyn's early urbanization, and some of the larger communities. Maps of different dates show roads and settlements.

Each of the selections has its own introduction, which identifies the author, puts the document in context, and briefly summarizes the content. The introduction is in a slightly smaller type size and separated from the transcribed document by three asterisks (* * *). The excerpts are presented in chronological order. At the beginning of the Notes for each selection is the citation of the source and an explanation of editing procedures, which vary somewhat depending on the original. In all instances, the editing has endeavored to make the material accessible to modern readers, while retaining the flavor of the original writing.

Travelers may come with their own biases. Historian and lawyer Benjamin F. Thompson has "Concluding Remarks on the Present Condition and Future Prospects of Long Island" in his well-known *History of Long Island* in the 1840s. He quotes from Timothy Dwight's comments on the insularity of Long Islanders (see Dwight's "Journey to Long Island, 1804" below). Thompson maintained that many of Dwight's conclusions were "the result of previously formed opinion, [rather] than of any thorough examination of facts as they really existed." Thompson noted that changes in agriculture and transportation in the half century since Dwight visited Long Island had significantly improved conditions. Travelers no longer had to await the winds or whims of a captain to sail, as Miranda had to do at Sag Harbor in 1784. Not only did steamships and the railroad reduce travel time, but they operated on regular schedules. Thompson acknowledged that Long Islanders had "stronger local attachments," but cites the whaling industry (then at its peak) as an example of Long Island's entrepreneurial enterprise. He boasted of the attractions of Long Island for travelers:

> To those whose means enable them to travel either for health or amusement, Long Island presents many solid attractions. The almost level surface of its southern and the agreeable inundations of its northern border; its extensive inland plains, woods, and forests, abounding in game for the hunter; the numerous streams, ponds, and bays, teeming with scale and shellfish of every kind; its fine air, with an illimitable [unlimited] water prospect in every direction, all hold out strong inducements to tempt and gratify the stranger. Since the introduction of turnpike roads in various parts of the island, with a very general improvement of common roads, agriculture has steadily advanced, till it has attained to a condition which equally surprises and delights the heart of the traveler and the patriot.[10]

Thompson realized that the railroad was "destined to work greater benefits to Long Island than have yet been realized." He expected further advances in agriculture, with more of the unimproved land "brought into profitable cultivation."[11] In time, the railroad became the greatest booster of

Long Island. It sponsored demonstration farms to encourage farming (and boost its own freight business) and published many booklets to bring visitors and residents (potential commuters). The selection from the LIRR's "Out on the Island" (1890) surpasses even Thompson in its praise of the region. Most of these selections portray Long Island and its people in a quite positive vein. Comments of travelers, residents, and other writers may need to be tempered, as Thompson reminds us, but they do succeed in portraying a by-gone past. Moreover, Long Island still has many "solid attractions" for visitors and residents in the twenty-first century.

Travelers often provide valuable descriptions of the landscape, communities, people, manners, and customs they observe. Their accounts and the other contemporary descriptions reprinted here provide information on the geography and topography of the region in the 150 years from the mid-eighteenth century to the end of the nineteenth century. Some writers describe the soil and agriculture, others religious practices and modes of travel, and many the landscape and the built environment. All of their observations and insights add to our understanding of the Island's past.

The contemporary descriptions of the landscape provide additional insights. The natural and cultural landscapes evolve and change over time. As John Brinckerhoff Jackson has observed, "landscape is history made visible."[12] Long Island in the eighteenth century was a rural and maritime region. Agriculture continued to be dominant through the nineteenth century, but much of the land was undeveloped, as is evident from Nathaniel Prime's description of the natural features in 1845. Small villages and hamlets did develop and Old Bethpage Village Restoration recreates a crossroads settlement of this pre-industrial period.[13]

Brooklyn, on the western end of the island, pioneered as America's first suburb in the early nineteenth century. It evolved into a large city and together with western Queens became part of New York City at the end of the century. Suburbs spread east and some Long Island seaside communities attracted summer visitors. Long Island evolved further in the twentieth century with the growth of population and suburbanization, construction of highways and parkways, development of shopping centers and large malls, and expansion of business and industry. Metropolitan New York spread, and many suburbs matured in the late twentieth century and became more diverse. Yet Suffolk remains the leading agricultural county in the state in terms of the wholesale value of its products, while its population grows and development continues. Doubtless there will be other future changes which we cannot now imagine. It is sometimes hard to envision in the twenty-first century the Long Island of a hundred or 250 years ago. *Journeys on Old*

Long Island can transport you back to those earlier days and enable you to discover and explore the past. Enjoy the trip!

Acknowledgements

Victoria Aspinwall, Long Island Studies Institute secretary, entered most of the documents on the computer, assisted in copy-editing, and patiently proofread the selections numerous times (invariably finding a few errors each time). After my retirement in 2000, the conference and publication activities of the Long Island Studies Institute for which I had responsibility were transferred to the Axinn Library where the Institute's collections were housed. I appreciate the support of Daniel Rubey, Dean of the Axinn Library and Information Services, and Geri Solomon, currently Acting Director of the Institute. At the Long Island Studies Institute, Debra Willett and Bronwyn Hannon, as well as Gary Hammond and Mildred DeRiggi of the Nassau County Museum staff, provided assistance at various times.

Many librarians have been helpful as I sought materials, illustrations, and information for the notes. I am grateful to Hofstra's reference librarians, particularly Janet S. Wagner and Deborah Dolan. Among the many other librarians who helped are Luise Weiss at the Middle Country Library, Mark Rothenberg at the Patchogue-Medford Library, Myrna Sloam at Roslyn's Bryant Library, and Dorothy King and Diana Dayton at the East Hampton Library. Long Island historian Richard Ryan shared information on Dr. Alexander Hamilton's trip. Maria Cobb and Vivienne Shaffer at the Lefferts Homestead provided information on the house and family. Professor Joann P. Krieg, in addition to recommending the publication as mentioned earlier, suggested the title and reviewed my introductions to the Charles Brockden Brown and Walt Whitman selections. Dorothy B. Ruettgers assisted my editing in numerous ways.

I appreciate permission to reprint copyrighted selections from: North Carolina University Press (Hamilton's "Itinerarium"); University Press of Virginia (Washington's "Tour"); Harvard University Press (Dwight's "Journey"); and the Brooklyn Historical Society (Blanchard's "Visiting Long Island"). Finally, I appreciate the work of the many other Long Island historians who have assisted this publication by their own work in the field; they are acknowledged in the notes.

Notes

1. George Fox, the founder of the Friends, visited America in 1672. Entries from his journal relating to Long Island are reprinted in *"The People Called Quakers": Records of Long Island Friends, 1671-1703,* edited by Natalie A. Naylor (Interlaken, NY: Empire State Books and Hofstra University, 2001), pp. 121-26. Excerpts from the journals of Quakers Roger Gill and Thomas Story (1699) are included in "The Rise and Growth of the Society of Friends on Long Island and in New York City," by Henry Onderdonk, Jr., (1878), reprinted in ibid., pp. 131-36. Onderdonk mentions the visits of English Quaker women ministers Alice Curwen in 1676 and Joan Volkins in 1680. These are just a few of the many Friends who visited Long Island, which was one of the centers of Quakerism in the colonial period.

2. In *New York History* 14 (April 1933): 152-63; this is vol. 31 in the *Proceedings* of the New York State Historical Association. (For additional information on Hedges, who married Morton Pennypacker in 1936, see note no. 1 to Francisco de Miranda's "Country Excursions and Visits on Eastern Long Island, 1784," below.)

3. Martineau is quoted in *Long Island as America: A Documentary History to 1896,* edited by James C. Bunce and Richard T. Hammond (Port Washington: Kennikat Press 1977), pp. 134-35. Another famous traveler, Andrew Burnaby, made brief comments in his *Travels through the Middle Settlements in North America in the Years 1759 and 1760,* 1798 (Reprint; New York: Augustus M. Kelley, 1970), p. 119. There were also many less well-known travelers who wrote about Long Island. St. George Tucker visited Jamaica and Flushing in 1786 (see "A Virginian in New York: The Diary of St. George Tucker, July-August, 1786," edited by Bettina Manzo, *New York History* 67 [April 1986]: 193-94). John Fanning Watson in an unpublished 1855 manuscript in the Winterthur Museum's Library in Wilmington, Delaware, describes an 1855 railroad trip to Thompson's Station (today's Brentwood). The *Brooklyn Daily Eagle* published the Rev. Fitch Reed's letters from Sag Harbor in 1819 to his younger brother in Dutchess County. As a circuit rider for the Methodist Episcopal Church, he had an opportunity to travel throughout Suffolk County and most of his observations focus on that area (*Brooklyn Daily Eagle,* January 15, 1893, p. 17).

One needs to be careful, however, about the authenticity of accounts. "Christmas on Old Long Island," purported to be "Excerpts from the memoirs of a Boston gentleman" (unnamed) who spent Christmas in 1733 with Dutch relatives in Cow Neck (Port Washington). It appeared in Oyster Bay's *North Shore Almanac* in 1933 and was reprinted in *Stories of Roslyn and Long Island,* edited by June Selby (Roslyn: [Roslyn Public Schools], 1928-1935), typescript in the Bryant Library, Roslyn. I suspected that it was written in the twentieth century and hence did not include it in this collection.

4. *Exploring the Past: Writings from 1798 to 1896, Relating to the Town of East Hampton, New York,* edited by Tom Twomey (New York: Newmarket Press, 2000), pp. 301-6. This valuable collection also includes excerpts on East Hampton from several travelers (the best-known of whom are Timothy Dwight and John Howard Payne) and has selections from many nineteenth-century historical accounts of East Hampton. Bryant's *Picturesque America* was reprinted by American Heritage in 1974.

5. William Cobbett (1763-1835) lived in what is now New Hyde Park in 1817-1819 (he rented an estate, which had been Governor Thomas Dongan's country residence). During his stay on Long Island, Cobbett wrote *Grammar of the English Language* (1818), *A Year's Residence in the United States of America* (1818), and *American Gardener* (1819). His *Year's Residence* focuses on his farming, particularly of rutabaga (a Swedish turnip). This book was reprinted by Sutton in 1983, by A.M. Kelley in 1969, and by Southern Illinois University Press in 1964. Adelphi University has a William Cobbett collection in their library. On Cobbett, see George DeWan, "A Maverick's Rowdy Odyssey," *Newsday,* November 7, 2000; Charles Reichman, "William Cobbett, Pioneer of the Long Island Rutabaga," *Long Island Forum* 52 (Winter 1989): 34-37; and James Sambrook and Elizabeth Thornton, "William Cobbett," *British Romantic Prose Writers, 1789-1832,* First Series, edited by John R. Greenfield, *Dictionary of Literary Biography,* vol. 107 (Detroit: Gale Research, 1991), pp. 35-67.

6. Natalie A. Naylor, editor "A 'Mid-Summer Outing,' Visiting Long Island in 1893," parts 1 and 2, *Long Island Forum* 62 (Summer 1999): 8-23; 62 (Fall 1999): 4-15.

7. Many of the reprints are in facsimile editions. See, for example, Adriaen Van der Donck, *A Description of the New Netherlands,* edited by Thomas F. O'Donnell (Syracuse: Syracuse University Press, 1968); David P. DeVries, *Voyages from Holland to America in the 17th Century* and Charles Wooley (Wolley), *A Two Year Journal in New York* (1678-80), reprinted in their entirety in *Historic Chronicles of New Amsterdam, Colonial*

New York, and Early New York, edited by Cornell Jaray, 1st series (Port Washington: Ira J. Friedman, 1968). Daniel Denton, *A Brief Description of New York* (1670) is printed in *Historic Chronicles of New Amsterdam, Colonial New York, and Early New York,* edited by Cornell Jaray, 2d series (Port Washington: Ira J. Friedman, 1968); portions are reprinted in *Roots and Heritage of Hempstead Town,* edited by Natalie A. Naylor (Interlaken, NY: Heart of the Lakes Publishing, 1994), pp. 192-96. Jasper Dankers and Peter Sluyter's *Journal of a Voyage to New York . . . in 1679-80* was reprinted in 1966 by Readex Microprint, and sections were retranslated in the 1980s. See Charles T. Gehring and Robert S. Grumet, "Observations of the Indians from Jasper Danckaert's Journal, 1679-1680," *William and Mary Quarterly,* 3d Series, 44 (January 1987): 104-20. Selections from early colonial descriptions can be found in Bunce and Harmond, *Long Island as America,* pp. 6-12, 37-40.

8. Examples of such accounts include: Clifton Johnson, "A Jaunt on [Eastern] Long Island," in *New England and Its Neighbors* (New York: Macmillan, 1911); Charles Hanson Towne, *Loafing Down Long Island* (New York: Century, 1921); Raymond H. Torrey, Frank Place, Jr., and Robert L. Dickinson, *New York Walk Book* (New York: American Geographical Society, 1923), pp. 26-30, 137-49 (there are also later editions); Frederick Simpich, "Spin Your Globe to Long Island," *National Geographic Magazine* 75 (April 1939): 413-60; William Oliver Stevens, *Discovering Long Island* (New York: Dodd, Mead, 1939; reprinted by I.J. Friedman, 1969); Federal Writers' Project, *New York: A Guide to the Empire State* (1940, reprinted 1962), and *New York City Guide* (1939, reprinted 1969); Howell Walker, "Long Island Outgrows the Country," *National Geographic* 99 (March 1951): 237-326; Suzannah Lessard, "The Suburban Landscape: Oyster Bay, Long Island," *New Yorker* 52 (October 11, 1976): 44-79; Christopher Morley, "Suburban Life in Roslyn [1920s]," in *Christopher Morley's New York* (New York: Fordham University Press, 1988), pp. 317-74; Marion Hunt Berg Homire, *Grandmother Burned Peachpits* (Old Field: Privately printed, 1992), a memoir of growing up in East Meadow in the 1910s and 1920s.

9. The individuals whose portraits or homes were included in those histories often paid for the privilege and thus helped finance the publication of the book. For information on earlier historians, see Richard P. Harmond, "Doing and Not Doing Long Island History: The Long Island Historians from Wood to Weeks," *Long Island Historical Journal* 13 (Spring 2001): 175; reprinted from *Journal of Long Island History* 15 (Fall 1978): 16-24.

10. Benjamin F. Thompson, *History of Long Island from its Discovery and Settlement to the Present Time,* edited by Charles J. Werner, 3d. ed., 3 vols. (New York: Robert H. Dodd, 1918), 3:275-77. Thompson died in 1849, but his third edition was not published until 1918; it was reprinted in 1962. A similar section on "The Present Condition and Future Prospects" appeared in his two-volume, 1843 second edition, which has minor variations in some of the wording, but not in the substance (2:298-303).

11. Thompson, *History of Long Island,* 3:280.

12. Quoted by Helen Lefkowitz Horowitz, "J.B. Jackson and the American Land," in John Brinckerhoff Jackson, *Landscape in Sight: Looking at American,* edited by Helen Lefkowitz Horowitz (New Haven: Yale University Press, 1997), p. x.

13. Nassau County's museum village interprets Long Island's rural heritage. Old Bethpage Village Restoration preserves many houses and structures which have been moved to the site. It is open from March to December; (516) 572-8400.

Itinerarium, 1744

Dr. Alexander Hamilton

Alexander Hamilton was born in Edinburgh or its environs in Scotland in 1712.[1] His father, Dr. William Hamilton, was a divinity professor and principal at the University of Edinburgh. Alexander received a medical degree from Edinburgh in 1737. Two years later, the young Hamilton came to Annapolis, Maryland, in order to practice medicine (his older brother John was a minister there). After an extended illness, Hamilton set out on May 3, 1744 on a journey north "only for health and recreation."[2] He kept a record of his journey which he titled, "Itinerarium," from the Latin word for an account of a journey.

Hamilton traveled by horseback with his slave Dromo to New York City. To reach New York, they crossed from Perth Amboy in New Jersey to Staten Island and then took another ferry to Long Island. It took them a half hour to cross the Narrows. Before he reached the Brooklyn ferry to Manhattan, he wrote, "I rid a bye way where, in seven miles' riding, I had 24 gates to open." Dromo asked a black girl if they were on the right road "to [New] York," but she replied to him in Dutch which he could not understand. Hamilton described the route they traveled in Kings County: "The road here for several miles is planted thick upon each side with rows of cherry trees, like hedges, and the lots of land are mostly inclosed with stone fences."[3]

Hamilton reached New York on June 15 and stayed in the city several days. He met John Milne, a minister in Shrewsbury, New Jersey, who was planning to go to Albany where he had been the rector at St. Peter's Church for nine years. Hamilton agreed to accompany him to Albany. The excursion up the Hudson by sloop took two weeks.

After he returned from his trip upstate, Hamilton remained in New York City a few days. He met two Boston merchants, Henry Laughton and Benjamin Parker, with whom he decided to travel to Boston. On July 10, Hamilton, Dromo, and the two Boston traders set out for New England via Long Island. They traveled the length of Long Island to Orient (Oyster Ponds) and crossed Long Island Sound to New London. The selections below are reprinted from this segment of his trip. Then the party headed north in Rhode Island, through Massachusetts, and along the coast from Boston to southern Maine. On the return trip, Hamilton and Dromo rode along the Connecticut coast and did not return to Long Island.

Hamilton spent only three days on Long Island and obviously it was a convenient short cut (the return trip from New London to New York City took twice as long and involved crossing several ferries and fording streams).[4] The party traveled from Jamaica to Hempstead, then headed northeast to Huntington and traveled along the North Shore through Setauket, Riverhead, and the North Fork to Orient. Their route east from Huntington was probably the North Country Road, approximately today's Route 25A and, on the east end, Route 25. Hamilton's account gives us a good picture of the conditions travelers encountered in the mid-eighteenth century and a glimpse of taverns and other accommodations. The three bachelors flirted with the servant girls and were entertained in a Setauket tavern by another traveler's gymnastic tricks.

Carl Bridenbaugh edited Hamilton's full journal from which these sections on Long Island are excerpted. He refers to Hamilton as a "truthful traveler" and characterizes "his accurate and comprehensive reporting" to be "unequaled in any other colonial travel account."[5]

After his return to Annapolis, Hamilton resumed his medical practice and married Margaret Dulany in July 1747. He was elected to the colony's Assembly in 1752, and served one term. He died in his Annapolis home in 1756 at the age of 44.

* * *

York Ferry—Long Island—Jamaica

Tuesday, July 10th. Early in the morning we got up, and after preparing all our baggage, Messrs. Parker, Laughton, and I mounted horse and crossed the ferry att seven a'clock over to Long Island. After a tedious passage and being detained sometime att Baker's,[6] we arrived a quarter after 10 att Jamaica, a small town upon Long Island just bordering upon Hampstead Plain. It is about half a mile long, the houses sparse.[7] There are in it one Presbyterian meeting, one English, and one Dutch church.[8] The Dutch church is built in the shape of an octagon, being a wooden structure. We stopt there att the Sign of the Sun and paid dear for our breakfast, which was bread and mouldy cheese, stale beer and sower cyder {sour cider}.

Reformed (Dutch) Church in Jamaica, built 1716

Hampstead {Hempstead}

We set out again and arrived att Hampstead, a very scattered town standing upon the great plain to which it gives name. We put up here att one Peter's[9] att the Sign of Guy of Warwick where we dined with a company that had come there before us and were travelling southward. There was a pritty girl here with whom Parker was mightily taken and would fain have staid that night. This girl had intermitting fevers. Parker pretended to be a doctor and swore he could cure her if she would submitt to his directions. With difficulty we perswaded Parker to mount horse.

Att 4 a'clock, going across this great plain,[10] we could see almost as good a horizon round us as when one is att sea, and in some places of the plain, the latitude might be taken by observation att noon day. It is about 16 miles long. The ground is hard and gravelly, the road very smooth but indistinct and intersected by severall other roads which makes it difficult for a stranger to find the way. There is nothing but long grass grows upon this plain, only in some particular spots small oak brush, not above a foot high. Near Hampstead there are severall pritty winding brooks that run thro' {through} this plain. We lost our way here and blundered about a great while. Att last we spyed a woman and two men at some distance. We rid up towards them to enquire, but they were to wild to be spoke with, running over the plain as fast as wild bucks upon the mountains. Just after we came out of the plain and sunk into the woods, we found a boy lurking behind a bush. We wanted to enquire the way of him, but as soon as we spoke the game was started and away he run.

Huntington

We arrived att Huntington att eight a'clock att night, where we put up at one Flat's {Platt's} att the Sign of the Half Moon and Heart.[11] This Flat is an Irishman. We had no sooner sat down when there came in a band of the town politicians in short jackets and trowsers, being probably curious to know who them strangers were who had newly arrived in town. Among the rest was a fellow with a worsted cap and great black fists. They stiled him doctor. Flat told me he had been a shoemaker in town and was a notable fellow att his trade, but happening two years agoe to cure an old woman of a pestilent mortal disease, he thereby acquired the character of a physitian, was applied to from all quarters, and finding the practise of physick a more profitable business than cobling, he laid aside his awls and leather, got himself some gallipots, and instead of cobling of soals {soles}, fell to cobling of human bodies.[12] Att supper our landlord was very merry and very much given to rhiming. There were three buxom girls in this house who served us att supper, to whom Mr. Parker made strenuous courtship. One was an Indian girl named Phoebe, the other two were Lucretia and Betty, but Betty was the top beauty of the three.

Wednesday, July 11. We left Huntington att half an hour after six in the morning, and after riding 5 miles stonny road, we breakfasted att a house upon the road att the Sign of Bacchus.[13] Then proceeding ten or eleven miles farther, we forded Smithtown River, otherwise called by the Indians, Missaque {Nissequogue}. We baited {fed and rested} our horses att a taveren where there was a deaf landlady.[14] After half an hour's rest we mounted horse again and rid some miles thro' {through} some very barren, unequal, and stonny land. We saw the mouth of Smithtown River running into the Sound thro some broken sandy beaches about eight miles to our left hand N.N.W., and about 24 miles farther to the northward, the coast of New England or the province of Connecticut.

Brookhaven, or Setoquet {Setauket}

We arrived att a scattered town called Brookhaven, or by the Indians, Setoquet about two a'clock afternoon and dined att one Buchanan's there. Brookhaven is a small scattered village standing upon barren, rocky land near the sea. In this town is a small windmill for sawing of plank, and a wooden church with a small steeple.[15] Att about 50 miles' distance from this town eastward is a settlement of {Montaukett} Indians upon a sandy point which makes the south fork of the island and runs out a long narrow promontory into the sea almost as far as Block Island.

While we were at Buchanan's, an old fellow named Smith called att the house. He said he was a travelling to York {New York City} to get a license or commission from the Governour to go a privateering and swore he would not be under any commander but would be chief man himself. He showed us severall antick tricks such as jumping half a foot high upon his bum without touching the floor with any other part of his body. Then he turned and did the same upon his belly. Then he stood upright upon his head. He told us he was 75 years of age and swore damn his old shoes if any man in America could do the like. He asked me whence I came and whither I went. I answered him I came from Calliphurnia and was going to Lanthern Land.[16] He swore damn his old shoes again if he had not been a sailor all his life long and yet never had heard of such places. Mr. Parker made him believe that he was a captain of a privateer, and for a mug of syder {cider} made him engage to go on board of him upon Friday next, promising to make him his leutenant, for nothing else would satisfy the old fellow. The old chap was mightily elevated at this and damned his old shoes twenty times over. Att last he wanted to borrow a little advance money of Parker, which when he found he could not obtain, he drank up his cider and swore he would not go.

We took horse again att half an hour after 5 o'clock, and had scarce got a mile from Brookhaven when we lost our way but were directed right again by a man whom we met. After riding 10 miles thro' woods and marshes in which we were pestered with muscettoes {mosquitoes}, we arrived att eight o'clock att night att one Brewster's where we put up for all night, and in this house we could get nothing either to eat or drink and so were obliged to go to bed fasting or supperless.[17] I was conducted up stairs to a large chamber. The people in this house seemed to be quite savage and rude.

Thursday, July 12. When I waked this morning I found two beds in the room besides that in which I lay, in one of which lay two great hulking fellows with long black beards, having their own hair and not so much as half a nightcap betwixt them both.[18] I took them for weavers, not only from their greasy appearance, but because I observed a weaver's loom at each side of the room. In the other bed was a raw boned boy who, with the two lubbers, huddled on his cloths and went reeling down stairs making as much noise as three horses.

{Riverhead}

We set out from this desolate place att 6 a'clock and rid 16 miles thro very barren and waste land. Here we passed thro a plain of 6 or eight miles long where was nothing but oak brush or bushes two foot high, very thick, and replenished with acorns; and thinly scattered over the plain were severall old naked pines at about two or three hundred foot distance one from another, most of them decayed and broken. In all this way we met not one living soul nor saw any house, but one in ruins. Some of the inhabitants here call this place the Desart of Arabia. It is very much infested with muscettoes. We breakfasted att one Fanning's.[19] Near his house stands the county court house, a decayed wooden building, and close by his door runs a small rivulett {Peconic River} into an arm of the sea {Peconic Bay} about 20 miles' distance, which makes that division of the eastren end of Long Island called the Fork.

Southold.

This day was rainy, but we took horse and rid 10 miles farther to one Hubbard's where we rested half an hour, then proceeded eight miles farther to the town of Southold,[20] near which the road is levell, firm, and pleasant, and in the neighbourhood are a great many windmills. The houses are pritty thick along the road here. We put up att one Mrs. More's in Southold.[21] In her house appeared nothing but industry. She and her grandaughters were busied in carding and spinning of wool. Messieurs Parker and Laughton were very much disposed to sleep. We ordered some eggs for dinner and some chickens. Mrs. More asked us if we would have bacon fried with our eggs; we told her no. After dinner we sent to enquire for a boat to cross the Sound.

Att night the house was crowded with a company of patchd coats and tattered jackets, and consequently the conversation consisted chiefly in "damne ye, Jack," and "Here's to you, Tom." A comicall old fellow among the rest asked me if I had come from the new country. His name, he told me, was Cleveland, and he was originally of Scots parentage. I told him then his genuine name must be Cleland. We asked him what entertainment we could have att the Oyster Pond {Orient} where we designed to take boat to cross the Sound. "Why truly," said he, "if you would eat such things as we Gentills {Gentiles} do, you may live very well, but as your law forbids you to eat swine's flesh, your living will be but indifferent." Parker laughed and asked him if he took us for Jews or Mahometans {Mohammedans or Muslims}. He replied, "Gentlemen, I ask pardon, but the landlady informed me you were Jews." This notion proceeded from our refusing of bacon to our eggs att dinner.

While we were att supper there came in a pedlar with his pack along with one Doctor Hull, a practitioner of physick in the town. We were told that this doctor was a man of great learning and very much of a gentleman. The pedlar went to show him some linnen by candle light and told him very ingenuously that now he would be upon honour with him and recommend to him the best of his wares, and as to the price he would let him know the highest and lowest att one word and would not bate {take less than} one penny of 6 shillings a yard. There passed some learned conversation betwixt this doctor and pedlar in which the doctor made it plain that the lawers, clergy, and doctors tricked the rest of mankind out of the best part of their substance and made them pay well for doing of nothing. But the pedlar stood up mightily for the honour of his own profession and affirmed that they made as good a hand of it as any cheat among them all. "But then," added he, "you have something to handle for your money, good or bad as it happens." We left this company att 9 a'clock att night and went up stairs to bed, all in one chamber.

Oyster Pond[22]

Friday, July 13. We took horse after 6 in the morning and rid 5 or 6 miles close by the Sound till we came to one Brown's who was to give us passage in his boat. Then we proceeded 7 miles farther and stopped att one King's to wait the tide, when Brown's boat was to fall down the river to take us in.[23] The family att King's were all busy in preparing dinner, the provision for which chiefly consisted in garden stuff. Here we saw some handsome country girls, one of whom wore a perpetuall smile in her face and prepared the chocolate for our breakfast. She presently captivated Parker, who was apt to take flame upon all occasions. After breakfast, for pastime, we read

Orient (Oyster Ponds)

Quevedo's Visions[24] and att one a'clock dined with the family upon fat pork and green pease {peas}. Att two a'clock we observed the boat falling down the river, and having provided our selves with a store of bread and cheese and some rum and sugar in case of being detained upon the water, that part of the Sound which we had to cross being 18 miles broad, we put our horses on board 10 minutes before three and set sail with a fair wind from the Oyster Pond.

Sound

Att three a'clock we passed the Gutt, a rapid current betwixt the main of Long Island and Shelter Island caused by the tides.

Shelter Island—Gardiner's Island

Att a quarter after three we cleared Shelter Island, larboard {starboard}, upon our weather bow. Gardiner's Island[25] bore east by north, starboard, about three leagues' distance. This island is in the possession of one man and takes its name from him. It had been a prey to the French privateers in Queen Anne's war, who used to land upon it and plunder the family and tennants of their stock and provisions, the island lying very bleak upon the ocean just att the eastermost entry of the Sound betwixt Long Island and the main of Connecticut.

Fisher's Isl.—Two-tree Isl.

A little to the northward of this lyes Fisher's Island, and about 3 or four leagues' distance upon our larboard we saw a small island called Two-Tree Island because they say there are only two trees upon it which are of a particular kind of wood which nobody there can give a name to, nor are such trees to be seen any where else in the country.[26]

Notes

Source: *Gentleman's Progress: The Itinerarium of Dr. Alexander Hamilton, 1744,* edited by Carl Bridenbaugh (Pittsburgh: University of Pittsburgh Press, 1992), pp. 89-96 and 227-28. First published for the Omohundro Institute of Early American History and Culture. Copyright © 1949 by the University of North Carolina Press; renewed 1976 by Carl Bridenbaugh. Used by permission of the publisher. The *Itinerarium* initially was published in 1907 in a privately printed limited edition transcribed and edited by Albert Bushnell Hart. The manuscript is owned by the Henry E. Huntington Library of San Marino, California.

Editor Bridenbaugh followed the original text except to modernize paragraphing, punctuation, and capitalization "in the interest of clarity and readability." Spelling was not standardized in the eighteenth century and was often phonetic. Notes have been renumbered and Bridenbaugh's verbatim notes are identified at the end by his bracketed initials [CB]. Notes by the editor for this publication are identified by her initials (NAN). Her explanations in the text and within Bridenbaugh's notes are in braces (or wavy brackets), {thus}. Richard A. Ryan, Curator of the Walt Whitman Birthplace Association and Director of the Townsend Society of America, has carefully researched Hamilton's journey, and information he graciously provided on the locations where Hamilton stopped is identified in the notes by his initials (RAR).

1. Dr. Hamilton was not related to the better-known American patriot, Alexander Hamilton, who wrote the majority of the *Federalist* papers and served as the first United States Secretary of the Treasury. He was born in the British West Indies in 1755 and thus was not yet born when Dr. Hamilton made the trip described here (NAN).

2. Hamilton, *Gentleman's Progress,* p. 3 (NAN).

3. The gates were to ensure that cattle did not roam at will. Hamilton, *Gentleman's Progress*, pp. 40-41 (NAN).

4. Nearly a century later, the Long Island Railroad (LIRR) also tried to shorten the trip from New York City to Boston by constructing a route through Long Island to Greenport. A few years after the railroad line was completed, the technological problems of bridging the many rivers and streams along the Connecticut coast were solved and the LIRR went into bankruptcy. See Edwin Dunbaugh, "New York to Boston via the Long Island Railroad," in *Evoking a Sense of Place* (Interlaken, NY: Heart of the Lakes Publishing, 1988), pp. 75-84 (NAN).

5. Bridenbaugh, "Introduction," in Hamilton, *Gentleman's Progress,* p. xi. On Hamilton's tour of Long Island, see also George DeWan, "A Magical History Tour," in *Long Island: Our Story,* by Newsday (Melville: Newsday, 1998), p. 103 (NAN).

6. Baker's Tavern was located near the intersection of today's Flatbush and Fulton Avenues in Brooklyn (RAR).

7. A visitor {to Jamaica} of some ten years later spoke of "Houses on one Story and a stoop to each, a roof longer than the Stud, Odd appearance." Samuel Curwen, "Journal of a Journey from Salem to Philadelphia in 1755," Essex Institute, *Historical Collections, 52* (1916): 52, 78 [CB].

8. For fifty years after its founding, the Presbyterian was the only church in Jamaica. In 1702 a Reformed Dutch congregation was formed, but the church was not built on the south side of Fulton Street until 1715. Grace Church (Anglican) was erected in 1734. Benjamin F. Thompson, *History of Long Island* (New York, 1839), pp. 387, 391-92, 395 [CB].

Thompson published a two-volume edition in 1842, and prepared a 3d edition before he died in 1849 which was posthumously published in 1918 in 3 volumes, edited by Charles Warner (Reprint; Port Washington: I.J. Friedman, 1962). The references in this more accessible edition are 2:590, 597, 613, 627 (NAN).

9. Peters is the name of an old family in Hempstead, but the public house referred to must have been the Pettit Tavern at the sign of the Guy of Warwick. Bernice Schultz, *Colonial Hempstead* (Lynbrook, NY, 1937), pp. 24, 245 [CB]. Schultz's book was reprinted under her married name, Bernice Schultz Marshall, by I.J. Friedman in Port Washington in 1962 (NAN). There was a Peters Tavern in Hempstead in 1744, however, operated by Hulet (or Hewlett) Peters which was located on the north side of what is now Fulton Avenue, west of the intersection with Main Street (RAR).

10. Hempstead Plain {or the Hempstead Plains} was a prairie in the middle of a forest which served as an admirable grazing area for cattle. Ralph H. Gabriel, *The Evolution of Long Island* (New Haven, 1921), p. 30 [CB]. Gabriel's book was reprinted in 1960 by I.J. Friedman in Port Washington (NAN).

On the Hempstead Plains, in addition to the descriptions below in Samuel Latham Mitchill, "The Traveler's Guide to Nassau Island, 1807," and Nathaniel Prime's "Long Island in 1845," see also: Gabriel Furman's 1845 depiction, "The Hempstead Plains," reprinted in *The Roots and Heritage of Hempstead Town*, edited by Natalie A. Naylor (Interlaken, NY: Heart of the Lakes Publishing 1994), pp. 197-200; Carol Neidich, "The Hempstead Plains and the Birdfoot Violet," *Long Island Forum* 51 (Spring 1988): 54-62; and George DeWan, "The Prairie That Was," in *Long Island: Our Story,* by Newsday (Melville, NY: Newsday, 1998), p. 11 (NAN).

11. This was undoubtedly Philip Platt's Tavern which was located at what is now the southeast corner of Park Avenue and East Main Street (Route 25A) in Huntington. George Washington stopped there in 1790 when it was operated by Obediah Platt (RAR). See Romanah Sammis, *Huntington-Babylon Town History* (Huntington: Huntington Historical Society, 1937), pp. 82-83 (NAN).

12. Gallipots were small earthenware jars which were used for medicines (NAN).

13. The Sign of Bacchus tavern was in present-day Northport (RAR).

14. This may have been owned at this time by the Norton family. Today it is known as the Epenetus Smith tavern (RAR). Its original location was on the northwest corner of Middle Country Road (Route 25) and North Country Road (at the junction of Routes 111 and 25A), which is now the site of the Smithtown Presbyterian Church. The tavern building has been moved east on Middle Country Road (Route 25) and is one of the buildings preserved by the Smithtown Historical Society, which uses it for education programs; 631-265-6768 (NAN).

15. Buchanan's was operated by Arthur and his brother William Buchanan (RAR). The Caroline Church of Brookhaven in Setauket was built in 1729, and is the oldest Episcopal church in Suffolk County (NAN).

16. Calliphurnia (also spelled Caliphurnia and Calphurnia) may have been a reference to the area where Sir Francis Drake anchored off the west coast of what is today's California. That would have been virtually *terra incognito* in the mid-eighteenth century for those on the east coast of America. Lanthern Land (or Lanternland) was probably a reference to François Rabelais, *Pantagruel* (1538, 5th book, chapter 33), where Lanternland, "an island four days' sail from Satinland," was the "land of literary charlatans, whose inhabitants are graduates in arts, doctors, professors, and prelates." See E. Cobham Brewer, *Dictionary of Phrase and Fable* (1898); and Alberto Manguel and Gianni

Guadalupi, *The Dictionary of Imaginary Places* (New York: Macmillan, 1980), p. 205 (NAN).

17. Brewster's was on the northeast corner of the intersection of today's Middle Country Road (Route 25) and Rocky Point Road (Route 21), (RAR). Thomas R. Bayles, in a 1976 leaflet reprinting selections from the Long Island portion of Hamilton's manuscript, identifies this as "Pfeiffer's country store at Middle Island in later years." See "Dr. Hamilton's Trip Through Long Island in 1744" (NAN).

18. Inns of the time rented a bed or space in a bed rather than a private room (NAN).

19. Fanning's was located on the south side of today's West Main Street, west of Osborn Avenue. James Fanning built the Suffolk County Courthouse (RAR).

20. Curwen speaks of stopping on the eighteenth stage of his journey with Captain Hubbard, the Southold collector. Curwen, "Journal," p. 77. Southold was settled by people from New Haven {in 1640} and was one of the oldest settlements on Long Island. Epher Whitaker, "The Early History of Southold, Long Island," New Haven Historical Society, *Papers* 2 (1877): 2 [CB]. Hubbard's was at the northwest corner of Main Road (Route 25) and Love Lane (RAR).

21. Mrs. Abigail (or Widow) Moore's was on the northeast corner of Main Road (Route 25) and Boisseau Avenue (RAR).

22. Oyster Pond {or Ponds} was really a peninsula on the easternmost extremity of the North Fork of Long Island where the town {hamlet} of Orient now stands. Thompson, *History of Long Island,* p. 245 [CB]; in the 1918/1962 edition of Thompson's, *History*, 2:243 (NAN).

23. This may have been Captain Daniel Brown's which was probably located on Stirling Avenue which runs along Stirling Creek in present-day Greenport (earlier known as Stirling). The inns of Constant Booth and Orange Webb were also on Stirling Avenue, but King's has not yet been located (RAR).

24. *Quevedo's Visions* was one of the novels of the Spaniard Francesco Gomes de Quevedo y Villegas (1560-1645), [CB].

25. Gardiner's Island was purchased from the Indians in 1639 by Lion Gardiner, who named it Isle of Wight, but even before Hamilton's visit it had come to be known as Gardiner's Island [CB]. Gardiner also had received a grant from the English crown in 1639. See Roger Wunderlich, "Lion Gardiner, Long Island's Founding Father," *Long Island Historical Journal* 10 (Spring 1998): 172-85. Gardiners Island remains in the hands of the family in 2001. See Steve Wick, "Gardiners Island: What Next?" in *Long Island: Our Story,* p. 67 (NAN).

26. Fisher's Island is politically part of the Town of Southold, although geographically it is less than two miles from the Connecticut shore. Two-tree (or Two Tree) Island is located off the coast of Connecticut, in the Niantic River harbor (NAN).

Home Life During the American Revolution, 1776-1783

Femmetie Hegeman Lefferts

Femmetie (or Femmetia) Hegeman Lefferts (1760-1847) witnessed the events she describes in Flatbush as a young girl. She later recounted these stories to her children and grandchildren in the Lefferts family homestead which was located on the east side of Flatbush Avenue near today's Maple Street. The Lefferts family donated the home to New York City and it was moved a few blocks to Prospect Park in 1918. The Lefferts Homestead is now a Children's Historic House Museum which can be visited.[1]

Most of the fighting in the Battle of Long Island (or the Battle of Brooklyn) occurred on August 27, 1776, but the events described at the beginning of this account occurred a few days earlier. The impact of the Revolutionary War and occupation on civilians is still the untold story of the American Revolution on Long Island. Lefferts' account provides a view from the perspective of a young girl who lived close to the fighting in Brooklyn in August 1776. The family fled their home which was burned by the troops on August 24, together with the neighboring houses of Leffert Lefferts and Jeremiah Vanderbilt.[2] The Hegemans rebuilt their house during the war. Lefferts' account reminds us that Dutch continued to be spoken in western Long Island more than a century after the English had gained possession of New York. The Hegemans owned several enslaved Blacks and we get a glimpse of their situation, albeit through the perspective of the white family. (Nearly one-third of the population in Kings County in 1771 were African Americans, nearly all of whom were enslaved.[3])

After the events described in this account, Femmetie Hegeman married her neighbor, the widower Pieter Lefferts in 1784. Pieter Lefferts (1753-1829) had served as a lieutenant in the American forces during the war and subsequently held public office. They had a son, John Lefferts (1785-1829), and a daughter, Seytie (1791-1850), before Femmetie was widowed in 1791. She lived with her son who was elected to a number of public offices including the U.S. Congress and New York State Senate. John Lefferts married Maria Lott (1786-1865) in 1823 and they had two children, (Phebe) Gertrude Lefferts and John Lefferts [Jr.]. When her father died in 1829, Gertrude was only five years old and her brother was two years younger. Thus, Gertrude Lefferts grew up in a household with her widowed mother (Maria Lefferts), paternal grandmother (Femmetie Hegeman Lefferts), and younger brother. No doubt she had heard her grandmother recount her experiences during the Revolution many times. Femmetie lived to be 87 years old; she died in 1847, a year after Gertrude Lefferts married John Vanderbilt.[4]

Lefferts Homestead, 1901

Gertrude Lefferts Vanderbilt (1824-1902) recorded her grandmother's stories in an appendix to her *Social History of Flatbush.* In her introductory comments, Vanderbilt writes, "we can vouch for this as being an unembellished account of what she herself saw and did; and therefore it has the merit of being strictly true."[5] Although these oral histories were not written down for more than a century, they do have the mark of authenticity. They provide a unique civilian perspective on the war and occupation through the eyes of a young woman as she remembered her experiences decades later.

* * *

The morning on which the British troops landed was one of the loveliest we had had that summer. The sky was so clear and bright that you could scarcely think of it as a day which was to bring so much sorrow. I was then just sixteen years old, and my sister was a little older. Father was very feeble—he died of consumption after the close of the war—and, as we had no brothers to protect us, when the news reached us that the army was advancing in the direction of our village, Mother concluded to leave the house and go to a cousin of hers who had a large farm some miles eastward. Accordingly, the great farm-wagon was brought to the door, and such articles of furniture as could be easily removed were placed on it. Our faithful old Negro man, Caesar, received instructions from Father to take his little grandson, Cato, with him, and to drive the cattle through the farm lane to the woods beyond, while Mink, his son, who was a tall, strong, young fellow, was set to watch the premises, and, if possible, to protect the house. Before these arrangements were completed, the rumor reached us that the soldiers were rapidly approaching. The whole village was in commotion. Nothing, as yet, was to be seen of our troops. Women and children were running hither and thither. Men on horseback were riding about in all directions. Farmers might be seen cleaning up their rifles, and half-grown boys practicing shooting at a mark. As I stood near our wagon, which was being loaded, I could see the old Dutch school-master open the door of the little red school-house. The boys rushed out with a shout; it proved to be a longer holiday than they then dreamed of. The advancing army was just beyond the hills. There was an almost incessant firing in that direction. The whole care of the farm, and the management of everything, came upon Mother on account of Father's illness; she was fully equal to any emergency, as many of the women in those days were, but her manners were very quiet and gentle, so that when we all became very much excited over the approach of the British troops, she alone remained calm and proceeded to make the necessary arrangements. General [George] Washington had placed General [Nathaniel] Greene in command of this part of Long Island, and fortifications had been thrown up in Brooklyn and Flatbush to guard the approach to New York. An entrenchment was thrown up in Flatbush a little to the south of us, and a small redoubt, on which a few pieces of artillery were mounted, was put up at the north of us, on a spot which is now in Prospect Park, Brooklyn, and is called the Battle Pass. From these arrangements we knew that the enemy was expected in the line of our house. As my father was ill, and my sister and self were two young girls more full of life and spirit than of discretion, Mother had resolved to seek our safety in flight. Not very brave, you say? Well, perhaps it was not. But I think if any of you young girls were in the line of an approaching army of English and Hessian soldiers, your mother would do the same.

I can bring before me as if it were but yesterday the scenes of our preparations for flight. Diana, the old cook, Caesar's wife, stood with her hand on the crane, which she had turned on its hinge outward from the great open fireplace, ready to hang the iron pot upon the trammel when the mistress should give the order. But the mistress, in neat homespun short gown and petticoat, after the fashion of the Dutch farmers' wives, stood with her finger on her lip, silently planning before she spoke. Father, in his high-backed chair, sat leaning his hand on the cane he held before him, while my sister and I were endeavoring to extract a promise from Caesar that his care should be extended to our pets which we were holding up before him. We had killed a calf that morning. There were no butchers' shops in those days among the Long Island farmers. "You need not cook dinner to-day, Dian," said Mother. "Put all that is left of the calf on the wagon; we must not be a burden upon our friends. Caesar has harnessed up the farm-horses to the large wagon, and we will put it in such things as we can save. We shall go and stay for a while with Cousin Jacobus."

Cousin Jacobus lived about two miles eastward. Just then old Betty came in; she had brought some herbs for my father's cough. Betty was the wife of the last chief of the Canarsie Indians, a tribe who had once owned land in the west end of Long Island. I am sorry to say that both the chief and his wife were often the worse for liquor. Betty was very fond of my mother. The attachment had sprung up under the following circumstances. In the course of a violent storm years before, Mother, looking from the window, saw a woman, without any protection from the rain, seated on a rough stone wall that fenced off our wheat-field from the public road. Touched with pity, Mother sent Caesar to bring the forlorn creature in the house and to give her a place at the kitchen fire.

"Why, Betty, is it you? Why didn't you come in?" asked my mother, as the object of her pity proved to be the old chief's wife.

"Because," replied Betty, "I wanted to know if I had any friends; so I waited to see who of the neighbors would call me in."

"Why, Betty, you knew I was your friend," said Mother.

"I thought so once—I know it now," said the old woman; and from that day she was true to my mother's interest upon every occasion. Knowing that we should leave, she came with a supply of herbs for father and the news that the British army was approaching. She told us that the American troops stationed along the western shore were retreating over the hills toward Flatbush; that Lord Cornwallis with the English soldiers was on the march, and that the Hessian troops had landed. This last piece of information was incorrect; the Hessians under General [Philip] de Heister were daily expected, but they did not come to Flatbush until some days later. The constant although irregular firing in that direction gave weight to Betty's news, and, when the wagon was brought to the door, my sister and I were all excitement, rushing wildly about the house and bringing the most useless things to Caesar to put in the wagon. Mother coolly took out whatever did not seem to her necessary, reserving space only for such household articles as were in her judgment best to save. The very first thing placed on the wagon was the great Dutch Bible with its huge brass clasps and brass corners. Then the little stand was brought on which this heavy Bible always rested. The old Dutch clock was carefully lifted in, and some one or two articles of furniture, and our clothing. The horses were getting very restive under the firing, which could now be heard distinctly from beyond the western woods.

"Come, Femmetia," Mother called to me again, "you must drive. Where is Gertia?"

"Come, girls, come," exclaimed my father, somewhat impatiently; but, even after we were all seated in the wagon, and I held the long whip over the heads of the horses, ready to give them the signal to go, he himself delayed us with the many parting admonitions he gave to Mink, who was to be left in charge of the barnyard.

"Go as far as Yost Williamse's lane," said my father. "I will leave word there as we pass how much farther you must drive them."

I, almost unconsciously, had given the horses a tap on their ears with the point of my whip; it only needed this in connection with the constant sound of firearms to start them.

"Hold on, Femmetia. How can you be so impatient? Seytie," turning to my mother, "do keep that child quiet."

"But, Father, it was you who hurried us just a moment ago."

Mother shook her head at me. By this time the horses had stopped, and old Caesar had come up to us again, and now stood listening to my father, with one hand upon the wagon side.

"You know all our year's grain is stacked in the east lot, Caesar; if you can get them to spare it, it would be well. But I'm afraid it will be burned to save it from falling into the hands of the British. Oh, dear! We never had a more plentiful harvest."

"Never mind," said Mother hopefully, "we are not any worse off than our neighbors. You will bring on another coughing spell if you stay here in this dusty road. Let us go on. Whip up, Femmetia."

"No, no!" said my father, laying his hands on the reins, "hadn't we better stop at Axtell's and see if he can do anything about saving that grain?"[6]

"We may have to seek greater favors than that of Colonel Axtell," said Mother. "Let us not begin already to ask for help. If it is best to burn the grain crop, let it go. Our people will not destroy it sooner than is necessary."

Caesar turned toward the house, and we drove on. Father and Mother looked back at the old homestead with heavy hearts. There were tears in Mother's eyes, although she tried to speak cheerfully for Father's sake.

It was late in the afternoon before we reached the farm-house of Cousin Jacobus. They welcomed us very kindly, and were anxious to hear all we could tell them about the landing of the British. I had a great deal to say about the patriotic things I was going to do, which made Mother anxious about me and quite reconciled to having me out of the way in this quiet place.

That evening a bright light, as of a large fire, shone westward against the sky, and the next morning a heavy smoke brooded over our village. Father took a stout cane to lean on, and my sister and I helped him climb a little eminence which commanded a view in that direction. He looked very pale, and sighed; his step seemed more feeble than ever.

"I think the fire is directly in the line of our house," he said.

Youth is very hopeful, so we girls said many encouraging things, and would not believe in disaster. We were young and happy, the sky was bright, the birds were singing all around us, and we could not bear to think of anything gloomy. We did not know then that to the westward, just in the woods beyond where as children we had played, there were heaps of dead and dying.

Father was probably thinking of what might be even then happening in the village, for he seemed unusually sad, and we noticed that he trembled, as if he felt weak and feeble. I think that our merry tones jarred upon him. He could not bear to see us so light-hearted, knowing the perils of our people, and the desolation even then threatening our dear village. We were sure that the British had already been driven back to their ships. He shook his head sadly and said: "I am afraid the old homestead is burned down, children!"

Father was right. When, after the Battle of Long Island, we returned home, before we reached the village we could see the tall old trees that had stretched their arms so protectingly over our roof; they were all charred and blackened by the flames. Yes, Father was right; the old homestead was burned down.

Two of our neighbors' houses, as well as our own, were burned to the ground. This was done by order of Lord Cornwallis, because they offered a defense behind which the American riflemen could reload, and from which they could discharge their firearms.

When we returned to the village we were obliged to live in the house of friends who left when we did, but remained longer from home. What a scene of desolation met us on our return! There had been a most reckless destruction and waste of property. What could not be used was broken and destroyed.

Our church was used for the accommodation of prisoners and the sick, and the wounded soldiers were placed in the old school-house.[7] Three of our neighbors who had left the village had their houses turned into hospitals for the American officers as the sickness increased. There had been very heavy rains all through the autumn of 1776, and an epidemic had broken out, arising from the effluvia [sewage] connected with the British and Hessian encampment. Many of our neighbors and friends were taken ill with this fever, and very few of those who were seized survived. Food was scanty; even the little to be obtained by hard work we were likely to be robbed of at any moment by the lawless plunderers who had followed in the train of the army.

Some of the houses seem to have been used indiscriminately as stables for horses and as barracks for soldiers. The fences were torn down, the gardens trampled on, the crops destroyed. The roads were so cut up by the passage of artillery wagons that, as it proved to be a very rainy season, they were almost impassable. There was scarcely a family in the whole town which was not visited by the camp fever. I was very ill, and poor Mother had the care of me during all that dreary autumn, as well as of Father, who seemed to be very much prostrated, and to cough more than ever. We were all depressed in consequence of the discouraging rumors which were circulated as to the general state of the country. The newspapers reached us rarely. The *New York Journal and General Advertiser,* printed by John Holt, near the Coffee House, was a very warm advocate of the American cause. It was sometimes brought to us by the prisoner officers who were billeted on the inhabitants after the capture of Fort Washington.[8] This hopeful little sheet was handed from neighbor to neighbor, and it helped to cheer us up in those dull November days. There were two other newspapers of which we often obtained copies from the British officers: *The New York Gazette and Weekly Mercury,* printed by Hugh Gaine, and Rivington's *New York Gazetteer, or the Connecticut, Hudson's River, New Jersey and Quebec Weekly Advertiser*—such was its ambitious name. The last mentioned of these papers left us in doubt about everything, except the loyalty due to the King of England.

You may imagine how difficult it was for us to get the papers when I tell you that the Fulton Ferry, that great thoroughfare of to-day, was then only crossed by occasional rowboats.[9]

My mother was very active and energetic; she was naturally of a cheerful disposition, and disposed to look upon the bright side of things. She would not allow us girls to sit down and mope over our discomforts, but insisted upon our sharing with her the support of the family. Old Caesar had managed to keep some of our cows hidden in the woods at the end of the farm lane. Mother set aside every morning as much milk as Father needed, but she would not reserve any for herself nor for us girls. She sold milk and butter to the British officers; they paid a good price for it, and this was our main dependence that winter. We used to spin and knit a great deal, for Mother would not allow us an idle moment. I was very fond of reading, and I would hide away ends of candle to read by when the rest of the family were asleep. All my education was in the Dutch language; I never went to an English school in my life, but I taught myself to read English, so that I would take up an English newspaper and read it aloud to my sister in Dutch, or, reading a Dutch book, I could translate it into English for the prisoner officers as rapidly as if it was written in English.

It was useless to try and raise grain that year, for the fences were all destroyed, and our beautiful farm was laid waste. Our faithful Caesar managed, however, to pasture some of the horses of the cavalry officers in the wood-lots at the back of the farm, out of sight of the road, and that was very profitable. I must tell you of something in this connection which afforded us much amusement.

We had a wood-lot at the north end of the farm, known familiarly as Nova Scotia. There was no undergrowth, and, as the grass was luxuriant, here the horses were pastured. One morning an English officer came in great haste to Caesar, asking for his horse. Caesar, who had had no great opinion of British troops, seeing the trouble their coming had given, replied, without looking up from his work, that the horse was in Nova Scotia. "How dared you send my horse to Nova Scotia?" demanded the Englishman, getting very red in the face. The old colored man looked up in surprise, but he merely said that "Master had ordered it to be sent there." The officer stamped his foot in rage. "I tell you I want my horse; I meant to use him this very day. What right had he to send him away?" Caesar thought his conduct was certainly remarkable, inasmuch as there was no better pasture than Nova Scotia lot for miles around. In great rage the Englishman advanced toward the house. He was too much of a gentleman to be rude to a young girl who received him with politeness, and when I met him at the door the struggle between his anger and the desire to appear calm kept him silent. I invited him in, and, knowing him to be the owner of one of the finest horses in the pasture-lot, I sent Mink to bring down "the Financier." The struggle to repress his pent-up indignation was ineffectual. You may imagine his embarrassment when, in the midst of his reproaches, he looked up and saw his spirited horse come gayly cantering down the farm lane. He was a kind-hearted man, and very much of a gentleman. He could scarcely forgive himself for being so rude, and he tried in every way to make reparation for his conduct. He was a fast friend of ours after that, and was enabled by his position to do us many an act of kindness, which in our defenseless state we certainly needed. Caesar was not as reticent as we wished him to be, and when the officers got hold of the story, they joked him for months after about the disposition which the rebels had made of his horse.

All Mother's energies were now directed to gaining a home, so that she might make Father more comfortable. It was almost impossible to get building materials. With the money she had saved she purchased some lumber from a neighbor, but it was not sufficient to complete the house. The room intended for my sister and myself was not floored all the way across. This was fun for me, but my sister did not view it in that light. It is strange what different dispositions may be in the same family. I looked on the bright side of everything, Sister on the dark side. I thought of our unfloored room as a good joke, she as a great misfortune. On the first night that we went up to our room, I skipped over the beams to the flooring as nimbly as a squirrel. While she stood trembling at the other side, in the doorway, insisting that she could not get over, I stood coolly combing out my long hair and teasing her.

"I can never get over," she said dolefully.

"Oh, yes, you can; it is very easy. I like it. Mother wants to get a board laid from the door to the bed, but I sha'n't let her. It's better so. It's such fun. Besides, we have only to go to the edge, and we can look right down to the room below. I like it better than our room in the old house. If you don't come soon I shall put out the light and go to bed." She knew this was what I would be quite likely to do, for I was, I confess, fond of teasing her.

"Oh! now don't; I shall break my neck, and then Mother will have the care of me as well as Father."

"Oh, no, she wouldn't. That would be the end of you and all your troubles. Still, if you're going to be so serious, I suppose I must come."

Then I skipped across to her, and, leading her just half way over, let go her hand. Of course she screamed, and Mother opened the door below. "Hush-sh-sh, girls! You'll waken your father."

My sister appealed to Mother for help, but the door had already closed below. Before I had time to relieve my "prisoner," as I called her, we heard the heavy bare foot of Diana approaching. She came to the room beneath and called up to us:

"Dere's a hull lot of sogers [soldiers] jes come inter de barn. Spec dey'll kill all what's lef of de chickens."

It was no new thing. We were constantly being plundered. There was no redress for the depredations daily committed. One pair of our farm-horses had been taken from the harrow, even while Caesar was using them. I remarked to my sister that is was a "harrowing case." She wouldn't laugh. I can't say whether she felt so disheartened at our loss that she did not appreciate my poor attempt at wit, or whether she understood so little English that she did not see it. We always spoke Dutch in the family. We only used English in speaking with the prisoners who were billeted upon us, and to the British officers. To return to Dian, who was standing below, her arms akimbo, looking up at us:

"You jes come down," she said.

The hint was enough. I helped my sister to cross the room to the safe flooring, and rushed down stairs to Diana. Good, faithful soul, I was her favorite and her accomplice in all her attacks upon the enemy. Mother never knew how many scouting parties of two [which] she and I formed that winter to watch our premises. She had concealed weapons at the kitchen-door—an old rifle and a broomstick; with these we proceeded to the barn, dodging from the great walnut-tree to the corn-crib, and from there flitting behind the wagon-house, until we reached the shadow of the great barn. It was moonlight. I often wonder now that I could ever have been so fearless, but I was young and knew no danger or cause for alarm. Besides, I had perfect faith in my leader. Dian and I were fast friends, and she had never failed in any of our expeditions against the invaders of the poultry-yard. She had confided to me the plan she would have pursued had she been in Caesar's place when they stole the horses, and I had accredited her with the victory she might have gained.

In this instance it was by stratagem that we were to conquer. She had privately surveyed the field of action before calling me, and the moonlight had enabled her to recognize in the thieves some of the members of the company who were appointed to protect (?) the town. Concealed between a corn-crib and the barn, she thrust her rifle through a hole in the side door, I at the same time flinging a stone against the barn to attract the notice of the parties within to the fact of their close proximity to the rifle. The moonlight fell upon the weapon pointed at them by unseen hands. It was enough; we were left in possession of the field. Mother knew nothing about the raid until the next day, when Dian told her that we were to have roast fowls for dinner.

We could not buy any nails for building, so that we were obliged to use those taken from the ruins of the burned houses. The prisoner officers used to meet with us and other young girls of our age, and help us straighten the nails there gathered. Thus the ruins got to be a place of fashionable resort. The young people collected there for an afternoon's chat, but Mother, who did not look with friendly eyes on the attentions of all these young officers, insisted that there was quite as much talking and flirting as there was work. The young girls of our age, of course, could not but sympathize with the prisoners, and as the officers had little to beguile their time, both parties had an excellent excuse for meeting there, and boasted very much of their industry, as people are apt to do when work and pleasure are united.

I have heard that four hundred prisoners were billeted in the southern towns of Kings County. The only regiment left in Flatbush after the Battle of Long Island was the Forty-second Regiment of Highlanders.[10]

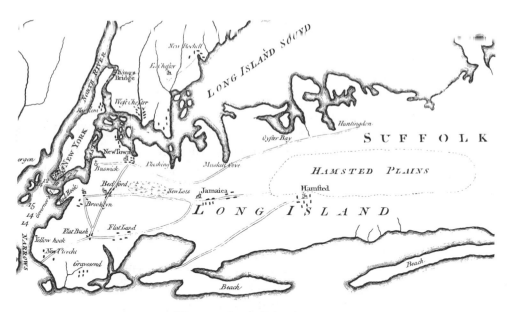

Western Long Island, 1776

There was little protection for property at this time; appeal to law was impossible; indeed, people acted as if there was no law. Everything in the shape of personal property was kept at the risk of the owner. The cattle were not safe unless watched vigilantly. Mother went on one occasion to our neighbor, Colonel Axtell, and submitted to him the fact that all our cows had been driven off in spite of her remonstrance. She was a great favorite among her neighbors, and the Colonel listened to her story. After conferring with his English friends, he sent us word that Caesar might go on a certain day to a place which he named, and from among the herd of cattle which he would find there he might point out those which belonged to us. It was a great relief to see Caesar let down the bars, and turn the herd once more into their accustomed pasture. From this you may see how insecure property was, and with what audacity we were plundered. Our household articles of value we were obliged to conceal. Many persons hid boxes containing valuables in their fields and gardens. It has been asserted that some of this hidden treasure was never taken up, but this is very doubtful.

Our spoons, tankard, and such pieces of silver tea-service as every Dutch housekeeper at that time possessed were placed in a box and hidden under the hearthstone. The insecurity of the hiding-place was made evident to us by Mink, who was not in the secret. He remarked in Dutch to his father, old Caesar, that some evil spirit must have taken lodging under the hearth, for it seemed loose and uneven. The Negroes were so superstitious that the supposed presence of an evil spirit would have insured it from their examination, but we felt that it was insecure if it attracted any observation whatever, and with the assistance of Caesar, who was fully to be trusted, we found for it another hiding-place.

A neighbor of ours related to us her experience in this matter. She had secreted a number of gold coins in one of those round, ball-shaped pincushions which the Dutch matrons sometimes wore suspended by a ribbon at their side. A party of English soldiers, on entering the room, noticed this novelty (as it was to them) in the good lady's dress. One of them playfully, although not very politely, cut the ribbon with his sword, and the whole party had a boisterous game of ball with the pincushion. Once or twice it bounced in the ashes of the broad, open fireplace, from which it was snatched up and tossed again from hand to hand. To show any anxiety would have betrayed the value of the property, so that the owner was obliged to continue her work unmoved, although, had they torn the cushion in their rough play, she would have lost all the money she had saved when the war broke out.

Not only was our property insecure, but our homes were liable at any time to be invaded, and seclusion was almost impossible; there were at various times soldiers billeted upon us arbitrarily without our consent, and often without compensation. A Waldeck regiment, commanded by Colonel De Horn, was quartered upon our village in this manner, as were also some soldiers who had fought in Canada through the French war, and afterward a Saxon regiment. In addition to this, the quiet of our homes was invaded by companies of soldiers marching from place to place. I remember one evening that we were all, even sick Father, turned out of the house by a small company of soldiers who took possession. Fortunately, they soon received marching orders, and they left as suddenly as they came.

The American prisoners had our warmest sympathy. They were on parole, and were not guarded strictly; they could go about where they chose.[11] When the French fleet under Count D'Estaing was expected, these prisoners went daily to see the vessels from the hill.

I took no pains to disguise my sympathy for the American prisoners and my warm interest in the cause of freedom. My sister sometimes begged me not to express my opinions so openly in the presence of the British, and Mother checked me often, telling me that I was acting unwisely. On one occasion a line of artillery wagons was passing. The foremost driver, to avoid a muddy portion of road, turned his horses upon the sidewalk in front of our house. I was determined that the second should not do the same; I rushed out to frighten the horses, and succeeded so well that they overturned the wagon I was obliged to retreat precipitately, and Mother had to meet the storm I had raised. An old German doctor, who was a frequent visitor at our house, laughed immoderately at my heroic attack upon the artillery and my subsequent discomfiture. I can see him now as he stood giving a description of the whole scene to a tall Hessian officer. He turned to me, exclaiming between the paroxysms of laughter:

"Oh, vat a heroine vas our leetle Femmetia! She attack dese big artillery-mon! She attack him wis a gun? Oh, no! wis a broomsteek! eh, Fem? a broomsteek!"

Then he broke out afresh, and the contagion extended to the tall Hessian, whose name was so impressed upon me by the very vividness of the whole scene that I can recall it to this day, unpronounceable as it is. When the old doctor saw me blushing deeply, mortified as I was at his description, his kind heart misgave him, for I was a great pet of his, and, patting me affectionately on the head, he said:

"Navair mind; she's our brave leetle lady, Captain Bumbbochk, and een moije vrouw [pretty woman], eh?"

The old doctor was very fond of a joke, and I knew that he was telling Father the story over again soon after, for I heard his voice in Father's room, and he was laughing as loudly as before.

We were, as I have said, subjected to constant exactions, from which we had no means of redress. On one occasion, as old Caesar was plowing, in the almost hopeless endeavor to cultivate our vegetable garden, a soldier came up and demanded the horses for the British service. Caesar, always true to us, promptly and indignantly refused to take them from the plow. Little Cato, who was an interested spectator, ran to the house to inform Mother of the predatory design of the redcoat. Father overhead the child's account. He had a high fever, and had been ill in bed for some time. Under the excitement of anger and fever united, he rose and dressed himself. Taking his heavy cane, he went to the field, and with the aid of Caesar he administered such correction to the soldier that he sought safety in flight. Strange to say, the exertion cured Father of the fever. He broke out in a profuse perspiration, and, although he was much exhausted, he had no fever afterward, and was able to sit up in his arm-chair for the rest of the day.

Large sums of money were loaned by the inhabitants of Kings County for the advancement of the American cause. The agent for collecting this money was intrusted by Governor [George] Clinton with blank notes signed by himself. These blanks the agent filled out with the sum given. The greatest secrecy was necessary in collecting this money, as it was attended with imminent danger to all concerned. Through her thrift, economy, and industry, Mother was enabled to appropriate five hundred pounds to this object. This she gave in small sums at a time, and on one occasion, as she was counting out the money into the hands of the agent, she saw, on looking up, a British officer enter the door-yard. For the Major to escape from the house was impossible, and had he been seen his life would have been forfeited.

"Femmetia," said my mother, "hurry out to meet that officer. Don't let him come in this room as you value your life."

"Talk as fast as you can, Fem, and be as entertaining as possible," said the Major, looking anxiously toward the approaching figure.

"Let my sister come with me," said I, rather timid at accepting so great responsibility.

"No! no!" said my mother imperatively. "Too much depends on it. Don't fail us now, child!"

She looked sternly at me, and I felt she was right, for the consciousness of danger had already brought the color to my sister's face; it must depend upon me alone to divert any suspicion, should such be aroused, on the part of the Englishman.

I hurried out of the room as they rapidly gathered up the coin they had been counting, and Mother went to look for a hiding-place for the Major, who was an old friend of ours. I could hear the doors opened and closed; I could hear a word in Dutch now and then; happily, our visitor could not understand it; but I did my best to look unconscious, and I believe I succeeded. I had been in the habit of expressing my opinions pretty freely, and, if I chatted on this occasion more rapidly than usual, the officer probably thought that I was in good spirits, and would be rather more entertaining company than if he went in the next room to look for my father and mother. He staid [stayed] what appeared to me an unreasonably long time, and left without a suspicion of who was under the same roof with himself, and of the treason being enacted almost within his reach.

Never before nor since have I had such weighty reasons for striving to attract attention to myself, and this was the only time during the war that Mother ever expressed gratification that I had succeeded in entertaining an English officer.

Notes

Source: "Appendix" in Gertrude Lefferts Vanderbilt, *The Social History of Flatbush: and Manners and Customs of the Dutch Settlers in Kings County* (New York: D. Appleton, 1881), pp. 330-45. A second edition, published posthumously in 1909, included three additional chapters; the Appendix in that edition is pp. 370-85.

Editing changes are minimal. Some of the punctuation has been modernized; titles of newspapers have been italicized and "Negro" has been capitalized, consistent with today's usage. The Hegemans would have been speaking Dutch. Vanderbilt wrote phonetically when she tried to reproduce African American and German accents in English.

1. The Lefferts Homestead is located in the Children's Corner near the Willink Entrance of Prospect Park on Flatbush Avenue at Empire Boulevard (718-789-2822).

2. John J. Gallagher, *The Battle of Brooklyn, 1776* (New York: Sarpedon, 1995), p. 91. Gallagher states that the American forces burned the houses; Femmetie Lefferts attributes the burning to the British soldiers.

Femmetie's mother's maiden name was Seytie Suydam; her father was Evert Hegeman. Their oldest daughter (Femmetie's sister), Cornelia (Nelly), married Peter Cornell before the events described here. Gertrude (Gertie) Hegeman never married. Femmetie named her own daughter, Seytie (1791-1850), after her mother.

3. Edgar J. McManus, *A History of Negro Slavery in New York* (Syracuse: Syracuse University Press, 1966), p. 199.

4. Gertrude did not use her first name, Phebe, which is the English form of Femmetie. Gertrude's husband, Judge Vanderbilt, was an invalid in his last decade and died in 1877 at the relatively young age of 58. Gertrude herself outlived her younger brother and her only child who died in 1893 and 1895 respectively. She died in 1902 at the age of 78 (the second edition of her *Social History of Flatbush* was published posthumously). Biographical information on the Lefferts family is from Shirley G. Hibbard, "Research Report on Five Women Associated with the Lefferts Homestead," August 1992, typescript at the Lefferts Homestead; and Tenis G. Bergen, *Genealogy of the Lefferts Family, 1650-1878* (Albany, 1878), pp. 83, 86.

5. Vanderbilt, *Flatbush,* p. 330 (1881 edition; p. 370 in 1909 edition).

6. William Axtell's country house, Melrose Hall, was in Flatbush. He was a member of the King's Council and colonel of a regiment of provincial forces, the "Nassau Blues."

7. The Dutch Reformed Church at this time was a stone church built in 1699. Although it was ransacked by the British, it was in use until 1793 (their third church was built in 1796).

8. Fort Washington in northern Manhattan (located near what is now Fort Washington Avenue, between 181st and 186th Streets), surrendered to the British on November 15, 1776.

9. The Fulton Ferry began to operate steam ferries in 1814 across the East River where the Brooklyn Bridge was later built. (The Brooklyn terminus of the ferry was where the Empire Fulton Ferry State Park is now located.) Sailboats and rowboats could be hired to cross the river from Brooklyn to Manhattan as early as 1642.

10. The 42nd Royal Highland Regiment was also known as the Black Watch. See Gallagher, *Battle of Brooklyn,* p. 183.

11. For a first-hand account of life in Flatbush by an American prisoner on parole, see Col. Alexander Graydon, *Memoirs of a Life, Chiefly Passed in Pennsylvania, Within the Last Sixty Years* (Edinburgh: William Blackwood, 1822), pp. 255-334 (a copy is in the East Hampton Library). A twenty-year-old Philadelphian wrote a letter in 1781 from her family's summer home in Flatbush, which provides a Loyalist perspective. See "Letter of Miss Rebecca Franks," *Pennsylvania Magazine of History and Biography* 23 (1899): 303-9, reprinted in P.M. Zall, *Becoming an American: Young People in the American Revolution* (Hamden, CT: Linnet Books, 1993), pp. 94-98.

Heroism on Occupied Long Island, 1776-1783

Augustus Griffin

Augustus Griffin (1767-1866) was born and died in the town of Southold where he had lived virtually all his life. His Terry and Griffin ancestors had lived on the North Fork for several generations. Griffin taught in an Orange County school from 1790-1794, but spent most of his adult life in Oysterponds at the eastern end of Long Island (today's Orient). There he taught school and at various times operated a general store and inn.

Griffin began keeping a diary in 1844, and collected "many facts and incidents." With the assistance of one of his sons, he published his *Journal,* which is based on his memory and diaries. John Orville Terry, in his preface, stated that Griffin was "well known for his literary tastes and indefatigable application to the subject," and described the *Journal* as "an invaluable repository of facts, connected with the early settlement, character, and actions of our ancestors."[1]

Griffin's *Journal* has been long prized for its genealogical data on the early settlers of Southold, but the focus in these selections is on the home front during the Revolution. Griffin was a boy during those years; he was nine years old when the war began and sixteen when peace was concluded. The incidents he recounts probably are ones he heard from others later in life rather than witnessed himself. Several of the selections recount "domestic resistance" by women on the home front. Doubtless some of his stories may have been embellished and romanticized over the years of retelling. Nonetheless, this oral tradition, recorded by a local historian, is part of the history and folklore of the region and provides a glimpse of the vicissitudes of life on occupied Long Island during the Revolutionary War years.

* * *

What hearts, what fortitude, what sublimity and heroism of soul must have actuated our mothers, grandmothers, and their invaluable husbands, to submit and cheerfully make all these unparalleled sacrifices, that their children and descendants might become the partakers of that sweetest of all earthly fruits—Liberty!

In these days of bustle, excitements, sorrow and trouble, Peter Griffin, of Southold, who, with his interesting family of six promising children and wife, left this island.

In those seasons of trial and peril, Peter was owner and master of a fine sailing sloop. By good management and great attention to the alongshore business, in such a vessel, he had realized a handsome support; but now, in

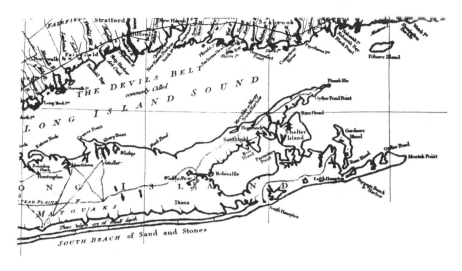

Eastern Long Island, 1776

consequence of the British cruisers, his situation, as to doing business coast-wise, was critical. In crossing from the main to the island, he was often in imminent danger. Once, in the autumn of 1776, he arrived safe in Oysterpond Harbor in the morning. After landing, he proceeded to the inn of Aunt Hannah Brown, as she was called in those days, who kept an inn. After inquiring whether there were any of the enemy in the place, and learning that there was not just at that time, he called for a breakfast. Soon after he and his men had seated themselves at the table, a child came running into the room, and screaming at the top of its lungs, "The troops are coming; the troops are coming!" And, sure, they were within half a mile, on horseback. Captain Griffin and his men immediately ran across the fields to his small boat, then at the landing. They launched her, and boarded the vessel about the time the troops reached the shore, within twenty-five rods of the vessel. They drew up abreast, dismounted, and gave Griffin's sloop the contents of their guns. Before they could reload, Griffin, who was a marksman, took from the cabin his old King's arms, and, without ceremony, returned the fire. At this, they, in much confusion, took refuge behind the nearest house. With much tact and skill in charging his piece, he made several shots at them, which kept them skulking and dodging until he could weigh anchor and be off. Several of the bullets discharged from his gun lodged in the house, which now [1857] is owned by the heirs of the late George Champlin. A year or so after this, Captain Griffin lost his vessel, being captured by the English sloop-of-war *Swan*. The *Swan* was several times in Southold Harbor. At one time, while on shore, Captain Asknew, her commander, was surprised by a party of Yankees, who attacked him as he was pushing off from shore in his barge for his ship. These Yankees fired into his barge, wounding him in his foot, which lamed him for life. I saw him there in 1780.[2]

It is said, and no doubt it is a fact, that these parties of horse which often came to Oysterponds, were Tories [Loyalists] of Long Island. . . .

Richard Brown, the fourth of his family, in succession, known in his day, as Ensign Brown, died at the commencement of the Revolutionary War, aged about seventy-seven years. His wife, who was, when a girl, named Hannah Hawk, was at the time of his demise, about sixty years of age, with an excellent constitution and a strong mind, she entered the melancholy state of widow-hood. Her family, with those of a number of grandchildren, who were orphans now, made her household large; yet, it appears she proved to the world, and her neighbors that wisdom, prudence and discretion, marked her every movement in the government of the charge committed. Soon after the death of her husband, she commenced keeping a Tavern, or Inn; over this establishment she presided with circumspection and dignity. At this time, Long Island was in the possession of the British, and Oysterponds was swarming with British, Hessians and Tories. It was in the Autumn of 1777, on a pleasant evening, that a file of armed soldiers, without ceremony, entered the house of Mrs. Brown. The officer ordered Mrs. Brown to open the door of the room containing the liquors instantly, or he would stave it down. At this threat, accompanied with a horrid oath, she rushed between them and the door, against which she placed her back. He appeared a moment astonished at such fortitude, but collecting himself swore her instant destruction; and with great violence thrust the muzzle of his gun against the door on each side of her person, and as near as he could without hitting her. The marks of those thrusts remained visible for more than sixty years after. She stood facing and thus addressed him, "you unfeeling wretch, you hired tool of a tyrant, your conduct is worse than a savage, my situation you see here, is lonely, I am without a human protector; but know you, Mr. Officer, surrounded as you are with men and arms, that I despise your threats, and if you pass the threshold of this door, you will first pass over my lifeless body." Such language pronounced with emphasis, and true self possession from a lone woman, at such a time and place, was too much for his cowardly soul to withstand. He quailed, muttered and grumbled a hasty retreat. . . .

In the summer of 1781, two whale-boats, manned with twenty men, landed at Southold harbor, and marched up about a mile to Joseph Peck's Inn, made free with his liquors and provisions, abused his family and wounded him seriously with their weapons; they then left for their boats, insulting and robbing the inhabitants by the way. Near their boats was the house of Mr. Constant Lhommedieu, which they entered with words and actions becoming heathens. Mr. Lhommedieu, mildly spoke to their leader, at which he raised his cutlass at Mr. L's. head. Mrs. L. saw it and with true fortitude, rushed between this fiend and her husband, and received the blow on her naked arm. Her arm was broke, but her husband's life was saved. The wretch, at seeing such self-devotion and conjugal purity, in haste left, wondering who could think of subduing a nation of such women and wives. . . .

Who is not familiar with the part so wisely played by the heroic wives, mothers and daughters of the Revolutionary War? Shining examples of their self-denial, their patriotism, constancy, and courage, have come down to us; but the hallowed story of their efforts, sufferings, and trials, is yet unportrayed in colors adequate to the touching, affecting story.

Abigail Moore was the daughter of Robert Hempstead, of Southold. . . . [Her first husband was John Ledyard, her second Micah Moore. Widowed a second time on the eve of the Revolution, she had seven children, four of whom were under ten years of age. She was fifty years old.] The scenes which she was destined to witness, and lived to pass through, occasioned by an eight years' war, were trying and dreadful, especially in the forlorn state of widowhood. In the immediate neighborhood of Mrs. Moore, were quartered numbers of the English and German soldiers. These last carried terror in their movements. Their language, to us, was a jargon.

Amidst and surrounded by these, she conducted her house with piety and wisdom.

It was on a certain evening, during this struggle, that she was placed in a situation to test her fortitude. An officer, with a drawn sword, entered her house with several soldiers. Her children, frightened, came around her for protection. The officer, in a rough voice, observed, "Madam, I am informed [that] you harbor deserters here. If it is true, by the Eternal God, I will lay your house in ashes before morning!" Mrs. Moore heard this threat and oath with perfect calmness, looked him full in the face, and said, "Sir, I am a widow, but feel myself perfectly secure under the protection of that Providence which has thus far sustained me. My trust is in God; I have no fears from man. Allow me to request who was your informer?" He quickly replied, "That man," pointing to Elnathan Burts, who stood present.[3] She as readily answered, "He is a liar; and, if you choose, I will prove him that, and more." They left.

Fanny, Mrs. Abigail Moore's only daughter by her first husband, Captain Ledyard, was on a visit to Groton, at her uncle's, Colonel Ledyard's, when he was massacred at Fort Griswold, in September 1781. She, as an angel of mercy, and alive to every tender feeling of humanity, was the first to enter the Fort to administer to the wounded and dying, who were left in and near the Fort after the enemy had left this scene of their fiendish cruelty and slaughter. With all the divine emotions of pure, affectionate woman, she flew to the wretched, disfigured, distressed group, whose bodies were covered with blood. She washed their wounds, allayed their parching thirst, and did all in her power to alleviate and assuage their pains and acute distress.[4]

The self-denial, patriotism and courage of our Revolutionary women merit a conspicuous page in the volume of American History. Many of them were truly mothers in Israel.

Mrs. Deborah Townsend, the amiable wife of Jothom Townsend, of Queens County, New York, deserves a notice for her fearless stand and strength of mind in the cause of her country.

It was in the summer of the year 1777, when the British had full possession of Long Island, the arduous cares of a family of children and their wants devolved on Mrs. Townsend. Her husband had joined the army of Washington; he had been honored with the commission of Captain. His fine farm was situated at what is called "Cedar Swamp" [Old Brookville], Queens County. It was in the morning, while the lonely Mrs. Townsend was immersed in the attentions incident to a household of children, and when she was preparing for baking, that a small party of British cavalry rode up to the house, dismounted, and abruptly entered the apartment where Mrs. Townsend was busied in her domestic duties. The officer, with warmth, apart from every vestige of civility, demanded of Mrs. Townsend the keys of the grainhouse, as, he observed, his horses must be fed immediately. She, with dignity and self-possession, hesitated a compliance; told them she had not any grain for them. He replied, with a threat, that if she did not instantly deliver them up, he would split the door down. He proceeded, as if to execute his fiendish promise. She, without a second thought, seized a large bread shovel, which she wielded with such consummate courage and skill over his head, that, astonished and confounded, he and his men soon made a hasty retreat, exclaiming, with warmth, "If this woman is a sample of the wives of our opponents, it is useless to think of subduing them."

In October, 1850, John K. Townsend took me out in his carriage to the farm of his late father, Jotham Townsend, at Cedar Swamp, of a little more than two hundred acres. From the handsome sight on which the spacious house and out-buildings stand, you can see every field and orchard on the place.

It was here, in this secluded retreat, that Mrs. Townsend, their mother, resided when she displayed such an undaunted, fearless and determined resolution. Such decision of character and contempt of fear, lonely and unprotected as she was, truly merits a panegyric. I was also shown the family cemetery. Two marble stones show the resting-place of the bodies of their parents. It is about one hundred rods from the house, on the borders of a beautiful grove. . . .

Woman has, in every age of the world, evinced patriotic zeal in national conflicts for the liberties and happiness of her country and family.

Many and glowing instances are recorded of their fearless and daring intrepidity. At certain times, it would seem their courage bordered on rashness. In our own favored and happy country, when struggling for its independence, the personal bravery and heroism of many of the wives and daughters of our Revolutionary fathers astonished, and often dismayed, their heartless invaders.

From 1776 to 1783, Long Island was solely under British rule. In the year 1778, foreign mercenaries were quartered in and around Southold. Generally, their movements and address were unpleasant and forbidding, especially when entering a house for favors.

It was on a summer's day in the year last mentioned, that a small party of light horse hastily rode up to the house of Major John Corwin, of Mattituck, and the officer, in a rough voice, demanded of Mrs. Corwin, (her husband being absent) some grain for their horses, and, to enforce this order and show the consequence of his authority, he, with a commanding air, observed: "Madam, your situation warns you to an immediate attention to my request. To abuse my authority, is to rush to destruction." Mrs. Corwin was unmoved, no-wise daunted, and coolly replied that she had no food for him nor his horses. "Well," said he, with a harsh oath, "here is a fine piece of wheat across the road; it will answer for our horses, and we'll have it." With that, he made for the bars which opened into his field of grain. At this move, she, with a spirit almost superhuman, commanded him instantly to desist, at his peril; "for," she said, "although I am alone and unprotected, and in your power, I am a stranger to fear, and defy your threats. The first horse that enters that wheat field I will shoot instantly dead." With this daring resolution, and, suiting the action to the word, she seized her husband's old King's arm, which stood loaded behind the door, and took her station to consummate her purpose.

The wheat field was not touched. They left, muttering curses and praises on the women. Mrs. Corwin, previous to her marriage, was a Miss Mapes. She died on Christmas day, in 1850, in her ninety-first year. . . .

The day succeeding that on which the British burnt New London, in September, 1781, and massacred the garrison at Fort Griswold, at Groton, they passed over the sound to Long Island, and landed, many of them, at Oysterpond point, traveled up the road, about two miles, to this village. Their actions and disorderly conduct carried terror to the inhabitants. Mr. Jeremiah Vail, who had just heard of their merciless cruelties at New London and Groton, with emotions of no common excitement viewed them coming up the road. His wife—called Betsey, but named Elizabeth—displayed great self-possession and fortitude. She saw them approaching the house, without order or discipline, and very furious. Mr. Vail kept a house of entertainment, but at this time had no liquors except two hogsheads of good cider. The thought of this cider flashed across her mind, and the consequences that would follow should they find it. She went forthwith, alone, to the cellar, knocked out the bungs [stoppers] of the hogsheads containing the liquor, and, by an almost superhuman effort, turned them in a position so that their contents were soon all flooding the ground floor. She then ascended the stairs in time to meet the unwelcome countenances and forbidding expressions of this ruthless gang, who entered the house more like demons than civilized beings. Their looks she described as awful—having not slept probably within the last forty-eight hours, and besmeared visibly with the blood of her murdered countrymen at Groton. They flourished their swords, and uttered oaths of vengeance on American rebels; seized and bound Mr. Vail, and confined him in the garret. They searched every room, pantry, and closet, in search of, as they said, "something to drink." Finding nothing, the cellar was next resorted to. They there soon discovered they had been successfully foiled in their wicked purpose. The ground had drank the liquor, and was still sober. Like mad men, they ascended to the room of Mrs. Vail, and demanded her reasons for depriving them of refreshments. She very deliberately replied: "You are the enemies of my country; I have nothing for you; you have no business here; threats nor oaths don't alarm me. If I have done wrong, I am responsible to my husband, not to you. You will not eat or drink in this house, if I can prevent it." She expected violence; but they left the house very soon after, muttering curses for her devotion and fortitude. Mrs. Vail was the daughter of Charles and Elizabeth Glover, of Oysterponds.[5]

Notes

Source: Augustus Griffin, *Griffin's Journal* (Orient: Privately printed, 1857), pp. 126-27, 135-42, 185-86, 193-94. The Oysterponds Historical Society reprinted this in a facsimile edition in 1983 with a *Supplement to Griffin's Journal* (Orient: Oysterponds Historical Society, 1983), which has biographical notes on Griffin and a new index.

Only minor editorial changes were made in the selections, e.g., to correct a few typographical errors. Griffin's notes are identified by his initials [AG]; the editor's by her initials (NAN).

1. John O. Terry, "Preface," to *Griffin's Journal*, p. 7. Terry was a local poet and "philosopher" who had written a poem about Griffin which he had published in 1850. One of the stanzas states: "His mind is a record of ages and dates,/ And his knowledge to others with pride he relates—/ Grand-fathers, grand-mothers, great-uncles and aunts,/ All start into life from his memory's haunts." From "Augustus Griffin, Esq.," reprinted in *Supplement,* not paginated. On Terry, see Mildred H. Smith, "The Homespun Poet of Oysterponds, John Orville Terry," *Journal of Long Island History* 8 (Winter-Spring 1968): 12-25 (NAN).

2. Although no independent collaboration has been located for this and other incidents described here by Griffin, *Rivington's Gazette,* the Loyalist New York City newspaper, reported on February 26, 1778, that "Peter Griffen" was one of "a gang of ruffians" who "stripped the schooner Clio of her sails, rigging, &c, which they carried off and have no doubt sent across the Sound." Quoted by Henry Onderdonk, Jr., in *Revolutionary Incidents of Suffolk and Kings Counties,* 1849 (Reprint; Port Washington: Kennikat Press, 1970), p. 71. None of the other persons or incidents Griffin mentions are included in Onderdonk's book which he compiled from various newspaper accounts and primary sources. Although Onderdonk had published his *Revolutionary Incidents* before Griffin published his *Journal,* clearly Griffin was not drawing on it. Onderdonk also published a companion book, *Documents and Letters Intending to Illustrate Revolutionary Incidents of Queens County* in 1846 (also reprinted by Kennikat in 1970), and a 2d series, *Documents and Letters Intending to Illustrate Revolutionary Incidents of Queens County* (Hempstead: Lott van de Water, 1884). Onderdonk left an unpublished manuscript of a second series on Suffolk and Kings counties, which is in the Brooklyn Historical Society (NAN).

3. Elnathan Burts was an inhabitant of Southold—a man of not much repute—about thirty years of age, living with his father in a small house one half mile east of Ashmomogue Beach. While the British were quartered at Southold, he was much with them, and, as it appears, it was for no good purpose. In the spring of 1781, his neighbors attempted to arrest him for some mischievous act—[the neighbors were] John Boiseau, Nat Lhommedieu, Stephen Baily, Thomas Ledyard, and Joshua Horton, all young men. Horton, who was foremost in pursuit, was shot dead by Burts, who then went and took refuge with the British. Some year or two after this murder, Burts died of the small pox [AG].

4. Mr. Jephsa Latham was in the Fort at the time, and survived the awful catastrophe. I knew him well, and have heard him tell the doleful tale [AG].

5. For other accounts of women's heroism during the Revolution, see Edna H. Yeager, "Long Island's Unsung," *Daughters of the American Revolution Magazine* 109 (October 1975): 908-14; Edna H. Yeager, "Long Island Women in the Revolution," *Long Island Forum* 40 (January 1977): 10-11; and William Donaldson Halsey, *Sketches from Local History* (Bridgehampton: Privately printed, 1935), pp. 179-81. Halsey includes some of the incidents described by Griffin, but also others, including one commemorated in "The Ballad of Pudding Hill." The village of East Hampton still has a Pudding Hill Lane (NAN).

Country Excursions and Visits on Eastern Long Island, 1784

Francisco de Miranda

Francisco de Miranda (1750-1816) is sometimes known as "The Precursor of Spanish-American Independence" for his efforts to liberate the Spanish colonies. Miranda was born in Venezuela, attended the University of Caracas, and traveled in Spain for two years in his early twenties. He became a captain in the Spanish infantry and, after being stationed in North Africa, was sent to Cuba in 1780. Spain then was allied with France against England in the war the United States was fighting. Miranda assisted at a battle at Fort Pensacola in Florida and helped secure funds for the French fleet which enabled it to assist in the victory at Yorktown, effectively ending the Revolutionary War.

Despite these miliary successes, Miranda was convicted of engaging in contraband trade. To escape a prison sentence and appeal the decision, he left Cuba and embarked on a whaling ship for the United States. (He finally was exonerated of the charges in 1799.) Miranda landed in North Carolina in June 1783 and visited the Carolinas before sailing to Philadelphia where he met George Washington and other important men. Miranda traveled through New Jersey to New York City. In February 1784, he spent several days on western Long Island, then headed up the Hudson to visit the Saratoga battlefield. After traveling in Connecticut for nearly a month, he crossed the Sound to eastern Long Island in August where he remained ten days before resuming his trip through New England. Miranda sailed to London from Boston in December 1784.

Miranda had an eventful career after his visit to the United States. He spent two years in England where he unsuccessfully tried to get the government to help liberate the Spanish colonies. When the French Revolution broke out, he volunteered and served as a general in the republican army. Then Miranda returned to London where he resumed his efforts to liberate Venezuela, and went to America trying to organize an expedition from New York in 1805. In 1810 he accompanied Simón Bolívar to Venezuela where the government had been overthrown. General Miranda took command of the troops, helped organize a government, and ruled as a dictator. When the Venezuelan revolution collapsed in 1812, Miranda was arrested and died in disgrace in a Spanish prison in 1816. He did not live to see the successful liberation of Venezuela and other Spanish colonies in the Western Hemisphere. In his homeland, a monument, erected in 1986, is inscribed: "Miranda took part in all the great movements of world politics in his lifetime: The independence of the United States of North America, the French Revolution, and the Independence of South America."[1]

Francisco de Miranda. From a crayon portrait drawn in 1786, presumably by Heinrich Lips von Kloten. In the Lavater collection of portraits, National Bibliotek, Vienna, Austria.

Miranda kept a diary and diligently saved his papers, although his manuscripts remained in a private collection until the twentieth century. The Venezuelan government purchased his papers in 1926 and returned them to Caracus. In 1926, William Spence Robertson published in the original Spanish the portions of his diary dealing with Miranda's 1783-1784 visit to the United States. This translation of the Long Island sections was by Ettie Hedges Pennypacker in 1937. The full diary of his travels in the United States was not translated and published in English until 1963.[2]

John S. Ezell, who edited the 1963 English edition of Miranda's travels, characterizes Miranda's diary as "one of the better travel accounts dealing with the United States." Miranda was sympathetic to Americans and did not have preconceived biases. Ezell concludes that it provides a "charming and enlightening narrative" of life in the United States which is "well substantiated."[3]

In the sections pertaining to Long Island which are reprinted here, Miranda describes winter excursions by sleigh to Brooklyn, the Hempstead Plains, and Rockaway. Later, en route to Boston in August, he took a boat from New London across Long Island Sound to visit Dr. and Mrs. Nathaniel Gardiner. Miranda landed on Shelter Island, stayed with Thomas Dering one night, and then proceeded to East Hampton. After two days, he was ready to sail to Newport, but had to wait several days in Sag Harbor for a boat and favorable winds. With poor accommodations and "no society in which to mingle," Miranda's comments on Sag Harbor are quite negative. It is interesting to compare his descriptions with those of Timothy Dwight who visited two decades later (see Dwight's "Journey to Long Island").

* * *

[February 1784] The weather having improved 'tho painfully cold, with rivers and bay frozen, I resolved to make a short excursion to Long Island. At 12 o'clock I went aboard the ferry (as they call it) accompanied by Jack

Dutch Church and Houses in Brooklyn, 1766

McEvers, a youth of 18 years, who had with much courtesy agreed to go with me. Looking for a favorable place to cross the Sound,[4] among the great number of pieces of floating ice which covered it, we arrived safely at Brooklyn in about fifteen minutes. Brooklyn is a small place, situated on the opposite shore, on Long Island, and has about 150 houses occupied mostly by poor people.[5] Here we ate in the principal tavern—a very good one.

We took a sledge {sleigh} to continue the excursion because all the country and roads were covered with at least 2-1/2 to 3 feet of snow. At 2 o'clock we left Brooklyn, passing through Bedford—a small place which is located less than four miles on the road to Jamaica. At half past three we stopped at a tavern which they call the "Half-way House"[6] to warm up a little as our feet, hands, ears and noses were almost frozen. After a glass of wine we felt more comfortable and resumed our journey, the sledges running like lightning. At five o'clock we arrived at Jamaica, at the house of a Mr. Charles McEvers, my young companion's father, who welcomed us with extreme hospitality. He has three young daughters between fourteen and eighteen years of age, very good looking and fairly well educated, two young sons also, and a brother-in-law, Captain [Thomas] Bibby. This Captain was the aide-de-camp to General {Simon} Fraser in the Saratoga campaign. McEvers' wife had died {in childbirth} a few months before.[7] His daughters are Miss Mary, Miss Nancy and Miss Eliza. They are very intelligent and literary minded, Miss Nancy in particular. In this gracious company we enjoyed the evening, and the next day after breakfast, at the wish of Mr. McEvers, we continued our journey in the sledge. At ten o'clock

Howard's Halfway House

all except the ladies, for whom it was too cold, set forth to visit Hempstead plain, about six miles from Jamaica. The ground was covered with snow, and gazing over the wide expanse I could fancy it to be a great lake, or even the sea, for on the horizon line snow and sky were blended into one.

They say that the plain is 20 miles long and seven wide. Here we proceeded to visit two prominent families who lived on the outskirts four miles on, the wife and children of Col. {Gabriel} Ludlow, and further the daughter of Judge {George Duncan} Ludlow,[8] the places half a mile apart. This last place was a very beautiful country house where we enjoyed the quiet of the surroundings.

Three or four miles further on is an elevation called Success Hill, on the summit of which is a small lake, Success Pond, at all times full of water with plenty of fish and extraordinarily deep.[9] The view from here is very pleasing: one can see both ocean and sound and the land of Connecticut. At about three o'clock we came back to Jamaica. The rest of the day was spent in literary conversation by the fireside of our sociable Colonel.

The next day, after breakfast, Mr. McEvers and I made another excursion in the sledges, towards the southern part of the Island, around a place called Rockaway, which is twelve miles from Jamaica.[10] The roads are very smooth and pleasant. It is a fine location and everywhere there are houses, ponds, woods and evidences of agriculture. At three o-clock we werc back, having covered thirty miles in 2–1/2 hours without tiring the horses.

We spent the evening in the same pleasant company as the preceding one and the next day I returned to New York, as the extreme cold prevented further excursions to the country and really made me wish to stay in my comfortable apartment in the city.

At twelve we took our sledges, accompanied by my friend young McEvers, his brother, and our generous host, Mr. McEvers, who desired to go with me to New York. About two we arrived at the outskirts of Brooklyn where we stopped to examine the fortifications which were constructed by the British. . . .[11]

Long Island is considered by New Yorkers the Hesperides of America,[12] and without doubt in the summer the country, roads, waters, woods and cultivated land appear to one like a garden. The quality of the soil, the products, etc., are very similar to those of the Jerseys.[13] The principal produce is Wheat, Rye, Indian Corn, and Oats—the general yield of Wheat and Rye is from eight to twenty bushels for one planted, but in many instances it produces upwards of forty from one. Indian Corn is produced from two hundred to three hundred and fifty from one. The staple of the Island is neat Cattle {cows}. Great numbers of Sheep are also raised and before the late war Long Island was noted for breeding some of the best horses in America. The testimony I have received from Col. William Floyd and Mr. [David] Gelston, natives of this country, well educated and upright, proves these statements.[14]

This island is probably 140 miles long and from 9 to 15 wide. Its fruits are very choice—conspicuous among them being the apple called Newtown Pippin, which is considered superior to all other varieties in the world. Long Island's population is estimated at 30,000. There are probably 90,000 cattle and 100,000 sheep on the island. . . .[15]

{On February 20, Miranda left for West Point. After traveling upstate and in Connecticut and Rhode Island, he visited friends on eastern Long Island for a few days.}

{August 20, 1784.} There were two boats leaving New London, one for Rhode Island and one for Long Island. I decided to visit Dr. and Mrs. {Nathaniel} Gardiner, who had invited me. About seven we sailed, with Capt. Clark Truman,[16] in company with two New York merchants. At 12 o'clock the merchants got off the boat with their horses at Oyster {Orient} Point, opposite Plum Island, 22 miles from New London. At 1:30 I arrived at Shelter Island eight miles further. The owner of a small house near the ferry offered me every hospitality. He gave me horses and accompanied me to my destination, the house of Mr. [Thomas] Dering[17] two miles on, where I arrived about four o'clock. This good old man was concerned about his health, being hardly able to leave his bed. He rose and with his son received me, the rest of the family being away. They arrived home about dusk and after all were together and had had prayers, the old man retired. We went to supper with Dr. and Mrs. Gardiner, after which we conversed around the table and retired. I confess that I was a little fatigued.

In the morning after breakfast we walked around the Island with the Doctor. There are about 2,000 acres wooded with timber and firewood, and only ten or twelve owners. From the heights we could see Gardiner's Island, across Gardiner's Bay. This bay is broad and safe. The British Navy occupied it for a long while in order to observe the French ships at Newport, Rhode Island.

When we returned to the house I had the pleasure of reading for the first time the book entitled *Magnalia Christi Americana: or, the Ecclesiastical History of New England,* by the Reverend Cotton Mather, in the presence of Parson [Rev. Enoch] Huntington of Middletown, who happened to be there for a visit. This book is one of the most curious documents that can be imagined, full of fanaticism and the wrong way of thinking, which was prevalent at that time over the continent, yet it had the dignified support of the New Haven code![18]

We had supper in the American style out of doors (a picnic) and afterwards I took a chair {carriage} in company of Dr. Gardiner, and young Mr. Dering who desired to accompany us to the dock of the ferry, which is about two miles from the house. We took a boat and sailed against the tide for three hours, arriving at Sag Harbor at 8:30. At 9 we took a chair and at 10 arrived at East Hampton, seven miles away. Here Dr. Gardiner has his house.[19] We had a very good supper and entertainment under his excellent roof, which rewarded us for the hard journey.

Sunday and the Church. Dr. {Nathaniel} Buell preached a very long and tedious sermon which held us up to 12:30. . . .[20] Returned to the house in company with Dr. Sage and Miss Gardiner, sister of my friend Dr. Gardiner,[21] with whom we had an enjoyable time. The ladies went to church again immediately after the meal and we went a littler later for a ride.

This is an agricultural community with a large population. The inhabitants have a good character and resemble the people of Connecticut. The place is estimated to have about 100 houses and a public library with 200 old volumes, the majority of them theological books. We returned home for tea and in the same jovial company spent the rest of the evening.

At 8 o'clock in the morning, after breakfast, the Doctor and I traveled to Sag Harbor with intention to take the boat which sails to Newport. It was nine o'clock when we arrived. We thought the Captain about to sail as agreed, but he was not ready, and did not propose to go to Newport, so I had to stay in a dreadful place to wait an opportunity.[22] I passed the time in observing a whale boat and talking with the crew, examining the whaling equipment. These boats go to the Brazilian coast for whales. They are brigantines of about 160 tons. The crews for the main part are Indians, among whom you can find the best harpooners, and some commissioned officers, who behave with decency and circumspection—never getting drunk nor misbehaving, so we observe these Indians are as capable and prudent as any other people. The implements are Harpoons and Ropes. The first are thrown to kill the whale and the rope to pull. Inside, near one of the masts they have a furnace of brick with two kettles in which they melt the fat. The first product is put in barrels and is called whale oil—the second is "Esperma-city" {spermaceti}, and is placed in earthen vessels.[23] Note the exertion and courage required in this industry. I was told that from this whole neighborhood 400 whaling ships went out during the last war.

Having spent the morning writing, I went to lunch at 11 with Dr. Gardiner, his wife and two young ladies from Shelter Island who were walking to East Hampton. Mr. Huntting, his companion, also joined us. Upon their departure I had in mind to keep my promise to call that afternoon on Squire [David] Gelston,[24] an old friend I had met in New York, who lived four miles away. While drinking my coffee another old friend, Mr. L'Hommedieu, joined me and urged me to visit him at his house seven miles distant.[25] After the meal we proceeded together to Squire Gelston's where we had tea and supper with the family. It was surprising to observe the simplicity and narrowness of these people's lives—their houses very small and quite lacking in ornament and comfort—and at the same time to note the high ideas they have in their heads. The first of these men is a member of the Assembly and the other a New York State Senator. Their houses and furniture are of the simplest, though the first man has a few books, among them a curious collection of English Poetry by [Mather] Bayle [Byles].

Later we returned to Sag Harbor to seek the boat for Newport. No boat in sight; I had to be patient and spend the time reading as the place is one of the worst you can imagine. Still no boat, no society in which to mingle.

That evening Capt. Latham came to say that he sails for Newport tomorrow morning. God permit it to be so. With expectations I arise early and write in my diary to date. Nine o'clock and no boat to be seen. Afternoon and boat not in sight. The Captain did not choose to sail. I began to feel myself growing ill. In the afternoon Dr. Gardiner took me to visit Mr. and Mrs. Jacob Conkling. To coffee afterwards and to read till the hour of retiring.

Next day the wind was wrong for sailing and I amused myself reading and watching the sailors wrestling and jumping, the exercises of these robust and healthy whale fishermen. Paid my bill to Mr. Wm. Duvall the Inn keeper for the night in his miserable hotel which he calls "Sag Harbor Coffee House," where you could not get a cup of coffee fit even for medicine.

Next day we sailed at 6 a. m., slowly with slack wind through Gardiner's Bay where the English navy were stationed {during the Revolutionary War}. We passed Gardiner's, Fishers and Block Islands and saw Montauk Point, where the native {Montaukett} Indians number about 50 families. Here is the best land on {this lengthy island, or} Long Island.[26] After sighting Point Judith we passed the light house of Newport, five miles from the city at 11 o'clock p. m., and at 12 arrived at the end of our 70 mile trip.

Notes

Source: The Long Island section of Miranda's diary, with an introduction by Ettie Hedges Pennypacker, appeared in the *Nassau County Historical [Society] Journal*, in two parts: "Francisco de Miranda's Visit to Long Island in 1784," 1 (Summer 1937): 5-8, and "The Journal of Miranda," 1, nos. 2-3 (1937-1938): 56-58. Some of her notes (identified as [EHP]) have been edited here and full publication information is provided for the books she cited. Doubtless she had used *The Diary of Francisco de Miranda, Tour of the United States, 1783-1784, The Spanish Text,* edited by William Spence Robertson (New York: Hispanic Society of America, 1928). The Long Island sections are on pp. 53-56 and 94-98 in this published version of the diary in Spanish. The first full English translation of Miranda's travels in the United States is in John S. Ezell, ed. *The New Democracy in America: Travels of Francisco de Miranda in the United States, 1783-84,* translated by Judson P. Wood (Norman: University of Oklahoma Press, 1963); the Long Island sections are on pp. 78-81, and 127-32.

Pennypacker's insertions in the text are in brackets, [thus]; the editor's insertions for this volume are indicated by braces or wavy brackets {thus}. Notes by Pennypacker are indicated by her initials in brackets [ELP]. All other notes are by the editor for this volume. Only minor changes have been made in Pennypacker's text and notes, including italicizing the titles of books and shifting full identification of names from footnotes to the text; her capitalization of words has been retained. Where Wood's translation differs substantively from Pennypacker's, it is pointed out in the notes and cited as *New Democracy.* (I consulted my colleague, Dr. Ignacio Götz, who is from Venezuela, to determine the correct translation.)

1. Bibliographical information on Miranda, is from: Pennypacker's introduction (1: 5-7); Robertson's Introduction which is in English (pp. xiii-xxxii); Edith H. Shephard, "A World Citizen Visits Shelter Island: Francisco de Miranda, Venezuelan Patriot on Tour in 1784," *Long Island Forum* 53 (Summer 1990): 73-80; William Spence Robertson, *Life of*

Miranda, 2 vols. (Chapel Hill: University of North Carolina Press, 1929); Joseph F. Thorning, *Miranda: World Citizen* (Gainsville: University of Florida Press, 1952); and Ezell, *The New Democracy in America,* pp. Xv-xxxii. The monument quotation is cited in Shephard, "World Citizen," 53: 79. Shepherd had used a privately published booklet, "Miranda's Visit to Long Island" which undoubtedly was Pennypacker's translation.

2. Ettie Pennypacker (1879-1970) was the librarian in the East Hampton Library for fifty-six years; she retired in 1955. Her notes provide additional information on eastern Long Island personages. She first presented her paper on Miranda at a meeting of the Nassau County Historical and Genealogical Society in Hempstead on January 21, 1937. Her translation of Miranda's Long Island tour was also privately printed in a pamphlet in 1937, *Francisco de Miranda's Visit to Long Island in 1784.* Her article, "Colonial Travelers on Long Island," was published under her maiden name, Ettie C. Hedges, in *New York History* 14 (April 1933): 152-62. She married Morton Pennypacker in 1936, who was a well known Long Island historian. He collected Long Island materials which became the core of the East Hampton Library's excellent local history collection.

3. Ezell, *New Democracy,* pp. xxx, xxxi, xxxii.

4. Miranda crossed the East River (not Long Island Sound) on the ferry to reach Brooklyn from Manhattan, but the East River was sometimes called the Sound at that time.

5. Pennypacker had translated "gente pobre" as "middle class people," but Wood's "poor people" is a more accurate translation and has been substituted here (in Ezell, *New Democracy*, p. 78).

6. The Half-way House was Howard's. See Eugene L. Armbruster, *The Eastern District of Brooklyn* (New York: Privately printed, 1912), pp. 60-63 [EHP]. William Howard built the inn in 1699 and his grandson William Howard was operating it during the Revolution. Armbruster, ibid.

7. In Wood's translation, McEvers is the uncle rather than father, and it is Capt. Bibby's wife who had died.

8. Judge Ludlow possessed a library worth twelve hundred pounds at the time his house was destroyed by fire in 1773. The *New York Mercury* for December 27th, says: "About 10 o'clock last Thursday morning, the house of the Hon. George Duncan Ludlow, Esq., third Judge of the Supreme Court of this Province, at Hempstead Plains (Hyde Park), took fire and was burnt to the ground with almost everything therein contained, but providentially no lives were lost. Mr. L. had been in New York the day before and was scarce three hours at home before his house was all in flames. The fire originated, as is supposed, by means of some sparks that found their way through the cracks of the old chimney and communicated to the wooden work of one of the rooms above. The loss Mr. Ludlow sustains by this accident cannot be less than three thousand pounds, for besides the loss of his furniture, plate, etc., a library worth twelve hundred pounds is entirely consumed." (This house was rebuilt and was occupied by his daughter at the time of Miranda's visit, but later during the occupancy of the famous William Cobbett was again consumed by fire on May 26th, 1819), [EHP].

The Hempstead Plains were marked on many early maps. Miranda was not alone in describing the Plains as a sea. On the Hempstead Plains, see note no. 9 in Hamilton's "Itinerarium" above. The English writer William Cobbett lived in the area known today as New Hyde Park from 1817-1819, and wrote, *A Year's Residence in the United States of America* (see above, p. 7 n.5). Evers identifies Col. Ludlow being in DeLancey's (Loyalist) Brigade and indicates they were attainted and had their estates confiscated *(New Democracy,* p. 79 n.). Ludlow's estate was sold in November 1784, after Miranda's visit.

Both Ludlows were prominent in the British government in New Brunswick where they resettled. See Benjamin F. Thompson *History of Long Island from its Discovery and Settlement to the Present Time,* 3 vols., 1918 (Reprint; Port Washington: I.J. Friedman, 1962), 2:569-70.

9. The "small lake, Success Pond," is today known as Lake Success; it is in northwestern Nassau County, near the Queens border.

10. Miranda probably visited in today's Far Rockaway, though the term "Rockaway" then covered a large area: today's East Rockaway and the Five Towns area (Inwood, Lawrence, Cedarhurst, Woodmere, and Hewlett) in southwestern Nassau County, as well as what is now Far Rockaway and the entire Rockaway peninsula in southern Queens County. See also Charles Brockden Brown's "Jaunt to Rockaway, 1793" below.

11. Pennypacker omits Miranda's summary comments on the Battle of Long Island and his description of the remaining fortifications. Miranda wrote: "New Fort, the principal fortification, is a very well constructed parallelogram with four bulwarks, spacious moat, solid storehouse, well water, and barracks; it can easily shelter a garrison of 1,600 men. Two or more positions, built with equal judgment and intelligence, serve as outposts. Likewise one can see there the lines and remains of the American entrenchments, which the British wanted to attack in {August} 1776" (Evers, *New Democracy,* p. 80).

12. The word in Spanish is "Hesperia." The Hesperides refers generally to western land, and in Greek mythology specifically to a garden where golden apples were grown at the western end of the earth.

13. From 1676-1701, what we know as New Jersey was divided into East and West Jersey which is probably why Miranda (and Pennypacker) used the plural "Jerseys."

14. William Floyd was a signer of the Declaration of Independence; his estate in Mastic Beach is now a National Historic Park site; (631) 399-2030. David Gelston (1734-1828) represented Southampton in the provincial congresses in 1775 and 1776; his daughter Phebe married Floyd's son Nicoll in 1789. Thompson *History of Long Island,* 2:166 n., 363-66. On Floyd, see also James F. Skurka, "William Floyd, Long Island Patriot" (M.A. thesis, Hofstra University, 1979). On Gelston, see also note no. 24 below.

15. The length of the Island is actually 118 miles and it is 20 miles in width at its widest. The population six years later in the 1790 federal census was 36,949—12 percent in Kings County, 43 percent in Queens County (which included present-day Nassau County), and 45 percent in Suffolk County.

16. See Frederic Mather, *Refugees of 1776 from Long Island to Connecticut* (Albany: J.B. Lyon, 1913), p. 254 [EHP]. Mather identifies Truman as "probably from Sag Harbor," but born in New London in 1736. Pennypacker omits Miranda's footnote description of Truman as "a great babbling liar" (Evers, *New Democracy,* p. 127). Miranda became frustrated later when he had to wait several days for Truman to leave Long Island and cross the Sound so he could resume his New England trip.

17. Dering was the Chairman of the Committee of Safety during the Battle of Long Island. (See *Journals of the Provincial Congress* [Albany: T. Weed, 1842], p. 594.) He died September 26, 1785, age 65 years, 4 months, 10 days. Henry P. Dering was a son, age 21 in 1784. Another son was Sylvester Dering, then 25. His daughter Elizabeth Dering married Dr. Nathaniel Gardiner on January 27, 1784. She was born in 1760 [EHP]. Like many other Long Island patriots, Dering moved to Connecticut during the British occupation of Long Island during the Revolution. Evers identifies Henry Dering (whose name he erroneously spells "Derin") as a "pioneer in wool production on Long Island" (*New Democracy,* p. 127 n. 47).

18. Wood translates the final phrase in the paragraph as "is a worthy companion of the extraordinary Blue Laws of New Haven!" (Evers, *New Democracy,* p. 128; this section is p. 95 in Robertson's Spanish edition).

19. Known as the "Brown House" and occupied by his father, Col. Abraham Gardiner, before the Revolution. It was used as British Headquarters by Sir Henry Clinton and other officers and in 1937 was occupied by Winthrop Gardiner [EHP].

20. Buell (1716-1798) was the minister in East Hampton from 1746-1798. On Buell, see John Turner Ames, "Leading the Way: The Political Force," in *Awakening the Past: The East Hampton 350th Anniversary Lecture Series,* edited by Tom Twomey (New York: Newmarket Press, 1999), pp. 67-72. In Wood's translation, Buell delivered an "extremely dull and wearisome sermon." Pennypacker omits Miranda's reference to Buell's refusal to baptise an infant until the father, who had only been married a few months, publicly confessed his pre-marital fornication. Miranda wrote, "I have never in my life suffered greater shame. What barbarity!" Evers points out, "Public confession of sins was not an uncommon practice at this time." See *New Democracy,* p. 129.

21. Both of Dr. Gardiner's sisters were married. They were Mary and Rachel. Miranda does not indicate which he here refers to. Mary since 1772 was married to Isaac Thompson of Islip. She at that time was 36, and Rachel (then 33) was married to Maj. David Mulford, son of Col. David Mulford, and was then the mother of David Mulford two years old, and Phebe Gardiner Mulford, 15 days [EHP].

22. Wood translates this as the "terrible inn" in Evers, *New Democracy,* p. 129.

23. Miranda here describes the first vessels sent from Long Island into southern latitudes after whales. They were fitted out by Dr. Nathaniel Gardiner and his brother Capt. Abraham Gardiner, then 21, and father of David Gardiner (1784-1844), author of the *Chronicles of the Town of East Hampton* (New York: Bowne, 1871), [EHP]. Whale oil was used in lamps and to grease machines, while spermaceti, from the head of sperm whales, was used for candles and to oil precision instruments. Sag Harbor became an important whaling port in later decades.

24. David Gelston was from 1777 to 1785 a member of the New York Assembly from Suffolk County. At the time of Miranda's visit he was Speaker of the Assembly. He became collector of the Port of New York in 1801. His son Maltby was for years the president of the Bank of the Manhattan Co. in New York and married Miss Margaret Jones whose sister was the wife of Gov. DeWitt Clinton [EHP].

25. Miranda refers to Senator Ezra L'Hommedieu of Southold on the North Fork, whose brother Samuel lived in Sag Harbor and owned a ropewalk. See Shephard, "A World Citizen Visits Shelter Island," *Long Island Forum* 53 (Summer 1990): 80 n. 7.

26. The sentence, "Here is the best land on Long Island" is omitted in Wood's translation in Evers, *New Democracy,* p. 132; it is part of a footnote on Montauk in the Spanish version (p. 98) which Pennypacker incorporated in the text.

Tour of Long Island, 1790

George Washington

George Washington (1732-1799) is the most famous traveler to visit Long Island. He was first on Long Island in 1756 when he was on his way to or from Boston in February and March to see Governor William Shirley of Massachusetts to settle a dispute over who had command of troops in the Shenandoah Valley. Local tradition in Greenport is that he stopped at an inn there, and a New London diary has some evidence that he traveled across Long Island Sound, but Washington's own records are inconclusive.[1]

Washington returned to Long Island on August 23-24 and 26, 1776 to review fortifications in Brooklyn. The Battle of Long Island was fought August 27 and Washington was in Brooklyn during the fighting that day. Although his forces suffered a major defeat, he supervised the successful evacuation of the troops across the East River to Manhattan on the evening of August 29 through the early morning the next day.[2]

New York City was the first capital of the United States under the Constitution for eighteen months. George Washington was inaugurated on the balcony of Federal Hall on April 23, 1789. Six months before his better known five-day overland tour, Washington came to Long Island one morning to visit the Prince Nursery in Flushing in October 1789. He wrote in his diary of this visit:

> Saturday 10th. Pursuant to an engagement formed on Thursday last—I set off about 9 Oclock in my Barge to visit Mr. Prince's fruit Gardens & shrubberies at Flushing on Long Island. The Vice President {John Adams}—Governor of the State {George Clinton}, Mr. {Ralph} Izard {Senator, South Carolina}, Colo. {William Stephens} Smith {son-in-law of Adams}, and Majr. {William} Jackson {military aide} accompanied me.
>
> These gardens, except in the number of young fruit Trees, did not answer my expectations—The shrubs were trifling and the flowers not numerous.
>
> The Inhabitants of this place showed us what respect they could, by making the best use of one Cannon to salute.[3]

A few days before the visit to Flushing, Washington had written in his diary, "Had conversation with Colo. {Alexander} Hamilton on the propriety of my makg. a tour through the Eastern states during the recess of Congress to acquire knowledge of the face of the Country the growth and Agriculture there of and the temper and disposition of the Inhabitants towards the new government who thought it a very desirable plan and advised it accordingly."[4] On October 15, Washington embarked for Boston and his "tour through the Eastern states." This trip took nearly a month, included several days in Boston, and, of course, covered many more miles than his Long Island trip. It also was more elaborate with militia escorts, speeches, and celebrations.

As a farmer with a large plantation at Mount Vernon, Washington was interested in soil conditions and agricultural yields, which together with his comments on the food and lodging dominate his entries for his Long Island tour. Washington's policy was to accept neither hospitality nor free lodging when he was on a presidential tour. Because of the sparsity of good taverns on Long Island, the owners of private houses who entertained him probably had agreed to accept money—hence his descriptions of private houses which took money. Washington rode in a coach with his military aide, Major William Jackson, and was probably accompanied by several servants, perhaps a "coachman, postilion, valet, and footman." He ate his main meal at 3 p.m. and covered about 160 miles in the five days, traveling about seven and a half hours a day.[5]

Local historians have hypothesized that Washington may have chosen his route and stops on Long Island in order to thank those involved in his Revolutionary War spy ring. Plaques and historical markers (most erected in the 1930s), have marked many of the sites or actual houses where Washington stopped on his 1790 tour; some of these markers are no longer in place. The oral tradition in families and communities have provided additional details about Washington's visit which are not documented in his diary. References to extant historical markers and oral traditions are included in the notes.

* * *

Monday 19th. Prevented from beginning my tour upon long Island to day from the wet of yesterday and the unfavourableness of the Morning. . . .

Tuesday 20th. About 8Oclock (having previously sent over my Servants, Horses and Carriage I crossed to Brooklin and proceeded to Flat Bush—thence to {New} Utrich—thence to Gravesend—thence through [{blank; Canarsie to}] Jamaica where we lodged at a Tavern kept by one Warne—a pretty good and decent house. At the House of a Mr. Barre, at Utrich, we dined.[6] The Man was obliging but little else to recommend it. He told me that their average Crop of Oats did not exceed 15 bushls. to the Acre but of Indian Corn they commonly made from 25 to 30 and often more bushels to the Acre but this was the effect of Dung from New York (about 10 Cart load to the Acre)—That of Wheat they sometimes got 30 bushels and often more of Rye.

The land after crossing the Hills between Brooklyn & flat Bush is perfectly level, and from the latter to Utrich, Gravesend and in short all that end of the Island is a rich black loam. Afterwards, between [{blank; Canarsie}] and the Jamaica Road it is more Sandy and appears to have less strength, but is still good & productive. The grain in general had suffered but little by the openess, and Rains of the Winter and the grass (clover &ca.)

appeared to be coming on well. The Inclosures are small & under open Post
& Rail fencing. The timber is chiefly Hiccory & Oak, mixed here and there
with locust & Sasafras trees and in places with a good deal of Cedar. The
Road until I came within a mile or two of the Jamaica Road, calld the middle
road kept within sight of the Sea {Jamaica Bay,} but the weather was so dull
& at times Rainy that we lost much of the pleasures of the ride.

From Brooklyn to Flat bush is called 5 miles—thence to Utrich 6—to
Gravesend 2 and from thence to Jamaica 14—in all this day 27 Miles. . . .

Wednesday 21st. The Morning being clear & pleasant we left Jamaica
about Eight O'clock, & pursued the Road to South Hempstead passing along
the South edge of the plain of that name—a plain said to be 14 miles in
length by 3 or 4 in breadth witht. {without} a Tree or a Shrub growing on it
except fruit trees (which do not thrive well) at the few settlemts. thereon. The
Soil of this plain is said to be thin & cold and of course not productive, even
in Grass.[7] We baited {ate} in South Hemstead (10 Miles from Jamaica) at
the house of one Simmonds, formerly a Tavern, now of private
entertainment for Money.[8] From hence turning off to the right we fell into
the South Rd. at the distance of about five miles where we came in view of
the Sea {Bay} & continued to be so the remaining part of the days ride, and
as near it as the road could run for the small bays, Marshes and guts, into
which the tide flows at all times rendering it impassible from the height of it
by the Easterly Winds. We dined at one Ketchums wch. had also been a
public House but now a private one receivg. pay for what it furnished.[9] This
House was about 14 Miles from South Hemstead & a very neat & decent
one. After dinner we proceeded to a Squire Thompsons such a House as the

Squire Thompson's house is now Sagtikos Manor,
an historic house museum in West Bay Shore. Photograph, c. 1945.

last, that is, one that is not public but will receive pay for every thing it furnishes in the same manner as if it was.[10]

The Road in which I passed to day, and the Country were more mixed with sand than yesterday and the Soil of inferior quality; Yet with dung wch. all the Corn ground receives the land yields on an average 30 bushels to the Acre often more. Of Wheat they do not grow much on acct. of the {Hessian} Fly {infestation} but the Crops of Rye are good.

Thursday 22d. About 8 Oclock we left Mr. Thompson's—halted a while at one Greens distant 11 Miles and dined Harts Tavern in Brookhaven town ship five miles farther.[11] To this place we travelled on what is called the South road described yesterday but the Country through which it passed grew more and more Sandy and barren as we travelled Eastward, so as to become exceedingly poor indeed but a few miles further Eastward the lands took a different complexion we were informed. From Harts we struck across the Island for the No. side, passing the East end of the Brushey Plains and Koram {Coram} 8 Miles—thence to Setakit {Setauket} 7 Mi. more to the House of a Captn. Roe which is tolerably dect. {decent} with obliging people in it.[12] The first five Miles of the Road is too poor to admit Inhabitants or cultivation being a low scrubby Oak, not more than 2 feet high intermixed with small and ill thriven Pines. Within two miles of Koram there are farms but the land is of an indifferent quality much mixed with Sand. Koram contains but few houses. From thence to Setalket the Soil improves, especially as you approach the Sound; but is far from being of the first quality—still a good deal mixed with Sand. The road a cross from the So. to the No. Side is level, except a small part So. of Koram but the hills there are trifling.

Friday 23d. About 8 Oclock we left Roes, and baited {rested and fed} the Horses at Smiths Town at a Widow Blidenbergs[13]—a decent House 10 Miles from Setalkat—thence 15 Miles to Huntington where we dined and afterwards proceeded Seven Miles to Oyster-bay, to the House of a Mr. Young (private & very neat and decent) where we lodged.[14] The house we dined at in Huntington was kept by a Widow Platt and was tolerably good.[15] The whole of this days ride was over uneven ground and none of it of the first quality but intermixed in places with pebble-stone. After passing Smithstown & for near five Miles it was a mere bed of white Sand, unable to produce trees 25 feet high; but a change for the better took place between that & Huntington, which is a sml. village at the head of the Harbour of that name and continued to improve to Oyster-bay about which the Lands are good and in the Necks between these bays are said to be fine. It is here the Lloyds own a large & valuable tract, or Neck of Land from whence the

British whilst they possessed
New York drew large supplies
of Wood and where, at present,
it is said large flocks of Sheep
are kept.[16]

Saturday 24th. Left Mr.
Youngs before 6 Oclock, and
passing Musqueto {Glen} Cove,
breakfasted   at   a   Mr.
Underduncks at the head of a
little bay; where we were kindly
received and well entertained.[17]
This Gentleman works a Grist &
two Paper Mills, the last of

Hendrick Onderdonk House in
Roslyn (now George Washington
Manor). Photograph, c. 1930.

which he seems to carry on with Spirit, and to profit—distc. from Oyster bay
12 Miles. From thence to Flushing where we dined is 12 more & from thence
to Brooklyne through Newton {Newtown/Elmhurst} (the way we travelled
and which is a mile further than to pass through Jamaica) is 18 miles more.
The land I passed over to day is generally very good, but leveller and better
as we approached New York. The soil in places is intermixed with pebble,
and towards the Westend with other kind of stone which they apply to the
purposes of fencing which is not to be seen on the South side of the Island
nor towards the Eastern parts of it. From Flushing to New Town 8 Miles, &
thence to Brooklyn, the Road is very fine, and the Country in a higher State
of Cultivation & vegitation of Grass & grain forwarded than any place else I
had seen—occasioned in a great degree by the Manure drawn from the City
of New York. Before Sundown we had crossed the Ferry and was at home.

Observations

This Island (as far as I went) from West to East seems to be equally
divided between flat, & Hilly land—the former on the South next the Sea
board & the latter on the No. next the Sound. The high land they say is best
and most productive but the other is the pleasantest to work except in wet
seasons when from the levelness of them they are sometimes (but not
frequently having a considerable portion of Sand) incommoded by heavy &
continual rains. From a comparitive view of their Crops they may be
averaged as follow. Indian Corn 25 bushels—Wheat 15—Rye 12—Oats 15
bushels to the Acre. According to their accts. from Lands highly manured
they sometimes get 50 of the first, 25 of the 2d. & 3d. and more of the latter.
Their general mode of Cropping is—first Indian Corn upon a lay, manured

in the hill, half a shovel full in each hole (some scatter the dung over the field equally)—2d. Oats & Flax—3d. Wheat with what Manure they can spare from the Indian Corn land. With the wheat, or on it, towards close of the snows, they sow Clover from 4 to 6 lb; & a quart of Timothy seed. This lays from 3 to 6 years, according as the grass remains, or as the condition of the ground is, for so soon as they find it beginning to bind they plow. Their first plowing (with the Patent, tho' they call it the Dutch plough) is well executed at the depth of about 3 or at most 4 Inches—the cut being 9 or 10 Inches & the sod neatly & very evenly turned. With Oxen they plough mostly. They do no more than turn the ground in this manner for Indian Corn before it is planted; making the holes in which it is placed with hoes the rows being marked off by a stick. Two or three workings afterwards with the Harrows or Plough is all the cultivation it receives *generally*. Their fences, where there is no stone, are very indifferent; frequently of plashed trees of *any & every* kind which have grown by chance; but it exhibits an evidence that very good fences may be made in this manner either of white Oak or Dogwood which from this mode of treatment grows thickest, and most stubborn.[18] This, however, would be no defence against Hogs.

Notes

Source: George Washington, *The Diaries of George Washington, Vol. 6, January 1790-December 1799,* edited by Donald Jackson and Dorothy Twohig (Charlottesville: University Press of Virginia, 1979), pp. 62-67. Reprinted with permission of the University Press of Virginia.

Jackson and Twohig explain their editing procedures on pp. xv-xvii. They retained spelling, contractions, abbreviations, punctuation, and capitalization as in the original manuscript, but added periods to abbreviations, lowered superscripts, and changed dashes at the end of sentences to a period and capitalized the following word. Their editorial insertions are in square brackets [thus]; but [{*blank*}] indicates a space that Washington left blank in the original. Jackson and Twohig's notes have been shifted to endnotes where full citations for sources were added from their bibliography and grouped at the end of the note. Additional insertions in the text for this edition are in braces or wavy brackets {thus}. In the notes, those by Jackson and Twohig are identified as [DJ/DT] and those added for this edition by (NAN).

Earlier editions of Washington's *Diaries* were edited by Benson J. Lossing (1860) and John C. Fitzpatrick (1925). Most of Washington's original diaries are in the Library of Congress, but the one which includes his brief 1789 visit is in the Detroit Public Library, and the diary with the 1790 Long Island tour is at the Virginia Historical Society in Richmond. George Washington, *The Diaries of George Washington, Vol.1, January 1748-65,* edited by Donald Jackson and Dorothy Twohig (Charlottesville: University Press of Virginia, 1976), pp. xlvi.

1. Stephen Decatur, "Washington on Long Island," *New York History* 21 (July 1940): 303-15. Washington's household account books were in possession of Decatur's family and

Decatur was the author of *Private Affairs of George Washington* (see note no. 3 below*)*. On Washington's 1756 visit, see also Ettie C. Hodges, "Colonial Travelers on Long Island," *New York Historical Association Proceedings/New York History* 14 (April 1933): 161-62; Romanah Sammis, *Huntington-Babylon Town History* (Huntington Historical Society, 1937), pp. 215-18; and Leslie Elhoff, "Washington on Long Island," parts 1 and 2, *Long Island Forum* 13 (February and March 1950): 23 (NAN).

2. John J. Gallagher, *The Battle of Brooklyn, 1776* (New York: Sarpedon, 1995), pp. 92, 95-96, 99, 110; see also articles by George DeWan in *Long Island: Our Story* (Melville, NY: Newsday, 1998), pp. 120-24; and Myron H. Luke and Robert B. Venables, *Long Island in the American Revolution* (Albany, NY: New York State American Revolution Bicentennial Commission, 1976), pp. 19-31 (NAN).

3. William Prince's Linnean Botanic Garden at Flushing, Long Island, had been established by his father, also William Prince, in 1737. Although Prince's extensive nurseries for plants and trees had been severely decimated by British depredations during the Revolution, the gardens and orchards had largely recovered by 1789, and GW {George Washington} often ordered fruit for his table from Prince. Stephen Decatur, Jr., *Private Affairs of George Washington, from the Records and Accounts of Tobias Lear, Esquire, His Secretary* (Boston: Houghton Mifflin Co., 1933), pp. 62, 93 [DJ/DT]. George Washington, *The Diaries of George Washington, Vol. 5, July 1786-December 1789,* edited by Donald Jackson and Dorothy Twohig (Charlottesville: University Press of Virginia, 1979), 5:458, 459.

The Washingtons held a formal dinner every Thursday; the same men (and their wives) had attended dinner on the preceding Thursday. Martha Washington did not like to travel by boat, so she, Eleanor Parke Custis (her daughter from her first marriage), Abigail Adams, and her daughter, Abigail Adams Smith, went by carriage to meet the men for dinner at a tavern in Harlem (ibid., 5:459), (NAN).

The Prince Nursery had been established by William Prince's grandfather, Robert Prince, in 1737 and continued by his son, William Prince [Sr.]. See also Timothy Dwight's references to the Prince nursery during his 1804 "Journey to Long Island" (NAN).

4. GW had appointed Alexander Hamilton secretary of the treasury on September 11, 1789 [DJ/DT] 5:452-53.

5. Decatur, "Washington on Long Island," pp. 312-13, 314 n. On Washington's visit, see also George DeWan, "An LI Victory Tour," in *Long Island: Our Story* (Melville, NY: Newsday, 1998), pp. 158-60 (NAN).

6. "One Warne": probably William Warne, who is listed in the 1790 census as living in Jamaica. The 1790 census for New Utrecht contains no entry for "Barre" but does list a William Barry, whose household consisted of eight whites and five slaves. *Heads of Families at the First Census of the United States Taken in the Year 1790: New York* (Reprint; Baltimore: Genealogical Publishing Co., 1966), {pp. 150, 98}, [DJ/DT], 6:64. Decatur identified the blanks in the first day's entries as Canarsie and indicated that Warne operated the Jamaica Inn. See his "Washington on Long Island," pp. 309, 311 (NAN).

Washington did not take a direct route from Brooklyn to Jamaica. He may have diverted southward to Flatbush and Gravesend to see the terrain of British operations preceding the Battle of Long Island in 1776. The "Queens Head" tavern in Jamaica where he stayed was on today's Jamaica Avenue near Parson's boulevard. It remained in operation until demolished in 1906. A 1905 photograph is in Vincent F. Seyfried and William Asadorian, *Old Queens, N.Y. In Early Photographs* (Mineola: Dover, 1991), p. 26.

7. Early maps depicted and many early visitors commented upon the Hempstead Plains, prairie land which extended over a large portion of the middle of present-day Nassau County. See note no. 9 above in Hamilton's "Itinerarium" for articles on the plains. The northern part of the Town of Hempstead seceded in 1775 from the southern Loyalist part of the town; this was confirmed by the state after the war in 1784. What is now the Town of Hempstead was originally called "South Hempstead" (NAN).

8. The village seal of Hempstead depicts Washington standing by his carriage in Hempstead. Many historians have assumed that Washington stopped at the well-known Sammis Tavern in Hempstead; see, for example, Bernice Schultz, *Colonial Hempstead* (Lynbrook: Review-Star Press, 1937; reprinted under name Bernice Schultz Marshall in 1962), pp. 164, 247. However, Washington's identification of it as "Simmonds," a private house, and his notation that he turned off to the right when leaving are evidence against it being the Sammis Tavern. Decatur identifies the house as "Simonson's" or "Simmonson's," which was later Anderson's inn ("Washington on Long Island," p. 312). Elhoff concurs and indicates that Simmonson's was located diagonally opposite the Sammis Tavern ("Washington on Long Island," p. 55. Abraham Simonson and William Simonson are listed in South Hempstead in *Heads of Families, N.Y. . . . 1790*, p. 156 (NAN).

The Sammis Tavern dated from the seventeenth century and continued as a tavern into the twentieth century. Nehemiah Sammis, who operated the tavern during the Revolutionary War and in 1790, was a noted Tory which is another reason Washington was unlikely to stop there. Nonetheless, there is a bronze tablet on the site of the Sammis Tavern on the northeast corner of Main Street and Fulton Avenue in the village of Hempstead. It was unveiled in 1927 when the Historical Committee of the Long Island Chamber of Commerce made a pilgrimage along Washington's route. See "George Washington's Presidential Tour of Long Island Retraced Over His Route of 1790," *Proceedings of the New York State Historical Association*, vol 25 / *Quarterly Journal* 8 (1927): 248 (NAN).

9. "One Ketchums": A number of Ketchams were living in Huntington in 1790. Fitzpatrick identifies the house as "Zebulah Ketcham's Inn." *Heads of Families, N.Y.*, pp. 163-65; and *The Diaries of George Washington, 1748-1799*, edited by John C. Fitzpatrick, 4 vols. (Boston: Houghton Mifflin, 1925), 4:117 n.2 [DJ/DT], 6:65.

The town of Huntington divided in 1872, when the southern part became the Town of Babylon. Zebulon Ketcham's household had ten whites and one slave (*Heads of Family*, p. 165). Family tradition is that Washington presented a gold ring to one of the Ketcham girls (see Elhoff, "Washington on Long Island," p. 55). A plaque in Copiague (Merrick Road and Deaville Boulevard) marks the site of Zebulon Ketcham's farmhouse. The Winterthur Museum in Wilmington, Delaware, has a wainscot armchair which belonged to the Ketchams; it has a nineteenth century plaque stating that Washington had sat in it. See Dean F. Failey, *Long Island is My Nation: The Decorative Arts & Craftsmen, 1640-1830*, 2d ed. (Cold Spring Harbor: Society for the Preservation of Long Island Antiquities, 1998), p. 9-8 (NAN).

10. "Squire Thompsons": probably Judge Isaac Thompson's Apple Tree Neck farm in {the Town of} Islip. Thompson (1743-1816) married Mary Gardiner (d. 1786) in 1772, and five years after her death he married Sarah Bradnor, who died in 1819. At the time of GW's visit, Thompson's household consisted of five whites and four slaves. Benjamin F. Thompson, *History of Long Island from Its Discovery and Settlement to the Present Time*, 2 vols., 2d ed. rev. (New York: Gould, Banks, & Co., 1843), 1:451; *Heads of Families, N.Y.*, p. 165 [DJ/DT], 6:65. In the more accessible twentieth-century edition of Thompson's *History*, the reference to the Thompsons is 3:299. See Benjamin F. Thompson, *History of*

Long Island from Its Discovery and Settlement to the Present Time, 3 vols., 3d ed., rev. by Charles J. Werner, 1918 (Reprint, Port Washington, NY: I.J. Friedman, 1962). Isaac Thompson's house, which had been occupied by British troops during the Revolution, is now Sagtikos Manor, an historic house museum on Montauk Highway (Route 27A) in today's West Bay Shore (NAN).

11. "Harts Tavern": probably run by Gilbert Hart, listed in the 1790 census for Brookhaven. Hart, whose household consisted of five whites, owned no slaves (*Heads of Families, N.Y.,* p. 160), [DJ/DT], 6:65. Hart's Tavern was located at the northern end of River Avenue, near the Lakeview cemetery on the north side of Montauk Highway (Route 27A) in present-day Patchogue. Hart family tradition is that a group of boys who were roasting sweet potatoes on a fire offered Washington one and he gave them an English shilling which the family preserved. Green's tavern was in Sayville. See Kate Wheeler Strong, parts 1 and 2, "When Washington Came in 1790," *Long Island Forum* 16 (August 1953): 155, 157 (reprinted from *Long Island Forum* 3 (May 1940): 97-98 (NAN).

12. An historic marker marks the site of Austin Roe's tavern on the northwest corner of Bayview and North Country Road (Route 25A) in Setauket. The house itself was moved in 1936 and is privately owned (it is north of Old Post Road between Gnarled Hollow Road and Coach Road). Roe (1748-1830) was a member of the Culper Spy Ring. It is said that he broke his leg when dismounting to greet Washington. On the Roe House, see Howard Klein, *Three Village Guidebook: The Setaukets, Poquott, Old Field, & Stony Brook,* 2d ed. (East Setauket: Three Village Historical Society, 1986), pp. 98-100. On the Culper Spy Ring, see George DeWan's articles in *Long Island: Our Story,* pp. 136-39; Corey Ford, *A Peculiar Service* (Boston: Little, Brown, 1965); and Morton J. Pennypacker, *George Washington's Spies on Long Island and in New York* (Brooklyn: Long Island Historical Society, 1939; vol. 2 published by East Hampton Free Library, 1948), (NAN).

13. Widow Ruth Blydenberg's house stood until the 1930s; the land is now just west of the Smithtown Library at the intersection of Routes 25 and 25A. A plaque on a boulder marks the site (NAN).

14. Daniel Youngs had been a captain in the Royal (Queens County, Loyalist) Militia during the Revolutionary War. He may have cooperated with the Townsends in Oyster Bay; Robert Townsend was a member of the Culper Spy ring (see note no. 12 above). Youngs' family tradition is that Washington kissed 18-year-old Keziah Young on the cheek and she never let anyone else kiss her there (see Strong, "When Washington Came in 1790," p. 155). The Youngs house, a private home, stands at the corner of Cove Neck and Oyster Bay Cove Roads. An historical marker notes Washington's visit (NAN).

15. The Widow [Mary Carll] Platt's tavern was located at the southeast corner of today's East Main Street (Route 25A) and Park Avenue in Huntington until 1860. An historic marker, which no longer stands, had stated: "Platt's Tavern. President Washington was a guest here April 23, 1790. Early Town meeting site." Oral tradition in the family is that eight-year-old Sarah Williams saw Washington's entourage pass on Oyster Bay Path while the Cold Spring Harbor schoolhouse was being built. She said someone in the party helped raise a rafter, and Washington left a dollar for the workmen. The West Side ("Bungtown") School was on the south side of today's Route 27A, northwest of where St. John's Church now stands in present-day Laurel Hollow. See Sammis, *Huntington-Babylon Town History,* pp. 82-83, 133-34; and Henry Onderdonk, Jr., *Revolutionary Incidents of Suffolk and Kings Counties,* 1849 (Reprinted: Port Washington: Kennikat Press, 1970), p. 264 (NAN).

16. In the Long Island Sound between Oyster Bay and Huntington Bay, the peninsula known as Lloyd's Neck was divided among four brothers of the Lloyd family when the British attacked Long Island in Aug. 1776. During its occupation of the island, the British army despoiled the extensive strands of timber on the Lloyd farms. The 50,000-cord stand on the farms of Joseph Lloyd (1716-1780) and John Lloyd (1711-1795) was reduced to one quarter its original size. Henry Lloyd (1709-1795), who remained a loyal subject of the king, received £5,834 14s. 1d. for the loss of timber and other damages to his farm. The farm of James Lloyd (1728-1810) probably suffered similarly. Dorothy Barck, ed., *Papers of the Lloyd Family of the Manor of Queens Village, Lloyd's Neck, Long Island, New York, 1654-1826,* 2 vols. (New York: New-York Historical Society, 1927), 2:777-78, 828 [DJ/DT], 6:66.

Two of the early Lloyd houses survive and are now historic house museums. The Lloyd Harbor Historical Society maintains Henry Lloyd's 1711 house located on the edge of Caumsett State Park. The Society for the Preservation of Long Island Antiquities operates the Joseph Lloyd Manor House (completed 1767). See Jean B. Osann, *Henry Lloyd's Salt Box Manor House,* rev. ed. (Huntington: Lloyd Harbor Historical Society, 1982); and Kenneth Scott and Susan E. Klaffky, *A History of the Joseph Lloyd Manor House* (Setauket: Society for the Preservation of Long Island Antiquities, 1976), (NAN).

17. "Mr. Underduncks": Hendrick Onderdonck (Onderdonk, b. 1725 {died 1809}) built New York's first paper mill at Hempstead {. . . Harbor, present-day Roslyn} in 1768. Onderdonck may have had a number of partners in the venture, among them his son Andrew, a Henry Remsen, and possibly Hugh Gaine, editor of the *New York Gazette and Mercury.* At the time of GW's visit, Onderdonck's household consisted of eight whites and seven slaves. Mary Powell Bunker, comp., *Long Island Genealogies,* 1895 (Reprint; Baltimore: Genealogical Publishing Company, 1976), p. 316; Leander Bishop, *A History of American Manufactures from 1608 to 1860,* 3 vols., 1868 (Reprint; New York: Augustus M. Kelley, 1966), 1:200; Lyman Horace Weeks, *A History of Paper Manufacturing in the United States, 1690-1916* (New York: Lockwood Trade Journal Co., 1916), pp. 37, 60; *Heads of Families, N.Y.,* p. 152 [DJ/DT], 6:67.

Hendrick Onderdonk's home is now the core of the Washington Manor Restaurant in Roslyn (1305 Northern Boulevard, opposite the clock tower). The Roslyn High School has a mural in the library depicting Washington's visit to the paper mill painted by Robert Gaston Herbert in 1937 under the auspices of the Works Projects Administration (WPA). Onderdonk's grist mill on Main Street is under reconstruction by Nassau County. A replica of the paper mill, built near the original site on Paper Mill Road in 1915, is in the Gerry Pond Park in Roslyn. A plaque on Washington Manor Restaurant commemorates Washington's visit to Onderdonk's home and his paper mill. The plaque, installed by the Nassau County Historical Society in 1985, states, "According to legend, during a demonstration of the paper-making process, the president made a sheet of paper." It is more likely that he may have watched the paper-making process. See Roy W. Moger, *Roslyn, Then and Now,* 2d ed., edited by Myrna L. Sloam (Roslyn: Bryant Library, 1992), pp. 16-18, 62-63; and Decatur, "Washington on Long Island," p. 315 (NAN).

18. A photograph of an example of a surviving splashed ("plashed") tree or living fence in Melville is in Bernie Bookbinder, *Long Island: People and Places, Past and Present* (New York: Harry N. Abrams, 1983), p. 84 (NAN).

A Jaunt to Rockaway, 1793

Charles Brockden Brown

Charles Brockden Brown (1771-1814) was an early American writer. He was born in Philadelphia to a Quaker family and after an apprenticeship studying law moved to New York City and turned to literary pursuits. One of his earliest writings was this travel letter (an "epistolary narrative") which was first published in the *Literary Magazine.* This genre enabled an author to project his own character and emotions on what he observed.[1]

Brown and his two companions (whom he refers to only by initials) traveled by stage coach from Brooklyn to Rockaway via Jamaica. In prefatory comments omitted here, Brown denies at length his ability to adequately describe the countryside. Nonetheless, he does provide an interesting description of the trip. Brown recounts in considerable detail the facilities provided for bathers to change their clothes. The first night they used a hut which had pegs for their clothes and a tub to wash off the sand. The next day Brown used an innovation pioneered at Rockaway—a bathhouse on wheels which horses pulled into the ocean.[2] Despite his rather negative view of the excursion, Brown's account provides an interesting description of an encounter with the natural landscape at a time when Rockaway was just beginning to become a resort destination.

Brown would later write *Alcuin: A Dialogue*, which was reprinted as "The Rights of Women" and six novels, the best known of which were *Wieland* and *Ormond.* After he returned to Philadelphia in 1801, he was a merchant, editor of two literary magazines, and continued to write. He was a prolific author in a variety of genres and is recognized as "the most important of early American novelists."[3]

* * *

Dear R.

What possible amusement can you expect from *my* recital of a jaunt to Rockaway? I cannot dignify trifles, or give to vulgar sights a novelty, by making them pass through my fancy. That fancy, you well know, has no particle of kindred to that of poet or painter, and nobody should pretend to describe, who does not look through the optics of either painter or poet. . . .

Remember, it is a picture of myself, and not of the island, that you want: and such, how disreputable soever it may be to the painter, you shall have. I have some comfort in thinking that most of the travellers to Rockaway are but little wiser and more inquisitive than myself.

In the first place, then, we left J.'s at one o'clock. The day was extremely fine, and promised a most pleasant ride. You may suppose that we were most agreeably occupied in the prospect of a journey which neither of the three had ever made before: but no such thing. We thought and talked of nothing but the uncertainty of getting seats in the stage, which goes at that hour from Brooklyn, and the reasonable apprehension of being miserably crowded, even if we could get seats. Such is my aversion to being wedged with ten or twelve in a stage coach, that I had previously resolved to return, in case of any such misfortune. So I told my friends, but in this I fibbed a little, for the naked truth was, that I wanted a pretext for staying behind; having left society in New York, the loss of which all the pleasures of Rockaway would poorly compensate.

We passed the river, and after dining at the inn, were seated in the coach much more at our ease than we had any reason to expect. We rode through a country altogether new to me, twelve or fourteen miles (I forgot which) to Jamaica. Shall I give you a peep into my thoughts? I am half ashamed to admit [to] you, but I will deal sincerely with you. Still, say I, my consolation is, that few travellers, if their minds were laid as completely open to inspection, would come off from their trial with more credit than myself.

I confess to you then that my mind was much more busily engaged in reflecting on the possible consequences of coming off without several changes of clothes in my handkerchief, and without an umbrella to shelter me from sunshine and rain, than with the fields and woods which I passed through. My umbrella I had the ill luck to break as we crossed the river, and as to clothes, I had the folly, as usual, to forget that Rockaway was a place of fashionable resort, and that many accidents might happen to prolong our stay there four or five days, instead of a single day; and yet think not that I was totally insensible to passing objects. The sweet pure country air, which was brisk, cool and fresh enough to make supportable the noon-tide rays of a July sun, to the whole force of which my seat beside the driver exposed me, I inhaled with delight. I remember little, however, but a country, pretty much *denuded of its woods* (as Sam. Johnson would say),[4] a sandy soil; stubble fields, houses fifty years old, a couple of miles from each other, and most of them, especially those furthest on the road, exact counterparts of such as we see in Dutch and Flemish landscapes; four-wheeled rustic carriages, of a most disproportioned length, crazy and uncouth, without springs, entered from behind, and loaded with women and children, pigs and chickens; not a single carriage of elegance or pleasure to be met with, though overtaken by half a dozen gigs, going to the same place with ourselves.[5]

We reached Jamaica at five o'clock, and here we staid [stayed] one hour. A glass of lemonade, a plentiful ablution in cold water, and a walk with B. in a church-yard opposite the inn, were all the surprising events which distinguished this hour. This island is one of the oldest of European settlements in North America, and we therefore expected to find in this churchyard some memorial of ancient days, but we were disappointed. There were many grave-stones, broken or half sunken, or blackened by age, but the oldest date was within forty years. The church, though painted anew and furbished up lately, was about seventy years old, as an inscription on the front informed us. There was another [church] of a much more antique cast within view, but we did not approach it.[6]

I hope you will be sparing of your questions respecting Jamaica, for I can answer none of them. I asked not a single question statistical or topographical of our hostess. I did not count the houses, and therefore can form no notion of the population. It is a spacious, well-looking village, many of whose houses appear to be built as summer retreats for wealthy citizens, and that is all I can say of it.[7]

During our second stage, I was placed much more at my ease than during the first. I was seated beside a pretty little girl, whom all the company took care to inform, that they thought her pretty. For my part, her attractions made little impression on my fancy. To be infirmly delicate in form, to have a baby-like innocence of aspect, and a voice so very soft that it can scarcely be heard, are no recommendations to me. She prattled a good deal about a squirrel and canary-bird which she had at home, and that respectful attention was paid to a pair of very sweet *lips,* which the *words* that fell from them would never have obtained. The rest of our company were men, and I have not wit enough to extract any oddity or singularity from their conversation or appearance. Two of them, you know, were my companions, and the other two cheerful and well-bred strangers.

I, for the most part, was mute, as I usually am, in a stagecoach and among strangers. Not so my two friends. B. finds a topic of talk and good humour in every thing, and J.'s amenity is always ready to pursue the other's lead. I forget all their topics, except a very earnest discussion of the merits of different lodging-houses, at the sea side, and many sympathetic effusions, drawn forth by the *shipwreck* of another coach. On the first head we concluded to go to the house nearest the sea, one Ben Cornwall's, our purpose being as much to gratify the eye as the touch, and there we accordingly arrived, pretty late on a chill, moist and cloudy evening.

There are few men who are always masters of their spirits, and mine, which had not been high through the day, fell suddenly some degrees lower, on stepping out of the carriage into the piazza of the house. This place appeared, at the first glance, to want at the same time the comforts and seclusion of a private house, and the order and plenty of a public one. The scene without was extremely dreary, and the vicinity of the sea, not being a quarter of a mile distant, gave us very distinctly the music of his multitudinous waves.

Our curiosity would not allow us to go to bed, till we had touched the ocean-wave. We, therefore, after a poor repast, hastened down to the beach. Between the house and the water, is a wide and level expanse of loose white sand, which is a pretty good sample of Arabia or Zaara [Sahara], as I have heard them described. Tell me, you who have travelled, whether every country, in the temperate zone, of moderate extent and somewhat diversified, contains not samples of every quarter of the globe?

The air was wet to the touch and saline to the taste, but the novelty of the scene, to which a canopy of dark clouds, with a pale star gleaming now and then through the crevices, tended to increase, buoyed up my spirits to their usual pitch. To my friend B. this novelty was absolute. He never before saw the ocean; but to me it was new only as I now saw it, at night. Seven years ago I found my way to the margent [border] of the sea, between Sandyhook and the mouth of the Raritan. I took a long peregrination [journey] on foot, in company with two friends, and shall never forget the impression which the boundless and troubled ocean, seen for the first time, from an open beach, in a clear day, and with a strong wind blowing landward, made upon me. It was flood-tide, and the sandy margin formed a pretty steep shelf. The billows, therefore, rose to a considerable height, and broke with great fury against it; and my soul was suspended for half an hour, with an awe, a rapture which I never felt before. Far different were my feelings on *this* occasion, for the scene was no longer new to me, and the scene itself was far less magnificent. There was scarcely any wind, the tide was ebb, and the shore declined almost imperceptibly.

As we came to this place for the purpose of bathing, and had so short a time to stay, we thought we could not begin too early, and therefore stript [stripped] immediately, notwithstanding the freshness of the air, and what is of greater moment, our ignorance of the shore.

Up, pretty high upon the shore, is an house, no better than a fisherman's hut. 'Tis a mere frame of wood, boarded at the sides and top, with no window, and a door-way. The floor is sand, and there are pegs against the wall to hang clothes upon. There is a tub provided for cleansing the feet from the sand, which when wet clings to the skin like bird-lime. Towels, which are furnished at the house, we brought not with us.

Is there any thing, the advantages of which are more universally and constantly manifested, than order? Its value is seen in the most trivial matters, as in the most momentous. This room was pitch-dark, and we were wholly unacquainted with it: and yet by the simple process of hanging our clothes, as we take them off, on a peg, and putting them on in the same order reversed, there is no difficulty. Some of us were not so wise as to practise this order, and, of consequence, were condemned to grope about half an hour longer than others, in the dark, for stockings, sleeve-buttons, hats, and handkerchiefs.

What would physicians say to standing naked on a bleak night, with the wind at east, while the billows broke over you for ten minutes? There is an agreeable trepidation felt, while the scene is new, and the sudden effusion of cold water must, methinks, produce powerful effects of some kind or another.

As we were early comers to this house, we were honoured each with a room to himself. There were twenty or thirty persons to be accommodated, besides a numerous family, in a wooden house of two stories; so that we could not but congratulate ourselves on the privilege thus secured to us. The chamber, however, allotted to me was a little nook, about seven feet long and three wide, only large enough to admit the bedstead and him that slept in it. In such excursions as these, however, hardships and privations, are preferable to ease and luxury. There is something like consciousness of merit in encountering them voluntarily and with cheerfulness. There is a rivalship in hardihood and good humour, more pleasurable than any delights of the senses. A splenetic [irritable] or fastidious traveller is a great burden to himself and to his company, and ought, through mere generosity, to keep himself at home. In saying this, I am conscious, that in some degree, I pronounce my own condemnation, but I hope I am not very culpable.

My friends rose at day-light next morning, and went to bathe. They gave me warning, but I heeded it not. My little nook had half melted me with heat, and I felt as if unqualified for the least exertion. I was sorry to have lost the opportunity and rose, when the sun was high in the heavens, with some degree of regret. But more lucky than I deserved to be, I found a country wagon at the door, ready to carry down any one that chose, to the strand [beach]. I went down with another.

This was a far different bathing from that of the night before. The wagon carries us to the water's edge, and there we may undress at our leisure amidst a footing of clean straw, convenient seats and plenty of napkins [towels]. The wagon receives us directly from the water and carries us home, without trouble or delay. On this occasion the sun was just warm enough to be comfortable, and the time o'day exactly suited to the bath. Such is my notion of the matter, but I doubt whether any body else will agree with me. Sunrise and sun-set are the usual bathing-times.

After breakfast, we took a walk along the strand. My pastime consisted in picking up shells; in sifting and examining the fine white sand; in treading on the heels and toes of the wave, as it fell and rose, and in trying to find some music in its eternal murmur. Here could I give you long descants on all these topics, but my vague and crude reveries would only make my dull epistle still more dull. The sun at last broke out with the full force of midsummer, and we panted and waded through the sand, homeward, with no small regret that we had ventured so far. We Americans in general have feeble heads: those of us, I mean, who were not born to dig ditches and make hay. A white hat, broad-brimmed, and light as a straw, is an insufficient shelter against the direct beams of the sun. What must we have suffered on this occasion when the vertical rays fell on a surface of smooth white sand? We were almost liquefied before we reached the house.

The company, at this house, was numerous, and afforded, as usual, abundant topics of speculation. Some were young men, in the hey day of spirits, rattling, restless, and noisy. Some were solid and conversible, and some awkward and reserved. Three ladies, married women, belonged to the company: one of whom said nothing, but was as dignified and courteous in demeanor as silence would let her be: another talked much, and a third hit the true medium pretty well. I did not fail to make a great many reflections on the passing scene, which, together with a volume of Cecilia, made the day pass not very tediously. . . .[8]

My friend, I have grown very tired of my story. I believe I will cut short the rest, and carry you back with me next morning, to New York, in a couple of sentences. The weather on the morrow was damp and lowering, but it cleared up early. We were again agreeably disappointed in our expectations of a crowded stage, and after breakfasting at Jamaica, reached town at one o'clock. On my return, I was just as unobservant of the passing scene as before, and took as little note of the geography of the isle. Set me out on the same journey again, and I should scarcely recognize a foot of the way. I saw trees and shrubs and grasses, but I could not name them, *being as how* I am no botanist.

Perhaps, however, I mistake the purpose of such journies, which is not to exercise the reasoning faculties, or to add to knowledge, but to unbend, to dissipate thought and care, and to strengthen the frame and refresh the spirits, by mere motion and variety. This is the language which my friends hold; but I confess, mere mental vacuity gives me neither health nor pleasure. To give time wings, my attention must be fixed on something: I must look about me in pursuit of some expected object; I must converse with my companion on some reasonable topic; I must find some image in my own fancy to examine, or the way is painfully tedious. This jaunt to Rockaway has left few agreeable traces behind it. All I remember with any pleasure, are the appearance of the wide ocean, and the incidents of bathing in its surges. Had I been a botanist, and lighted upon some new plant; a mineralogist, and found an agate or a petrifaction; a naturalist, and caught such a butterfly as I never saw before, I should have reflected on the journey with no little satisfaction. As it was, I set my foot in the city with no other sentiment, but that of regret, for not having employed these two days in a very different manner.

Notes

Source: William Dunlap, *The Life of Charles Brockden Brown: Together with Selections from The Rarest of His Printed Works, from His Original Letters, and from His Manuscripts Before Unpublished.* 2 vols. (Philadelphia: James P. Parke, 1815), 1:58-67.

Editing changes have been minimal. Brown's spelling and punctuation have been retained, except that spaces before colons, semi-colons, and question marks have been eliminated. Elipses (three dots) indicate omissions. Insertions in the text by the editor for this volume are in brackets; all notes are by the editor.

1. For additional information, see Joann P. Krieg, "'This Jaunt To Rockaway': An Eighteenth-Century Excursion," *Long Island Forum* 52 (Spring 1989): 52-57; and the selection below, "Rockaway on 'Old Long Island's Sea Girt Shore.'"

2. See Vincent Seyfried and William Asadorian, *Old Rockaway, New York in Early Photographs* (Mineola: Dover, 2000), pp. 3-4.

3. Biographical information on Brown is from Philip Barnard, "Brown, Charles Brockden," *in American National Biography,* edited by John A. Garraty and Mark C. Carnes (New York: Oxford University Press, 1999), 3:657-59. See also entries on Brown in various volumes of the *Dictionary of Literary Biography* (Detroit: Gale Research, 1985-1988), 37:69-81, 59:26-35, 73:21-28; and Steven Watts, *The Romance of Real Life: Charles Brockden Brown and the Origins of American Culture* (Baltimore: Johns Hopkins University Press, 1994).

4. Dr. Samuel Johnson (1709-1784) was an English writer and lexicographer.

5. A gig was a two-wheeled, horse-drawn carriage.

6. There were three churches in Jamaica at the time of Brown's visit. The Presbyterian stone church was built in 1699, a hexagon-shaped Dutch Reformed Church was built in 1715, and the Anglicans built their first church in 1734. Each of their buildings was replaced in the nineteenth century. Brown probably visited Grace (Episcopal) Church and saw the nearby Dutch Church. See engravings on p. 10 and 99 above.

7. Today's King Manor Museum in Jamaica was still an eighteenth-century Dutch-style house when Brown visited. Rufus King, a signer of the Constitution and U.S. Senator, bought the land in 1805 for a country home and expanded the house in the Federal style. It is now owned by New York City and is open year-round (King Park, 150th Street and Jamaica Avenue; 718-206-0545).

8. *Cecilia; or Memoirs of an Heiress,* was a novel by the English writer, Fanny Burney (1752-1840). It was published in five volumes in London in 1782 and printed in the United States in 1793.

Journey to Long Island, 1804

Timothy Dwight

Timothy Dwight (1752-1817) had deep roots in New England. Born in Northampton in western Massachusetts, his maternal grandfather, the famous Jonathan Edwards, and his great-great-grandfather, Solomon Stoddard, were among his ministerial ancestors. Dwight graduated from Yale in 1769 and returned there as a tutor (instructor) after teaching school for two years. Dwight and his fellow tutors introduced *belles lettres* into the classical curriculum which was dominated by Latin and Greek. In addition to teaching seventeenth and eighteenth century authors, they wrote poetry themselves and literary historians later dubbed them the Hartford or Connecticut Wits. Timothy Dwight's criticism and defiance of the college trustees in holding commencement exercises led to his forced resignation in 1776.

Dwight had been studying theology with his uncle, the Reverend Jonathan Edwards, Jr., and was licensed to preach in 1777. That same year he married Mary Woolsey and became a chaplain at West Point. In 1779, after his father died, Dwight returned to Northampton to support his mother and younger brothers. He farmed, taught school, and did supply preaching on weekends. Dwight accepted a call from the Greenfield Church in Fairfield, Connecticut, where he was ordained to the ministry in 1783. Appointed president of Yale College in 1795, he preached regularly in the college chapel, taught *belles lettres* and rhetoric, introduced science into the curriculum, began to transform Yale into a university with the introduction of legal and medical instruction, and "nurtured academic excellence within the sphere of Christian values."[1] Dwight was the acknowledged leader of the Connecticut clergy in his day and an advocate of the "New Divinity." He was a Federalist in his political views and defended the preferred status of the Congregational Church and the "legal establishment of the public worship of God."[2]

Dwight traveled during college vacations to restore his health and kept a journal during these trips. After unsuccessfully trying to imagine how the land might have appeared a century earlier, he decided to describe the current scene. He hoped to enable future generations to know "the appearance of their country" during the time of his journeys. He also wanted to correct the distorted view of New England presented by European writers. Although he adopted the literary style of letters "addressed to an English gentleman," he wrote them primarily for his own countrymen.[3]

On several occasions Dwight considered publishing his travel writings, but he did not do so during his lifetime. On his deathbed, he asked his friend and colleague, Professor Benjamin Silliman, to see that his travel accounts were published. With the assistance of his sons, *Travels in New England and New York* was published posthumously in four volumes in 1821-1822, and reprinted in London in 1823. "Journey to Long Island" is in the third volume. The selections reprinted here are from the 1969 edition of his *Travels* edited by Barbara Miller Solomon and published by Harvard University Press. Some sections that do not enhance our understanding of Long Island in the early nineteenth century are not included here, but the content of the omitted sections is briefly noted.

Dwight made a number of visits to Long Island, but these writings are based primarily on his visit from May 9-28, 1804. On that trip, he traveled across Long Island Sound to Huntington and went west along the north shore, through Smithtown and Setauket to Riverhead and Orient. He then crossed Shelter Island to Sag Harbor and headed east on the south fork to East Hampton. On his return route, Dwight traveled on a southern route through Southampton, Westhampton, Amityville, Hempstead, Flushing, Jamaica, and Brooklyn to New York City. He did not go through the town of North Hempstead nor northern sections of the town of Oyster Bay.

Dwight described the settlements (e.g., "a pretty village"), appearance of houses and churches ("new and neat"), the soil, the landscape, and the character of the people ("industrious and thrifty"). Dwight was an unabashed booster of his native region and viewed Long Island through his New England eyes. Long Island had few streams for waterpower and the flat terrain resulted in "generally dull scenery." He felt that even the "fantastical scenery" at Napeague Beach on the Montauk peninsula compared unfavorably with beaches at Cape Cod. He did not believe that education on Long Island was up to New England standards. His negative comments on the Montaukett Indians reflect the prejudices of his day. But in Suffolk County, having been settled by New Englanders, the inhabitants remain "New England people" and Dwight generally regarded their manners, morals, and religion favorably. (Three-fourths of his pages on Long Island are devoted to Suffolk County.) Though he felt the "appearance of the country" improved in the western part of the island, he criticized the morals and religion of the people; horse racing was popular and many did not observe the Sabbath. He felt Long Islanders were insular, that few looked beyond their own small hamlets, and the most talented left for New York City or the "allurements of the continent." Despite his critical eye, Dwight's account, as Barbara Solomon observes, "is invaluable as a contemporary record and interpretation." It is a unique detailed depiction of Long Island at the beginning of the nineteenth century.[4]

* * *

LETTER I

Passage from Norwalk to Huntington—Lloyd Neck—Town of Huntington—Smithtown—Setauket—Brookhaven—Riverhead—Its courts—Southold—Oyster Point— Fishers Island—Plum Island

Dear Sir,

In company with Professor D—, of Yale College, Mr. S[tuart?], one of the tutors, and Mr. D[wight], a graduate of that institution, I set out {from New Haven}, May 9, 1804, on a journey to Long Island.[5] The first day we rode to Greenfield, twenty-four miles; and the next, to Norwalk, nine. Here we continued till Monday the 14th, the wind being unfavorable for passing the Sound. On Monday, at five o'clock in the morning, we embarked with our horses on board the Huntington ferryboat.[6] After leaving Norwalk River, the mouth of which is a good harbor for vessels of less than one hundred tons, the wind became very feeble, shifted suddenly and frequently throughout the whole day; and, what was very tedious, shifted in almost every instance in such a manner as to retard our progress. We had breakfasted early and on meager diet, and were miserably provided with food, both as to quantity and quality, for the day. My companions ate merely to satisfy the corrodings of hunger. I fasted till after three the succeeding morning. To add to our troubles, a thunderstorm overtook us in the mouth of Huntington harbor at nine o'clock in the evening. Our quarter deck was leaky, and permitted the rain to descend upon us in streams, not at all resembling those of Helicon.[7] Time, patience, and apathy, however, helped us through the train of our difficulties; and, at half after two, we landed at the usual place. Here we found a very decent house. The family arose with a great deal of good nature and entertained us very kindly and very well. We went to bed between three and four, rose at ten, and between eleven and twelve pursued our journey to Setauket: twenty-five miles.

Huntington is an ancient settlement, the westernmost of those in the county of Suffolk which were formed by colonists from New England. The township extends from north to south through the whole breadth of the island, ten or twelve miles, and about the same distance from east to west.[8] The town is built six miles from the northern shore, at the head of a bay, named Huntington Bay, and during the Revolution the principal station for the British ships of war in the Sound. This bay is large and deep enough to receive the greatest number of vessels which ever assemble at any single place, furnishes good anchorage, and is safe from all winds. Its mouth is formed by two peninsulas, or, as they are here termed, *necks:* Eaton's, on [the] east; and Lloyd, on the west. On the former of these is a lighthouse. Few places more demand such a structure or furnish for it a more commodious situation. The rocks which project from this neck and are a continuation of its base into the Sound have in several instances proved fatal to seamen. Captain Keeler, a worthy and intelligent inhabitant of Norwalk, returning from the West Indies after a prosperous voyage, entered the Sound on the 16th of January in the year 1791. I then resided at Greenfield and distinctly remember the day, and never saw a winter day which was more pleasant. In the evening there arose a tremendous storm. The brig was driven upon these rocks, and every person on board perished.[9]

Lloyd Neck is a large and valuable estate belonging to a respectable family of that name, which has been in possession of it for a long time.[10] It is connected at the western end with the township of Oyster Bay by a narrow strip of sand. On the southern side of this peninsula is a pretty, romantic retreat named Queens Village, and handsomely celebrated by the late Gov. Livingston, of New Jersey, in his Philosophic Solitude.[11] I visited the place formerly, and thought it not undeserving of the character attributed to it by that gentleman.

The town of Huntington we left on our right, intending to pass through it upon our return. As we failed of accomplishing this design, I am able to describe it only as it appeared to me many years since. It was then loosely and indifferently built. As we now passed by it, several good houses and a well-looking church, newly erected, showed us a handsome addition to its former appearance.[12] The inhabitants at the time to which I refer were esteemed sober, industrious, and religious. The Revolutionary War affected them unhappily in all these respects. Within a few years past several revivals of religion have extensively renewed their ancient character. The soil of the township is light, warm, moderately good, and well suited to all the productions of the climate.

Huntington lies about three miles south of the general line of the north shore. The country from Huntington to Setauket is, on the middle road {Middle Country Road, now Route 25}, (that which we took) formed of interchanging hills and valleys, and a few plains, none of them extensive. The greater part of it is forested, principally with oak and chestnut, but with an interspersion of hickory, cherry, and several other kinds of trees.

The best land which we saw on this day's journey is in and about Smithtown. Here we dined or rather wished to dine, the inn at which we stopped, and the only one on the road, not having the means of enabling us to satisfy our wishes. In this humble mansion, however, we found a young lady about eighteen, of a fine form and complexion, a beautiful countenance, with brilliant eyes animated by intelligence, possessing manners which were a charming mixture of simplicity and grace, and conversing in language which would not have discredited a drawing room or a court. Her own declarations compelled us to believe, against every preconception, that she was a child of this very humble, uneducated family; but nothing which we saw in the house could account for the appearance of her person, mind, or manners. I was ready, as I believe all my companions were, when we left the spot, to believe that some

>   Flowers are born to blush unseen,
>   And waste their sweetness on the desert air.[13]

A small church stands near this inn in the midst of a hamlet consisting of ten or a dozen houses. Not far from this little collection runs a sprightly millstream, an object which in this region will engage the attention of every traveler.

Smithtown extends about half across the island, and is ten or twelve miles in length from east to west. It is formed almost universally of scattered plantations. The soil, taken together, is, I suspect, inferior to that of no township in this county. It received its name from two families, both named Smith, which first settled in it, and from which a considerable part of its present inhabitants derive their origin.[14] Their number of the year 1790 was 1,022; in 1800, 1,413; and in 1810, 1,592.

In this township, near its southern limit, is a pond, having the Indian name of *Ronkonkoma,* which is said by authority that cannot be rationally questioned to rise regularly throughout seven years, and to fall with the same regularity through the following seven. No water except from subjacent springs runs into it or out of it. It abounds with perch. I will not vouch for the truth of the story.

Brookhaven is a township lying immediately east of Smithtown, extending east and west on the road nineteen miles, and from the north to the south side of the island, a distance varying here from thirteen to eighteen miles.

Setauket, the principal village in this township, is built near the north shore, and like Smithtown and Huntington is an ancient settlement. The number of houses within the compass of a square mile may be forty or fifty, thinly dispersed and with a few exceptions old and indifferently repaired. The village contains two churches: a Presbyterian and an Episcopal, both ancient and ordinary, the latter in a ruinous condition.[15] The soil is sandy and light, but capable by a judicious cultivation of producing good crops.

Brookhaven contains several other villages and hamlets, besides a number of scattered plantations. In 1790, the number of its inhabitants was 3,224; in 1800, 4,022; and in 1810, 4,176.

Brookhaven is the largest township on the island.

We lodged at the hospitable house of the Hon. S. Strong, where we spent our time very pleasantly until Thursday morning, being detained by a violent northeast storm accompanied by a heavy rain.[16] We then rode to a village in the township of Southold named Mattituck, having passed through the

The Setauket Presbyterian Church (*left*) was built in 1812. Setauket's Caroline Church (*right*) is the oldest Episcopal church on Long Island (1712).

remainder of Brookhaven, the township of Riverhead, and a part of Southold: thirty-six miles.

When you read this, you may not have before you a map of Long Island. It will not be amiss, therefore, to give you here a general view of its geography.

Long Island is divided into three counties: Kings, on the western point; Queens, in the middle; and Suffolk, on the east, containing at least two thirds of the whole island.[17]

Kings contained in 1790, 4,495; in 1800, 5,740; and in 1810, 8,303 inhabitants. Queens contained in 1790, 16,014; in 1800, 16,893; and in 1810, 19,336 inhabitants. Suffolk contained in 1790, 16,440; in 1800, 19,464; and in 1810, 21,113 inhabitants. The island contained in 1790, 36,949; in 1800, 42,097; and in 1810, 48,752 inhabitants.

Queens County is about thirty miles in length; Suffolk, about one hundred. Kings and Queens counties contain each six townships; and Suffolk, nine. Three of these townships, Oyster Bay in Queens, Huntington, which borders on it, and Brookhaven, extend across the breadth of the island. In Queens County, Newtown, Flushing, and North Hempstead lie on the northside, and Jamaica and Hempstead, on the south. In Suffolk, Smithtown, Riverhead, and Southold are on the north; and Islip, Southampton, and East Hampton are on the south. Shelter Island, the remaining township in Suffolk County, lies between the two great eastern arms of Long Island, to be hereafter described.

When you remember that five townships occupy the whole extent of one hundred miles on the north shore of this island, you will not be surprised to find two of them spreading through a moderate day's journey, nor to be told that the inhabitants, though considerably numerous on paper, are yet in each township to a great extent scattered in a very thin dispersion.

During the first part of this day's journey, the country was formed of hills and valleys as before. We passed several hamlets in the township of Brookhaven, called *Drowned Meadow* {now Port Jefferson}, *the Old Man's* {Mount Sinai}, *Miller's place* {Miller Place}, and *Wading River,* partly in Brookhaven, and partly in Riverhead.

At Miller's place, and in several others, the prospect of the Sound and the Connecticut shore is very extensive and attractive.

During the second part of our journey this day, the country was chiefly a plain, occupying almost the whole distance from Wading River, which is fourteen or fifteen miles from Brookhaven, to Southold, near thirty miles.

The road over this plain is generally excellent. On the soil, I shall make some observations hereafter.

Riverhead is the shire town of this county {i.e., the town where the county seat is located}. It was formerly a part of the township of Southold, and was incorporated in 1792. Its name is derived from Peconic River, the principal stream on the island. This river rises in the middle of the island, and running from west to east, empties its waters into the great bay in the eastern end, known by several names, by one of which, viz., Peconic, I shall denominate it hereafter. The courthouse, a poor decayed building, and a miserable hamlet containing about ten or twelve houses stand near the efflux of this river.

From this account of the courthouse you will naturally suspect that the business of lawyers and sheriffs is not here in very great demand, nor in very high reputation. The suspicion is certainly well founded. The county court, or court of common pleas, sits here twice annually, assembles on Tuesday; and, after having finished its whole business, adjourns almost always on the succeeding day.

The court of oyer and terminer sits once in a year. It assembles on Tuesday at ten o'clock, finishes all its business, and adjourns almost always on the succeeding day also. In twenty years it has never sat later than till Thursday evening.

No lawyer, if I am not misinformed, has hitherto been able to get a living in the county of Suffolk. I entertain a very respectful opinion of the gentlemen of the bar; but both you and they will cheerfully agree with me in saying that this exemption from litigation, while it is a peculiar, is also a very honorable characteristic of this county. Not far from this hamlet is a spot of ground about three miles in diameter, which, as I was informed by good authority, is covered with shrub {or scrub} oaks and pines, not more than five or six feet in height. In the whole tract there is not a single tree of the usual size, although it is surrounded by a forest of such trees.[18] The cause of this phenomenon in a place where the soil is substantially the same with that of the neighboring country, it is not easy to assign.

Six or eight miles before we arrived at Mattituck, the country on both sides of the road was chiefly settled in scattered plantations; and the inhabitants appeared generally to be in comfortable circumstances.

Riverhead contained in the year 1800, 1,498 inhabitants; and in 1810, 1,711.

Mattituck is a hamlet in the township of Southold.

Friday, May 18th, we rode through Southold to the ferry. Thence we crossed to Shelter Island; and, passing over it, crossed a second ferry to *Hogs Neck* {North Haven}, a peninsula united to Southampton by a long narrow isthmus of sand, bare only at low water. This isthmus we traveled over when it was covered by the tide one fourth of a mile in length, and in different places to the depth of two feet. Then by a very circuitous course we proceeded to Sag Harbor.

The country from Mattituck to Southold is almost a perfect level, and the road very good.

Southold is a more considerable settlement than any other through which we had passed. The houses are generally better, more numerous, and more compactly built. The inhabitants, who are chiefly Presbyterians, have erected a church, which is the principal ornament of their town.

Southold contains two parishes: the town and Oysterponds. From the town to Oysterponds {Orient} Point is ten miles: five to the beach which connects the point with Long Island, and five thence to the extremity of the point.

The parish of Oysterponds which occupies this ground is only one mile in breadth, but is populous. The land is good, and the people are industrious and thrifty. A considerable number of the inhabitants are fishermen. The agriculture has lately been much improved, but the people suffer not a little from ecclesiastical contentions. It contains a Presbyterian church and has a settled minister, but there are many sectaries {sectarians or religious dissenters}. The houses are about as numerous as in Southold and of as good an appearance.[19]

The township of Southold includes also several islands. Of these the largest is Fishers Island, lying eight miles southeast of New London. It is nine miles in length, and contains about four thousand acres. The surface is uneven, and the soil moderately good. It feeds a great number of sheep, with a few neat cattle {cows}, and yields a considerable quantity of wool, butter, cheese, and corn. It was originally purchased by His Excellency John Winthrop, Esq., formerly governor of Connecticut; and is now the property of Francis B. Winthrop, Esq., of New York.[20] Southwestward of Fishers Island are two islets, named the Gull Islands, on the least of which is built a lighthouse.[21] These stand in a rapid tide called the *Horserace,* by which, had they not a base of solid rock, they would long since have been washed away.

Immediately southwest of these islands, or rather west southwest, lies Plum Island, separated from Oysterponds Point by a channel three fourths of a mile wide, called Plum Gut, through which also runs a strong and rapid tide. This island was first purchased by Samuel Wyllys, Esq., of Hartford, about the year 1667, for a barrel of biscuit and a hundred awls and fishhooks. The original proprietor was Wyandanse {Wyandanch}, called by Dr. Trumbull Wyantanse, one of the principal sachems of Long Island.[22] Afterwards it fell into the hands of a Mr. Beebee, of Plymouth, some of whose descendants are said lately to have had in their possession a manuscript history of the settlement of that colony, now supposed to be lost. This island contains about eight hundred acres of excellent land, and is inhabited by six families. Its waters abound in fine fish. Anciently it was called the Isle of Patmos, I suppose, from its solitary situation.

There are also two or three islands in Peconic Bay included in this, of which the largest is Robins Island.

All these islands, except the last, lie in a line, and in the general direction of the north shore of Long Island in this region, and were very possibly a part of it in distant ages.

In the year 1790, Southold, then including Riverhead, contained 3,219 inhabitants; in the year 1800, without Riverhead, 2,200; in the year 1810, 2,613.

I am, dear Sir, yours, etc.

LETTER II

General observations on the northern parts of Long Island, and on the stones and sand of which it is composed—Cultivation of wheat—Account of the Hessian fly—Forest trees—Fruit trees—Improvement in agriculture—Scarcity of brooks and millstreams—Fisheries

Dear Sir,

In the summary account which I have given of this part of our journey, you have undoubtedly concluded that many particulars were omitted which might have been mentioned with advantage. The truth is, this country is not distinguished like others through which I have traveled by a succession of varieties, continually inviting the eye, and furnishing a fund of materials for observation. A general sameness spreads over its face; and in an excursion of twenty or thirty miles a traveler may be said, in a sense, to have seen it all. I have, therefore, chosen to throw together the remarks which occurred to me during this part of my progress.

Long Island, from Huntington to Southold, and probably from a considerable distance further westward to Montauk Point, is, like the peninsula of Cape Cod, Nantucket, Martha's Vineyard, and a considerable tract in the southern part of Massachusetts, a vast body of fine yellow sand, rising in many instances from one to two, and in some to near three hundred feet above the level of the ocean.

Of the same sand is formed Shelter Island also; and, I presume, most others in this neighborhood, both within and without Peconic Bay. Of the same material is formed the immense beach, extending everywhere as a barrier against the ocean, in front of the great bay which reaches on the south side of the island from Hempstead to Southampton, about eighty miles, and communicates with the Atlantic by a few narrow inlets. Like the beach formerly described on the eastern shore of Cape Cod, this also is tossed into innumerable wild and fantastical forms. On a multitude of grounds in different places, the yellow sand, as on Cape Cod, is covered by a thin stratum of white sand, sometimes naked, but generally overspread with the layer of soil; and, as on that peninsula, so here in Riverhead, Southold, East Hampton, and Southampton, the sand in several places has been blown away to a considerable depth, leaving a number of small tracts absolutely desolate and useless.

When we commenced our journey on this island, I proposed to my companions to examine with a continual and minute attention the stones of every size which should be visible to us throughout all the parts of our progress. This examination was made by us all with great care, and was extended to the stones on the general surface, to those washed out in hollow roads, to those uncovered on the summits and sides and at the bottom of hills, to those found in the deepest valleys, and to those which were dug out of a considerable number of very deep wells. The result of this examination was that all the stones which we saw were, without an exception, destitute of angles, limited by an arched exterior, appearing as if worn by the long-continued attrition of water, and in all respects exactly like those which in a multitude of places we found on the beach of the ocean. In ten or twelve instances, possibly a few more, we observed small rocks of granite on our road. Everyone of these exhibited what I thought plain proofs of having been

washed for a considerable length of time, and strongly resembled rocks of
the same kind which have been long beaten by waves. I will not say that no
other traveler would have considered these rocks as exceptions, but to my
eye they exhibited manifest appearances of having been long worn by water.
If this opinion be admitted, we did not find, in a progress of more than two
hundred miles, a single stone which did not exhibit proofs of having been
washed for a considerable period.

On Montauk Point, the stones have a different aspect, being angular, and
wearing the common appearance of the granite rocks so generally found in
New England. After we had passed Jamaica in our way to New York, we
found a similar change in the stones, most of them being here also angular,
and presenting no evidence that they had ever been washed. Between these
limits the stones are universally *aquatic,* if I may be allowed for the sake of
succinctness to give them this name.

From this extraordinary fact it would seem to be a natural conclusion that
the great body of this island, or, perhaps more properly, the materials of
which it is composed, were at some former period covered by the ocean; and
by a cause, which cannot now be discovered, were thrown up into their
present form. As there are in it no vestiges of a single volcano, the attribution
of its origin to volcanic eruptions must be gratuitous. Were we to admit the
existence of such a cause, its operations would in no measure account for the
actual phenomena. Nor does it seem reconcilable with facts to suppose that
this mass of earth was thrown up to such a height by any movements of the
ocean. . . .[23]

The surface of Long Island along the north shore is from Wading River
to the western point a continual interchange of hills, valleys, and plains, but
without any distinguished specimens of the beauty which might naturally be
expected from such a variety of surface. Throughout the whole extent there
is nothing which approaches toward the appearance of a mountain; nothing
bold and masculine; and, except in a few of the necks or points, nothing
particularly soft and elegant. From Wading River eastward, the country is
almost an absolute level.

The soil on the north side has but two considerable varieties. It is either
the thin mold already mentioned as covering the layer of white sand and of
no great value, or a loam of a yellowish brown, spread from the depth of one
to perhaps three or four feet, mixed with an abundance of gravel, and by a
skillful husbandry capable of being rendered eminently productive. It is not,
however, friendly to grass. We traveled through this country in the month of
May, when New England is universally covered with a fresh and glowing
verdure, promising by its brilliancy the future luxuriance of the pastures and

meadows. Here, with a small number of exceptions, chiefly in Huntington and Brookhaven, the natural verdure was faint and bluish, indicating that the soil whence it sprang was unfavorable, and the cultivation imperfect. The meadows created by the plow yielded a considerable growth of clover and herds-grass.

To wheat the best soils of this island are peculiarly suited. In favorable years they have often yielded with a good dressing of manure, particularly of whitefish, from thirty to forty bushels an acre. To maize they are less congenial. This, however, I learned from information, the season not being far enough advanced to enable me to judge from inspection.

Flax has heretofore been cultivated with success, but for two years past the crop has failed. A black rust has settled in spots on the rind or coat, eaten it through, and destroyed its texture. Happily this evil, unknown till within this period, is already decreasing.

The Hessian fly has some years seriously injured the wheat, but generally has done little mischief.

So far as I have been able to learn, this insect, so insignificant in its appearance, and yet so important by its ravages on the labors and happiness of mankind, was first found in a field of wheat on or near the Hessian encampment in the neighborhood of Brooklyn, and opposite to the city of New York. This was in the year 1784. Thence it spread at the rate of about twenty miles a year through most parts of the northern and middle states, faster with and slower against the southwest wind. So many descriptions of this insect have been given to the public that a minute account of it must be unnecessary here. . . . The maggot perforates the stalk of the wheat, cuts off the interior rind together with the principal part of the vessels, and lives upon the juice which would otherwise supply nutriment to the ear. Wheat is its favorite food. Its greatest ravages are accomplished in the autumn, when for want of wheat it will sometimes destroy rye and barley. The yellow-bearded wheat, having in the exposed joints a stalk nearly solid, is more secure than any other kind against this enemy; but yields less, is more exposed to the injuries of winter and spring, and, when made into bread, becomes dry much sooner than the bald wheat. Upon ground also which has been manured with ashes, as the wheat grows more gradually and with a firmer stalk, it is less exposed than when sown after a dressing from the stable. When it is sown late in the season, it commonly escapes the ravages of the fly in the autumn; and, unless destroyed by the frosts in February and March, may with a good degree of probability be expected to yield a crop. But, notwithstanding these and all other remedial efforts, the mischief which it accomplishes is prodigious. Twenty years since {c. 1784}, I was informed by a merchant in

West Greenwich, whose business gave him the best opportunities of knowing, that the inhabitants of that parish before the arrival of the fly used to export annually ten thousand bushels of wheat, but were then obliged to import three thousand. Where grass or maize does not furnish the farmer a substitute, the evil is still greater. In Connecticut, the cultivation of wheat has for more than twenty years been in a great measure discontinued {written 1804}.

Nothing can more strongly exhibit the dependence or the littleness of man than the destruction of his valuable interests by such minute, helpless beings; nor can anything more forcibly display the ease with which his Maker punishes his transgressions. . . . The Hessian fly, as I observed, is less than a gnat; and, when settled in its usual manner on the ground, is commonly visible, being seen only as it rises in small clouds immediately before your steps. It is feeble and helpless also in the extreme, defenseless against the least enemy, and crushed by the most delicate touch. Yet for many years it has taxed this country annually more perhaps than a million of dollars. . . .[24]

A great part of this island is still forested. Formerly, four-fifths of the county of Suffolk were considered as barrens, i.e., not literally, but tracts of poor land, left to nature, and regarded as incapable of useful cultivation. A considerable part of these tracts is now devoted to agriculture. Still, a great proportion of the county is a mere wood, so great a proportion that the city of New York, and many other places, are to a considerable extent furnished with fuel from this source. One half at least of these forests, as I judged, is yellow pine; the rest is made up of oak, chestnut, hickory, etc. The trees of every kind are low and small compared with those of New England. I should estimate them at a medium between the common New England forests and the largest on the peninsula of Cape Cod. Until they have grown about thirty feet, they appear thrifty; but afterwards, though increasing considerably in height and somewhat in bulk, are stinted, indicating the want of sufficient nourishment to continue their growth. From Huntington throughout our circuit to Brooklyn, not a single large tree was visible from the road.

Fruit trees abound everywhere on the north side of the island, particularly those which belong to the garden. The houses in great multitudes are encompassed by them, and vast numbers stand in the highways. No land in the United States appears to suit them better. Nowhere do they more generally or in greater abundance yield fruit of an excellent quality, nor are they anywhere less injured by frost or exposed to fewer enemies. The tree yielding the Madeira nut succeeds better here than on the opposite shore of Connecticut. Of these advantages the inhabitants have availed themselves in a commendable manner.

Their agriculture has within a few years been greatly improved. For a considerable period before the fifteen years preceding the date of this journey {in 1804}, the land had become generally impoverished by a careless husbandry, in which the soil was only exhausted, and no attempts were made to renew its strength. The usual consequences of this culture (but too common on the continent as well as here), such as miserable crops, discouragement, and listlessness on the part of the farmer, prevailed everywhere. Within this period the inhabitants, with a laudable spirit of enterprise, have set themselves to collect manure wherever it could be obtained. Not content with what they could make and find on their own farms and shores, they have sent their vessels up the Hudson and loaded them with the residuum of potash manufactories; gleaned the streets of New York; and have imported various kinds of manure from New Haven, New London, and even from Hartford. In addition to all this, they have swept the Sound, and covered their fields with the immense shoals of whitefish with which in the beginning of summer its waters are replenished. No manure is so cheap as this where the fish abound; none is so rich; and few are so lasting. Its effects on vegetation are prodigious. Lands which heretofore have scarcely yielded ten bushels of wheat by the acre are said, when dressed with whitefish, to have yielded forty. The number caught is almost incredible. It is here said, and that by persons of very fair reputation, that one hundred and fifty thousand have been taken at a single draft. Such upon the whole have been their numbers, and such the ease with which they have been obtained, that lands in the neighborhood of productive fisheries are declared to have risen within a few years to three, four, and in some cases to six times their former value.

You will easily believe that the fetor {offensive odor}, of which I complained in a former letter, was at least equally troublesome here. Wherever the fish were gathered in considerable quantities near the road, their effluvia filled the atmosphere, and made our journey sufficiently unpleasant. The farmers, however, by the force of habit and the prospect of gain are reconciled to this odor. Indeed many of them must, I think, be insensible to it, for they feed their swine in the near neighborhood of their houses, and some of them directly before their doors, with the fish called horsefoots, the remains of which yield a smell still less supportable.[25]

Among the serious disadvantages under which the inhabitants of the tract already described labor, the want of water is the greatest. At the time when we passed through it, streams of every size are usually full. Yet we saw, if I remember right, during the first twenty-four miles of our journey but one small brook, which is in Huntington, and the millstream mentioned above in the account of Smithtown. In Setauket, however, we found three small brooks. Between this village and Southold, a distance of more than forty miles, we crossed but one: viz., Wading River, an insignificant rill, from two to perhaps six feet in breadth. The want of millstreams obliges the inhabitants to have recourse to windmills, which are erected in all these settlements except the hamlet through which we passed in Smithtown. The want of brooks to water their cattle forces them in many instances to dig basins in the earth near their houses. During the wet seasons these excavations furnish them with a tolerable supply, but the water is often muddy and bad. In rare cases this want is relieved by ponds; but even these have their inconveniences, particularly during the hot season, when they become corrupted and unhealthy. Their wells also must commonly be dug to a great depth before they will yield a sufficient quantity of water. A traveler accustomed to the wells, brooks, and millstreams of New England is apt to wonder in what manner these people can live comfortably under this embarrassment.

The best lands on both sides of the island are, with some exceptions, the *points;* or, as they are sometimes termed, the *necks.* They have usually a stronger soil and are often enriched by a variety of marine shells, deposited here through a long succession of ages by the Indians, converted with a gradual decay into valuable manure, and thus supplying the nutriment drawn off by vegetation. Not unfrequently also are these lands furnished with springs, which break out on the shore, both above and below the high watermark, and with tide mills erected on the inlets in their neighborhood.

The small breadth of this island and its numerous inlets accommodate the inhabitants, almost everywhere, with a harbor near to their doors, and enable them to convey their produce to market with little expense. In the ocean also, they find, on both sides, a considerable portion of their food, and materials for half of their commerce. Fish of most kinds found in this climate abound in the waters of this island. Within a few years, however, oysters have in several places greatly decayed, particularly at Blue Point in the southwestern part of Brookhaven. The oyster beds at this place were not long since supposed to be inexhaustible, and supplied not only the inhabitants of Long Island, but the inhabitants of New York, the county of Westchester, and the south shore of New England, with immense quantities of this valuable fish. Now they have become lean, watery, and sickly, and have declined still more in their numbers than in their quality. Formerly they were large and well flavored; now they are scarcely eatable; and, what is worse, there is reason to fear they will soon become extinct.

Bass are caught in vast numbers along the shore.

I am, Sir, yours, etc.

LETTER III

Shelter Island—Sag Harbor—The peninsula of Montauk—Indians who inhabit it—Lighthouse—East Hampton—Manners of the inhabitants— Honorable efforts of the people to maintain the government of law and to discountenance vice—Settled from New England—Suffolk County— Gardiners Island—Bridgehampton—Southampton—Canoe Place— Westhampton—The Fireplace

Dear Sir,

The ferry from Southold to Shelter Island is attended with the inconveniences usual in places where there is too little traveling to defray the expense of good accommodations. We found neither wharf, nor ferry stairs, on either side. The shore was a gradual slope. We were, therefore, obliged to ride to the boat, and with much difficulty to force our horses into it by leading them over the gunwale. The boat itself was inconvenient, and was managed by a single man. The breadth of the ferry is three fourths of a mile. To make us amends for these troubles, the weather was perfectly serene and pleasant; and we crossed the strait without any accident.

Shelter Island lies in Peconic Bay, at about an equal distance from Southold and Hogs Neck {North Haven}; and, with that peninsula, renders the bay a secure harbor for vessels not drawing more than four fathom. The passages on both sides are perfectly safe. There is, however, little reason to believe that this bay can ever be much used as an anchoring ground, unless by the ships of an enemy. In the Revolutionary War it was frequently occupied by the British shipping.

The Indian name of this island was *Manhansack-Ahaquashuwornock,* signifying an island sheltered by other islands. Its present name, intentionally a translation of the original one, ought to be *Sheltered Island.* It is about seven miles in length from north to south, about five in breadth, and not far from thirty in circumference. Its area is between eight and nine thousand acres. Its surface is much more undulating than that of the neighboring country. A great number of small hollow grounds are dispersed over it, containing usually a considerable quantity of water, and covered with a thick growth of swamp shrubs. These spots are unsightly and indeed offensive to the eye, but they furnish the farmer with the great convenience of water for his cattle. There is not, I believe, a spring on this island above high watermark. The forest growth, which consists of oak, chestnut, etc., is thinly planted, and chiefly without underwood. The British cut down a great part of the wood during the Revolutionary War, and thus greatly lessened the value of the lands. Three thousand cords were taken from the estate of Thomas Dering, Esq., a man of such excellence of character as would, if anything could, have disarmed the spirit of plunder.[26]

The soil is lighter and thinner than that of the good lands on Long Island. Yet in a field belonging to General Dering, it yielded under a skillful husbandry between thirty-nine and forty bushels of wheat an acre, the year preceding the date of this journey.[27] Exclusive of grass, for the growth of which it is rather too dry, it seems well fitted for all the productions of the climate. To sheep it is peculiarly suited: the sweet feed which it yields being remarkably grateful to that animal; and the snow lying ordinarily so short a time as very little to interrupt the pasturing of cattle. The wool of the Shelter Island flocks is thought inferior to none in this country.

The property of this island is principally in the three families of Dering, Havens, and Nicholl.[28] It was incorporated in 1788; and in 1790, contained 201 inhabitants; in 1800, 260; and in 1810, 270.

To the credit of the inhabitants, especially of the principal proprietors, it ought to be observed that they have customarily made considerable exertions to support schools and to obtain the preaching of the Gospel.

Two of our company left us here, and proceeded immediately over Hogs Neck to Sag Harbor, and thence to East Hampton. We spent a considerable part of the day at the house of General Dering. In the afternoon this gentleman politely accompanied us to the ferry, and assisted us not a little to obtain a comfortable passage. The wind being boisterous, we sent our horses over first, and followed them without accident, although not without disagreeable apprehensions. We then found our way, with some difficulty, over Hogs Neck; and proceeded, unpleasantly enough, through the waters which overflowed the long, narrow, and winding isthmus connecting this peninsula with Southampton. Thence we had a circuitous, solitary, and tedious ride to Sag Harbor, where the hospitality of Mr. D. amply compensated us for the troubles of the journey.

Sag Harbor is a pretty village, lying partly within the township of Southampton, and partly in that of East Hampton. It is situated on a mere mass of sand. The harbor, which is excellent and the only good one for a great distance on the eastern end of the island, allured the inhabitants to this unpleasant ground; not unpleasant from the want of prospect, but because it furnishes unpleasant streets and walks, and is unfriendly to every kind of vegetation. The village contained at this time about 120 houses, the principal part of which are on a winding street terminating at the shore; the rest, on some other streets of less consequence. Many of the houses, outhouses, and fences are new and neat; and an appearance of thrift, elsewhere unknown in this part of the island, is spread over the whole village. Several of the inhabitants have acquired considerable wealth by commerce and fishing, both of which have been regularly increasing since the Revolutionary War. When we were on the spot, there were three, and there are now (1811) six ships employed in the whale fishery on the coast of Brazil, each of which is supposed on an average to return annually with one thousand barrels of oil.[29] The other vessels owned here may amount to fifty. Mechanical business is also done here to a considerable extent. Shipbuilding particularly is carried on with skill, spirit, and success. There is a printing office in this village, the only one on the island, except at Brooklyn. The inhabitants have a small Presbyterian church, old and of design ill repaired, a much larger one being necessary to accommodate their increasing population.[30]

Sag Harbor is now and probably will continue to be the most considerable village in the eastern part of Long Island. The number of inhabitants at the date of our journey was about 850; in 1810, they amounted to 1,168.

We left Sag Harbor, Saturday morning, May 19th, and rode to East Hampton. Our journey lay on a sandy, solitary plain, covered with oaks and yellow pines, through which flowed a small brook or two, the first seen by us in traveling sixty miles. In the neighborhood of East Hampton, we passed by a considerable field blown in the same manner, although in a less degree, as those formerly described on the peninsula of Cape Cod. Here also, I saw, for the first time since I left that peninsula, the beach grass, the extraordinary and the only preventive of that misfortune.

When we arrived, we found that our companions had gone to Montauk Point. After dinner we followed them, in company with the Rev. Mr. {Lyman} B[eecher], the minister of East Hampton, as far as the beach which unites the peninsula of Montauk to Long Island.[31]

On the Way to Montauk

Here my remaining companion left me to visit the point. Mr. B[eecher] and myself, in the meantime, examined the fantastical scenery presented by this spot. The beach has been thrown up by the conspiring force of winds and waves in the same manner as those which are annexed to the peninsula of Cape Cod, but is far less wild and magnificent. This tract was, however, once a plain of firm ground, but occasionally overflowed. Mr. *Benjamin Hodges,* now (1811, {TD}) living on Montauk, at the age of ninety-six years, remembers this fact. It is named Niepeag: *Niep,* water; *eag,* land.[32]

This peninsula is nine miles in length, and generally from two to three in breadth. Its surface is uneven, nowhere in the proper sense forested, but ornamented in several places by groves and scattered trees. The soil is a mixture of loam and gravel, yielding short, sweet grass, and furnishing good beef and mutton. With a few small exceptions, it is owned by the citizens of East Hampton, being a vast common within that township, on which the cattle of the inhabitants are fed promiscuously during the mild season. The number of proprietors is about one hundred and twenty.

A few years since, a large pond of fresh water {Fort Pond}, about five miles from the point, was broken in upon by the ocean; and from that time has been replenished with oysters, of a good size and flavor. These are principally caught by some Indians, the remains of the Montauk tribe, who live near the pond and sell them for corn, cider, and other commodities.

The Montauk Indians are a branch of the Mahicans, as is proved decisively by their language.[33] I have not been able to ascertain their number, but it is very small. Like those mentioned in the account of Stonington, and all others residing among the English, they have lost the proud and warlike spirit of their ancestors, and assumed in its stead a tame, stupid character. The amount of all their aims is to acquire the bare necessaries of life, and to doze away their remaining time in that sluggish inactivity which is the middle stage between intellectual and animal existence. A few of them are employed in fishing; and, when at sea, are said to perform their duty well; but as soon as they have returned and received their wages, they become mere Indians again, expending their hard earnings chiefly for rum, the only enjoyment which they appear to covet.

There are four or five English families on this peninsula. These unfortunately are from two to three miles apart, so that each house is a hermitage. One of them has the care of the {Montauk} lighthouse, a structure eighty feet in height, standing in an elevated situation on the point, distinguished soon after the colonization of this country as a landmark of the first importance. Perhaps no building of this useful kind was ever erected on this side of the Atlantic in a spot where it was more necessary for the preservation of man.[34]

About twelve hundred acres of this peninsula are still in the possession of the Indians. The fee of the land is not theirs, but they hold it partly by lease and partly by permission. It is a remarkable fact that a number of words in their language are the same with the corresponding words in the language of a tribe discovered by Sir Alexander Mackenzie between three and four hundred miles from the Pacific Ocean.[35]

It is also remarkable that none of the stones on the surface of the peninsula, except those which are now within the reach of the waves, show any marks of having been washed by the ocean.

Clinton Academy, c.1900. The East Hampton Historical
Society now has changing exhibits in the restored building.

Between the beach and the town of East Hampton, the land is generally undulating, moderately good, settled, and under culture.

The town of East Hampton is built principally on a single street, running very nearly from northeast to southwest. Its site is a perfect level. It is compactly built, and contains an ancient Presbyterian church, an academy, and about one hundred dwelling houses. The academy is resorted to by a considerable number of students, and with a little more spirit and enterprise on the part of the people might be rendered extensively useful.[36] The houses are generally of long standing. I saw but a single new one, and that was erected where another had been lately pulled down. Scarcely any of them are painted. In other respects they are generally in a tolerable state of repair. The passion for appearance, so far at least as building is concerned, seems, hitherto, to have fastened very little on the inhabitants of East Hampton. A general air of equality, simplicity, and quiet is visible here in a degree perhaps singular. Sequestered in a great measure from the world, they exhibit scarcely a trace of that activity which everywhere meets the eye in New England. There is, however, no want of the social character; but it is regulated rather by the long-continued customs of this single spot, than by the mutable fashions of a great city, or the powerful influence of an extensive country intimately connected in all its parts, and controlling by the general opinion and practice the personal conduct of every inhabitant. Living by themselves more than the people of most other places, they become more attentive to whatever is their own, and less to the concerns of others. Hence their own customs, especially those which have come down from their ancestors (and these are almost all that exist among them), have a commanding influence on their conduct. Removed to a great distance from most of their countrymen, reports may be easily raised and for a long time circulated among them without any contradiction, if a few individuals who may be regarded as the traveling members of their community should happen to unite in the wish to keep them alive. Thus the character of a person even in the most public life, if living at a distance, may by such individuals for an indefinite period be completely inverted. If a villain, he may pass for a man of worth; if a man of worth, for a villain. Thus also any event or any conduct may be misstated and misbelieved, and often without a remedy. I have rarely been struck with so much surprise as at finding the strange and mistaken apprehensions of some discreet and worthy people in this town concerning several individuals of distinction in their own state: men whom I perfectly knew, and with some of whom I had been long and intimately acquainted.

You are not from these things to suppose the inhabitants of East Hampton to be in an uncommon degree either injudicious, or ignorant. They are as respectable for their understanding and in other things as well informed, read as much and converse as well as most of their countrymen. But their insular and remote situation precludes them from the means either of acquiring sound information, or detecting that which is false, concerning persons and facts existing in different parts of their country. Hence, as in the same circumstances all other people would be, they are exposed to misjudge, because their confidence can be, and often is, abused; while the detection of the abuse is beyond their power. In truth, they are better acquainted with many subjects deeply interesting to man than most of their countrymen.

Their moral and religious character also are much above the common level. By this I do not intend that they are free from loose and profligate manners, but that the town contains a larger number of virtuous citizens, that morality and religion hold a higher place in the public estimation, and that transgressions of their dictates are felt by men of any reputation to be more dangerous, than in most other places.

As a proof of the justness of this opinion it may be observed that a society has been voluntarily established here for the express purpose of strengthening magistrates in the prevention and punishment of petty crimes, exposing all licentiousness, and promoting every kind of virtuous conduct. The measures of this society, in which all or nearly all the respectable inhabitants of the town are united, have in an eminent degree been harmonious, useful, and happy. They have not merely formed a constitution, assembled, deliberated, and resolved, according to the spiritless and useless examples of too many such societies, but have executed their resolutions in a manner highly honorable to their character. Vice has been really discouraged, virtue really strengthened; and the execution of law in those inferior cases in which it is but too frequently unexecuted, and which thus lay the foundation of no small part of human degeneracy, really promoted. At the same time, while their measures have been firm and energetic, they have been cautious and prudent. Their prudence has ensured them success, and their success has invigorated their energy. May the blessing of heaven rest upon all who are engaged in this excellent design, and upon every justifiable effort for its accomplishment.

Equally honorable to these people are their industry and frugality, their exemplary behavior at church, their spirit of good neighborhood, their mutual decency and respect, and the interest which they take in the enjoyments and sufferings of each other. I need not say that they have their faults; but I can say truly, I wish that the inhabitants of this country generally had as few.

These observations are extensively applicable, with some qualifications, to the county of Suffolk at large.

I have already observed that this county was originally settled from New England. A considerable number of the colonists came from Lynn, and others probably from some of the other towns in the neighborhood of Boston. These planted themselves near the western end of the island. The Dutch, who had already begun some small plantations in that quarter, quarreled with them, and finally drove them away.[37] They then removed to Southampton and stationed themselves without molestation. Here they were joined by other emigrants from the same colony.

In the year 1640 the colony of New Haven purchased and settled Southold, the Indian *Yennecock.* The same year, the colony of Connecticut purchased a tract containing a great part of the townships of Oyster Bay and North Hempstead, and placed on it a considerable number of settlers. All these settlements were from the beginning claimed by the colonies of Connecticut and New Haven. Southampton sent representatives to the General Assembly of Connecticut twenty years, from 1644 to 1664. In 1663, the plantations in the neighborhood of the Dutch settlements sent a petition to the legislature of Connecticut, praying to be taken under their jurisdiction. The legislature voted that they would "use such just and lawful means as God should put into their hands for the indemnity and safety of these plantations, until His Majesty should make known his royal pleasure on this subject."[38] In the year 1664, the Dutch surrendered New York {New Netherland} to Colonel Nicolls; and Long Island was thenceforth annexed to that province.[39] The inhabitants of Suffolk County, however, have always been and now are in every other respect New England people. Descended from one source, they have to this day sustained one character. From their neighbors in the two western counties they are distinguished by their names, their pronunciation, their manners, their attachment to the education of their children, their intelligence, their morals, and their religion. All these are of New England origin. The very manners, which I distinctly remember to have been forty years since the prevailing manners of such places and people as I visited at that time, and better and happier in many respects than those which have been substituted for them, are now the manners of a great part of this county. The insular situation of the inhabitants, while it has precluded them from many motives to improvement, has also preserved them from many sources of corruption. Their houses and churches are less tidy and beautiful; but their minds are more susceptible of religious impressions, and their lives less stained by vice.

The old New England hospitality which welcomed a guest because he was a stranger, a neighbor, or a friend, and not because it coveted an opportunity of displaying wealth and taste, or acquiring admiration, prevails generally throughout this county. A traveler is received with an air of frankness and goodwill which he cannot distrust, and which endears his entertainment much more than manners, however polished, or accommodations, however convenient. He feels that he has been received not only with civility, but with kindness, and leaves the house of his host with affection.

In passing through this county a traveler is forcibly struck with a sense of stillness and sequestration from the world. Every place seems to him a retirement. Noise and bustle clamor at such a distance that the din is not heard. Profound contemplation and playfulness of mind scarcely meet with an interruption. Everything indicates and cherishes repose, and he will hardly believe that disorder and disturbance of any kind can here intrude upon the peace of man.

A gum tree, of the kind which is here called the Balm of Gilead, or the black poplar, is now growing before the house of Mr. William Huntting, of this town. The stem was a branch wafted upon the south shore by the ocean. There it was found by a member of Mr. Huntting's family, and set out where it now stands.[40]

Gardiners Island, or the Isle of Wight, lies across the mouth of Peconic Bay, between Plum Island and Montauk, and is about seven miles in length, and one in breadth, containing not far from three thousand acres. The soil is excellent and yields very plentifully wheat, maize, and grass, and furnishes excellent beef and mutton, cheese and wool. It was purchased originally by Lion Gardiner, Esq., who commanded the fort at Saybrook several years, and was also granted to him by James Torrett [Farrett], the British nominal proprietor of the whole island.[41] Mr. Gardiner began a settlement here in 1639, the first British settlement within {what is now} the state of New York. From this original proprietor it has descended regularly in his family to the present owner {1804}, John Lion Gardiner, Esq. Until lately, it was an entailed estate: now it is holden in fee simple. Its Indian name was *Munshongonuc* [Monchonock]; and signified *a place where a multitude of Indians had died:* like the character given of Carthage when it is styled *the grave of Europeans.*[42]

It is believed here, and generally along the southern shore of the island, that fruit trees cannot be cultivated with success when they are exposed to the sea winds. That these winds blow here with great strength and are very damp is certain, but that they destroy or prevent the growth of fruit trees, particularly apple trees and pear trees, is questionable. On the land of the Rev. Mr. B[eecher] at East Hampton, I saw a considerable number of young trees which were very flourishing. I saw also several orchards in places entirely open to these winds which were well grown and prosperous, and some of them in full blossom. It may therefore be concluded that this opinion has been hastily taken up. Yet so extensively has it been adopted that there are few orchards and very few fruit trees of any kind in this township or Southampton, and indeed very few for sixty or seventy miles along the shore.

East Hampton is uncommonly healthy, as is evident from the number of old people which it contains. Notwithstanding the frequency, dampness, and strength of the sea winds, the inhabitants appear to be liable in no peculiar degree to any particular disease except the hypochondria. This evil is said to be unusually frequent here, at Bridgehampton, and at Southampton. What is called *land air* can hardly be said to be breathed at all at East Hampton; and the people are healthy from the same cause which produces the health of seamen.

East Hampton contained in 1790, 1,497 inhabitants; in 1800, 1,549; in 1810, 1,484.

On Monday, May 21st, we left our friends in East Hampton, and rode through Bridgehampton and Southampton to Westhampton: twenty-six miles.

Bridgehampton is a parish of Southampton. Its surface is agreeably undulating; the soil better, or better cultivated, than any tract of the same extent on our journey; and the houses are in more instances neat in their appearance. We saw no village in this parish.

There has lately been a considerable revival of religion, both here and in East Hampton.

Southampton is said to have been formerly a flourishing settlement, the whaling business having been vigorously pursued and become a source of wealth to the inhabitants.[43] At present, it wears the aspect of decline. Some of the houses are better than any in East Hampton, but the general appearance is less agreeable and prosperous. The town is not so compactly built, and the inhabitants are said to be less industrious.

The soil of Southampton is more sandy and light than most of that through which we had traveled.

Southampton contained in 1790, 3,408 inhabitants; in 1800, 3,670; and in 1810, 3,899. This increase is probably all found in the village of Sag Harbor.

From Southampton to what is here called *the Canoe Place,* about four miles, the country is a succession of disagreeable sand hills, a considerable part of which are blown, like the grounds formerly mentioned in the description of Cape Cod, and exhibit a desolate and melancholy aspect. These hills were once cultivated, but from the poverty of the soil and the ravages of the wind appear to have been finally forsaken.[44]

From the Canoe Place, where there are two or three indifferent houses, to Westhampton, the country is a mere forest, chiefly of yellow pines. The surface is a plain; the soil, a lean sand; the trees are small and unthrifty; and the road is difficult and tedious. In this part of our journey we met with nothing that was agreeable except the solemn roar of the ocean, the prospect of the great bay already mentioned, the magnificent beach by which it is bounded, and the immeasurable waters lying beyond it. These objects occurring in several instances through vistas opened in the forest were highly sublime, and amid our otherwise unvaried scenery peculiarly delightful.

Westhampton is a parish of Southampton, and a scattered settlement. It is here commonly designed by the dismal Indian name *Ketchaboneck*, properly the name of a point of land within its limits. To complete the list of unfortunate titles of this abused place, two hamlets belonging to it are termed *Quogue,* or *Speonk.* Yet here, on a point of land south of the road, we found good accommodations, obligingly furnished at an inn kept by a Mr. Howell.

The next morning, the 22nd, we left Westhampton, and rode to Douglas' in Islip, through the remaining part of Southampton, a part of Brookhaven, and a part of Islip: thirty-six miles. We dined at Carman's in what is called *the Fireplace* {now the hamlet of South Haven}, in {the Town of} Brookhaven, and fared comfortably; but were obliged to lodge at a miserable house, half in ruins, kept by very poor and very ignorant people: the inn at which we intended to lodge having been preoccupied by some sportsmen from New York, who had come hither to catch trout.

The country from Howell's to the Fireplace is a continuation of the same plain, almost wholly forested, less sandy, less covered with pines, and more productive of oaks. The road also, being on a firmer surface, was generally better; but in some instances was still sandy and tedious. The settlements, though few, were more numerous; and, together with several fields of wheat growing vigorously on the borders of our road, varied the generally dull scenery of this region. The preceding day we had crossed a few rivulets; this day we found a greater number, and among them several fine, sprightly millstreams. One of these, which runs by Carman's, is named Connecticut {now Carmans} River, the largest after Peconic in the island, and replenished with fine trout. From this spot the road became still firmer; the forests, more and more composed of oaks; the wheat fields, more numerous and flourishing; the settlements, though thinly scattered, more frequent; and the country, universally more pleasant. While we were at Douglas', a thunderstorm passed over us, and the rain distilled plentifully through the roof and sides of our shelter. Part of our company were disagreeably sprinkled while in bed, but experienced no distressing consequences from the wetting. Our horses, which passed the night without any other hay than sedge, had more reason to complain than ourselves.

I am, Sir, yours, etc.

LETTER IV

Islip—Hempstead plain—Grouse plain—Huntington—Oyster Bay—
Hempstead—North Hempstead—Flushing—Mr. Prince's fruit
yard—Jamaica—Ride from Jamaica to Brooklyn—Bushwick

Dear Sir,

Wednesday morning, May 23rd, we pursued our journey through the remainder of Islip, through Huntington, Oyster Bay, Hempstead, and a part of Jamaica: thirty-eight miles.

The country on this day's journey, until we came to the border of Hempstead plain, generally resembled that which was last described, but in all the particulars mentioned in that description became more and more pleasant. Of Islip I know nothing beyond what I have already said, except that the township includes three or four islands of no importance, and contained in 1790, 609 inhabitants; in 1800, 958; and in 1810, 885.

Near the western border of the township of Huntington, we passed through a hamlet consisting of about a dozen neat houses, all of them new and built in a modern style.[45] This was the first settlement of any importance which we saw after leaving Southampton, a distance of about sixty miles, and the first indication of the neighborhood and commercial influence of New York. Soon after we left this village, we turned to the northwest, over a country of an indifferent appearance, containing a few miserable settlements, but principally covered with a forest of pines and an underwood of shrub oaks. Four of five miles from the commencement of this forest, we entered upon what is called *the Grouse,* or *Bushy plain,* the southeastern border of Hempstead plain, extending about three or four miles in breadth. From this ground we entered Hempstead plain, and dined at a place called the Isle of Pines, situated near its center.[46]

Hempstead plain is a continuation of the vast level which extends from the Canoe Place to Jamaica, about eighty miles, and occupies throughout this distance the southern half of the island. It is not interrupted by a single hill. About twenty miles from the eastern limit it is covered with yellow pines, then with a mixture of pines and oaks, then with oaks only, until within a few miles of Hempstead plain the pines make their appearance again. The eastern division of this level is unfit for agriculture and useful only as the basis of a forest. Thence to the western boundary of Huntington the soil becomes gradually better, and thence to the border of Hempstead plain it is almost absolutely barren. From the southern border of this level a number of points {necks or peninsulas} shoot out into the great bay, which are generally covered with a good soil, and owned by men of property and consideration. Several of them have long been entailed estates.

That part of this extensive level which is called Hempstead plain is distinguished from the rest only by the appearance of the soil, which is a dark, rich-looking mold, or a brown loam spread over a coarse gravel; and by its vegetation, which from the earliest knowledge of European settlers has, with the exception of the little spot called *the Isle of Pines,* been nothing but a long, coarse, wild grass. Many attempts, as I am informed, have been made to cultivate this ground, but without success. It is now what it ever has been, a mere and very indifferent pasture.

The Grouse plain is distinguished from it by nothing except its covering, which, instead of grass, is formed of shrub oaks: the most shriveled and puny that I ever met with, scarcely exceeding in size a large whortleberry bush. On this ground there is always a multitude of grouse, the heath cock and hen of New England; and hither a great number of sportsmen annually repair from Long Island, New York, and the county of Westchester to hunt this bird, hardly any amusement being more coveted in this quarter.

The forested parts of this great level abound with deer. A large number of these are every year killed by hunters, and are carried chiefly to New York, where they never fail to command a good price.

Hempstead plain is, I presume, the easternmost of those *"American prairies,* which are too fertile to produce forest trees;" unless it should be thought that the little cluster of pines amid which we dined vitiates its title to this extraordinary character. To my eye, both now and in two excursions which I made to it formerly, the appearance of its border strongly resembled that of a lake. Its length is about sixteen miles from east to west; its greatest breadth eight, and its least five. Like Montauk, it is almost entirely a common, and supplies indifferent pasturage and a sufficiency of water throughout the mild season for a great number of cattle. The Isle of Pines, at a distance, resembles not a little a real island.[47]

Between the western limit of Huntington and Hempstead, we passed through the southern part of the township of Oyster Bay. Heretofore, I had repeatedly passed through the northern. This tract is undulating and fertile. It is also better supplied with springs and brooks, and wears more proofs of prosperous industry than many other parts of the island. In two of these excursions also, I passed through North Hempstead; and in one of them, through Flushing into Newtown. These townships have a good soil, and a surface in many places not unpleasant. In several places they exhibit, particularly the two last, a cultivation which within a few years has been greatly improved. In Flushing, Mr. Joseph Prince, and afterwards his son, Mr. William Prince, have for many years collected, raised, and sold the greatest number and variety of valuable fruit trees ever seen in a single spot on this continent. These they have extensively spread through the United States, and have even sent them to several parts of Europe. They may, therefore, be fairly reckoned in the list of benefactors to their country.[48]

In these townships the effects of their vicinity to New York are abundantly conspicuous, in the wealth of the farmers, and in the beauty of the villas with which they are handsomely ornamented.

Oyster Bay contained in 1790, 4,097; in 1800, 4,548; in 1810, 4,725 inhabitants. North Hempstead contained in 1790, 2,696; in 1800, 2,413; in 1810, 2,700 inhabitants. Flushing contained in 1790, 1,607; in 1800, 1,818; in 1810, 2,230 inhabitants. Newtown contained in 1790, 2,111; in 1800, 2,312; in 1810, 2,437 inhabitants.

Hempstead is a small and rather pretty village, containing several neat houses, an Episcopal and a Presbyterian church, both decent, and a courthouse: this being the shire town of Queens County. The ministers of both churches preach in them a part of the time only, having other congregations under their care.

Hempstead lies on the southwestern skirt of the plain, and on some gently rising grounds by which it is bordered in this quarter. In the year 1790, the township, which is extensive, contained 3,828 inhabitants; in 1800, 2,413 [4,141][49]; in 1810, 5,804.

From the village of Hempstead to Jamaica the appearance of the country continually improved. The surface was still plain, but the soil was sensibly better; the forest trees, now appearing singly or in groves, were larger and more thrifty; the cultivation was more skillful; and the produce was more vigorous. The influence of New York was continually more and more evident until we arrived at Jamaica.

Jamaica is the largest and handsomest village in this county, containing about a hundred houses,

Saint George's (Episcopal) Church, Hempstead, 1735-1821

Presbyterian Church, Jamaica, 1699-1813

three churches: a Dutch, a Presbyterian, and an Episcopal; and an academy, of long standing {Union Hall}, but supported with less spirit and uniformity than could be wished. The houses are built principally on a single street, running from east to west, and are generally good. The churches are not distinguished for their beauty. This town, from its neighborhood to New York and from having long been a customary resort for the inhabitants of that city, has acquired a polish not visible in the towns further eastward. Its buildings and fences are neater; and the manners of its inhabitants have more of what may be called a city air: in persons of refinement and virtue, extremely agreeable; but in such as are vulgar and vicious, pert, impudent, gross, and profane. The latter manners are unhappily the most common and the most prominent in all such places, are the most visible to every traveler; and enter, perhaps, more than they ought into the estimate which he forms of their character. In such a place I have often felt that if life were not now and then refreshed by the refined sentiments and conduct of the small number, the coarse and protuberant vices of the clumsy and insolent multitude would render it intolerable. But, happily the gentleman, now and then found, reanimates the spirits under the stupor into which they sink within the contagion of the market man.

In the year 1790, Jamaica contained 1,675 inhabitants; in 1800, 1,661; and in 1810, 2,110. Jamaica and Hempstead, with a strip of Oyster Bay, occupy the whole of Queens County on the southern shore.

Thursday morning, May 24th, we rode to New York to breakfast, through the remainder of Jamaica, a small corner of Bushwick, and the township of Brooklyn. The country between Jamaica and Brooklyn, being generally owned by persons who have grown rich with the aid of New York, and being manured from the streets and stables of that city, is under high cultivation. The soil also is naturally good, a stiff loam approximating to clay, and differing materially from any which we had seen on this island. I remember no spot of the same extent where the produce of so many kinds appeared so well. The wheat, winter barley, flax, and oats were remarkably fine; and, wherever the country was cultivated, as almost all of it was, its face resembled a rich garden. The surface here is generally undulating, and in some places rough: the ridges and points of the hills being formed of ragged rocks. This discord was, however, particularly agreeable to me, as I had been wearied with the monotony of the scenery which we had left behind us. The buildings on this part of the road are generally good, and are surrounded by neat appendages. Upon the whole, I thought this part of our journey peculiarly agreeable.

About two miles west of Jamaica, as I estimated the distance, we quitted the smooth, circular stones which before we had found everywhere except on Montauk, and came suddenly upon such as were universally rough and angular. These continued to the ferry.

In the course of this journey I was struck with the diversity of the progress of vegetation in the different places which we visited. We left New Haven on the 9th of May, and arrived at Huntington on the 15th. Here we found the vegetation at the same stage at which we had left it at New Haven. After we left Brookhaven, it became gradually more and more backward until we arrived at Southold. On the 19th, we reached East Hampton. Here, notwithstanding the lapse of time, we found it several days behind that of New Haven when we left it, and at least a fortnight later in the whole. We passed through the southern parts of Huntington and Oyster Bay on the 23rd. At that time the vegetation in these places had scarcely overtaken that which we had left at New Haven. On the 24th, we rode from Jamaica to New York. Here the vegetation was advanced at least a week beyond that at New Haven, being more forward than we found it there on the 29th. The season at Jamaica, Bushwick, and Brooklyn was, therefore, three weeks earlier than in the south parts of Huntington and Oyster Bay. This difference can in no way be owing to the difference either of soil or climate, for both are in favor of these parts of Huntington and Oyster Bay: the soil being sandy and warm; the situation, several miles further south; and the distance of the two extremes, not more than forty. . . .[50]

Of Bushwick, as we passed through a corner of it only, I know nothing except that it is said to be pleasant and fertile; that it was settled by Dutch colonists, and is inhabited by their descendants; that it is possessed of the common prosperity of this neighborhood; and that in 1790, it contained 540 inhabitants; in 1800, 656; and in 1810, 798.

I am, Sir, yours, etc.

LETTER V

*Brooklyn—Prospect from the heights — The East River—Kings County
settled by the Dutch—Character of the inhabitants—Quakers—Return*

Dear Sir,

Brooklyn is the shire town of Kings County, directly opposite to New York. It is the largest and handsomest town on Long Island, and the most pleasantly situated. It is built on the summit and the sides of a pretty elevation, and commands a noble prospect of the East River, the city and county of New York, the Hudson, the shore of New Jersey beyond it, New York Bay and its islands, a considerable tract on Long Island, Staten Island, and the high hills of Navesink in the county of Monmouth {New Jersey}. The field of view is extensive, various, and rich, and includes a great multitude of the beauties both of nature and art. The city of New York is an object which in this country is singularly splendid; the groves are numerous and fine; the plantations are remarkably gay and fertile; and the villas rise in perpetual succession on the shores and eminences, embellishing the landscape and exhibiting decisive proofs of opulence in their proprietors. The waters here presented to the eye are charmingly diversified and nobly limited. An immense number of vessels, assembled at the numerous wharves, anchored in the streams, or moving in a thousand directions over their surface and over the great bay in which they terminate, present to the eye one of the liveliest images of vigorous activity which can be found in the world. For a view of all this fine scenery this elevation is probably the best position.

Brooklyn itself is a beautiful object, and from the opposite shore is seen with the greatest advantage. Several of the streets are straight and spacious.

View of Brooklyn, 1798

The houses are generally good; many of them are new, many handsome, very many painted white, and therefore cheerful and brilliant. The town contains three churches: a Dutch, an Episcopal, and a Methodist. The inhabitants are extensively descendants from the original Dutch settlers; the rest are a casual collection from all quarters. Their number in 1790 was 1,603; in 1800, 2,378; and in 1810, 4,402.

Brooklyn will long be remembered from the battle fought in its neighborhood by the British and Hessians. . . .[51]

The East River (as it is called) is a continuation of the Sound, and has probably derived its present name from its resemblance to a river in appearance. It is not far from a mile in breadth; and, being the principal harbor of New York, is always filled with shipping. The tide moves here with very great rapidity, and renders the ferry disagreeable, except at high and low water. We arrived just before high water and found the passage tolerably pleasant.

I have already observed that Kings County was principally settled by the Dutch. This is partially true of Queens County also. The general character of the Dutch settlers in the states of New York and New Jersey, I propose to give elsewhere. I know of nothing by which their descendants on Long Island are distinguished from their brethren.

The other inhabitants of these two counties are a mixed people, derived from many sources, and exhibiting a great variety of character. In religion they are Episcopalians, Presbyterians, Quakers, Baptists, Methodists, and nihilists {those who reject religious beliefs}. They are generally industrious, frugal, and thrifty. Their advantages for marketing are not exceeded. You will not wonder, therefore, that they are wealthy. The breeding of horses has for a long time been here a favorite business; and horse racing (of which Hempstead plain is the great theater), a favorite amusement. Wherever this kind of sport prevails, no man acquainted at all with human affairs will expect any great prevalence of morals or religion. There are few spots of the same extent, settled at so early a period, where these great concerns of man are less regarded. Young men, even of wealthy families, are usually taught scarcely anything more than to read, write, and keep accounts. The state of society is, therefore, humble, and involves very little of knowledge or sentiment. Intelligence is in truth disregarded by the body of the inhabitants, except as it aids them to the acquisition of property. The young men of ambition and enterprise, when they set out in life, generally quit their native soil and seek a residence in a superior state of society, or at least where they find more extensive means of business.

Brooklyn, 1820 (engraving of Francis Guy's Snow Scene).

In various parts of these two counties the Sabbath is considered by many of the inhabitants as scarcely sustaining a sacred character. It is devoted extensively to visiting, to amusement, and, during the seasons of mowing and harvest, not unfrequently to labor. In some places there are, for long periods, no ministers; in others the people are the prey of ignorant teachers, recommended by nothing but ardor and vociferation.

The clergymen who are actually settled in the ministry in these counties are, so far as I am informed, of the same respectable character possessed by those in other parts of this country; but the people are so generally split up into sects that their congregations are in most instances small.

The Quakers, the number of whom is considerable, differ little from their brethren elsewhere, except that they are more uninformed and more listless than in several other places.

The insular situation of these three counties has a very perceptible influence upon the inhabitants as a body. Their own internal concerns must always exist upon a small scale. Their views, affections, and pursuits must of course be always limited. Few objects can be presented to them, and few events can occur, of sufficient magnitude to expand thought, or of sufficient importance to awaken energy. Almost all their concerns are absolutely confined to the house, or to the neighborhood; and the neighborhood rarely extends beyond the confines of a small hamlet. Habitually bounded by these confines, the mind is neither very much inclined, nor very able, to look beyond them. Its views in most cases will, after a little time, be of choice occupied within these small circles; its affections will all center here; and its pursuits will break through only to reach the market. The tenor of life, therefore, will be uniform: undisturbed on the one hand, and tame on the other. What the mind might have been cannot be known, because it has never been stimulated to any attempts for the expansion of its views or the exertion of its powers. What it is may from one instance be easily conjectured in a thousand.

The inhabitants of this island are destitute of other advantages which contribute not a little to diffuse information and awaken energy. There is very little traveling here, besides their own. The attention excited, the curiosity awakened, and the animation produced by the frequent arrival of strangers are here in a great measure unknown. At the same time, comparatively few persons of talents and information reside here. There is nothing sufficiently inviting in the circumstances of the island itself to allure persons of this character hither from the continent; and the allurements of the continent are such as commonly to entice men of this description who are natives of the island to remove from it for the sake of obtaining them. A considerable number of such men both here are accordingly found in New York and elsewhere. The advantages derived from the conversation and example of persons distinguished for superiority of character are therefore enjoyed in a very imperfect degree, and that luminous spirit and those improvements in the state of society which they everywhere shed upon the circle around them are very imperfectly realized. Such, it would seem, must through an indefinite period be the situation of Long Island.

We continued in New York until Monday, the 28th, and then commenced our journey to New Haven, where we arrived the following day.

I am, Sir, yours, etc.

Notes

Source: Reprinted by permission of the publisher from *Travels in New England and New York* by Timothy Dwight, edited by Barbara Miller Solomon, Cambridge, MA: Harvard University Press, Copyright © 1969 by the President and Fellows of Harvard College. The "Journey to Long Island" is on 3:198-235 and Solomon's notes on 3:399-402 (a few of her identifications of individuals from earlier in the volumes have also been included in the notes below as well as the full citations of books). *Travels* was prepared by Dwight's sons from their father's notebooks and published in four volumes in 1821-1822. The "Journey to Long Island" is on 3:269-320 in the first edition. The Yale University Library has original manuscript notebooks in the Dwight Family Papers, but some have not survived, including those for the Long Island visit.

Solomon modernized spelling and punctuation and spelled out abbreviations, but retained italics as in the original edition. She identified individuals whom Dwight referred to only by an initial and added many references in her notes. Notes by Dwight are identified {TD}; those by his publisher in the first edition are identified as {Pub.}. (The title page lists

Timothy Dwight as publisher; presumably this was Dwight's son.) Solomon's notes are identified {BMS}, and her insertions in the text are in square brackets, [thus]. The editor's insertions in the text in this edition are in braces (or wavy brackets) {thus}, and her notes identified as (NAN). Omissions are marked by ellipses (three dots) and the content of the omitted sections is mentioned in the notes. Dwight's paragraphing has been retained as well as the topics listed in italics at the beginning of each letter. (If one of those topics is omitted from the text here, it has been deleted in the italicized summary.) Notes have been renumbered, but Solomon's number is included in the page citation (she numbered notes separately for each letter); notes by Dwight or the publisher were not numbered in either of the published editions.

1. The biographical information on Dwight is from Barbara Miller Solomon's "Introduction" in *Travels in New England and New York,* by Timothy Dwight, edited by Barbara Miller Solomon, 4 vols. (Cambridge: Belknap Press of Harvard University Press, 1969); the quotation is from 1:xix. Dwight's major literary work was an epic poem, *Conquest of Canaan,* most of which was written in the early 1770s, but not published until 1785. Dwight's wife, Mary Woolsey, was the daughter of Benjamin Woolsey (1717-1771), by his first wife, Esther Isaac. Mary Woolsey was raised by her stepmother, Benjamin's second wife, Ann Muirson, who was from Setauket. Woolsey's estate, Dosoris, was located in present-day Glen Cove. See Benjamin F. Thompson, *History of Long Island,* written 1849, 3d. ed., enlarged, 3 vols, 1918 (Reprint; Port Washington: I.J. Friedman, 1962), 3:543, 545; On Dwight, see also Kenneth Silverman, *Timothy Dwight* (New York: Twayne, 1969); and John R. Fitzmier, *New England's Moral Legislator: Timothy Dwight, 1752-1817* (Bloomington: Indiana University Press, 1999), (NAN).

2. Solomon, "Introduction," 1:xx. Connecticut did not end the preferred status of the Congregational Church until 1818. Dwight's *Theology: Explained and Defended in a Series of Sermons* was published posthumously in 1819. Those interested in the complexities of theological differences in New England can begin with Solomon's references in the notes to her Introduction (NAN).

3. Dwight, *Travels,* 1:1, 9 (NAN).

4. Solomon, "Introduction," 1:x. George DeWan concurs that Dwight's account is "unmatched"; see "A Critic Gives LI One Thumb Up," in *Long Island: Our Story,* by Newsday (Melville, NY: Newsday, 1998), pp. 161-62 (NAN).

5. Professor D and Mr. S may refer to Jeremiah Day and Moses Stuart. Jeremy Day (1773-1867), Yale 1795, twice succeeded his mentor, Dwight: first as head of Greenfield Academy, and second, as president of Yale. Though trained for the ministry, Day never held a pulpit. He was the author of mathematical text books and theological treatises. Moses Stuart (1780-1852), Yale 1799, after studying law was elected tutor at Yale 1802-1804, where he began the study of theology with President Dwight. After a short ministry at the First Church in New Haven, 1806-1810, Stuart undertook his life's work as professor of sacred literature at the Theological Seminary at Andover, Massachusetts (1810-1848). Mr. D. is doubtless one of Dwight's sons, perhaps Sereno Edwards Dwight, Yale 1803 {BMS}, 1:386 n. 5; 2:400 n. 4; 3:399 n. 1.

6. One fact concerning this boat well deserves to be recorded. The ferryman informed me that it was built and had been employed for some time, I have forgotten how long, in crossing this ferry antecedently to the Revolutionary War. It was now therefore more than thirty years old. This is a strong proof that the oak of New England and New York when

managed with skill furnishes a lasting material for shipbuilding. Very little had been done to keep this vessel in repair {TD}, 3:199.

7. Helicon refers to a range of mountains in Boeotia in ancient Greece. A temple and a grove sacred to the Muses stood nearby the famous fountains, one supposedly flowing from a place where the horse Pegasus struck his foot {BMS}, 3:399 n. 1.

8. Huntington included the town of Babylon until 1872; since then Huntington no longer extends the "whole breadth of the island" (NAN).

9. Capt. Benjamin Keeler, commanding the brig *Sally* of Stamford, Connecticut, on its return from the West Indies, ran into a snowstorm and struck a reef off Eaton's Neck, sometime between Christmas 1790 and New Year's Day 1791, not on January 16, according to Jeannette E. Rattray, *Ship Ashore! {A Record of Maritime Disasters Off Montauk and Eastern Long Island, 1640-1955}*, New York: {Coward-McCann}, 1955), p. 34 {BMS}, 3:399 n. 2.

Local historians of Eatons Neck also date the wreck of the *Sally* in December 1790. There have been many shipwrecks in this area of Long Island Sound because of hazardous reefs. The Eatons Neck Lighthouse was built on a cliff in 1799 and is Long Island's second oldest lighthouse (Montauk, completed in 1797, is the oldest). Eatons Neck Lighthouse is located in today's village of Asharoken (north of Northport). It has been on the National Register of Historic Places since 1973. See Harlan Hamilton, *Lights & Legends: A Historical Guide to Lighthouses of Long Island Sound* (Stamford, CT: Wescott Cove Publishing Company, 1987), p. 65 (NAN).

10. Henry Lloyd (1685-1763) was the first of the family to live on Lloyd Neck, taking up residence in 1711. For the history of Lloyd Neck and its ownership, see Peter Ross, *A History of Long Island* (New York and Chicago: {Lewis Publishing}, 1903), 1:89-90 {BMS}, 3:399 n. 3. Vols. 2 and 3 of this work were written by William Pelletreau and hence the work is sometimes cited as by Ross and Pelletreau. Lloyd Neck was part of the Town of Oyster Bay until 1886 when it was annexed by the Town of Huntington (NAN).

For additional information on the Lloyds and Lloyd Neck, see: *Papers of the Lloyd Family of Lloyd's Neck, New York,* edited by Dorothy C. Barck, 2 vols., *Collections of the New-York Historical Society, 1926 and 1927* (New York: New-York Historical Society, 1926-1927); Jean B. Osann, *Henry Lloyd's Salt Box Manor House,* rev. ed. (Huntington: Lloyd Harbor Historical Society, 1982); Kenneth Scott and Susan E. Klaffky, *A History of the Joseph Lloyd Manor House* (Setauket: Society for the Preservation of Long Island Antiquities, 1976); and George P. Hunt and the Lloyd Harbor Village Book Committee, *Tales of Old Lloyd Harbor: Historical Accounts of a Long Island Village in Archive, Legend and Personal Recollection* (Lloyd Harbor: Village of Lloyd Harbor, 2001). The Henry Lloyd (1711) and Joseph Lloyd (1766) Manor Houses are preserved as historic house museums; (631) 692-4664 (NAN).

11. The reference is to William Livingston's *Philosophic Solitude . . .* (New York, 1747). Queens Village is specifically mentioned in a prefatory poem by William P. Smith, p. x {BMS}, 3:399 n. 4.

12. The Presbyterian church was built in 1784 to replace an earlier church occupied and then torn down by British troops during the Revolutionary War. Huntington's "Old First Church" is in classic Georgian style and has been on the National Register of Historic Places since 1985 (NAN).

13. Thomas Gray, "Elegy Written in a Country Churchyard," lines 55-56: "Full many a flower is born to blush unseen, And waste its sweetness on the desert air" {BMS}, 3:399 n. 5.

The young lady who charmed Dwight was Phoebe McCoon (1786-1868). See Kathryn Curran, "'To Blush Unseen': A View of Nineteenth-Century Women," in *Long Island Women: Activists and Innovators,* edited by Natalie A. Naylor and Maureen O. Murphy (Interlaken, NY: Empire State Books, 1998), pp. 96-97 (NAN).

14. The Smithtown records seem to indicate that there was only one original Smith proprietor, Richard Smith {or Smyth}, (d. 1692). Six of his sons survived him. See William S. Pelletreau, *Records of the Town of Smithtown, Long Island, New York* (Smithtown, 1898), pp. vii-xiii, and passim {BMS}, 3:399 n. 6.

For a recent history of Smithtown, see Noel Gish, *Smithtown, New York, 1660-1929: Looking Back Through the Lens* (Virginia Beach: Donning Company and Smithtown Historical Society, 1996), (NAN).

15. There are now two handsome churches here {Pub.} 3:200 n.

The Episcopal Caroline Church was built in 1729, and is the oldest Episcopal church building on Long Island. After the Revolutionary War, many of its members who were Loyalists fled Long Island. The pulpit was empty until 1811, which probably accounts for the "ruinous condition" Dwight observed. The church interior was restored to its colonial appearance in 1937 and it has been on the National Register of Historic Places since 1991. The publisher's note refers to the present Presbyterian Church which was built in 1812, after the 1714 church Dwight saw had been destroyed by lightning. See Howard Klein, *Three Village Guidebook: The Setaukets, Poquott, Old Field & Stony Brook* (East Setauket: Three Village Historical Society, 1986), pp. 30-34; and *AIA Architectural Guide to Nassau and Suffolk Counties, Long Island,* edited by Robert B. MacKay, Stanley Lindvall, and Carol Traynor (New York: Dover, 1992), pp. 158-59, 162-63 (NAN).

16. Selah Strong (1737-1815) entered politics as a delegate to the provincial congress in 1775. After service as a captain in the Revolution, he became first judge of the county court of common pleas, 1783-1793, and state senator, 1792-1796 {BMS}, 3:399 n. 7.

17. Queens County included most of present-day Nassau County until 1899. After the three western towns of Queens and the Rockaway Peninsula joined New York City in 1898, Nassau County was created from the three eastern towns of Hempstead, North Hempstead, and Oyster Bay (NAN).

18. The 2,500 acre Dwarf Pine Barrens south of Riverhead in Westhampton include dwarf and scrub oaks and dwarf pitch pines. This is "one of the rarest plant communities on Earth, with only two other examples known, one in the New Jersey pine barrens and the other in New York's Shawangunk Mountains." Robert Villani, *Long Island: A Natural History* (New York: Harry N. Abrams, 1997), p. 116; see also pp. 100, 102, 116-21, 178 (NAN).

19. Orient had considerable turnover in ministers. The "ecclesiastical contentions" and sects that Dwight mentions may have stemmed from the controversial ministry of James Davenport in Southold two generations earlier. See Robert E. Cray, Jr., "More Light on a New Light: James Davenport's Religious Legacy, Eastern Long Island, 1740-1840," *New York History* 73 (January 1992): 5-27 (NAN).

20. Francis B. Winthrop (1787-1841, Yale 1804), a New York merchant, was married twice to relatives of Dwight's wife: Julia Ann Rogers, daughter of Moses Rogers of New York, in 1808; and her cousin Elizabeth Woolsey in 1816. In 1823 Winthrop moved to New Haven {BMS}, 3:339 n. 8.

21. Little Gull Island Lighthouse was completed in 1805. It was rebuilt in 1868 and automated in 1978. See Hamilton, *Lights & Legends,* pp. 193-97 (NAN).

22. Wyandanse, or Wyandanch (d. 1659), sachem of the Montauks who, on the death of his brother Poggatacut or Poygratasuck in 1652, became grand sachem of Long Island, was a loyal friend of the whites and an ally of Lion Gardiner; he helped prevent Narraganset raids during the Pequot War. (See Benjamin Trumbull, *A Complete History of Connecticut* [New Haven, 1797], p. 147.) Most of the land acquired on Long Island during this period, including Plum Island in 1659, was received, by deed, from him. Joseph Beebee of Plymouth, Massachusetts, bought the western half of Plum Island from Joseph Dudley, who had acquired it from Samuel Wyllys in 1686. His son, Samuel Beebee, possessed it in 1722 and was one of the island's first inhabitants. The family continued to hold property on Plum Island until 1835, when Noah G. Beebee sold the last 125 acres. See William Pelletreau, *A History of Long Island* {2 vols.} (New York and Chicago: {Lewis Publishing}, 1903), 2:438-39 {BMS}, 3:399-400 n. 9. See also note no. 10 above regarding this book (NAN).

Wyllys' purchase of Plum Island from the Corchaug Indians was confirmed in 1659 and also included a coat (Thompson, *History of Long Island,* 3:245-46). On Wyandanch, see John A. Strong, *The Algonquian Peoples of Long Island From Earliest Times to 1700* (Interlaken, NY: Empire State Books, 1997), pp. 213-15, 218-33; and John A. Strong, "Wyandanch, Sachem of the Montauketts: An Alliance Sachem on the Middle Ground," in *Awakening the Past: The East Hampton 350th Anniversary Lecture Series, 1998,* edited by Tom Twomey (New York: Newmarket Press, 1999), pp. 13-39. Plum Island has been owned by the federal government since 1897 and was the site of Fort Terry. Since 1954, it has been home to an Animal Disease Laboratory under the Department of Agriculture (NAN).

23. Dwight's three pages of comments on the scientific evidence of the formation of Long Island (3:206-9) are omitted here (NAN).

24. Dwight's remarks on other destructive insects (3:211-12) are omitted here (NAN).

25. Processing menhaden, mossbunkers, and other fish for fertilizer and oil was a profitable, but very odoriferous enterprise on eastern Long Island in the nineteenth century. See also references in selections below by Nathaniel S. Prime, "Long Island in 1845," and Walt Whitman, "Paumanok in Poetry and Prose" at note no. 7 (NAN).

26. Thomas Dering (1720-1785), a Boston merchant and father of Gen. Sylvester Dering, came to Shelter Island in 1760, to the estate he had acquired by his marriage to Margaret Sylvester, who had inherited the property of Nathaniel Sylvester, a settler of Shelter Island in 1652. See {Ross and} Pelletreau, *Long Island,* 2:456 {BMS}, 3:400 n. 1.

27. Sylvester Dering (d. 1820), a brigadier general of the New York state militia, was elected a member of the Assembly in 1804 {BMS}, 3:400 n. 2.

28. Nathaniel Sylvester sold a tract of a thousand acres on Shelter Island to George Havens (d. 1706) in 1700. The tract was divided among Havens' sons. A daughter of the Havens family married Gen. Sylvester Dering. The Nicoll {or Nicolls} family was descended from Mathias Nicolls who came to the colonies with Col. Richard Nicolls' expedition to subdue New Netherland. Mathias Nicolls purchased large tracts of land on Little Neck and Great Neck, Long Island. In 1695 Mathias' son William (d. 1723) purchased part of the estate of Giles Sylvester on Shelter Island; William Nicoll obtained more Shelter Island lands under the terms of Sylvester's will. William's son William (d. 1768), a member of the New York Assembly from 1739 to 1768, passed the Shelter Island estate on in the Nicoll family to his nephew William, who also succeeded his uncle in the Assembly. Samuel Benjamin Nicoll (1764-1828) was probably the proprietor of the estate at the time Dwight visited Shelter Island. See {Ross and} Pelletreau, *Long Island,* 2:443-62 {BMS}, 3:400 n. 3.

For additional accounts of Shelter Island history, see Clarence Ashton Wood, "Suffolk's Northeastern Towns," in *Long Island: A History of Two Great Counties, Nassau and Suffolk,* edited by Paul Bailey (New York: Lewis Historical Publishing, 1949), pp. 167-83; Ralph G. Duvall, *The History of Shelter Island, 1652-1932,* 2d ed. with a Supplement 1932-1952 by Jean L. Schladermundt (Shelter Island Heights: Privately printed, 1952); and Louise Tuthill Green, *Shelter Island: A Nostalgic Journey* (Dover, NH: Arcadia Publishing, 1997), (NAN).

29. Sag Harbor became a major whaling port in the decades after Dwight visited. See Dorothy Ingersoll Zaykowski, *Sag Harbor: The Story of an American Beauty* (Sag Harbor: Sag Harbor Historical Society, 1991), pp. 81-108 (NAN).

30. A large and handsome church has since been erected {Pub.} 3:216 n.

Dwight referred to the first church in Sag Harbor which was built in 1768; the publisher's footnote refers to an 1818 building which was replaced by the present "Old Whalers Church." Designed by Minard Lafever in Egyptian Revival style, it was completed in 1844, but lost its 200-foot steeple in the 1938 hurricane. See Thompson, *History of Long Island,* 2:181; and MacKay, Lindvall, and Traynor, *AIA Architectural Guide,* p. 155 (NAN).

31. Lyman Beecher (1775-1863), Yale 1797, trained for the ministry by Dwight, carried on his work in many spheres. Beecher, like Dwight, was convinced of the necessity of saving the West, and after serving parishes in East Hampton, Long Island; Litchfield, Connecticut; and Boston, Massachusetts, in 1832 moved to Cincinnati to be the first president of Lane Theological Seminary and minister of the Second Presbyterian Church. Similarly Beecher promoted the temperance movement and helped found a Domestic Missionary Society and the American Bible Society. The dominating father of a large family, Beecher succeeded in making ministers of all his sons, the best known of whom was Henry Ward Beecher; but one of his capable daughters, Harriet Beecher Stowe, achieved the greater fame {BMS}, 3:400-401 n. 4.

Another daughter, Catharine Beecher (1800-1878), was well known in the nineteenth century as an educator and author. She founded several female seminaries (secondary schools), trained teachers, and wrote *A Treatise on Domestic Economy* (1841), later revised in collaboration with her sister, Harriet Beecher Stowe, and published as *The American Woman's Home* (1869). See Kathryn Kish Sklar, *Catharine Beecher: A Study in American Domesticity* (New Haven: Yale University Press, 1973), (NAN).

32. Dwight credits John R. Gardiner, Esq., for this information in a footnote. Gardiner (1769-1816) was the seventh proprietor of Gardiners Island {BMS}, 3:217 n.

Gardiner recorded the Montauk vocabulary. See *Languages and Lore of the Long Island Indians,* edited by Gaynell Stone Levine and Nancy Bonvillain (Stony Brook: Suffolk County Archaeological Association, 1980), pp. 15-16. This area is now called Napeague Beach. There are many variations in the spellings of Indian names. William Wallace Tooker calls it Neapeague (with variant spellings, Napeagge, Napeag, Napeague), and also indicates it signifies the "water land." See Tooker's *Indian Place-Names on Long Island and Islands Adjacent With Their Probable Significations,* 1911 (Reprinted; Port Washington, NY: Ira J. Friedman, 1962), p. 156 (NAN).

33. The Mohegans and the Montauketts, as well as other native peoples on Long Island and in what is now southern New York and New England, spoke dialects of the Algonquian language. Modern anthropologists, however, would not designate the Montauk Indians as a "branch" of the Mohegans. See Gaynell Stone, ed. *The History and Archaeology of the Montauk,* 2d ed.(Stony Brook: Suffolk County Archaeological Association, 1993); John A.

Strong, *The Montaukett Indians of Eastern Long Island* (Syracuse: Syracuse University Press, 2001); and Strong, *Algonquian Peoples,* pp. 19-23 (NAN).

34. The Montauk Lighthouse was authorized by Congress in 1792 and has been on the National Register of Historic Places since 1969. The light has been automated and it is now a museum in Montauk State Park; (631) 668-2544. See Robert Heffner, "Montauk Point Lighthouse: A History of New York's First Seamark," *Long Island Historical Journal* 3 (Spring 1991): 155-66 (NAN).

35. Dwight credited John L. Gardiner with the information about Mackenzie in a footnote (3:218 n), (NAN).

Sir Alexander Mackenzie (1755?-1820), after spending several years traveling and trading with the Indians, published *Voyages from Montreal on the River St. Laurence, Through the Continent of North America, to the Frozen and Pacific Oceans; in the years 1789 and 1793* (London, 1801), {BMS}, 3:401 n. 5.

36. Clinton Academy began classes in 1785 and was the first incorporated secondary school in New York State (1787); it was in operation until 1869. See Natalie A. Naylor, "The 'Encouragement of Seminaries of Learning': The Origins and Development of Early Long Island Academies," *Long Island Historical Journal* 12 (Fall 1999): 11-30; and Sherrill Foster, "Clinton Academy: Its History and Architecture," *Long Island Historical Journal* 12 (Spring 2000): 181-93 (NAN).

37. The Southampton settlers first had landed in Schouts (Manhasset) Bay and tore down a Dutch coat of arms on a tree. Informed by the Indians, the Dutch arrested the English and sent them off. See Robert P. Schur, "The Hamptons of Suffolk," in *Long Island: A History of Two Great Counties, Nassau and Suffolk,* edited by Paul Bailey, 2 vols. (New York: Lewis Publishing, 1949), 1:212-13 (NAN).

38. Approximately quoted from Benjamin Trumbull, *A Complete History of Connecticut . . .* (New Haven, 1797), p. 272 {BMS}, 3:401 n. 6.

For recent discussion of the relationship of eastern Long Island to Connecticut (though the focus is on East Hampton), see Richard S. Dunn, "John Winthrop, Jr., of Connecticut: The First Governor of the East End," and Christopher Collier, "East Hampton: A Strategic Outpost of Connecticut in the 1660s," in Twomey, *Awakening the Past,* pp. 89-104, and 213-20 (NAN).

39. Richard Nicolls (1624-1672) was the first English governor of New York. Appointed by Charles II to head a commission to study and if necessary regulate the condition of the New England colonies and to capture New Netherland, within only a few years Nicolls succeeded in introducing an English government into New York without arousing the ire of the former Dutch inhabitants {BMS}, 3:401 n. 7.

40. William Huntting of East Hampton, Long Island, was the father of a Yale graduate of 1804, Jonathan Huntting (1778-1850), {BMS}, 3:401 n. 8.

41. Dwight no doubt means James Farret who conveyed the land to Lion Gardiner as agent for Lord Stirling. See Ross, *Long Island,* 1:28, 79-80 {BMS}, 3:401 n. 9.

42. Manchonake is the version given in Tooker, *Indian Place-Names on Long Island* (pp. 90-91), with the meaning "land of the departed " (NAN).

43. The Indians had hunted whales off shore, driving them onto the beach. The English settlers in the colonial period also pursued "shore whaling" to obtain whales on or near the shore. Very profitable from 1670-1730, this type of whaling declined as fewer whales were available close to the beaches. For a discussion of the effect this early phase of whaling had on eastern Long Island, see T.H. Breen, *Imagining the Past: East Hampton Histories* (Reading, MA: Addison-Wesley, 1989), pp. 141-276 (NAN).

44. Since the date of this journey I have been informed that the remains of a tribe of Indians called the *Shinnakaughs* [Shinnecocks] are the proprietors of these lands, and that some of them still undergo *Indian cultivation* {TD}, 3:223 n.

On the Shinnecocks, see *The Shinnecock Indians: A Culture History,* edited by Gaynell Stone (Stony Brook: Suffolk County Archaeological Association, 1983); and Rose O. Hayes, "An Ethnographic and Demographic Study of the Presqu'ile [Shinnecock]: The Adaptation of a Social Group in a Pluralistic Society," Ph.D. diss., SUNY Stony Brook, 1987); and John A. Strong, *"We Are Stll Here!": The Algonquian Peoples of Long Island Today,* 2d ed. (Interlaken, NY: Empire State Books, 1996). The Shinnecocks still survive and have opened the Shinnecock Nation Cultural Center and Museum on their reservation on Montauk Highway (Route 27), Southampton; (631) 287-4923 (NAN).

45. Dwight's reference is probably to what today is Amityville (NAN).

46. The "Isle of Pines" was also known as Island Trees, the Island of Trees, and Isle of Trees. When William Levitt developed the area in the late 1940s, he changed the name to Levittown. Island Trees is still the name of the school and water district. See Richard A. Winsche, *The History of Nassau County Community Place-Names* (Interlaken, NY: Empire State Books, 1999), p. 50 (NAN).

47. On the Hempstead Plains, see note no. 10, p.17 above in Dr. Alexander Hamilton's 1744 "Itinerarium" (NAN).

48. Dwight appears to have mistaken the first name of Mr. Prince. William Prince (c. 1725-1802) was the son of Robert Prince who planted and experimented with trees and shrubs for his own grounds. William Prince made a business of selling seedlings and attempted to breed new varieties, becoming one of the first nurserymen in America. After his retirement in 1793, his sons, William (1766-1842) and Benjamin, continued the business which was passed on to the younger William's son, William Robert (1795-1869), {BMS}, 3:401 n. 1. This became the Linnean Botanic Gardens and Nurseries which Prince operated until 1866. George Washington also had visited the Prince nurseries in 1789 (see introduction to Washington's "Tour of Long Island," p.53 above), (NAN).

49. For 1800 Dwight lists the North Hempstead figure for Hempstead. The correct number is inserted in the text, 4,141 {BMS}, 3:401 n. 3.

50. Dwight's two-page discourse of the effect of winds on climate (3:228-30) is omitted here (NAN).

51. The two-page account of the Battle of Brooklyn in August 1776 (3:231-33) is omitted. Dwight was not present during the conflict so his account is based on secondary sources (NAN).

The Traveler's Guide to Nassau Island, 1807

Samuel Latham Mitchill

Samuel Latham Mitchill (1764-1831) was a well-known physician and scientist in his day. Born in Plandome to a Quaker family, he studied medicine with Dr. Samuel Bard in New York City and at the University of Edinburgh. He was professor of chemistry, natural history, and agriculture at Columbia College (1792-1801) and at the College of Physicians and Surgeons in New York City, where he taught chemistry, natural history, botany, and "materia medica" (1807-1826). Mitchill helped to found and was active in the Society for the Promotion of Agriculture, Arts, and Manufactures, the American Geological Society, the Lyceum of Natural History (predecessor of the New York Academy of Sciences), and the *Medical Repository* which he edited for many years. He served terms in the state legislature and in Congress (Representative, 1801-1804 and 1810-1813; Senator, 1804-1809).

Mitchill was a prolific writer, primarily on scientific topics, and a member of numerous learned societies. His scientific knowledge was encyclopedic in breadth. He was particularly interested in popularizing scientific information and in practical applications. Although many of his pioneering works have been superseded, he has been called the "Nestor of American science." The Latin inscription on the monument which the State of New York erected for him in Greenwood Cemetery refers to him as "Doctor, scientist, citizen, senator," but also notes "His kindly disposition, simplicity of life, unshakable fidelity, love toward his friends."[1]

These selections are from a book Mitchill published anonymously. The first part is from a section that he entitles "Long, or Nassau Island." The New York colonial legislature had named Long Island the "Island of Nassau" in 1692, but that name was never in wide use. (In 1899, of course, Nassau became the name of the new county created from western Queens.) Mitchill gives particular attention to rocks and the large boulder known today as Shelter Rock. He provides three tours for travelers to New Utrecht, Rockaway, and Islip. Sea bathing, fishing, and hunting are the destination attractions, but Mitchill describes the landscape and built environment en route.

* * *

This piece of land, which forms the east and south sides of the bay and harbour of New-York, extends north-eastwardly about 120 miles, and terminates in a fork, the shorter extremity of which is called *Oyster-Pond* [Orient] and the longer, *Montauk-Point*. The land is very low, especially on the south side, and of course, not visible from any great distance at sea. The highest land on the island is called *Harbour-Hill.*[2] Its average breadth is estimated at about eight or nine miles. A ridge of hills runs almost the whole length of it on the north side, and completely divides its waters. The streams have, on this account, much shorter courses toward the Sound than on the side next [to] the ocean, and are, consequently, more rapid and precipitous.

The face of the country, on the one side of this elevation, which may be called the *Spine of the Island,* is exceedingly different from that on the other. On the north side it is variegated, uneven, and very much diversified with hills and dales; while, on the south, little else is discovered by the traveller than a flat surface, sloping gradually away toward the ocean. Stones and rocks are very frequent on the side next [to] the continent [i.e., the North Shore]; but, on the Atlantic side of the hills, a carriage may be driven many miles without the least impediment from them. Indeed, the tract which lies northward of the ridge, not only resembles the adjoining parts of the main land in its face and general appearance, but also in its fossils and mineral productions. It appears to have been separated from the continent, during the lapse of ages, by the encroachments of the salt water. . . .

On this [north] side of the island there are some solitary rocks, or enormous heaps of granite, which are too remarkable to be omitted in this description. To the eastward of the strait called Hell-Gate, all the considerable rocks are solitary masses of granite. These are scattered over the upland, and along the shores between high and low-water marks, and under the salt water of the bays and of the Sound. In the latter cases they are much frequented by fish, and many kinds of these animals are caught around them by the hook and line. Some of these detached or insulated rocks are of considerable size. The largest one of the kind is to be found in the town of North Hempstead. It is of a remarkable figure, forming a sort of irregular square, of the extent of about forty feet on the west, south, and east sides, and of nearly twenty on the north. It lies on the declivity of a hill, and its thickness above ground increases from ten or twelve feet; as you descend, to seventeen, or thereabout. The top of the rock is, to a considerable extent, pretty nearly level, and supports earth enough for a number of plants to grow. Among others a peach-tree, a yerva-mora (bozea), a species of cactus, a thorn-bush, an oak and a lilac, besides several other perennials and grasses. It is known in the records of the town by the name of the Mill-Stone Rock [Shelter Rock].

Supposing the rock to be uniformly thick, which is by no means an improbable supposition, then forty, the length, multiplied by thirty, the average breadth, gives a superficies [outer surface] of twelve hundred square fcct. This number, multiplied by seventeen, the supposed thickness, gives twenty thousand and four hundred cubic feet—A vast lump, indeed, of solid granite! and lying remote from all mountains and strata, for a distance of eight or nine miles at the least.[3]

This rock is considered as a mass of compact granite; not, indeed, that it has no cracks or fissures in it, but because all the pieces of which it is composed, and they are not numerous, are well fitted to each other, and show, by their shape and adaptation, that, as they are now in situ, they were once united into a whole.

There are, in the same town, other huge rocks of solitary granite, though not so regular and large as the one just described. And the well-known shoal of Old Success, in the Sound, near the mouth of Cow-Bay [Manhasset Bay], has, in its centre, a granite rock, whose top is sometimes bare, when the water around it is fifteen or sixteen feet deep. . . .

Between Long-Island and the continent there are several shoals, with rocks scattered over them, which are, apparently, sunken or wasted islands. These remains of what was, probably, in former days, upland of as great height as the neighbouring islands, afford strong evidence of the levelling power of the waves. One of these shallow places, whose rocks are frequently bare at low water, lies off the extremity of Cow-Neck [today's Sands Point], and occupies several acres near almost the middle of the Sound. From the damage sometimes done to vessels, by this shoal and its rocks, they are called *Executions*. Another sandy spot of many acres, with several large rocks appearing here and there above the little water which covers it, stretches far toward the main channel from the bottom of Great-Neck. These rocks are called the *Stepping Stones*.[4] Such of the islands enumerated as have not a rocky basis, will probably, in the progress of things, be washed down, and undergo a similar submersion. . . .

Tours in the Neighbourhood of New-York

1. *To New Utrecht.*

This is the nearest place for sea-bathing and air. It is a commodious house for lodging and entertainment, a little below the Narrows, in King's-county, on Long-Island. The best road to it, is from the village of Brooklyn, through Flatbush. On the road thither, the traveller may note several things connected with the history of the Revolution.

Proceeding along towards Flatbush, is seen the small hilly ridge, on which some skirmishing took place, between the two armies under Washington and Howe, about the end of August 1776. This is part of that spine or elevation of ground, which runs through the island, on the north side of the great plains, from New Utrecht to Southold.

At Flatbush there is a flourishing and respectable academy, called Erasmus-Hall. Boys are educated in common and classical learning, and regularly prepared for the higher studies of the college and university.[5]

This village is the county town. The prison and court-house are here. Many of its inhabitants are industrious and wealthy farmers, who enrich their lands with street manure and ashes from the city, and raise great crops of grain and grass. Hereabout may be seen some of the most productive agriculture in the state, or perhaps in any part of the union.

The principal inhabitants of this county are descendants of the Dutch settlers, who first encroached upon the natives in these parts. They have Dutch preaching in some of the religious meeting-houses, and many families learn no other language, until they are old enough to go abroad. But there are no Dutch schools, and, consequently, the language is on the decline.

The tavern at *Bath,* where the tourist goes for accommodation, is situated near the place where the British army landed in 1776. . . .[6] At this place, there is a broad view of the Atlantic Ocean, intercepted to the south and eastward only by Sandy-Hook and the lighthouse, and by Coney-Island and Gravesend point. Nothing can exceed the fine quality of the salt-water for bathing; nor the freshness of the southern breezes for invigoration. To increase the pleasures of the place, both the gunner and the angler may find his appropriate game.

2. *Tour to Rockaway.*

The route to Rockaway is from Brooklyn through the village of Jamaica, situated twelve miles to the eastward, in Queen's county. You may travel thither along the *old road,* through *Bedford,* and by the *half-way* house.[7] But a more agreeable and instructive route is by the *new-road,* over the Wallabogt bridge [Wallabout], through Bushwick and Newtown to Jamaica.

The mill-pond over which this bridge passes, belongs to the national [Brooklyn] navy-yard. In order to effect it, an act of congress was first obtained, granting permission to construct the bridge, and then an act of the state legislature, to incorporate the company. The road from Newtown and Flushing, is shortened 2 or 2-1/2 miles by it, and is not so heavy and sandy.

The navy-yard is inclosed with a stout fence. There is a marine guard there, to take care of the timber, vessels and public stores. Near the navy-yard wharf, lie the remains of the celebrated British prison-ship the *Jersey*, on board which upwards of 10,000 of the flower of the American youth were starved and poisoned to death by the enemy. These unfortunate victims of the Revolution were buried on the adjacent shore, and in digging down the bank, a few years ago, to make wharves and building sites, a vast quantity of their bones were dislodged and strewed over the shore. They were, however, collected by Capt. John Jackson, the proprietor of the neighbouring land, and re-interred at his expense, in a manner that does honour to his heart and feelings. It is meditated to set on foot a subscription, for a monument over their common grave. . . .[8]

Newtown is famous for its pippins [a variety of apples]. Its wood was greatly consumed by the enemy during the war; and the inhabitants now make great use of the peat from an extensive bog in the vicinity, for fuel. At this village, there is a Dutch, a Presbyterian, and an Anglican church.

In Jamaica, there are three similar religious houses; and an academy [Union Hall] for the education of youth.[9] This was formerly the county town in Queen's county, but the court-house having been burned, it was determined to build a new one, nearer the geographical centre of the county. In pursuance of this determination, they constructed it further eastward, in North Hempstead, on the north side of the great plains.[10] During the yellow fever at the city, in 1702, the legislature adjourned thence to Jamaica, to hold the sessions.

South of Jamaica is *Beaver Pond,* round which there have been many horse-races. Since the law passed discouraging that exercise, this place has been less frequented by jockies, and sportsmen of the turf, than formerly.[11]

About seven miles east of Jamaica, begins the prairie or savanna, called *Hempstead-plain.* It is about twenty miles long and three wide. It was naturally, or, at least, when the Europeans arrived, bare of trees, but covered with shrubbery and long grass. These have chiefly disappeared, except some andromedas, and plants of a smaller growth, on account of the vast herds of cattle and flocks of sheep with which it is pastured. These animals eat the plants very close, and give to this fine and neglected tract of land a barren appearance. It is not a common, appurtenant to the adjoining villages; but is a body of undivided land, belonging to the heirs and assigns of certain original patentees. And the owners are now so numerous and dispersed, that it is impossible to settle the titles and quotas, or to do any thing with it as property to be held in severalty. Individuals, however, encroach upon it in all directions, and are rapidly converting possessions into titles.[12] This plain is a noted resort of plover, and great numbers of these savoury birds are shot every year.

At Rockaway there is a great scope for exercise on foot, on horseback, or in carriages; as the country is very level, and free from stones. There is as fine bathing in the surf, as is found in any place upon earth. And there are several houses of shelter, on the sea-side, for the accommodation of ladies and valetudinarians [sickly persons]. At low-water, the surf-side of the beach is an excellent bottom to ride upon, and is equal to a turnpike road.[13]

The prospect of the unruffled ocean, is superb. All the vessels going in and out of New-York harbour, pass in sight. The lighthouse at Sandy-Hook, and the Neversunk hills are full in view. And the roaring and impetuosity of the waves, is sometimes truly sublime. In the adjoining bay, plenty of king-fish, sheep's head, and black-fish are to be taken, both in the seine and with the hook. And the variety of snipes, ducks, and plover, affords high gratification to shooting marksmen. During the warm season, a stage is kept regularly running from Brooklyn through Jamaica to Rockaway.

3. *Tour to Islip*

Instead of visiting Rockaway, you may travel strait onward to Hempstead village. . . .[14] Here was formerly an excellent school, kept by the Rev. Mr. [Leonard] Cutting, an accomplished classical scholar. . . .[15]

Passing from this village to Thomas Seaman's in the *Brushy* plains at Half-hollow-hills, you find yourself on the grouse ground of Suffolk County. After passing from the naked plains, you enter the shrubby oaks and pines, which form the brushy plains. Amidst these thickets live the heath-hens. And guides are to be procured at several of the houses on the road, to carry strangers to their haunts.

Travelling eastward to Islip, the angler may amuse himself in catching the large trout of the brooks, etc., may ride to Rockonkama pond [Lake Ronkonkoma], near the middle of the island, and take yellow perch; or he may venture into the south bay, in quest of the same kinds of fish that Rockaway affords.

Should the traveller incline to hunt deer, he may be gratified by making up a party and proceeding a few miles further eastward. Fixing themselves in convenient stations with loaded guns, the hunters wait the arrival of the deer, alarmed and driven along by others of the company who scare them with hounds. As the deer pass, the hunters shoot and kill as many as they can.

Patchague [Patchogue], 12 miles further, was formerly the rendezvous of the Blue-point oystermen. The quantities of oysters carried from the bay near the settlement, for more than thirty years, has been enormous. Latterly, however, they have failed remarkably; and oysters are at present nearly as dear at Patchague, as they are at New-York. Mulford's was formerly a house at which they might be got fried, in excellent order.

Should the expedition be undertaken in October and later, when the brent and wild geese arrive from the northward, the opportunities of killing them, and many smaller water fowl, at Smith's point in *Mastick* [Mastic] surpass every thing, perhaps, that any part of the island affords.[16] The flights of them seem innumerable and endless; and there are some stations, from which the gunners assail them with shot, at a most destructive rate.

For the information of travellers, it is proper to state that there is an act in force for "the preservation of heath-hens and other game," which was passed the 15th February 1791. This statute makes it penal to kill any heath-hen, within Queen's or Suffolk Counties, or any partridge, quail or woodcock, within Queen's, King's, or New-York Counties, between the following lines, to wit: heath-hen, partridge and quail, are protected by the law, from the 1st April, to the 5th October, and woodcock, from 20th February, to 1st July, annually. . . . [Describes penalties for violations.]

The forests of Suffolk County, furnish vast quantities of wood for the consumption of the city. Land that has been cleared of its growth of oak, is found to furnish another crop fit for fuel, in 48 or 50 years.

Notes

Source: *The Picture of New-York or The Traveller's Guide Through the Commercial Metropolis of the United States,* by A Gentleman Residing in This City (New York: I. Ripley, 1807), pp. 11-12, 14-18, 158-66, 175-78. Editing changes have been minimal; a few paragraphs have been combined and some capitalization modernized. Mitchill's spellings and use of italics have been retained. Insertions in the text are in brackets. All notes are by the editor for this volume.

1. The quotation is from Courtney R. Hall, "Long Island's Greatest Scientist," an undated clipping from the *Nassau Daily Review,* in the Nassau County Museum vertical files, Long Island Studies Institute, Hofstra University. Other biographical information on Mitchill is from Courtney Robert Hall, "Samuel Latham Mitchill, A Queens County Polymath," *New York History* 14 (April 1933): 113-24; Lyman C. Newell, "Mitchill, Samuel Latham," in *Dictionary of American Biography,* 7:69-71; and Keir B. Sterling, "Mitchill, Samuel Latham," in *American National Biography,* 15: 638-40. See also Daniel M. Tredwell, *Personal Reminiscences of Men and Things on Long Island,* 2 vols. (Brooklyn: Charles A. Ditmas, 1912), 1:166-70; Courtney R. Hall, *A Scientist in the Early Republic: Samuel Latham Mitchill* (New York: Russell and Russell, 1967); John A. Shiel, "Dr. Samuel Mitchill," parts 1 and 2, *Long Island Forum* 40 (October and November 1977): 192-97, 226-28; and Alan David Aberbach, *In Search of an American Identity: Samuel Latham Mitchill, Jeffersonian Nationalist* (New York: P. Lange, 1988).

2. In addition to being the name of the moraine (or "spine of the Island"), Harbor Hill is the name of an area in Roslyn Heights; Jaynes Hill in South Huntington is the highest point at 400 feet.

3. Shelter Rock is located on the west side of Shelter Rock Road, south of Northern Boulevard (Route 25A). It is fifty-five feet high, thirty-five feet wide and weighs an estimated five million pounds. See John Rather, "Shelter Rock Facing an Uncertain Future," Long Island section 14, *New York Times,* February 28, 1999.

4. Lighthouses were later erected at these locations which retain the historic names. Execution Rocks Lighthouse, north of Sands Point, was built in 1850, and Stepping Stones Lighthouse, off Kings Point, was built in 1877. See Harlan Hamilton, *Lights and Legends: A Historical Guide to Lighthouses* (Stamford, CT: Westcott Cove Publishing, 1987), pp. 23, 27.

5. Erasmus Hall was one of the first chartered academies in New York State. It became part of the Brooklyn public school system in 1896. The original wooden building today is preserved in a courtyard, surrounded by twentieth-century stone structures. See Natalie A. Naylor, "The 'Encouragement of Seminaries of Learning': The Origins and Development of Early Long Island Academies," *Long Island Historical Journal* 12 (Fall 1999): 11-30.

6. Bath or Bath Beach was on Gravesend Bay, near today's Bensonhurst Park. Mitchill briefly mentions the British troop movements in August 1776 (p. 161).

7. The Half-way House was Howard's. Francisco de Miranda also stopped there in 1784 (see his "County Excursions and Visits to Eastern Long Island" above). On Howard's see Eugene L. Armbruster, *The Eastern District of Brooklyn* (New York: Privately printed, 1912), pp. 60-63.

8. The Prison Ship Martyrs' Monument, designed by Stanford White, was dedicated in 1908. See "A Brief History of the Prison Ships and the Prison Ship Martyrs' Memorial," *Long Island Historical Society Quarterly* 1 (April 1939): 47-52. Mitchill reprints Philip Freneau's poem, "The Prison Ship," which is omitted here.

9. On Union Hall, see Naylor, "The 'Encouragement of Seminaries of Learning,'" 12: 19-23.

10. The court house in Jamaica was destroyed by the British during the Revolution. The courthouse in North Hempstead was authorized in 1785 and built on what is today Jericho Turnpike (Route 25) in Garden City Park. See Geoffrey Mahon, "Nassau's Difficult Birth," in *Long Island: Our Story* (Melville: Newsday, 1998), pp. 232-33.

11. Beaver Pond was located east of today's 150th Street. In 1906 it was filled in and Liberty Avenue now bisects its loction. The famous Union Course racetrack would later be built in this area (1823). See references to the horseracing in articles by Prime and Tredwell below.

12. The first major sale of the common lands of the Hempstead Plains was not until 1869 when Alexander T. Stewart bought 7,000 acres to develop Garden City.

13. On Rockaway, see also Charles Brockden Brown's, "A Jaunt to Rockaway" (above) and the poem "Rockaway" (below).

14. In sections omitted here, Mitchill mentions the Duke's Laws (enacted in Hempstead in 1665) and quotes provisions in his footnotes (pp. 167-74), and discusses unsuccessful efforts to divide the Hempstead Plains (pp. 174-75).

15. Mitchill had studied with Cutting who was rector of St. George's Church (1766-1784) and conducted a classical school in addition to his parish responsibilities. Before coming to Hempstead, Cutting had been a tutor and professor at Kings (later Columbia) College in New York City. See Benjamin F. Thompson, *History of Long Island,* 3d ed., enlarged, 3 vols, 1918 (Reprint; Port Washington: I.J. Friedman, 1962), 2:517.

16. On plovers, and hunting plovers and other birds on the Hempstead Plains, see Daniel M. Tredwell, "Personal Reminiscences of the South Side, 1839-1890s," below.

Camp Meetings in Musquito Cove and Flushing, 1830

James Stuart

James Stuart (1775-1849) was from Scotland where he had attended the University of Edinburgh. After an apprenticeship, he became a member of the Society of Writers to the Signet in 1798 and was collector of their widows' fund (1818-1828). He was involved in local government as a deputy lieutenant and justice of the peace. His Whig sympathies brought him into conflict with the Tory press, ultimately culminating in a dual in 1822 where he killed the man who had attacked him in a Glasgow paper. The trial attracted a great deal of attention, and the jury acquitted Stuart of the murder charge. Stuart came to America in July 1828, where he travelled throughout the country. After he returned to Scotland, he published an account of his travels, *Three Years in North America*. Stuart later became editor of a London newspaper for a few years and then was appointed inspector of factories in 1836.[1]

Stuart came to Long Island specifically to attend camp meetings. These outdoor religious services were a uniquely American development of religious revivalism. Camp meetings originated on the frontier in the early 1800s as a means of saving souls and revitalizing religion. Embraced by evangelical Protestantism, camp meetings spread throughout the country and were especially popular among Methodists in the nineteenth century. People came from a distance and literally pitched their tents for several days. The most famous camp meeting grounds included Ocean Grove on the Jersey Shore, Chautauqua in western New York, and Oak Bluffs on Martha's Vineyard, each of which evolved into summer resorts in the twentieth century. Sea Cliff, North Merrick, Jamesport, and Shelter Island Heights were among the camp meeting grounds on Long Island later in the nineteenth century. Camp meetings were held in many other locations as well. Stuart's account provides a detailed description of a camp meeting near Glen Cove (then known as Musquito Cove), and a briefer account of another camp meeting of "people of colour" near Flushing.[2]

After attending the camp meeting in Musqueto Cove, Stuart spent the evening in Oyster Bay. He describes that hamlet and the "wild country" through which he traveled the next day to Babylon to breakfast at its famous American House inn. Stuart's time on Long Island was brief—less than three days. As an outsider from Scotland and doubtless a Presbyterian, Stuart's views are particularly valuable. In addition to the overt religious purposes, the camp meetings were also a time for socializing and recreation. Camp meetings on the frontier sometimes had a reputation for undisciplined emotionalism, excessive drinking, and other "immoralities," which may have been what Stuart was anticipating. The rules he quotes obviously were to keep the proceedings under control, and he stresses the decorum. Stuart's descriptions of camp meetings and the communities where he traveled add to our understanding of nineteenth-century Long Island.

* * *

Some time after my expedition to Staten Island, an advertisement of a Camp-meeting to be held at Musquito Cove [Glen Cove] on Long Island Sound, came in my way. I expressed to the hotel keeper at Mount Vernon a wish to be present, and he and one of the friends who accompanied me to Staten Island, very good humoredly agreed to make a party to Long Island for a day. We hired a barouche [carriage], which is to be had at New York for four dollars a day, then crossing by the steam-boat ferry to Long Island and breakfasting at the village of Flushing, where are situated Mr. Prince's long established nursery grounds,[3] we reached that part of Musquito Cove where we understood the meeting was to be held at about twelve o'clock. The meeting was held within a forest or wood, where a sufficient number of trees had been cut to make such an opening as was required. The morning service was concluded some time before we arrived. From the high grounds, the view of the bay, of the shipping, and of the assembled multitudes with their carriages and horses was very striking. A great many of the people were straggling in the adjoining fields during the interval of service. The shipping, all of which had been employed in bringing persons from a considerable distance to join the meeting, consisted of five steam-boats, about sixty sloops and schooners, besides open boats. The number of horses and carriages was proportionably great. It was calculated that there were about 12,000 persons on the ground, certainly not less than 9,000 or 10,000.[4]

There seemed to be about a dozen clergymen, all belonging to the Methodist persuasion, in a large covered and elevated platform.

Benches were provided for the congregation, placed on the vacant or open space in front of the platform. The males were on the one side of the benches and the females on the other. There were benches for a great part of the assembled multitude, and the benches were surrounded on all sides by a close body of those who had only standing room. When the afternoon service commenced, the effect of this prodigious assemblage of people, all standing, lifting up their voices, and joining in praise of their Creator, was more sublime than those who have not witnessed such a scene can well imagine. The sermon, which was afterwards delivered, lasted for an hour and was distinctly heard all over the ground, for the most perfect order and silence prevailed. The clergyman preached from the 29th verse of the 10th chapter of the book of Numbers: "We are journeying unto the place of which the Lord said, I will give it you: come thou with us, and we will do thee good; for the Lord hath spoken good concerning Israel." The discourse seemed to me altogether faultless, and the address at the end was most remarkably impressive. The speaker in the conclusion alluded to the sect of Christians to which he belonged, the Methodists, but he meant, he added, to say "nought against other denominations of Christians who did good." After sermon, prayer, all kneeling, succeeded. Then a hymn was sung, and another clergyman, a very old man, coming to the edge of the platform, said that a friend whom they had never heard before was about to address them. Another clergyman, an aged person, then stepped forward to enforce, as he said, the invitation in the text, which he did very shortly and very skillfully, particularly, and with great earnestness, exhorting those members who had been lately added to their church, to communicate to their brothers, sisters, and friends, some idea of the happiness which they now enjoyed, that they might be induced to follow their example, and accept the invitation by joining the church even before the meeting was over.

The afternoon service was concluded as usual, with singing and prayer, and the most perfect decorum prevailed. The service continued for about two hours and a half.

I understood that this meeting was to last for about four days. Many people came from a distance of one hundred miles and upwards. The great objects of holding such meetings in this part of the country are to afford opportunities to persons whose situation, such as that of servants, prevents them from attending worship regularly on Sunday, of being present on the occasion when they are almost always indulged and allowed to avail themselves of it, and to keep people who have not yet turned their minds to religious subjects together for such a time that their attention must be arrested. It is conceived that extraordinary efforts ought frequently to be made by all those ministers of Christ who are faithful and do not neglect their duty. Such of the clergy as approve of the observance of numerous days for prayer meetings and of such assemblages as this, ascribe the wants of revivals, by which I merely understand the addition of any considerable number of converts at one time to any church, to the languor of the minister and to his making no further exertion than custom has established as a standard. They maintain that where the minister contents himself with preaching once or twice on the Sabbath, performing the professional duties required of him and nothing more, without questioning himself whether any thing more be required of him by the precepts of the religion he professes, the church becomes relaxed in discipline, and that the absence of any thing like a revival in such circumstances shows that those who believe in the Gospel of Christ must perform more ministerial and Christian duties, and must show more earnestness. I had a very different notion of what was meant by a revival of religion in the United States, both from what I had previously heard and from what I had been told since I was in this country by persons who consider every clergyman to be weak, and eccentric, and an enthusiast, who deviates from the ordinary routine of ministerial operation, or who shows the sincerity of his belief by using all the means in his power to obtain converts to that religion which he professes to believe.

The United States being free from any religious establishment, every one is not only tolerated in the exercise of the religion he believes, but is at full liberty without the fear, except in very few and very peculiar cases, of his temporal concerns being at all affected by his religious profession (whatever it may be), to embrace those religious doctrines which he conceives on due consideration are true. It follows from this state of things that there is much less hypocrisy in the professors of religion in this than in other countries. Those in this country who voluntarily go to a Protestant church, and who voluntarily pay for the ministration of a Christian clergyman may be generally (I do not mean to say universally), held to have made the necessary examination, and to be real believers of the doctrines of the Christian religion—whereas those from other countries who have travelled in the United States and who have put forth sneering and ill-founded statements on the subject of revivals, camp-meetings, etc., are generally Christians professing that religion merely because their parents did so, or because Christianity is the religion of their country, and not because they ever investigated its truth. . . .[5]

A contribution is at the camp-meetings made among the people in order to defray the expense of the ground, and of the necessary police to preserve order.

"The rules and orders for the government of the camp-meeting," printed on a card, were affixed to a great many of the trees on the neighbouring grounds. I tore off one of the cards in order to preserve a copy of the rules which follow.

I. Preaching, morning, afternoon, and evening at the sound of the trumpet from the stand.

II. During the time of preaching from the stand, not more than one person is to remain in each tent (except in cases of sickness), but all are to repair to the stand and come into the congregation.

III. No walking, talking, or smoking tobacco, or standing up while there are vacant seats is to be allowed within the circle of the tents in the time of preaching; no standing or walking on the seats at any time.

IV. No cooking or preparing victuals or setting or clearing of tables during preaching from the stand is to be allowed. This rule applies to those tents that keep boarders as well as others.

V. About ten o'clock in the evening the trumpet will be blown at the stand when all who have lodgings on the ground must retire to rest, and all who have not will be required to leave the ground.

VI. The owners or occupants of each tent shall be responsible for these rules and for any rude or improper conduct in their tents, and on complaint the tent shall be subjected to be removed.

These rules were most strictly observed, one person having been taken up on the evening before we arrived at the campground merely for selling cider. All sorts of liquor are prohibited, excepting tea and coffee. During the interval of worship, many of the people were walking about the adjoining grounds—others were in their tents, where the head of the family or some other person was praying, and in some of those tents, manifestations were occasionally given by the groans and exclamations of the people. There was less of these exclamations during the sermon than I had expected; the greatest order continued during the whole period of its delivery. Two of the clergymen had gowns and bands.[6]

When the afternoon service was concluded, we remounted our vehicle in order to reach Oyster Bay, where we proposed spending the night, before sunset. We stopped in our way at a small village two or three miles from the camp-meeting, where, though not at regular hours, a good dinner was quickly prepared. Oyster Bay is about forty miles from New York, in [on] Long Island Sound. The bay and village, which consists of straggling houses, are much resorted to as a summer retreat, are very beautiful, and the situation thoroughly retired. The hotel at Oyster Bay is large and was well filled on this occasion with people returning from the camp-meeting. We left it the next morning very early (between four and five o'clock), and ascertained that not a door had been shut during the whole night, nor even a window on the ground floor. We crossed the country before breakfast on the morning of our leaving Oyster Bay to Babylon, a village on the Atlantic side of Long Island about twenty miles off, chiefly through a very wild country consisting of thin soil overgrown with brush-wood, the chief inhabitants of which are wild deer, quails, and game, which are called here grouse and partridges, but which are very different from and very inferior to the birds of the same description in Britain. This tract of country is about seventy miles long and is greatly resorted to by the people of New-York as shooting-ground. No one is prevented from sporting over it as he likes. The [American] hotel at Babylon is deservedly famous for its breakfasts. We had the red sea trout in perfection, and the shell-fish called clams admirably prepared. From hence we retraced our steps to New York, passing through the very pretty village of Jamaica, as well as the grounds recently occupied by Mr. Cobbett, which did not seem particularly to require notice.[7]

Some time after I had attended this camp-meeting, I happened to go part of the way in the steam-boat with a great party of men of colour and their families who were proceeding to a camp-meeting under the charge of their own clergymen, who were men of colour. I never saw a happier set of people than they seemed to be, singing hymns in the boat, and regaling themselves with peaches of which they had tubsful. . . .

There was a camp-meeting of people of colour near Flushing on the 29th August. I accompanied a great body of them on Sunday morning from Hallet's Cove to Flushing.[8] Peaches and melons were at this time very abundant, and there were great quantities of them in the boat for the use of the people. Peaches were at this period selling for ninepence a bushel, and musk melons, of delicious flavour, at a penny for each. There were about 450 people in the steam-boat, the *Linnaeus,* of seventy tons on our trip to Flushing, and it required nice management to keep the people properly balanced on each side of the upper deck.

There might be about 3,000 or 4,000 people at this meeting. The preachers were all men of colour; one of them, though speaking the broken English, which is universal among the coloured people, possessed a great deal of natural eloquence, and was not at all deficient either in matter or manner. There were at this meeting a great many people from New York, who came in carriages by land; indeed, the multitude and variety of carriages were greater than at any race course I have seen in this country. Perfect order was maintained during the service, both in the forenoon and afternoon, but the contiguity of the village where spirits and fermented liquors of all kinds may be procured seemed to me unfavourable for that strict preservation of decorum which is indispensably necessary at such meetings. I left the ground when the afternoon service was finished.

Camp Meeting Grounds, Jamesport, c. 1910. Religious camp meetings continued to be held on Long Island. In Jamesport, camp meetings were conducted from the 1830s to the 1940s.

Notes

Source: James Stuart, *Three Years in North America,* 2 vols., 2d ed. (New York: J.&J. Harper, 1833), 1:263-65, 271-72, 2:322-23; in the 1833 Edinburgh edition, 2:412-17, 426-29, 554-55. The only editing change has been to standardize punctuation; Stuart's English spellings have been retained. Insertions in the text are in brackets, and all notes for this selection are by the editor (NAN).

1. Biographical information on Stuart is from *Dictionary of National Biography,* edited by Sir Leslie Stephen and Sir Sidney Lee, 22 vols., 1885-1901 (Reprint; London: Oxford University Press, 1921-1922), 19:90-91. The Signet was the seal of the early Scottish kings. A writer to the signet was a legal agent or clerk of the court.

2. "Musquito" was from the Matinecock Indian name for the area, "Mosquetah" (with variant spellings Musceata, Muskitoe, Musketo, Musketa, and Muchito), meaning "place of rushes." The English settlers also called this Musketa Cove and Moscheto Cove at various times. Residents felt the similarity of the name to the insect discouraged settlement and business, so they changed the community's name to Glen Cove in 1837. See Richard A. Winsche, *The History of Nassau County Community Place-Names* (Interlaken, NY: Empire State Books, 1999), p. 38.

3. Prince's Nursery began in 1737, and was in operation into the 1860s. See references to Prince's Nursery in George Washington's "Tour of Long Island" (including note no. 3), and Timothy Dwight's "Journey to Long Island," earlier in this volume; and George DeWan, "The Blooming of Flushing," in *Long Island: Our Story* (Melville: Newsday, 1998), p. 91.

4. To put these estimates in perspective, the population of the town of Oyster Bay in 1830 was less than 5,200, and all of present-day Nassau County had less than 15,000. The event also attracted people from a distance, as Stuart observes, but his estimate of the numbers attending may be exaggerated.

5. Omitted here are Stuart's reference to a revival in Baltimore and his general defense of revivals against the negative views of them by many English writers.

6. The "bands" refers to the two strips hanging down in front of a collar worn by ministers.

7. William Cobbett (1763-1835) was a well-known English journalist who lived on Long Island in what is now New Hyde Park in 1817-1819. (He rented the "Hyde Park" estate, which had been Governor Thomas Dongan's country residence). During this period Cobbett wrote *Grammar of the English Language* (1818), *A Year's Residence in the United States of America* (1818), and *American Gardener* (1819). His *Year's Residence* focuses on his farming, particularly of rutabaga (a Swedish turnip) and has been frequently reprinted, e.g., in 1964 by Southern Illinois University Press. Adelphi University has a William Cobbett collection in their library. On Cobbett, see George DeWan, "A Maverick's Rowdy Odyssey," *Newsday,* November 7, 2000; Charles Reichman, "William Cobbett, Pioneer of the Long Island Rutabaga," *Long Island Forum* 52 (Winter 1989): 34-37; and James Sambrook and Elizabeth Thornton, *British Romantic Prose Writers, 1789-1832,* First Series, edited by John R. Greenfield, *Dictionary of Literary Biography,* vol. 107 (Detroit: Gale Research, 1991), pp. 35-67.

8. Hallet's Cove was a settlement near the ferry at the end of today's Astoria Boulevard.

Journey Down the Island, 1835

Gabriel Furman

Gabriel Furman (1800-1854) was a lawyer whose avocations were history and collecting books. Born in Brooklyn, his father William was also a lawyer and involved in local politics as a village trustee and supervisor and county judge. Gabriel Furman attended Columbia Academy in Bergen, New Jersey. After working for five years from 1818 to 1823 with a company surveying and mapping the village of Brooklyn, he began to study law under Elisha King in Manhattan. Furman was appointed Justice of the Municipal Court in Brooklyn in 1827 and held leadership positions in St. John's Episcopal Church, the Brooklyn Dispensary, and Library Association (later the Apprentices' Library).

Pursuing his avocation, Furman compiled information on Brooklyn history which was published in 1825 as *Notes Geographical and Historical, Relating to the Town of Brooklyn, in Kings County of Long Island.* In 1828, he completed a draft of "A Sketch of the History of Theatres in the United States." He wrote "The Customs, Amusements, Style of Living and Manners of the People of the United States from the First Settlement to the Present Time," by 1844, and spent more than a dozen years writing "Long Island Antiquities and Early History with the Manners and Amusing Customs of Its Inhabitants." These works remained unpublished during his lifetime. He delivered a number of lectures in the early 1840s and edited Daniel Denton's 1670 work, "A Brief Description of New York, Formerly Called New Netherland," which was published in 1845.[1]

Furman was elected to the New York State Senate in 1838 and won the Whig nomination for lieutenant-governor in 1842. His defeat in the election brought an end to his political career, and he resumed his legal practice. Furman's personal and professional life declined in the mid-1840s, as a result of his addiction to opium. In 1846, he had to auction more than two thousand books from his personal library and sell his home to raise money. An unwise investment in a scheme to raise Captain Kidd's alleged treasure from the Hudson River forced him to sell the manuscript of "Antiquities," the balance of his library, and his other collections. Furman died impoverished at the age of 54. Later, Frank Moore acquired the "fragmentary manuscript" of "Long Island Antiquities" from a book dealer, combined it with Furman's earlier published Brooklyn history ("Notes"), and added a bibliography by Henry Onderdonk. Moore edited and published the three parts in 1874 under the title *Antiquities of Long Island.*[2]

There is much valuable social history of interest in Furman's *Antiquities,* including information on schools and education, churches and religious services, manners and customs, holidays and celebrations. As Furman himself acknowledged, much of his history is compiled from other books, though like many writers of his day, he does not cite his sources. In the selection here, Furman describes a journey he himself took by the mail-stage from Brooklyn to eastern Long Island, probably in 1835. The 110-mile trip took three days with overnight stops in Babylon and Quogue before reaching Sag Harbor and East Hampton.[3] In the opening paragraph, he refers to the changes brought by the railroad. By mid-1844, passengers could go to Boston by taking the railroad from Brooklyn to Greenport in less than four hours. They would then take a ferry across Long Island Sound to Connecticut to continue on to Boston. Furman is impressed by the beauties of the landscape on eastern Long Island and the casualness of the arrangements for mail delivery. He mentions how whales were spotted near the shore. He looks back nostalgically at the slower pace of travel before the changes in the 1840s brought by the railroad and turnpikes and the coming of tourists.

* * *

A mighty change has been produced in Long Island within the last few years, by the introduction of the railroad; now by its means travellers leave New York city after breakfasting and arrive in Boston between five and six o'clock the same evening. Only as late as 1835, the regular mail-stage left Brooklyn once a week on Thursday, having arrived from Easthampton and Sag Harbor the afternoon of the previous day; and this was the only conveyance travellers could then have through this island, unless they took a private carriage. The practice then was to leave Brooklyn about nine o'clock in the morning—they were not, however, particular as to a half hour—travel on to Hempstead where they dined, and after that, jog on to Babylon where they put up for the night. A most delightful way this was to take a jaunt—there was no hurry, no fuss and bustle about it; no one was in haste to get to his journey's end, and if he was, and intended going the whole route, he soon became effectually cured of it. Every thing went on soberly and

Northern View of Hempstead, 1842

judiciously, and you could see all there was to be seen and hear all that was to be heard and have time enough to do it all in; no mode of travelling ever suited our taste better; it was the very acme of enjoyment.

The next morning you left Babylon just after daylight—which in the summer was of itself worth living for—journeyed on to Patchogue where you got your breakfast between nine and ten o'clock with a good appetite for it, we warrant you. You would get no dinner this day, nor would you feel the want of it after your late and hearty breakfast, but travel along slowly and pleasantly until you reached the rural post office at *Fire Place* [Brookhaven hamlet], standing on the edge of a wood; here, if you have a taste for the beautiful in Nature, you would walk down the garden to look at the trout stream filled with the speckled beauties. Here you need give yourself no uneasiness about being left by the stage, as is the case in some of the go-ahead parts of our country—in this particular region the middle of the road is sandy, and the driver like a considerate man gives his horses an opportunity to rest, so that they may the better travel through this piece of heavy road. You might, therefore, after enjoying yourself at this spot, walk on leisurely ahead of the stage with a friend, and some one who is conversant with the country and its legends, and this walk would prove by no means the least pleasant part of your excursion, for many are the tales that you would hear of awful shipwrecks, of pirates and their buried wealth, of treasures cast upon the sea, and of all those horrors and wonders of which the ocean is the prolific parent. After walking for some two or three miles upon the green sward at the edge of the road, gathering and eating the berries as you strolled along until you were tired, you would find the stage a short distance behind you, the driver very complaisant, for you have much eased his horses in their journey through the heavy sand, and the passengers pleased to see you back in your seat again, that is, if you have done as every traveller ought to do, studied the comfort and convenience of your fellow-passengers as well as your own.

Shortly after sunset you would stop for the night, the second one of your journey, at a place called Quagg or Quogue. Here you might, after supper on a moonlight night in the beginning of August, if you were so fortunate as to be there at such a time as we were, cross the meadows with a guide and walk down to the sea-beach where, with no sound but the beating of the waves upon the shore swelling in from a waste of waters of three thousand miles and making the earth tremble under your feet, with scarcely a breath of air to move the hair upon your forehead, and nothing in sight for miles upon miles but the white sand hills glistening in the moonbeams on one side, and this world of waters on the other, you would more than at any other time realize the immensity of creation, and your own comparative insignificance. The following morning you would breakfast at Southampton after passing through a pine forest, in a portion which from the early hour and blindness of the road you would probably require a guide to go ahead of the horses with a lighted lantern. You would also this morning, before arriving at Southampton, cross the remains of the first canal constructed in what is now the United States by Mongotucksee, the chief of the Montauk Indians,[4] long before the white settlement of the country, and also traverse a region of hills known as the Shinecoc [Shinnecock] Hills on which not a tree has grown since they were known to man, certainly not since the European settlement of this island; and if you are wise, you would leave the stage near this canal, and with your friend cross these hills on foot, for the stage has to make a long circuit around their base, and you may leisurely walk over them in nearly a straight line, enjoying some most delightful views, which are not to be seen from any part of the road and reach the road on the opposite side before the stage has completed the circuit.

Sag Harbor would be reached in time for dinner, after which the mail stage would travel on to its final destination at Easthampton, arriving there just before sunset on Saturday afternoon, thus occupying nearly three days to traverse a distance of one hundred and ten miles, but most pleasant days they were, and no one has ever tried this mode of journeying through Long Island who had pleasure in view who did not wish to try it again. It would afford recollections for a life to make such a tour of this island to Montauk Point, going by the south road and returning by the north side; to stroll along the great south beach near Ammagansett on the hard level sand near the water's edge with nothing in view but the white sand hillocks crowned with scrubby bushes and occasionally at long intervals small thatched huts or wigwams on the highest elevations, with a staff projecting from the top. These huts were occupied at certain seasons by men on the watch for whales, and when they saw them blowing, a signal was hoisted on this staff. Immediately the people would be seen coming from all directions with their whaling boats upon wagon-wheels, drawn by horses or oxen, launch them from the beach and be off in pursuit of the great fish. You would see all through this region these whaling-boats turned upside down, lying upon a frame under the shade of some trees by the road-side, this being the only way in which they could keep them, having no harbors; four or five families would club together in owning one of these boats and in manning them.

This journey was then a most interesting one, from the variety of scenery and curious out-of-the-way occurrences. The whole south side of the island and also portions of the northern side are full of legends and stories of pirates, shipwrecks, and strange superstitions, of murders and buried treasures, which are revived from time to time by the actual discovery of Spanish dollars along the beach after unusually heavy storms; a large amount was found in this way as late as March 1842. It was worth the trouble of such a journey then, to witness the primitive manner of the post-office arrangements in various parts of the island, manifesting a degree of honesty in the whole community and confidence in each other to be met with in few other places in this world. The villages were in some instances a mile or two off the post road; in such cases the driver would stop and lay his package for the place intended on a particular rock inside of the fence by the road-side and would take up anything left there for him; at other times, as he was jogging along, he would throw out two or three newspapers, under a certain tree or shrub, all of which were sure to find their true destination. One morning on our journey down the island, we came to an old tree standing at the intersection of two roads with a box fastened to it without a lock; this was the post-office of that district; our driver deposited in it the letters and papers for that place, and took out those intended for carriage further east. These were the mail arrangements on Long Island even at that late period, and yet no instance was known of any letter of paper having miscarried.

But those things are all now passed, and such a jaunt can never again be taken; the old mail route is broken up, and now in place of travelling soberly along, we by means of railroads and turnpikes fly rapidly through the island. Now we will meet with hundreds of tourists for pleasure, where we met one at that period. It was then something of an undertaking to go to Montauk Point—now [c.1850] almost everybody goes there. Then there were few taverns, and in many places none; the inhabitants were delighted to see strangers and learn from them the news of the world; they were plain and hospitable in their manners, so that it was a peculiar pleasure to visit them. Now there are taverns or hotels everywhere, and in the summer they are filled. The people have ceased to offer their hospitalities, except to those with whom they are somewhat acquainted, otherwise from the great influx of strangers they might be much imposed upon. In place of that kind, open-hearted reception which you then met with from all the girls and young men in the eastern part of the island, you will find they have now the manners of the young people of our towns, and in order to have any intercourse with either sex, a previous formal introduction is necessary, and even after that, the frolicking, kind, good-humored attention you then received are now supplied by manners tinctured with distance and reserve. This change may have been inevitable, and, in fact, absolutely necessary,

The Long
Shoreman's
Home: Hauling
up the Skiff

from their change of circumstances and situation, with reference to the
travelling world, but yet it is much to be regretted.

Notes

Source: Gabriel Furman, *Antiquities of Long Island,* edited by Frank Moore (New
York: Boulton, 1874), pp. 242-50. The complete book is available on-line from Cornell
University's Making of America project (http://cdl.library.cornell.edul/moa). In 1968, Ira J.
Friedman in Port Washington reprinted a portion, under the same title. However, it is 271
pages whereas the 1874 edition totaled 478 pages. The reprint does not include Moore's
brief Introduction, the *Notes on the History of Brooklyn,* nor Onderdonk's bibliography).

Editing changes have been minimal. Some of the punctuation has been modernized and
a few of Furman's long paragraphs divided. All notes are by the editor (NAN).

1. The New-York Historical Society published portions of the "Customs" in issues of
their *New-York Historical Society Bulletin* in 1938-1939. Daniel Denton's "Description"
was published in volume 1 of *Bibliotheca Americana,* edited by William Gowans (New
York: A.T. Houel, 1849). Daniel Denton's work focuses on Long Island; excerpts from
Furman's edition, including his lengthy notes on the Hempstead Plains, are reprinted in
appendices to *The Roots and Heritage of Hempstead Town,* edited by Natalie A. Naylor
(Interlaken, NY: Heart of the Lakes Publishing, 1994), pp. 192-99.

2. Biographical information on Furman is from Stephen Clark, "Gabriel Furman:
Brooklyn's First Historian," *Journal of Long Island History* 10 (Spring 1974): 21-32.

3. See Sidney C. Schaer, "Horsepower Was Just That," in *Long Island: Our Story,* by
Newsday (Melville: Newsday, 1998), p. 177.

4. Furman described this also on pp. 58-59 in a section entitled "Traditions." The
"Devils Stepping Stones" is another Indian "tradition" he describes (pp. 56-57). Furman
devotes one-quarter of *Antiquities* to "Indians and their History." Much of this information
is dated and reflects the biases of his day. George DeWan refers to Mongontucksee's canal
as an "Indian myth" which Furman popularized. Later historical accounts repeated the
story, but John A. Strong reports there is no evidence in the documentary sources of its
accuracy. The Shinnecocks probably used Canoe Place for portage. Though a canal was
discussed since the 1820s, the state legislature did not vote funds until the 1880s; the canal
opened in 1892. See George DeWan, "The Canal Between the Bays," *Newsday,* October 26,
1999, p. A-34.

An English Quaker's Visit, 1839 and 1840

Joseph John Gurney

Joseph John Gurney (1788-1847) was born in Norwich, England, educated in boarding schools, and privately tutored in Oxford. At the age of seventeen, he joined the family's Gurneys Bank, but continued reading, particularly in Biblical studies. By the time he came to America as a traveling minister for the Society of Friends, Gurney was well-known for his social reform activities and his extensive biblical and theological writings. He was outspoken in England in temperance and the movement to end the slave trade. Gurney was following in the footsteps of many other Quakers who came to America to minister to fellow Friends.[1]

Gurney, however, had another reason for his trip; he wanted to see slavery first-hand. He did not speak out publicly against slavery until near the end of his visit, not wanting to antagonize Americans as some of his predecessors had done. He published a pamphlet criticizing Henry Clay's speech defending slavery in March 1839. Gurney recommended steps to end slavery in the United States, beginning with its elimination in the District of Columbia. This pamphlet, *Free and Friendly Remarks . . . on the Subject of the Abolition of North American Slavery,* was written while Gurney was on Long Island, recuperating from an illness. He had caught a "violent cold" which "rapidly became inflammatory" in January 1839. He explained that he was "laid up, at the house of some beloved friends at Flushing, by an illness of full three months' continuance."[2]

Gurney's pamphlet attracted considerable attention and he decided to visit the West Indies to study the impact of Britain's experiment with emancipation. On his return to the United States, Gurney met with Henry Clay and John C. Calhoun to discuss his findings, and Clay urged him to publish his views. Gurney began his *Familiar Letters to Henry Clay of Kentucky, Describing a Winter in the West Indies* during ten days he spent in Flushing in June 1840; he finished it in Rhode Island while attending the New England Yearly Meeting of Friends. Gurney criticized American slavery in this book which was published in New York and London after he returned to England. American abolitionists welcomed Gurney's book and reprinted it in *The American Intelligencer, a Monthly Newspaper* in May 1841.[3]

Gurney had left England in July 1837, and returned to his home, Earlham Hall, in August 1840. After returning to England, he wrote *A Journey in North America, Described in Familiar Letters to Amelia Opie,* based on the journal he kept during his three-year visit. He traveled extensively along the eastern seaboard, to the mid-west and south, and in upstate New York and New England. In the sections relating to Long Island which are excerpted here, he describes the countryside, particularly in the village of Flushing where he stayed for more than three months. Like many of the earlier visitors, he comments on the agricultural yields of the farms, but he also describes clams and ducks. He visited Quakers in Jericho and

Westbury, and refers to Elias Hicks, Long Island's most famous Quaker, whose name is associated with a schism among Friends in 1827-1828 between the "Hicksite" and Orthodox Quakers.[4] Gurney observes that Americans not only used first names in referring to neighbors and friends, but often nicknames. He comments favorably on their "remarkable willingness to help each other," citing as an example a cooperative effort in moving a house in Flushing. Gurney also describes some of the Quaker public meetings where he preached.

After Gurney returned to England, he continued efforts in the antislavery movement and joined his sister, Elizabeth Fry, in her activities in support of prison reform. Within the Society of Friends, Gurney espoused Evangelicalism and his name became associated with a schism in the New England Yearly Meeting between the Gurneyites and Wilburites in 1845.[5]

* * *

I look back on my stay in Long Island, during the three first months of 1839, with no common feelings of interest. It was indeed a time of some suffering from bodily indisposition, but there was much in it both to instruct and to enjoy. The Friends under whose roof I was, are the parents of an interesting family; and both they and their children were ever ready to minister to my comfort.

The village of Flushing stands on the coast of a beautiful bay near the north-western extremity of the island, and within a drive of an hour and a half from Brooklyn, which, as thou wilt remember, is on the East river, immediately opposite to New York. It is remarkable for its bright and pleasant dwellings. Many of these are on either side of a broad road which runs up a hill, into a well-cultivated district of the country. At the foot of this hill was the house of my kind host and hostess, and at the top of it, the residence of another family greatly endeared to me in the ties of intimate friendship. . . .

I know of no part of the United States more carefully cultivated than the neighbourhood of that village. The farms—each under the care of its own proprietor—are in excellent order. The country is also well wooded; and peculiarly agreeable are the residences (for the most part white frame houses) which are scattered over the district. Some of these are occupied by members of the Hicksite community, from whom, during my illness, I received many kind attentions. Land fetches a high price—in the immediate neighbourhood of the town, it sometimes sells for £50 per acre. A proportion of it is cultivated in nursery grounds. Indian corn here produces from 80 to 100 bushels per acre; and I was assured that the profits of the farmer average a high percentage. The produce of one farm of 200 acres, the year before, was 7000 dollars, besides the living of the family; but from this gross sum the expense of labour was to be deducted.

One of the common productions of the waters of Long Island sound is a shell-fish, called the clam, which, like the oyster, is a common article of diet. During some violent gales, which took place about this time, a bank, composed of a large species of this mollusc, with which they feed the hogs and poultry, was suddenly formed within a few miles of us on the southern coast of the island. It was said to be twelve miles in length, and sixteen feet broad; but the farmers of the country soon carted away the prize. The hogs break the shells for themselves, and so feed upon their contents. In one of our excursions we observed some of the Brant ducks which frequent this coast. Their plumage is white, black, and grey intermingled, and their shape peculiarly elegant. They are curiously eager and active in their manners, and are caught on this island (I believe as a delicacy for the table) in their passage from the north to the southern states.

On the coast of the sound, near Flushing, stands a seminary, belonging to the Episcopal Church, and in high reputation. Dr. Muhlenburg there presides over about 100 pupils. I had much pleasure in calling upon him in the course of one of my rides. He is a person of superior powers and high character, and generously devotes the whole of his time and fortune to his favourite institution.[6] On another occasion I spent a few hours at the beautiful residence of George Douglas, a gentleman from Scotland, of great wealth and liberality, who, in consequence of his having been the nephew and heir of a certain baronet, goes, in Long Island, by the name of *Lord Douglas.*[7] He is a person of warm religious feelings, and kindly invited me to spend a fortnight at his house—an obliging offer which I was in no condition to accept. On the opposite side of the small bay near which his villa stands, is the equally lovely abode of a country judge, which I frequently visited—being always sure of there receiving all needful refreshment, together with the kindest welcome.

Though my friend Douglas is dignified with the title of lord, I was rather amused by observing, during my stay in Long Island, and on other occasions, that almost all persons in America are in the practice of calling their neighbours, just as Friends do, by their simple names; and, in the country, the Robert, Samuel, and Thomas, often degenerate into the Bobby, Sammy, and Tommy. Young and old, poor and wealthy, seem all very much on a level—a condition of society which is sometimes followed by undesirable consequences. It is, however, accompanied by a remarkable willingness to help each other. The loghouse in the wilderness is built by the joint exertion of all the settlers in the neighbourhood; and the same kind of co-operation is to be observed where society is more advanced. I remember witnessing the removal *en masse* of one of the small frame houses at Flushing. It was drawn along to its new site by eighteen yoke of oxen—each neighbour contributing his portion of the animals required. On all such occasions, every one is expected to put his own or his bullock's shoulder to the wheel; under the implied compact, that when his day of need comes, he will be sure to meet with the same assistance.

After I had become a prisoner at large, I made the most of the opportunities which our daily rides afforded me, of observing the face of nature, in America, during the very early spring. Many were the hours of bright sunshine which we enjoyed from day to day, and now and then a little genial warmth was to be felt. But the chief beauty of colouring was in the blue of the sky above, and of the sea below; not a speck of verdure was to be seen. Well do I remember the singular effect of the universal brownness of the land, on a bright warm day, near the close of the 3rd month (March) when, from a high barren hill, called Mount Misery, we were viewing the surrounding country, and the noble expanse, Long Island sound.[8] In a few weeks after this time, the whole country rapidly became verdant; but afterwards there was scarcely the least appearance of vegetation. The greenness of the fields in winter (when the snow melts) and in the early spring, is a charm which must be sought in our own country.

My indisposition, during these months, was not so severe as to prevent my giving up a small portion of the time to religious engagements. With my faithful friend and brother, who had so long been my companion, I completed by degrees a family visit to the Friends of Long Island, partly resident at Flushing, and partly at Westbury and Jericho, from fifteen to twenty miles to the east. In both places the society is small, but our quiet intercourse with its members was to us a source of comfort and satisfaction. A few meetings for worship were also held with the public at large, in some of the neighbouring villages. Jericho, which is one of these, was the residence of Elias Hicks, who there exercised his ministry, and obtained an almost unbounded influence over the Friends in his neighbourhood—the great majority having joined his ranks at the time of the division. The old meeting-house, which is now occupied by his followers, was freely opened for us; and great was the number of this people that flocked, with their neighbours, to a meeting which we there appointed. My feelings were somewhat singular when I found myself in the seat which this bold advocate of unbelief had so long occupied. The glorious truths of the gospel of Christ were then freely declared; and whatever might be the ultimate effect produced, it was evident that many of these dissentients parted from us, after

Westbury Friends Meeting, 1869

the meeting, in the feeling of tenderness and love. Nevertheless, experience proves that when once persons have been betrayed into the denial of "the Lord who bought them," recovery to a sound state in religion, becomes a most difficult process.

At a small village near Flushing, a wealthy and liberal member of the Hicksite community has built a "free church," with which we were kindly accommodated for one of our public meetings. It is a curious evidence of the easy working of things in America, that this building—raised at the expense of a person of views so opposite to those of the Church of England—is now lent to an episcopal clergyman, who there performs his weekly service. The owner of the church lives on the coast of the Sound, in a large and handsome mansion, where we lodged after the meeting, and where I often received benevolent attentions. . . .[A year later, Gurney returned to Long Island.]

In the course of this little journey [to New Jersey], I was again rather heavily indisposed, and was glad to retreat once more, for a few days, to my retirement at Flushing. I had, however, another object in visiting that place; for I had long believed that it would be my duty to hold a meeting with the inhabitants under the old oaks, there being no suitable place of worship in the village, large enough to accommodate the people.[9] It was now the middle of the Sixth month (June), and notice had been given of the meeting to be held at five o'clock in the afternoon of the following First day. Seats had been provided in the open air for about 1000 people. The day was windy and lowering; and as one dark cloud after another moved rapidly across the sky, I could not but feel considerable anxiety, especially as my powers of voice appeared to be at a low ebb. But just before five o'clock, the sky cleared, the wind abated, and a multitude of people were seen flocking to the spot—large numbers of the upper class, and many more of the labouring inhabitants of the district, including the coloured people, and Irish Roman Catholics. The mixed assembly soon settled into silence, and I was enabled to speak to them for upwards of an hour, so as to be heard by all present. We were reminded that God is "manifest in his Son," and great was the attention which prevailed on the occasion. After the offering of prayer, we again fell into silence; and the meeting concluded in much order and quietness. Immediately afterwards a slight shower fell, which, had it occurred a few minutes sooner, would have robbed the meeting of its best and most solemn moments. . . .

[June 1841] After spending the First day at New York, I was accompanied by a kind friend and brother to Long Island, and held a large public meeting for the first time in the city of Brooklyn, where a revival of religion was said to have lately done much towards increasing some of the congregations. Afterwards we again visited our friends of Westbury and Jericho on that Island; and convened the public at the neat prosperous little town of Hempstead, on its northern coast. We then returned to New York, and took the steam-boat one early morning for Amboy [New Jersey], on our way to Philadelphia.

Notes

Source: Joseph John Gurney, *A Journey in North America* (Norwich, England: Privately printed, 1841), pp. 263, 265-70, 284-85, 361 (Da Capo Press reprinted the *Journey* in 1973). Editing changes have been minor and limited to modernizing some of the punctuation. Gurney's English spellings (e.g., neighbour) have been retained.

1. Among the English Quakers who came to Long Island in the seventeenth century were George Fox, Robert Hodgson, Roger Gill, and Thomas Story. See "George Fox's Visit to Long Island, 1672" and Henry Onderdonk, Jr., "The Rise and Growth of the Society of Friends on Long Island and in New York City," reprinted in *"The People Called Quakers": Records of Long Island Friends, 1671-1703,* ed. Natalie A. Naylor (Interlaken, NY: Empire State Books, 2001), pp. 121-44. Women were also "public friends" and such missionary activities were often within America and to the West Indies. See Natalie A. Naylor, "Preface" in *"The People Called Quakers,"* pp. 14-15; Hugh Barbour et al., "The

Orthodox-Hicksite Separation," in *Quaker Crosscurrents: Three Hundred Years of Friends in the New York Yearly Meetings,* ed. Hugh Barbour, et al. (Syracuse: Syracuse University Press, 1995), pp 108-9; and (for early nineteenth century travelers), David E. Swift, *Joseph John Gurney: Banker, Reformer, and Quaker* (Middletown, CT: Wesleyan University Press, 1962), pp. 185-88.

2. Gurney, *Journey,* pp. 260, 261. Gurney does not name the family, but does indicate (in a passage omitted in these excerpts, on pp. 263-64) that the parents and daughter were in Santa Cruz in the West Indies because of the wife's illness. Their sons were Gurney's companions when he was able to leave the house (he uses the phrase "prisoner at large") and rode about the countryside on horseback. Gurney's host was Joshua Kimber, a Quaker schoolteacher. See James Driscoll, "Flushing in the Early Nineteenth Century," in *Angels of Deliverance: The Underground Railroad in Queens, Long Island, and Beyond* edited by Wini Warren (Flushing: Queens Historical Society, 1999), p. 91 n. 28, citing unpublished Parsons Diary, 2:168.

3. Swift, *Joseph John Gurney,* pp. 226-29, 288; Gurney, *Journey,* p. 407.

4. Elias Hicks (1748-1830) was born in Rockaway, but lived most of his life in Jericho. His home still stands on Old Jericho Turnpike in Nassau County's Jericho Preserve. See Bliss Forbush, *Elias Hicks: Quaker Liberal* (New York: Columbia University Press, 1956). Gurney discusses some of the doctrinal differences between the Hicksites and Orthodox in his *Journey,* pp. 249-51; see also Barbour, *Quaker Cross-Currents,* pp. 100-131.

5. The Wilburites were the smaller group, but the schism spread to New York. The Hicksite and Wilburite groups were not fully reunited until the 1950s. Biographical information on Gurney is from Swift, *Joseph John Gurney.*

6. William Augustus Muhlenberg (1796-1877), rector of St. George's Episcopal Church in Flushing, had founded a boy's academy, the Flushing Institute, in 1827. After a decade, he expanded it into St. Paul's College and Grammar School and moved it north to a location on Flushing Bay which he named College Point. Muhlenberg left to become pastor of the free Church of the Holy Communion in Manhattan in 1847, and the school did not survive. One legacy is the name of the Queens neighborhood, College Point, and St. Paul's did become a model for later Episcopal boarding schools. Muhlenberg later founded St. Luke's Hospital in New York City, the Sisterhood of the Holy Communion (Protestant nursing sisters), and St. Johnland in Kings Park, a Christian utopian industrial community which was the origin of St. Johnland Nursing Home. See Alvin Wilson Skardon, *Church Leader in the Cities: William Augustus Muhlenberg* (Philadelphia: University of Pennsylvania Press, 1971).

7. Douglas bought land in the area now known as Douglaston in 1835. The railroad named its station for his son, William P. Douglas, who was a vice-commodore of the New York Yacht Club which donated land to them. See Vincent Seyfried, "Douglaston," in *The Encyclopedia of New York City,* edited by Kenneth T. Jackson (New Haven: Yale University Press, 1995), p. 342.

8. Mount Misery is near Port Jefferson. Gurney included in a footnote a poem about the view which he probably wrote himself (p. 268).

9. George Fox, founder of the Quakers in England, visited Flushing in 1672, stayed in John Bowne's house, and preached outdoors under the nearby oak trees. Known as the "Flushing Oaks" or "Fox Oaks," they were well known in the Quaker community and one survived until 1863. See Naylor, *People Called Quakers,* pp. 121-25.

Personal Reminiscences of the South Side, 1839-1890s

Daniel M. Tredwell

Daniel M. Tredwell (1826-1921) did not publish his two-volume *Personal Reminiscences of Men and Things on Long Island* until he was in his eighties. However, he took much of the information verbatim from a journal he began in 1838. Several decades later, Tredwell began to prepare for publication selections from the more than a thousand pages of his journal and notes. Although we have not followed his format of using a smaller type size for his quotations from his journal, the italicized dates preceding or within entries identify and differentiate them from his comments several decades later (where he has often noted parenthetically the year at the turn of the century).

Tredwell was born on the family farm in Milburn and early developed an interest in books, history, anthropology, and natural history.[1] He attended the district school, Joshua Healey's school in Brooklyn, and graduated from the Hempstead Academy in 1845. After settling in Brooklyn a few years later, he read law, but it is uncertain whether he was ever admitted to the bar. Tredwell worked briefly as a hotel keeper and on a newspaper before taking a position in the Kings County Clerk's Office and became the Chief Clerk of the Supreme Court in Brooklyn. After he retired in 1894, he worked in the title business for the rest of his life. Tredwell came back home to Hempstead often during his first decades in Brooklyn and some of his writings describe his experiences on Hempstead Bay in those years.

Tredwell wrote a number of books before publishing his *Personal Reminiscences.*[2] He collected landscape and genre paintings, books on Long Island, the Civil War, and other subjects that interested him. (The subtitle of his *Monograph on Privately Illustrated Books* is *A Plea for Bibliomania.*) He was a member of numerous clubs and societies, including the American Ethnological Society (later the Anthropological Institute of New York), the Faust Club of Brooklyn (which gave a bust of John Howard Payne to Brooklyn's Prospect Park), the Philosophical Club of Brooklyn, and the Rembrandt Club of art collectors and critics. Tredwell was active throughout his life until he died at 95. A biographer summarizes the value of his *Personal Reminiscences:* "Its appeal lies in its vivid evocation of ordinary life in a landscape familiar yet utterly changed and in the detailed descriptions of long-vanished customs such as sheep-parting and marshing. Its informal tone and gossipy detail provide 'the charm of local history.'"[3]

The first section is from Tredwell's "Prefatory" chapter where he reflects a bit nostalgically on the many changes in his own lifetime. Tredwell does not present

Daniel M. Tredwell, 1912

his reminiscences as "history." He writes that they "are simply a collection of personal experiences of the author, with an account of the customs and traditions which have passed out of use and out of general recollection." Of particular interest are his accounts of a family picnic, sheep parting, harvesting salt hay (the "marshing season"), gunning ducks, and plover shooting. These activities were commonplace in his boyhood, but are unfamiliar to most in the twenty-first century. In his journal entries of his trip to Sag Harbor in 1843, we have a traveler's account of the village during its boom years. The final entry reprinted here involves Alden Spooner and the "State of Long Island." This amusing incident alludes to the serious mid-nineteenth century movement for Long Island to secede from New York to become its own state.

Many of the journal entries were written when he was in his teens and he added quotations from the town records about the history of events he described. Those historical entries are omitted here, as well as most of his scientific writings, but there is much more in his two volumes of interest to today's readers. Although Tredwell modestly asserts his reminiscences "may or may not have historical value," they certainly do provide us with valuable first-hand detail of the social history of Long Island in the nineteenth century.[4]

* * *

The distinction of classes [in the 1840s] was much less marked than at the present [c. 1900]. Domestic service was a friendly and intimate relation of equals. The soil smiled with plenty, the bays swarmed with fish and the coverts [thick underbrush] with game. But all this old civilization so dear to us has been most iniquitously supplanted by the tyrannous bustle of the up-to-date man. Sixty-eight trains pass and repass daily within a few hundred feet of the old homestead where we were born [in Milburn, now western Freeport], and a journey in these early days to the City of New York, which consumed two days, is now performed in a less number of hours. . . .

The simplicity and economy of the household in those days were of the most vigorous character. Breakfast was usually at six in the morning, always by candle light in winter, dinner at twelve, and supper at six. Evening visiting was a common social entertainment during the winter months, quilting parties and gatherings at which hickory nuts, apples, new cider, crullers and doughnuts were among the refreshments, and in some more pretentious gatherings, dancing was not uncommon. But by far the most popular were the evening tea parties, when both old and young could participate.

The clothing worn in winter was made from the wool raised on the farm. These garments were emphatically the product of the farm, from the raw material to the made-up garments. The surplusage of the wool or cloth was sold, stockings were made from the same material. Of all the phases of the wool industry, from the raw material to its consummation, none were more fascinating than the spinning into yarn the wool rolls. We have watched the work for hours, when a child, of our grandmother, her comeliness and grace, "beyond the reach of art," as she moved up and down, back and forth, erect and dignified, beside the big wheel, which she kept whirling with one hand and held the wool roll in the other, and watched the spindle take up the yarn; these things spell-bound us, and eighty years have not effaced them from our memory. It transcends all the skill of the most accomplished professor in the art of gracefulness, and all perfectly natural. She was our Ariadne.[5]

The flax from which summer clothing was made was also raised on the farm. It was pulled, the woody part rotted, crackled, hatcheled, spun, woven and made into garments on the premises. These methods were true of nearly all the clothing worn, bed sheets and table linen were made of the same material. The leather for shoes was made from the hide of the cattle slain in the fall for winter supply of food for the household. It was tanned at the village tannery and made into shoes by an itinerant shoemaker who lived with the family while engaged on the work. And hence (from the animals killed for food) came the candles for the winter supply of light manufactured by a very simple process and called dips.

There were many products of the farm which brought in a small revenue. All kinds of truck [vegetables] were raised for home consumption, the surplusage sold. The principal cereals raised for market were Oats and Corn for which there was always a demand at the stores, where they were taken in payment for goods. Cattle, sheep and hogs were fatted and sold to herdsmen who purchased for cash, on the hoof, and drove them to New York for slaughter.

Sheep Parting

The sheep parting in the fall is of historical interest. It was the great holiday of the times. Here rogues, thieves and bullies congregated, creditors came in quest of debtors, dealers and traders of all kinds advertised their wares, horses were swapped and scrub races had; betting, gambling, drinking and fighting were in the order of the day's entertainment. To counteract these numerous evils, the town enacted a law that there should be no tavern or selling of liquor at the pens.

Tuesday, October 15, 1839. Went with father this day to the sheep parting to bring home our sheep that had been turned out on the plains last spring. The Hempstead Plains is one of the most marked features of Long Island. This tract of territory, being sixteen miles in length and containing sixty-four square miles, has a prairie-like appearance, and it is the common pasturage ground for the town of Hempstead. . . .

There seems to be no good reason why so many people should congregate at the Sheep Parting, except like sheep, one goes because another goes. It took place on the open Hempstead plains a little southwest from Westbury. Permanent pens had been erected upon the ground in which to confine the sheep while they were being reclaimed, otherwise there was not a structure, shed, tree or particle of shelter of any kind upon the territory proper on which this omnivorous fair was held except the temporary booths and tents erected by tradesmen and showmen.

There was a vast number of people gathered at this bleak and uninviting spot, summing up into the thousands. To natives of Queens County who had resided long from home, sheep parting and camp meeting were occasions to meet and greet old acquaintances, reunions not that they had either sheep or religious purposes to serve, but a fairly excusable object, the social. Everybody went to sheep parting and camp meeting. But with a large percentage, sheep parting was simply made the occasion for a great frolic of the masculine persuasion. The number of those who came for the ostensible purpose of the fair, or sheep parting, was comparatively small, and they generally transacted their business and went home; the fun followed. All the princes in small gambling were there, from Sam Wait and Nick Searing, with their sweat-cloths, to New York thimble riggers and experts at three card monte, and a limited number of representatives from the light-fingered fraternity.

In eatables and drinkables the commissariat was ample for any contingency. Patty Ann Wright was there with cake, gingerbread and vivant beer; oysters, watermelons by the wagon load. There was hot corn, a traffic monopolized by the darkey, and served with scrupulous neatness.

Among the amusements there was a troop of lofty tumblers, clowns, harlequins and pantaloons, whose wit and flexible bodies were marvelous exhibits.

But the most attractive, best patronized and most creditable sporting feature of the fair was the dancing, foot-racing, leaping and wrestling matches. These sports were carried on with order and decency by persons who were lovers of athletics. This was by far the most manly and respectable feature of the show. Officers of the law maintained order.

The fat woman who weighed four hundred pounds, more or less, and the skeleton man who weighed only sixty pounds, less or more—the former in a tent, the latter in a covered wagon. The purveyors of the two last itinerant marvels of human phenomena stood at the doors of their respective institutions proclaiming in Thrasonic [boastful] voices the merits of their *products.* All for one shilling. The above by no means exhausts the bill of fare.

It now being near the fall election, the politicians also made sheep parting the occasion for putting their goods on the market, and ventilated their righteous purposes of reform and expose the rascality of the other side. (A matter susceptible of easy proof.) A little outside of the main show ground, or aside from the sheep pens and on another part of the field, a stand had been erected by the Whigs on which was displayed a large poster, "Opposed to Selling the Marshes and Plains." Year after year propositions had been made, plans submitted and voted upon at town meetings, and committees appointed for dividing the common lands of the town, all of which, for reasons, failed in fruition, but it was nevertheless made a campaign issue when its agitation was likely to affect the popular vote. Not more than two hundred feet distant from the stand was another platform erected by the Democrats. At these two stands were holding forth respectively William McNeil and Bernardus Hendrickson and other local spoilsmen upon the great national questions of the day and the merits of their party candidates for the November election.

Some go to sheep parting for business, some for social intercourse, more for fun. The programme of entertainment is so extempore, varied and impulsive that one who goes for coarse fun can hardly fail of finding some agreeable comedy or comic tragedy. The ostensible purpose of sheep parting, originally participated in only by farmers, was to collect their sheep, which had been corralled by the keepers, and drive them home to house them for the winter, and fully and particularly set forth in the acts of the General Assembly of the people. . . .[6]

Family Picnic at Long Beach

Tuesday, July 26, 1842. Went yesterday on our annual family picnic to Long Beach. We were conveyed from the landing in the small boats of Daniel Smith, Samuel Tredwell and Daniel Tredwell to the head of Long Creek, where we embarked on a large sloop belonging to Daniel Smith. The company consisted of the families of Thomas Tredwell, John Tredwell, Daniel Tredwell, Samuel Tredwell, Benjamin Tredwell, Daniel Smith and Lester Bedell, consisting of fifty-one persons, representing three generations. We sailed down Long Creek to the beach, where we arrived at 9:30 o'clock and moored the sloop in deep water close to the bank, where we could walk to the shore on a gangplank. We roamed over the beach, bathed in the surf and swam in the still water. Some of our party gathered clams for a clambake. Everybody was enjoying himself generally. Dinner, which had been provided by each family, was served in common on the deck of the sloop under shelter of the mainsail spread over the deck as an awning. The dinner was the great feature of the day. All kinds of good things had been prepared and everybody had a good appetite. Cheer after cheer went up as dish after dish of chicken salad and pan after pan of baked beans were brought upon the table.

After dinner we took another stroll on the beach and at six o'clock got under way for home with the early flood [i.e., incoming tide]. The sail home was delightful, and we ventured outside New Inlet until we felt the ocean ground swell; when some of the women complained of sea sickness, we returned.

The wind was light; the weather perfect. Our progress homeward was slow and tedious; we did not arrive until after dark. The small boats were dispensed with on our return; it being now high tide, the sloop came up to the dock of Samuel Tredwell's landing, where wagons were in waiting to carry us home. Everybody had a good time, got sunburned, and the old folks and the children were very tired. Thus ended a very pleasurable day, a kind of family reunion, which will be repeated again next year, as it has been continued from immemorial time. . . .

The Customs of the Marshing Season

Foreword. Like the great plains, the marshes were the common lands of the Town of Hempstead. The marsh privileges were considered a great inducement to settlers. Sheep parting and marshing were institutions peculiar to Long Island, and so far as we know were unique.

On the south shore of Long Island, between the upland and the beach, or ocean, is a tract of meadow, or marsh land, consisting of about 50,000 acres, of which about 22,000 acres lie in Queens County and about 8,300 acres in the Town of Hempstead.

From the earliest history of the town efforts have been made to divide the common lands of the Town of Hempstead, consisting of the plain lands and these marshes, pro rata among the freeholders of the town. These efforts for various reasons have failed in fruition. . . .[7]

This tract of marsh land is perfectly level and is interspersed by creeks running in every conceivable direction, and being of every conceivable degree of crookedness, width and depth. A large portion of this tract of meadow produces a salt grass very healthful for cattle and sheep. And it being common land of the town, any townsman may harvest as much as he pleases, with only the restriction as to the time for the commencement of cutting. At the town meeting, or spring election, it was resolved by the good people of the town *viva voce* that the cutting of the marshes shall commence on a named day, usually Tuesday after the second Monday in September. Consequently, on the day previous, or the second Monday in September, the inhabitants go in their boats to locate a patent, or in other words, to select a desirable piece of grass not yet selected by any other person; but no one is permitted to cut until sunrise on Tuesday, under the penalty of the law. The cutting of hay on these marshes commenced early in the history of the English settlers, but the first act appearing on the records of the town regulating the cutting was on July 5, 1667. . . .[8]

From this time on, many acts were passed at the town meeting regulating the cutting of grass and many other matters concerning the marshes, until nearly one hundred years later, we find the . . . fully defined enactment on the town records [in 1761, confirmed in 1765]. . . . At every town meeting some enactment was passed regulating the cutting of grass on the marshes. The last act contained in the extant records of the Town of Hempstead was passed August 7, 1775.[9] It was merely confirmatory of former acts.

There is an unwritten common law among these honest people that the person first locating on a tract of marsh signified by setting up a rake, a pitchfork, a grindstone, or other device, has undisputed right to occupy against all subsequent comers. This right is never questioned.

My father had located a cluster of islands on Shell Creek, better known as Mud Hole Hassock. These patents were about three and a half miles from our landing place on the mainland. The landing place was private, belonging to our family, and we consequently escaped the ill consequences of common dockage and common curing ground. Such was the scarcity and so great the demand for curing ground that the highway commissioners were petitioned to set aside a piece of public ground for that purpose, which they did as a free spreading ground [1762].[10]

The grass when cut was brought in boats (large farmers had scows which would carry ten ordinary boat loads) to the mainland, usually the same day that it was cut, for a storm or a spring tide might carry it all away. Here it was spread out on upland to cure, and when cured it was removed to the barnyard and stacked, the cattle and sheep generally having access to it during the winter. They did not, however, eat much of it; it was very salt[y]. They enjoyed a little of it as a relish only. Milch cows were kept away from it, as it was said to dry up their milk.

This sedge hay harvest, or marshing, as it was called, was a season of hard work, but not without its pleasures. It was extremely healthful work. There were some who cut this hay to sell, and we believe it was sold at a profit. Farmers living out of the town who kept a large stock of cattle were generally the customers who purchased it. A two-horse load after it was cured would fetch about twelve or fifteen dollars. Some of the larger farmers who wintered a great deal of stock cut large quantities of this hay and had many men in their employ during the sedge harvest. Such usually constructed temporary huts or shelters of considerable dimensions on the marsh during this season. In these rude structures they slept, generally taking their meals in the open air, one of their number usually doing the cooking and preparing the meals. The cook was generally the greatest crank in the gang. He had a weakness for his profession and was always ventilating his peerless qualities as a caterer.

Eels, hard and soft shell clams, crabs and fish being obtainable in great quantities in the waters of the immediate creeks and bays, the farmers and their hands lived pretty generally upon these products, sometimes, however, indulging in the luxury of such game as snipe and duck. There was a great variety of game birds frequenting the waters and marshes of this part of Long Island, as the plover, canvasback duck, yellow leg snipe, marlin and others of the tribe, teal or brant.

Many of the plain countrymen are genuine sporting men of the old school, famous for coolness, unassuming and who do not in the fullness of experience claim entire immunity from nervousness in extreme cases, as a prolonged struggle with a twelve-pound sheepshead with a six-ounce rod and an ordinary trout line, and whose nerves do sometimes threaten *anesthesia* in looking into a flock of yellow leg snipe or marlin along the barrels of his fowling piece, but they never miss their game.

We recall with great pleasure the incidents of the nine days spent in the marshing camp, during which period we slept on the marsh, ate eel and clam

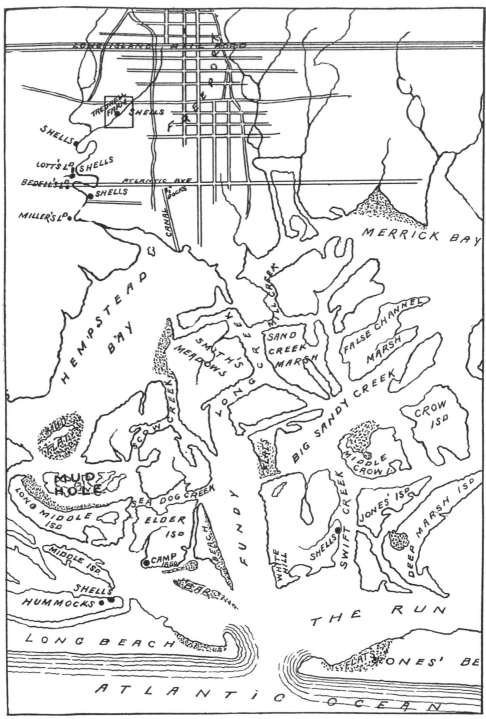

Map of Hempstead Bay and vicinity, c. 1850. The Tredwell farm is shown
in the upper left-hand corner, south of the railroad tracks. Mud Hole, the
site of the 1842 camp, is almost directly south.

chowder and smothered flounders, or fluke, with the mess. The methods of cooking were probably healthful, but not calculated to inspire the greatest enthusiasm for its classical neatness, or immaculate cleanliness, nor its conformity with the revised code of *Brillat Savarin.*[11]

Our *chef de cuisine* was phenomenal in science and artifice; one iron pot rendered service for boiling, stewing, roasting and for a variety of other purposes. The plates used were of pewter, spoons of the same material. Elegance and formality were not distinguishing characteristics of these camp meals, but they were served and eaten with an abundance of that appetizing sauce called in the old adage "hunger." Ovid observed that even the fingers could be used with grace at meals.

The vividness and detail with which our memory recalls, after a lapse of nearly fifty years, the small incidents of the old institution and its customs, all now passed into the realm of dreams, is an evidence of the deep impression made upon us and the intensity with which we enjoyed them. We believe many farmers looked forward with pleasure to the marshing season, as a relief to the monotony of their lives. They made a picnic of it. All is now passed and oblivion is fast closing over even the memory of these interesting local institutions.[12]

Monday, September 5, 1842. . . . According to a long-established custom, our gang were on the ground at Mud Hole Hassock early on Monday (this) morning and took possession of these hassocks under a ceremony very much like that under which Hendrick Hudson took possession of the Island of Manhattan, not, however, by the erection of our flag, but by the more significant symbols of putting up a rake in one place, a pair of cock-poles in another, our residence and grindstone in another, thus giving notice to the world that our claim was by prior discovery and would be defended against all or any subsequent claimant.

As no sedge could be cut on Monday, except for erecting huts, or some such necessary purpose, the day was spent in preparation, grinding scythes, mending rakes, etc. First, a hut or shelter was erected, and all hands were set to work in its construction. The site selected was on Shell Creek and which had been occupied for the past twenty-five years for the like purpose. There is no high ground on these marshes, but our home site was a trifle higher than the surrounding marsh, made so to some extent by the accumulations incident to occupancy. The soil, and consequently the vegetation, had changed in immediate proximity to our habitation. The vegetation was in a transition state and was already beginning to give evidence of upland tendencies, and a resemblance to fresh water products. All this greatly relieved the monotonous landscape.

A hardy shrub with strong woody fibre had taken possession of a little knoll around our hut and extended its sheltering branches over the less hardy aliens which from accident or selection had invaded our little plot. It is marvelous how soon after being rendered possible by leeching and bleaching that upland plants appear in favored spots on these marshes to the exclusion of all saline types.

Our household consisted of five men and myself, and accommodations, although necessarily the most primitive, must be provided for their protection from storms and for comfortable sleeping quarters. In fine weather we would be expected to take our meals in the open air. One of our gang took charge of the preparation of meals and the cooking, and the quantities of food consumed by these five men was truly astounding, although a large portion of our food was prepared on the mainland, such as bread, navy hard bread, pies, cooked ham, baked beans and many others; vegetables were cooked in camp; also clams, fish, eels and birds were served daily. We had an abundant supply of fruit and melons.

Everything now being in readiness for the opening of the season tomorrow, Tuesday, supper was served, and after smoking their pipes the men turned in and in a few minutes were sleeping as soundly as played-out children.

The novelty of the situation drove sleep from us, and after seeking in vain to sleep, thinking into forgetfulness, we crept silently out into the open air. It was a magnificent night. The moon and stars were reflected in flickering zig-zag lines upon the rippling waters. A slight mist like a curtain hung motionless over the distant creeks, but the solitude was painful. Now and then we were startled by the metallic cackle of a meadow hen or the muffled quack of a sheldrake. Otherwise it was the silence of death, save the ceaseless roll of the ocean.

Tuesday, September 6, 1842. The men were on hand at sunrise with a determination to send a freight of grass on shore on the morning flood tide, it being high water a little after ten o'clock, but alas, on the first stroke with the scythe, it was evident that we must suspend in consequence of the snails, the *Melampus-bidentatus.* These little creatures, not more than a quarter of an inch long were on the grass in countless millions and absolutely prevented the men mowing. They have a tough hard shell and in one stroke of the scythe its edge must necessarily come in contact with thousands—no scythe could endure it. This initial trouble was a little mollusc, an air-breathing animal with true lungs, whose habitat was in the mud at the roots of the sedge grass. He is emphatically a saline creature, but he is wonderfully fond of a little fresh water, and in the morning when the dew is on he ascends the stalk to get the pearly drop suspended on the tip of the sedge leaf, and in such vast numbers are these tiny creatures and so simultaneous are their movements that they would defeat any effort of the mower to cut through them.

Operations must therefore be suspended awaiting their pleasure; from this there was no appeal. However, they soon completed their pilgrimage, for having captured the coveted crystal drop, they descend to their mud homes and in half an hour the grass was entirely free of them. The mowers then went at the work with a will, and in less than two hours had cut sufficient grass for a freight and had commenced loading our transport with the hay, and at nine and a half o'clock our first freight was afloat on its way to the landing.

Wednesday, September 7, 1842. At nine o'clock this morning our transport was again freighted and on its way to the mainland, it being our intention to send two freights today, one on the morning flood and another on the afternoon. After the return of our boat she was again freighted and sent to the landing, this being the second freight today.

Thursday, September 8, 1842. It was very foggy this morning and our boat returned late, but was immediately freighted and sent on shore. In this manner the time passed, shipping one load a day, oftener two, except Sunday.

On Sunday, September 11th, we made an excursion to the Long Beach. Long Beach is about eight miles long, a continuous exchange of sand dunes and ocean strand [beach]. And we have heard people say that this stretch of seaboard was a bleak, dreary and unattractive waste. To this we beg to demur. It must be admitted, however, that the first impression of the landscape is barrenness, which instead of being dissipated, is probably intensified by the sparse vegetation of coarse stargrass, with here and there a sunny patch of wild flower in yellow and red. The star-grass, "Marrum" or sea mat, the roots of which penetrated to a depth of thirty feet in search of moisture, is a great protection to the dunes and to a great extent preserves the form and durability of the hills. In some localities on our sea coast where the sand is invading the upland, the artificial cultivation of marrum has stayed the invasion and large tracts of valuable land have been saved.

We differ from those who see no beauty in the beach landscape. As a whole, the strand, the dunes and the associated marsh to us is a landscape of unparalleled attractiveness. There is something restful and soothing in its silence and stillness. No sound save that of the monotonous old ocean upon the shingled beach in front of the sand hills, and the ceaseless cry of the sea gull performing its graceful evolutions overhead, now and then a snipe; but notwithstanding all this, the aggregate effect is solitude.

The eye cannot penetrate the length of these dunes westward. They melt into the horizon and their magnitude is intensified with an endless variety of form. These sand hills have an individuality. They are unlike any other hills. They are miniature mountain ranges, as unstable as the waves of the ocean beating at their base. They encircle deep and watered valleys, having a soil and healthful vegetation. As we stand on one of the greatest elevations facing westward, on our immediate right (the north) the white sand shades down insensibly by increased vegetation into the green landscape of the marsh with no sharp line of demarcation between beach and marsh. Next beyond to the north comes the West Run, a wide deep passage of water, like a trunk canal; it distributes all the waters of the floods and ebbs running west from and east to New Inlet. Farther still to the right, about one mile distant, by the aid of a field glass our camp is distinctly made out. Our boat that went on shore last night is just returning and will be ready for another freight tomorrow.

On the other side, the left, is the strand and the ocean, and here was a scene difficult to describe, but of unsurpassing interest. We counted within eye range from west to east sixty-four sailing vessels, sloops and schooners, coasters belonging to the various ports of the south side of Long Island, some going to, others returning from, New York and places on the Hudson. Farther out on the ocean there were within sight at the same moment eleven square-rigged ocean-going craft, some just completing their maybe long and tempestuous voyage, others outward bound.

There was a good full-sail breeze blowing from the westward and it was interesting to watch the change in position of the westward bound coasters. It was like a vast regatta. They were obliged to beat; one tack, "the long leg," would be off shore, and "the short leg" on shore. On the on-shore tack, some of them would stand close enough inshore so that we could hear the man in the jib sheets call out "let her come," or "hellum down" when in his judgment they were close enough inshore for safety, and this vast procession lasted until in the afternoon. As some passed out of sight in the distance others came in, until about five o'clock the whole coast was cleared, not a boat in sight save those entering our port. It seemed that the ocean had engulfed them, but that was not so. The weather outlook was threatening and they had prudently sought shelter in the side ports of Long Island. . . .

Monday, September 12, 1842. At six A.M. we were afloat with rod and gun to make a day for weakfish in Scow Creek, and peradventure any winged creature that may venture within our range. Weather fair, wind S.E.

Returned with fifteen pounds of weakfish and an empty gun. During the entire nine days of this picnic the weather was remarkably fine. We had but one short storm, many fogs, and among the casualties worthy of mention one was the sinking of our boat with a freight of hay on. It happened in this wise: We were getting ready to go on shore with a freight; a strong wind was blowing from the northwest and flood tide was making from the southeast. The boat was unmoored from the bank; before her crew were ready the tide swung her around against the strong wind, and between the two forces, wind and tide, acting in counter directions, she careened over, filled with water and sank. She was immediately towed to shallow water and unloaded. By this accident one trip was lost. The other casualty was the loss of a dinner through the stupidity of our cook. He upset two and a half gallons of clam chowder into the fire, putting out the fire, putting out the chowder, and seriously putting the workmen out of temper, who were obliged to satisfy their hunger upon hardtack, red herring and a short allowance of beans.

The second marshing week was enlivened by an affair in the bay which might have ended in a tragedy. It had been a custom from immemorial time for vessels, sloops and schooners, to lay at anchor in Long Creek with a clam basket up in the shrouds—a signal that they were there for trafficking in clams and would purchase, with cash, all that were brought to them. This was all legitimate, providing the sloops and schooners belonged to the ports of the South Side, and that those who caught and offered the clams for sale were inhabitants of the town. . . .[13]

Yesterday, September 13th, when the South Bay was swarming with a population of hay gatherers, a large strange schooner from New Jersey came into New Inlet, sailed up Long Creek and came to anchor opposite Skow Creek. Soon after she hoisted her basket, thus declaring her errand and soliciting trade of the native baymen. (The news immediately spread among the marshers that the strange vessel was a pirate.) This was an aggravated case, inasmuch that she came with six crews for clamming, all fully equipped with the latest contrivances of rakes and tongs preparatory for stealing a cargo of clams, and should no resistance be offered to do so peaceable, but forceably if necessary.

On learning these facts the trustees were notified and they proceeded this morning to enforce the law. They visited the schooner, followed by a long train of baymen in their boats and a whole fleet of marshmen. The trustees demanded that the schooner, being engaged in an unlawful traffic, immediately depart from these waters. To this demand the captain bluntly refused to comply, declaring that he had entered the port in stress of weather for water and provisions, that he "knew his rights and would maintain them by force against a gang of land pirates if necessary." This was impolitic language, and he was instantly informed by the indignant marshers and baymen that he had an option of leaving in thirty minutes, or they would burn his vessel. He still hesitated and wished to debate his rights, but when they proceeded to carry out their threat, he then hauled down his basket and was out of the inlet in an hour.

The captain of this schooner had a crew of about twenty men, which was force enough on any ordinary occasion to defy or overcome the South Side authorities with their immediately available force, or put out to sea at any moment when danger threatened. But he had made a mistake in coming into the bay during the marshing season. He had run unwittingly into a complete ambush.

The people of Hempstead had suffered too long these thieving incursions without redress to allow this one now in their power to escape without at least some healthful admonitions. No overt act had been committed, no clams had been taken by these foreigners; had there been, they would undoubtedly have been confiscated. The prompt and determined action of the marshers turned the threatened bloody tragedy of the New Jersey captain into a one-act comedy.

Saturday, September 17, 1842. Today we pulled up stakes for good. During all this marshing season the duty had been imposed upon us of supplying the camp with fish and fowl. We were complimented by the gang for our success in that department, with a chilling rejoinder from the cook, who had a contempt for our marksmanship, that he had never known game furnished at such reckless cost of materials. We did not, however, expect much from the cook, for unpacific relations had existed between us from the beginning, in consequence of our kindly suggesting the use of more soap in the kitchen economy.

The hired men, however, were not very particular in their tastes, and it was a merciful dispensation that they were not. When the Scotch hostess seized the cap from the head of one of her boys and boiled a pudding in it for Sam Johnson's dinner she made the most of her resources, and we will charitably think that our cook did his best with his limited means.

And now after all is over, so agreeably has the time passed that we do not realize that we have been away at all, but have passed through a hazy day-dream with no recognition of time. The greatest pleasures of life are probably those which come unsought, and the delicious unexpected compromise of idleness with labor was all disguised in agreeable results. The hustle and bustle immediately preceding the departure of our consignment of hay for the mainland and the delicious inactivity as we watched the product of our labor glide from its moorings and with a brisk south wind and a strong flood tide speed along Skow Creek toward its destination to add one more load to our acquisitions, was indeed a pleasurable leisure.

There are no delightful landscapes of forest and lawn embraced in these common lands to enamour the lover of bower and shade, but these marshes present a charming vista of hazy beauty unlike anything else in nature. And the creeks, the waterways, are labyrinthian and present novelties at every turn unknown to the most noted rivers of the world. . . .

Saturday Night at Milburn Corners [and Shooting Ducks on the Bay]

Saturday, November 19, 1842. Every Saturday night was market night, and there was a general gathering of the people of the Neck at the corner (now Milburn Corners) [Baldwin/Freeport]. We were greatly entertained last evening at the store of Tredwell & Frost (Milburn) in hearing some of the old veteran baymen and gunners, gathered about the store and occupying available soap boxes and barrel heads, relate experiences of great catches, great shots and wonderful flights of water fowl.

Ad Carman and Dick Smith made their boasts that they had cut down teal flying over White Hill point of marsh before a northwest gale at fifty yards distant seven times out of ten, and Dick Verity, with sinful sarcasm, offered to put up the bullion that he would bring home more birds than both of them by taking his chances on those which they missed. There was no reconciling some of their travestied statements, nor was there any happy middle ground or average on which to repose between their extremes—not falsehoods, but sarcasms. All were agreed, however, that the old veteran, Raynor Rock, at birds on the wing in rapid flight, was the most reliable shot on Long Island. Uncle Ben Raynor was as good as the best of them in his day, and Ira Pettit, of Christian Hook [Oceanside], had had an enviable reputation, now far past his prime. John Bedell thought he could average up with any of them now.

All this conversation was provoked by the introduction of the fact that Thomas Carman of Hick's Neck [Baldwin] had at some time previous killed thirty-four black ducks by one discharge of his fowling piece. This statement, as extraordinary as it may appear, was too well attested to be disputed. It created quite a sensation at the time. The Long Island newspapers and the city papers commented upon it, but some credulous people doubted it. Thomas Carman was an entirely trustworthy man and his word may be relied upon, and he vouches for its truth. We well remember the event, but cannot now give the date. The explanation, however, going with the statement being that the ducks were caught in a rift of the thin ice which was gradually closing as the two bodies of ice moved up with the flood tide, until in direct range from Carman's blind, and his shot raked the entire flock.

These baymen never used double barrelled guns, but carry two single barrels, and after discharging one into a flock, put the other in commission to take the rising birds. In this case Carman seized his other gun, but no birds arose; he had killed the whole flock, but it was found on examination that six of the birds had been drowned under the ice, where they dove after being wounded. This kind of entertainment is not of the true sporting man's hankering; it is wholesale slaughter.

The refinement and glory of a sportsman is not wanton destruction of life; genuine sporting is an inherited and humane accomplishment, and a man must be born to it as certain as he must be born a poet. A man may be taught to make a hole as wide as a barn door in a flock of ox-eye snipe and gather half a bushel of birds as a result or reward of his contingent luck shot, or he may wing-break a half-starved pigeon sprung from a trap fifteen or twenty yards off; but to stop a vigorous and healthy teal cutting through the keen frosty air of autumn, at daybreak, at the rate of eighty miles an hour, or to get a bead on a frightened woodcock as he flashes through the opening of a thicket of underbrush, entitles a man to a seat among the elders. It takes an eye, a hand and a heart which science cannot create. "It is born," says Squire Bob Akeley. "Reading and writing are inflictions of the schoolmaster, but a crack shot is the work of God."

Among the shooting legends of Long Island, one was related of a Bellport sportsman slaying one hundred and six yellow leg snipe sitting on the beach by discharging both barrels into them. But Mr. [John James] Audubon, the great naturalist, once condoned such an offense. He says he was present when one hundred and twenty red breasted snipe were killed by discharging three barrels into an enormous flock of them.

Many were the marvelous feats of powder and shot related by these amphibious, tarpaulin-skinned baymen, whose sense of humor is as keen as their instincts in hunting. And their adroitness in turning the statements of another into ridicule was unique and racy, but their wit and sarcasm were shown to the best advantage in describing the presumptuous methods of a city Nimrod in taking wild fowl.

The subsistence and being of these people is with the bay. It pervades their entire lives, and when they are not engaged in gunning, or in talking and speculating upon spring flights of snipe, autumn arrivals of sea fowl, nor dissertating upon marvelous hoardes of wild pigeons, then they were either fishing or talking of fishing, at which latter they were equally expert.

It is not always a salutary subject with South Siders, but we venture the statement generally that the most successful gunner and fisher is not infrequently tainted with Algonkin [Algonquian, i.e., Indian] blood.

Hecatombs of sea fowl, willet, marlin, curlew and plover, have fallen victims to the pleasure and profit of these craftsmen.

It was the verdict of the audience at the store that ordinary duck shooting was failing; nothing short of twenty-five or thirty birds could be considered a successful day's work, and in the season, which is short, there are at least two hundred and fifty professionals hunting, and twice that number of amateurs, on the south side of Long Island alone. The birds are getting scarce, but man pursues them from Florida to Maine on their migration, during which time they are constantly under fire. Annihilation is already in sight.

We may safely say that where we have seen the South Bay alive with web-footed denizens, there is not at this time (1880) one where there were thousands. When Thomas Carman, Floyd Smith and Dick Verity would take a skiff load of coot, duck and sheldrake in a day, their great-grandsons, with all the latest and most modern equipments of destruction, would have a struggle to bag (this is a modern invention; it took the place of the wheelbarrow as a game receptacle) enough for Sunday dinner, and still growing rarer. Within the memory of men now living, over fifty varieties of ducks frequented Long Island; now there are not half that number.

We have seen the November air thick with wild pigeons, so many that it was neither sport nor profit to shoot them. To the present generation of Hempstead South the wild pigeon is (1880) unknown, except the dressed and cooked variety. And the change was brought about chiefly by the rapacity and indiscretion of man. Of a frosty morning in the fall of 1846 we have seen the woods of John Tredwell and William Bedell swarm with wild pigeons. There were millions of them. In 1863 there were none worthy of mention, and in 1880 specimens for naturalists could with difficulty be obtained. Of birds, few existed in the State of New York in such numbers as the wild pigeon, and none have become extinct so quickly. It is now entirely a creature of the past. . . .[14]

Trip to Sag Harbor

Thursday, July 20, 1843. It now being our vacation, we were informed that some business of a family nature was to be transacted at Sag Harbor and that the option of this mission was offered to us, and it would be necessary to leave tomorrow (July 20th).

Today we were driven to Merrick, about five miles from Hempstead on the turnpike, to intercept the Sag Harbor mail stage, which leaves Brooklyn every Thursday morning at 9 A.M. At 2:30 P.M. the stage arrived at Merrick at Hewlett's Corner, opposite the residence of Doctor Wheeler. The stage was full, but room was made for us on top with the driver. From Merrick to Amityville the distance is about six miles (we get the distances from the stage driver). The road was very dusty. On reaching Amityville two passengers got out at South Side Hotel, which enabled us to get a seat inside. This was more enjoyable than the outside in the sun, and we took our book out to read, but the attractions of the country were much greater than the book. It is a singularly interesting piece of country; its contiguity to the ocean is the attractive feature. And then we had a traveling companion who took a great deal of pains to make himself ridiculous in relating his marvelous traveling experiences; he had visited many countries, and did all the talking, his hearers the thinking. During the afternoon we had a glorious shower, which laid the dust and made the traveling more agreeable. We arrived at Babylon at 6:30 P.M. Here we put up for the night at Carll's Hotel, Main Street.

Babylon (Sunguam's Neck) is a thriving village, with a general air of business pervading it. The people get up early and appear to have something to do, and set themselves about to do it.

Friday, July 21, 1843. We were called for an early start this morning and we left without breakfast. Our tedious and loquacious companion left us at Babylon and the last we saw of him he was disputing with a local hackman about fare to a certain place due north from Babylon, the hackman contending that the distance was fifteen miles, our traveled friend insisting with all the force of geographical facts on his side, that you can't go due north, or south, from any point on Long Island fifteen miles without driving off; that's where we left him.

The rain of yesterday made the ride of this morning delightful. The distance to Islip was five miles and we had a constant view of the Great South Bay and ocean beyond, and the distance was soon gone over. No stop was made at Islip except to water horses and leave the mail. We were soon on the road to Patchogue (Porchog), a distance from Islip of eleven miles, and nearly all the way in full sight of the ocean and an endless expanse of sand hills, going through Bayshore and Sayville, both thriving looking and well groomed little places. At Patchogue, which we reached at about 10 A.M., we took breakfast and changed horses.

Patchogue was named from a tribe of Indians who made it their headquarters. It is a lively little town of about seven hundred inhabitants with a number of hotels and some manufactories. Its greatest merit being that it is located upon the great thoroughfare from Brooklyn to Sag Harbor, and several other stage lines. It has two important business streets, Main Street and Ocean Avenue, and it has a considerable coasting traffic. Two of our company left here, and one got on. After breakfast we started for the next stopping place, Fire Place [Brookhaven hamlet]. Did not stop at Bellport, a much more important place, but a little off the road.

Fire Place, formerly Connetquot, was distant from Patchogue nine miles, where we arrived at 3 P.M. One of our passengers left here. After leaving the mails for Fire Place, St. George's Manor [Manorville] and Mastic, we proceeded on to Moriches. Fire Place is a small hamlet of six or eight private houses, a hotel, church and schoolhouse, the rest being mills. It is a tidy looking place nestled among willows and on the edge of a great forest, a charming place for retirement, or a recluse. Moriches is distant six miles over a territory where the leading impression is barrenness and sand. We arrived at 3 P.M., left the mail, changed horses and were off again for Quogue (also called Quanquanantuck)[15] . . . a distance of eight miles, where we arrived at 8 P.M. and remained all night. Just before we reached Quogue we struck a strong southeast wind loaded with moisture; it set us shivering.

Saturday, July 22, 1843. Had an early breakfast and were off again before sunrise, while the lighthouse at Shinnecock Point was yet flashing its rays. Our next stopping place will be Southampton, a random village built along a wide street two miles long called Main Street. It is distant nine miles from Quogue. Southampton has a reputation and a history. The travel today was slow; the road was heavy, but we had no dust. The landscape was interesting, but a desert of sand, with a few green patches to relieve it. It was a chromo landscape. A short stop only was made at Southampton and we hurried on to Bridgehampton, a distance of six miles, over which we passed without incident, except a little hamlet, ironically called a centre of civilization, through which we passed, but did not stop. We were, however, in review of the entire population of men, women and dogs. From the glances we obtained of the motley crowd should say that they were of that class of the human family called primitive. We did not see a pair of shoes among them; they were all barefoot and nearly bareback, and appear to have solved the great philosophy of Diogenes, "getting along without things."

A short stop at Bridgehampton; we then pass tract after tract of territory marked on the school geography barren, and arrived at Sag Harbor at 4 P.M. Sag Harbor is indebted for its name to Saggabonac [now, Sagaponack], (meaning the place of ground nuts), a little place near Bridgehampton, for short called Sagg, and Sag Harbor, being the seaport of Sagg, was baptized Sag Harbor.

We immediately called upon Captain Budd, to whom we were accredited.[16] Our business was put down for the early part of the week, Captain Budd to notify other parties in the matter, the object of our visit.

This was satisfactory to us, as it would give us time (nearly a week) to do up the town and possibly to visit Montauk.

Sag Harbor is not an accident; it is a considerable village, situated directly on the bay, with ample water for all maritime purposes. It has a population of about three thousand and five hundred souls, and considering that it is a seaport and its population consists largely of sailors, it is orderly. The village consists of one principal street (Main Street), pretty solidly built upon for several blocks, and on which its business is transacted, with many side streets of private residences. On Saturday, the day of our arrival, it certainly made a lively show for business. It was the market day for the country people, who came from miles around, and country wagons and "hayseeders" possessed the town.

Two whalers have arrived within the past fortnight and are lying at the wharf, and one out in the harbor ready to sail for the Pacific on Monday. The arrival or departure of one ship gives Sag Harbor an excuse for going busy, but there are three here now and the business of the town essays New York activity. The financial and commercial importance of Sag Harbor is out of all proportion to its size and population. It has a population of about thirty-five hundred, many dry goods stores, grocery stores, outfitting stores for whalers, with ship chandlery stores and others. Sag Harbor has about $1,000,000 invested in the whaling and codfishing business, and has many packets and vessels engaged in the coasting trade. The income from its investments is about $15,000,000 annually; the profits arising therefrom mostly remain in Sag Harbor. Last year there were twenty-five arrivals of successful whalers at the port and thirty-five departures. There were 8,000 quintals of codfish shipped from this port, the result of the codfish enterprise. Sag Harbor is the oldest port of customs in the State of New York and the oldest principality on Long Island. Henry P. Dering was appointed Port Collector by George Washington in 1790, which office he held until his death in 1832 at the age of 91. . . .[17]

In the course of our conversations with Captain Budd during our stay he made this remark: "That a calamity was imminent with the whaling business. Whales are getting scarce, the profits are getting smaller and the expenses greater, and that he was shortening sail."[18]

Of the inhabitants of Sag Harbor as a class little can be said. They are just what one would suppose from a population made up in the manner they were; there is no marked famous or infamous class. But there are many learned and cultured people here, brought here through interest, and it was this class that gave status and character to Sag Harbor society. There are many wealthy and respectable citizens of Sag Harbor who commenced their career as ordinary seamen and rose to the rank of commanders, who are now retired capitalists, and who still maintain that the highest honors belong to those who have passed and graduated through the curriculum of a voyage around Cape Horn.

As a school for the study of ethnology and philology, New Bedford is the only port in the United States that outranks Sag Harbor. Nearly every insular nation of the globe is represented in their population, and many languages spoken.

Sunday, July 23, 1843. Weather very warm this morning. Took a walk from foot of Main Street up to Jefferson Street, crossed over to the cemetery and back to the hotel, the weather being too hot for an extended ramble.

In the afternoon walked up Division Avenue and Easthampton Turnpike, led on by a feeling of loneliness, the novel scenery, and the many pretty suburban residences, some palatial mansions, many of the little cottages with graceful verandas and charming green gardens, and yet in the midst of all this beauty we were sad; the truth is, we were homesick, and for the first time we began to realize it. We were a long way from home; at least twelve days intervened between us and home and friends. We walked down the turnpike towards East Hampton. Our thoughts must have been kindred to those which moved the young Ishmalite, John Howard Payne, as he stood alone in laughing Paris, in tears, whose "Home Sweet Home" has rendered East Hampton, only three miles distant from where we now stand and where Payne was born, immortal.[19]

Southampton

Wednesday, July 26, 1843. But with all the positive attractions of business, bustle and activity of Sag Harbor, we are repelled by its negative attractions. Its odoriferous atmosphere of whale oil and codfish fail to inspire us, and we seek relief now that we have closed the business which called us here.

Today we fortuitously made the acquaintance of a Southampton farmer by the name of Bishop who had, he informed us, just disposed of his load of hay and was about to return to Southampton in ballast, that is, one barrel of molasses and ten bags of shot consigned to a storekeeper at Southampton. We shipped with him for the voyage, of which we sadly repented. His old wagon was without springs and added to the clatter of the shelvings, took all the romance out of the trip, and when we arrived at Southampton we were too lame to get out of the wagon without assistance. Mr. Bishop, however, very kindly offered to keep us at his home during our stay in Southampton, and at the same time suggested that on Saturday morning he was going to

Quogue with a load of straw, and if we so desired, might accompany him to that place, remarking that the roads were heavy and while our carpet bag might have a berth on the straw, we would be obliged to walk a portion of the way. This presented no obstacles to us and we accepted thankfully.

Thursday, July 27, 1843. Our purposes in coming to Southampton, which is a charming place to look upon, were twofold, first, to escape the odors of Sag Harbor; second, that our ancestors originally settled in Southampton (formerly Agawam). . . . July 27th and 28th were spent at Southampton in researches and enquiries concerning our family (who came from Ipswich), but reached the conclusion that when the Tredwells left Southampton or Southold they had just cause for so doing, and that they brought everything with them that belonged to them. . . .

We explored the place pretty thoroughly and were charmed with the evidences of antiquity, cleanliness and holiness which pervaded everywhere. But its out-of-door antiquity is "sickened o'er with the pale cast of modernity." New and modern structures were sandwiched in among the old and venerable remains, whose duration is measured by centuries, but the old in the main is master of the field and its antique character is dominant. . . .

[Returning Home]

Saturday, July 29, 1843. Had a pleasant trip to Quogue. The walk was less painful than the ride from Sag Harbor to Southampton, and did not leave the results. Have determined to remain at Quogue until the stage leaves on Tuesday. While at Quogue we stopped at the boarding house of Mr. Cooper and fortuitously made the acquaintance of Hon. George Hall, formerly Post Master and Mayor of the City of Brooklyn, who was summering here. We fraternized; there was a degree of frankness and kindness in Mr. Hall's manner that won our confidence. He has a great consideration for young people. We walked together. . . .

Tuesday, August 1, 1843. We were fortunate in securing a back seat in the stage. The romance of the country failed to overcome our weariness and we at once fell asleep and did not awake until we had reached Patchogue, and then hunger awoke us. When we commenced this journey our notes were prolific in detail, but the novelty had worn off and our entries were like Mrs. Palmer's during her travels in the Malay Archipelago. Day after day she entered with painful detail in her diary her personal experiences in earthquakes, but so familiar had she become with the phenomenon that it assumed less and less importance until finally her diary closed day after day with: "Earthquakes as usual."

The stopping places on the road were reached and passed without comment or recognition until we reached Merrick, when with recklessness we offered Dr. Wheeler's farm manager six shillings to carry us to our home about two miles distant. We were joyfully received at home. We had accomplished a great journey and everybody was glad to see us, and we were happy, having been successful in the purposes of our journey.

Modern Sag Harbor

Since the above notes were made, now (1880) about forty years ago, modern Sag Harbor has had her calamity [1845 fire] and gone through all the stages of decline, from the highest prosperity down to zero; once started on the toboggan, there is no stopping place but the bottom, and Sag Harbor reached it. Not a whaling ship has entered her port in twenty years and grass grew in her streets, her immense warehouses fell into decay, her docks crumbled to ruins and her bustling streets became as silent as the oracle of Delphi. When Sag Harbor went into decline Southampton also fell into peaceful and pious slumber and for the same cause, a decline in the whaling industry.

But, like Sag Harbor, Southampton awoke one day. Some artists became attracted to the place and modern wealth became interested in its antiquity, simplicity and healthfulness. The Long Island Railroad saw and embraced its opportunity, and Southampton is now one of the most popular summer resorts on Long Island, the Mecca of the invalid.

A new era also dawned upon Sag Harbor, but on entirely different lines of wealth and beauty. It began a new existence, became the home of luxury and culture; magnificent residences now adorn its streets and avenues; the sand hills of its suburbs have been converted into boulevards; every variety of merchandise may now be procured in its bazaars. Its harbor and bay, once filled with whaling ships, are now filled with yachts and motor boats, and altogether, there is no more charming spot for summer residence, or for the permanent home of the man of leisure and retirement than Sag Harbor.

Nothing probably since the erection of the first Indian hut within the principality of Sag Harbor has contributed more permanently in sentiment and popularity to its already well-earned reputation than the noble response of Mrs. Russell Sage from her millions to the elevation of its social and educational possibilities and physical adornment.[20]

[Resources of Long Island]

Saturday, August 12, 1843. There is nothing remarkable in the great enthusiasm manifested by the early prospectors of this country concerning the resources of Long Island. There was probably no spot in America more prolific in animal life, or more fertile, than "This Fruitful Island near the Continent of Virginia in America named the 'Isle Plowdon or Long Isle.'"[21]

The forests were swarming with wild life; bears, wolves, foxes and deer were plentiful even down to within the memory of man; every variety of game known to the temperate zone flourished here, from the king of wild birds, the turkey, to the tiniest of the feathered creation.

The waters were teeming with every variety of game, fish, molluscs [mollusks], crustacea, etc.; even the whale and the seal were pursued with profit. Its brooks and streams have furnished the highest standard of trout fishing in the world. Three hundred years of vandalism have wrought great changes in the fauna of the island, and still there is an abundance of game in its uplands, marshes and waters, which rigid protection is necessary to preservation. No season has ever passed within our memory without one good sporting period of eight or ten days on the Great Hempstead Plains shooting the plain plover.

The Plover [and Shooting Plover on the Plains]

[*Saturday, August 12, 1843,* continued.] Some seasons have been much better than others, but there has been a gradual yearly decline. The plover migrates north in the early spring; he is not much sought after at that time, but on his return in August he is game worthy the nobility of the sporting fraternity.

There are a great many varieties of the plover. They are insectivorous feeders. The plain plover feeds upon grasshoppers and crickets and other insects, of which they consume vast numbers and which accounts for the great excellence of their flesh. It has been pronounced by epicures as equal to that of the woodcock.

Plover shooting differs from all other forms of sporting in the world. It is a characteristic of the entire plover family (*charadrinœ*) to be desperately afraid of man on foot, but entirely indifferent about him if on horseback, or walking at the side of a horse, or in a wagon. And the sportsman who risks his chances on foot, although the plains may be covered with birds, is pretty sure to return with an empty game bag.

The plover in many respects is a wonderfully stupid bird, yet for three hundred years his increasing knowledge of the efficacy of projectiles has kept pace with our steady improvement, and he has acquired a marvelous accuracy the range of modern shot guns. A plover feeding in the fields or on the great plains will permit a horse to approach within ten feet of him. But a man on foot, in the open, is fortunate indeed to get within a long gunshot of one in a day's pursuit.

Therefore successful hunting of the plover depends more in taking advantage of his weaknesses than in good marksmanship. Go on horseback, in a wagon, or lie in ambush, if you want success. There never has been a season within the memory of man when plover have not been fairly plentiful on the great plains, but the present is an exceptional one; in fact, they were never known to be so numerous, and great numbers have been taken not alone on the plains, but in the cultivated farm fields on the South Side, where they had better feeding and better cover.

Today, Saturday, still on vacation. We have accepted an invitation from some South Side friends to accompany them for a day's plover shooting on the great plains. We met them at the place agreed upon in the village, ourselves unequipped, however, for participating in the sport, going simply as a spectator. This was not a company of professional sportsmen, but a party of boys who were fond of shooting. The party, however, was rounded up by one professional gunner, who gunned for a living, and who knew the habits and call of every game bird on Long Island—Bob Akeley; we were under Akeley's charge.

We made our camp about halfway across the great plains northeast of Hempstead on a hollow that filled up with water in winter. Our journey to the ground along the plain edge was enlivened by the presence of thousands of larks. We never saw so many, but they seemed to follow us always at a respectful distance, however. The larks are gathering here from the north and will not move south until October unless a cold snap comes sooner. We also passed several parties on foot, or horseback and in wagons on the same errand as ourselves, their destination being farther east.

It must be remembered that the Hempstead plains is more than a mere potato patch. It embraces sixty square miles within its limits, and as a play and feeding ground for plover, fifteen or twenty square miles of private territory adjoining may be added, the latter of which for feeding and hiding is more serviceable to the plover than the former.

On reaching our camp and after rigging a blind with the long dry plain grass around a hole which had been used for the same purpose some previous season, we set out the decoys, tied our horses to stakes with about thirty feet of halter, that they might graze at their leisure, and awaited results. One of our horses was accustomed to a gun. He knew its meaning and did not flinch if discharged over his shoulders; the other was too nervous to be of service.

Two of our party were alternately to occupy the blind, the others to remain in, or under, the wagon. The birds were apparently indifferent, for they gave us a wide berth. After a period, however, four plover had espied the decoys and came with set wing directly for them. Just as they huddled (as is their habit) before lighting, a discharge from the blind dropped all four. It was impossible for the tenants of the wagon to restrain applause and a shout went up from the wagon. In half a second the air was thick with birds; they got up from everywhere.

This was the commencement of the day's sport, which lasted about three hours, the birds coming along in bunches of from two to ten. The day's work resulted in bagging eighty-two birds. It had been a restless day for the plain plover. There were many gunners and an incessant firing was going on. Some of it was miles away, others nearer. We could see persons on horseback a mile off; others in wagons, and some lonely fellows on foot, the latter doing good execution. There were so many birds on the wing that their chances, providing the hunter could hide, were as good as those encumbered with horses.

On our way home we fell in with a party from Jamaica with trained horses. They had had a great day's sport, and had taken over a hundred birds, but had been disappointed in the efficacy of their horses, which was due to the fact that so many birds were in motion.

The plain plover is a bird of broad wing and slow pinion movements. It makes slides through the air, but gets over the ground much more rapidly than it seems with his kind of jerky movement, and the gunner who is ambitious to take him on the wing is up against a problem fit for no sloven. Many game birds on flushing are intent only on getting away and they go straight from you. That's an easy problem, but the plover has a foolish curiosity to see the cause of his alarm, and he starts up at an angle crossing your longitude; that's another proposition, and as a reward for your skill, if an amateur, you are likely to secure a few tail feathers for your pains.

The stupid plover decoys easily. He has not wit enough to distinguish between the decoy of the yellow leg snipe and one of his own species. They spy the decoy at a great distance and they come sweeping down in their rough and tumble flight all in a heap before lighting; then is the time to fire.

Akeley's plover call did not seem to avail much; it was very weak. Their plaintive notes are not easily imitated by the human voice, and the plover detects the counterfeit very readily. He does not use his voice much in his day flights, but at night during the migrating season we have heard them at all hours. It is a plaintive "tuckset—peetweet."

This has been a delightful day's outing. We had a mess of our birds served at Hewlett's Hotel. The whole day's sport was accomplished between the rising and the setting of the sun.

The Tredwell homestead was located on the north side of West Merrick Road (see map, p. 148)

We love the country, the fields, the freedom, the air, the sunshine; this love is instinctively born within us, and does not wear out. We turn to the open blue sky with an instinct as keen and akin to that displayed by a city-bred dog in trying to bury his bone deep in the hearthrug of his unnatural environment.

Race: Fashion and Peytona

Saturday, May 3, 1845. Went to the Union Course today to witness the great contest between William Gibbon's "Fashion" (entered by Samuel Laird), eight years old, and carrying 122 pounds, and R. Ten Broeck's "Peytona," six years old, and carrying 115 pounds, so stated in the printed programme. This, like a former race of "Fashion" against "Boston," in which the former was the winner in 1842, claimed to be a contest of Northern and Southern methods of training, and consequently interested horse breeders all over the country.

The present match was for $20,000, $10,000 a side, four mile heats. The interest among the sporting men on this occasion was very great and called together a vast throng of people interested in horse flesh from all parts of the Union. The *New York Herald* published an extra on the ground between the heats.

The "Peytona" was the winner in consecutive heats in 7 minutes, 30-1/2 seconds, and 7 minutes and 45-1/2 seconds. As soon as the decision was announced the rush for home was terrific, every available means for conveyance was brought into requisition to get the vast multitude of spectators from the ground. The railroad company exhausted its capacity and left thousands on the ground to wait for a return train. . . .[22]

Governor Spooner

Tuesday, August 2, 1881. Attended the funeral of Alden J. Spooner at Hempstead, Long Island. Alden J. Spooner was born at Sag Harbor, Suffolk County, Long Island, February 10, 1810. He was a prominent figure in literary affairs in Brooklyn and Queens County for nearly half a century. He was a scholar and of fine attainments in the classics, an accomplished writer and journalist and a ready speaker, and stood high in his profession of the law, during the period of his active practice. He had been very successful in several fiercely contested law cases soon after his admission and while he was yet quite a young man. He had a chaste and well-developed imagination, and a peculiar humor.

He was Surrogate of Kings County, a member of the Queens County Bar. He founded the Long Island Historical Society; was a member and one of the projectors of the Hamilton Literary Association, Charter Member of the Brooklyn Library. He interested himself in the incorporation of classical schools at Hempstead and many other institutions of learning, and with Pierrepont Potter he visited the public schools on the south side while the former was superintendent. He was known and respected over all Long Island. In the City of Brooklyn his personal friends were Dr. Charles A. Storrs, A.A. Low, Seth Low, John J. Howard, Professor Raymond, Joshua M. Van Cott, John Greenwood, J. Carson Brevoort and many others. His humor was unique, adventuresome and daring. Many anecdotes might be related of him more noted for originality than prudence, as the one mentioned in the following rescript.

Mr. Spooner during the early part of his professional life resided at Hempstead and was a prominent factor in the affairs of the town. The latter part of his life, his retirement, was also at Hempstead, and it was here he died and was buried August 2, 1881.

Some day in the latter part of August 1847, we remember the circumstances with distinctness, although now nearly thirty-five years ago. We were walking on Main Street in the village of Hempstead in company with Alden J. Spooner, journalist, lawyer, etc., whom we regarded with great veneration. We met Doctor Webb, of Hempstead, who extended his hand and saluted my companion as Governor Spooner. No importance was thought to attach to the salutation believing the title Governor merely complimentary with no other signification. We continued our walk to the hotel, when the proprietor, Stephen Hewlett, also address Mr. Spooner as governor, and still we did not regard it as having any import above the flexible title of squire, captain, colonel, as marks of respect which are always being more or less used in suburban places regardless of any import.

Twenty-five years after in a discussion before the Philosophical Society, the chairman in ruling declared that Governor Spooner had the floor. We were more strongly impressed on this than any former occasion that there must be some reason for calling Mr. Spooner governor. . . .

Alden J. Spooner was one of the many old time Long Islanders who never became reconciled to the rude and uncourtly treatment of the proposition to enroll Long Island on the galaxy of Union Statehood. The claim had been advocated by some of the most estimable citizens of Long Island, and the legislature memorialized away back in the "Twenties" and again in the "Thirties." . . . This project with some of its advocates was a hobby and to others was urged as a political measure. Some of the most influential citizens of Long Island were among its advocates, chief of whom in enthusiasm was Alden J. Spooner. . . .

But notwithstanding the brave resolves and the righteousness of their cause, these respectable Long Islanders could not create a *de facto* state, but they had the right and they did resolve it a state as the next best thing, for at one of their sessions, after many hours discussion and the immolation of hecatombs of squab and other connestables [comestibles], did solemnly vote and declare Long Island to be a free and independent state, and in the same spirit proceeded in the election of officers for the newly created commonwealth, which resulted in the election of Alden J. Spooner, Governor.

All this transpired prior to the year 1841, as will presently more fully appear. Now it so transpired that just after the election of General [William Henry] Harrison as President of the United States in 1841, his friends throughout the country resolved to honor the occasion of his election by a grand national dinner and jubilee to be celebrated at Niblo's Garden, New York, and to which duly accredited delegates were to be admitted from every State in the Union.

Governor Spooner prorogued the convention, and jointly with his cabinet resolved that the new state of Long Island was entitled to recognition and to a seat at the great national feast or celebration on an equal footing with the other States, and consequently fully accredited credentials were prepared and issued to the four selected delegates from the most stalwart and imposing members of the Long Island Convention to attend the jubilee.

And on the day and hour, Governor Spooner, at the head of his delegation, formed in line at the entrance of the Garden to demand admission. The Massachusetts delegates, headed by Governor Winthrop, were just in advance, and as they entered and were announced the throng inside burst into cheers.[23] As they passed in, Governor Spooner advanced with the delegation. Behind him Fanning C. Tucker, full 6 feet 4 inches high, leading, and John Tredwell, nearly as tall but more graceful in carriage, following, and others of impressive stature and manners. They gravely marched up to the usher, who, by the way, was a Louisiana man. Governor

Spooner solemnly handed out the credentials, and whispered, "Delegates from the State of Long Island." Forgetting all his history and geography amid the confusion inside in consequence of the entrance of the Massachusetts delegation, the usher roared out, "Delegates from the State of Long Island please enter." They did enter and took their seats amid thunders of applause, which broke out again and again as the ludicrous facts dawned upon the convention.

The joke was soon explained to the managers of the banquet, who enjoyed it as greatly as the Governor and his delegates. The scheme was so cleverly planned and so adroitly executed that no effort was made to expel or to ask the retirement of the Long Island delegates who had so ingeniously gained admission, and they remained through the proceedings. And Alden J. Spooner, then only a little over thirty years old, had the honor of replying to the toast, "The Brand New State of Long Island," which he did in a manner said to have been the most consummate and finished piece of oratory of his life.

And thus through this little unprecedented nervy humor, Alden J. Spooner won his spurs as Governor, and the recognition of Long Island as a full-fledged State of the National Union *de jure* if not *de fact*.[24]

Notes

Source: Daniel M. Tredwell, *Personal Reminiscences of Men and Things on Long Island,* 2 vols. (Brooklyn: Charles Ditmas, 1912, 1917), 1:15-16, 86, 88-89, 128-29, 135-48, 150-59, 161-66; 2:197, 324-26, 328-29. Editing changes have been minimal. Some short paragraphs have been combined and titles of newspapers (originally within quotation marks) changed to italics. Tredwell's spellings have been retained, but some of his punctuation standardized. Most of the subheads are taken from Tredwell's headings at the beginning of chapters. Except for a few references in the notes by Tredwell which are identified as [DMT], all notes are by the editor for this edition; her insertions in the text are in brackets [thus].

1. Milburn was an early name for the area which is now in northwestern Freeport and eastern Baldwin. The Tredwell farm was located on the north side of today's Merrick Road, east of Milburn Creek and Pond in western Freeport. See Tredwell's map of the South Side.

2. Titles of his other published publications include: *A Catalogue of Books and Pamphlets Belonging to Daniel M. Tredwell, Relating to the Great Civil War* (1874); *Monograph on Privately Illustrated Books, A Plea for Bibliomania* (1881, revised 1892); and *A Sketch of the Life of Apollonius of Tyana: or the First Ten Decades of our Era* (1886). His *Apollonius* was reprinted in 1996 by Kessinger in Kila, Montana.

3. Biographical information on Tredwell is from Robert P. Rushmore, "A Sketch of the Life and Works of Daniel M. Tredwell," *Journal of Long Island History* 12 (Fall 1975): 5-22; the quotation is from p. 19.

4. Tredwell, *Personal Reminiscences,* 1:13

5. In Greek mythology, Ariadne gave Theseus the thread that enabled him to find his way out of Minatour's labyrinth.

6. Tredwell has another entry on sheep parting three years later (not included here) where he noted, "a declining interest in these doings." He attributed "the great diminution in the attendance of respectable farmers" because many had "ceased keeping sheep" (1:149).

7. Tredwell quotes from 1723 town records and refers to legislation in 1743. The 1723 meeting is reported on p. 400 of Liber D [DMT] and published in the *Records of the Town of North and South Hempstead* (hereafter cited as *Hempstead Town Records),* 8 vols. (Jamaica: Long Island Farmer Print, 1896), 3:65-66, but with slight variations in language from Tredwell's quotation.

8. Tredwell quotes the text of the 1667 town regulations. He does not cite a source, but it can be found in the published *Hempstead Town Records,* 1:237-38.

9. Tredwell quotes these regulations from the town records. See *Hempstead Town Records,* 4:351-52 (1761), 5:11-12 (1765), and 5:478-79 (1775).

10. See *Records of the Town of North and South Hempstead,* Liber E, p. 70 [DMT]. In the published *Hempstead Town Records,* 3:240.

11. Anthelme Brillat-Savarin (1755-1826) was a French gourmet who wrote *Physiologie de Goût* (1825) on the art of dining.

12. On the marshing season, see also Julian Denton Smith, "Ma'shin' Seas'n," *Nassau County Historical Society Journal* 34 (1975): 13-20; originally in ibid., 10 (Summer 1947): 31-37.

13. Records of the Town of Hempstead, Liber E, p. 449 [DMT]. In *Hempstead Town Records,* 4:195-96, with slight variations in spelling and capitalization. This legislation, quoted by Tredwell but omitted here, restricted clamming to residents of the town.

14. Long Island gunning interests ("an amalgam of professional gunners, guides and hotel and boarding house keepers") opposed restrictions and Long Island was exempted from the state's ban on use of the battery in the nineteenth century. Many hat makers, including William L. Wilson's large millinery factory in Wantagh, used bird feathers for decoration. State and federal legislation enacted in the early twentieth century limited spring gunning, feather hunting, and commercial hunting of wildfowl. See E. Jane Townsend, *Gunner's Paradise: Wildfowling and Decoys on Long Island* (Stony Brook: The Museums at Stony Brook, 1979), pp. 18-21. In the twenty-first century, there are numerous bird sanctuaries and protected bird nesting areas on Long Island.

15. Omitted here is Tredwell's statement, "the termination *ogue* in Indian proper names on Long Island means *fish.*" Quogue is the name of a type of clam, but this derivation of "ogue" is unsubstantiated.

16. Dorothy Ingersoll Zaykowski indicates that Captain John Budd operated a cooperage and shipyard in North Haven. A bridge connected North Haven to Sag Harbor. See her book, S*ag Harbor: The Story of an American Beauty* (Sag Harbor: Sag Harbor Historical Society, 1991), pp. 27, 348.

17. Dering's home in Sag Harbor is preserved by the Society for the Preservation of Long Island Antiquities (SPLIA) as the Custom House museum. It is located on Garden and Main Streets (next to the Whaling Museum) and open from June to October; information, (631) 692-4664.

18. Whaling in Sag Harbor peaked in the 1840s. See Zaykowski, *Sag Harbor,* pp. 81-110; and Steve Wick, "Sag Harbor's Heyday" and "In Search of Whales," in *Long Island: Our Story,* by Newsday (Melville: Newsday, 1998), pp. 163, 168-70.

19. Payne's family had lived in East Hampton and he later visited his grandparents there, but he was born in New York City in 1791, as Tredwell himself later noted in his journal entry for an 1873 visit (2:302). On John Howard Payne, see Robert P. Rushmore, "'The Village of East-Hampton,' A Sketch by John Howard Payne [1838], Edited with an Introduction and Notes," *Long Island Historical Journal* 10 (Fall 1997): 25-38; and Peter Goodman, "Payne's Sweet Home," in *Long Island: Our Story,* p. 173. The Home Sweet Home Museum at 14 James Lane can be visited; 631-324-0713.

20. Margaret Olivia Slocum (1828-1918) married widower Russell Sage in 1869. One of America's wealthiest women after her husband's death in 1906, Oliva Sage was the "Lady Bountiful" of Sag Harbor in the early twentieth century. Her mother was Margaret Pierson and maternal grandfather John Jermain, both old Sag Harbor families. Sage bought her grandparents' home in 1869 and later the larger Benjamin Hunting home on Main Street, which now houses the Sag Harbor Whaling and Historical Museum. Among her philanthropies in Sag Harbor were contributions to build Pierson High School, John Jermain Memorial Library, Mashashimuet Park, Union Chapel in Noyac, the brick railroad depot, and money to finance publication of William Wallace Tooker's *Indian Place Names on Long Island.* See Zaykowski, *Sag Harbor,* pp. 188, 191, 242, 273-85. Mrs. Sage also donated to many welfare and religious causes in the northeast and established the Russell Sage Foundation. She assisted many educational institutions and founded Russell Sage College.

21. The quotation is from a grant by King Charles I to Sir Edmund Plowden in 1632. See *Collections of the New-York Historical Society for the Year 1869* (New York: New-York Historical Society, 1870), 2:218.

22. This event was commemorated in a Currier and Ives lithograph. See Bernie Bookbinder, *Long Island: People and Places, Past and Present,* 1983 (Reprint; New York: Harry N. Abrams, 1998), pp. 141-43. On horseracing on Long Island, see also Nathaniel Prime's comments below in "Long Island in 1845."

23. Harrison was elected in 1840 and took office in March 1841. Tredwell may have misidentified the office Winthrop held or the name of the governor. Thomas Lindall Winthrop (1760-1841) had served as Lieutenant-Governor, 1826-1832. His son, Robert Charles Winthrop (1809-1894), was a Whig Congressman from Massachusetts in the 1840s, Senator in 1850, and defeated for governor in 1851. (Their ancestor, John Winthrop, had been a colonial governor of Massachusetts.) The governor of Massachusetts in 1840 was Marcus Morton, while John Davis was governor in 1841-1842. See *National Cyclopaedia of American Biography,* 6:217, 7:504-5; *Dictionary of American Biography,* 10:416-17; and Robert Sobel and John Raimo, eds. *Biographical Directory of the Governors of the United States, 1789-1978* (Westport, CT: Mechler Books, 1978), 2:702.

24. In the 1830s and 1840s, there was a serious movement for statehood for Long Island (some of Tredwell's information on this has been omitted here). A song, "The Long Island State," was written by George Stowe of Jamaica in 1848 and published in the *Long Island Democrat* that year. See Harrison Hunt, notes for *The Long Island State* audiocassette recording by the Old Bethpage Singers, 1984.

Benjamin F. Thompson, Long Island historian and lawyer, supported statehood for Long Island in 1849, as "her invincible right to a separate and distinct political existence." (*History,* 3:29-80). Walt Whitman supported this proposal in an article in the *Brooklyn Standard* in 1861, which is reprinted in *Walt Whitman's New York: From Manhattan to Montauk,* edited by Henry M. Christman (New York: Macmillan, 1963), p. 106.

Rockaway on "Old Long Island's Sea Girt Shore"

Rockaway (today's Far Rockaway) was the earliest Long Island "watering place" or resort area (see Charles Brockden Brown's "Jaunt to Rockaway, 1793" above). The Rockaway Marine Pavilion, built in 1833 with a large dining room and 160 rooms to accommodate guests, soon attracted the elite of New York society.[1] "Rockaway," or "On Old Long Island's Sea Girt Shore" was a popular song in the mid and late nineteenth century which well describes the attractions of the sea shore and ocean surrounding Long Island.

The words of this ballad are variously attributed to George Pope Morris (1802-1864) and Henry John Sharpe. Morris was born in Philadelphia, but moved at an early age to New York. He worked in a printing shop and began publishing poems in New York newspapers when he was only 15 years old. His best-known poem was "Woodman Spare That Tree." Many of his popular poems and songs were later published in collected editions. Morris founded the *New York Mirror* in 1823, and edited this and other literary newspapers for more than three decades. Known as General Morris (he was a Brigadier General in the militia), he is one of the "Knickerbocker school of literati."[2] Benjamin F. Thompson, in a contemporary (1849) account says that Henry John Sharpe, Esq. wrote the words for his friend Henry Russell. "Esquire" probably indicates that Sharpe was a lawyer, but efforts to locate information about him have been unsuccessful. Henry Russell (1812-1900), a popular English-born singer and composer who was in the United States from c. 1833-1845, set the poem to music in 1840. Thompson said the song was "faithfully descriptive of this delightful spot."[3] Regardless of who wrote the words, they capture the experience that innumerable people enjoy at Long Island's beaches to the present day.

* * *

Rockaway
On old Long Island's sea girt shore
   Many an hour I've whil'd away,
In list'ning to the breaker's roar
   That wash the beach of Rockaway. [Chorus]
Transfix'd I've stood while nature's lyre
   In one harmonious concert broke,
And, catching its promethean fire,
   My inmost soul to rapture woke.
     Oh! oh! oh! oh! oh! oh! [+ Chorus]
Oh, how delightful 'tis to stroll
   Where murm'ring winds and waters meet,

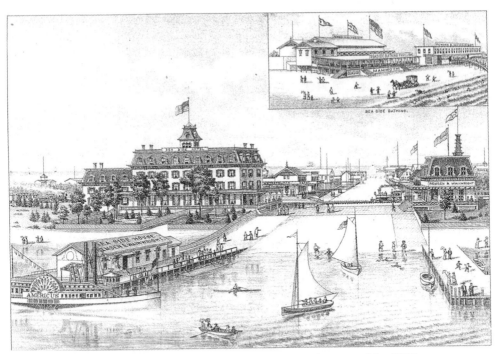

The Sea Side House on Rockaway Beach opened in 1881.
The largest hotel in the world, it could accommodate
400 guests and had 1000 bathing houses.

Marking the billows as they roll
    And break resistless at your feet;
To watch young Iris, as she dips
    Her mantle in the sparkling dew,
And, chas'd by sol, away she trips
    O'er the ho-ri-zon's quiv'ring blue.
        Oh! oh! oh! oh! oh! oh! [+ Chorus]
To hear the startling night-winds sigh,
    As dreamy twilight lulls to sleep;
While the pale moon reflects from high
    Her image in the mighty deep;
Majestic scene where Nature dwells,
    Profound in everlasting love,
While her unmeasured music swells,
    The vaulted firmament above.
        Oh! oh! oh! oh! oh! oh! [+ Chorus]

Notes

Source: The words in this version are from an undated broadside in the Library of Congress published by H. De Marsan in New York City. The four lines of the opening chorus are repeated at the end of every verse in the original, but indicated here as [+ Chorus]. This primary source indicates neither the author of the words nor music; American Memory website: memory.loc.gov (accessed June 27, 2001). "Rockaway" is printed (with minor variations in some of the wording) in: Benjamin F. Thompson, *History of Long Island*, 3d edition (written in 1849, but not published until 1918), edited by Charles J. Werner, 3 vols. (Reprint; Port Washington: I.J. Friedman, 1972), 2:538; W.W. Munsell, *History of Queens County, New York* (New York: W.W. Munsell, 1883), pp. 168-69 (which indicates George P. Morris probably wrote it at the Marine Pavilion in Far Rockaway); and Stanley A. Ransom, *Songs of Long Island* (Plattsburgh, NY: Connecticut Peddler Enterprises, 1997), p. 35.

The song was recorded in 1984 by the Old Bethpage Singers on an audiocassette, *"The Long Island State" and Other Patriotic, Comic, Sentimental and Descriptive Songs of Nineteenth Century America.* Harrison Hunt's notes for the recording indicate only that it was composed by Henry Russell. Stanley A. Ransom, who recorded the song in 1997 on audiocassette and compact disk, *My Long Island Home,* attributes the words to Henry John Sharpe. A web site on "The Music of Henry Russell" attributes the words to Sharpe: pdmusic.org/russell (accessed June 27, 2001).

1. The main building of the Marine Pavilion was 235 feet long with two wings, 75 and 45 feet long. See Thompson, *History of Long Island,* 3d ed., 2:536-37. Although the Marine Pavilion burned in 1864, other large hotels and smaller boarding houses continued to maintain Rockaway as a resort, particularly with the coming of two railroad lines in 1869 and 1872. Far Rockaway was incorporated as a village in 1888, and its population in 1890 was 2,288. For comparisons, the population of the village of Hempstead was 4,831 in 1890; Rockaway Beach had 1,502; Inwood, 1,277; Lawrence 620; and the entire Town of Hempstead, 23,756. See Vincent Seyfried and William Assadorian, *Old Rockaway, New York in Early Photographs* (New York: Dover, 2000), pp. viii, 1-2, 8-10; *Eleventh Census of the United States: 1890, Report on Population,* 1:250.

Rockaway was part of the town of Hempstead until 1898, when the Rockaway peninsula became part of greater New York City. Averne-by-the-Sea had been incorporated as a village in 1895, and Rockaway Beach in 1897. They, together with Far Rockaway, unsuccessfully tried to secede from New York City in 1915 and 1917. See Henry Isham Hazelton, *The Boroughs of Brooklyn and Queens, Counties of Nassau and Suffolk, Long Island, New York, 1609-1924,* 7 vols. (New York: Lewis Publishing, 1925), 2:1,012.

2. Biographical information is from Philip Barnard, "George Pope Morris," *American National Biography,* ed. John A. Garraty and Mark C. Carnes (New York: Oxford University Press, 1999), 15:894; and Evert A. Duyckinck, *Cyclopaedia of American Literature* (New York: C. Scribner, 1856), p. 349, University of Virginia's Library of Early American Fiction website: etext.lib.virginia.edu/eaf/authors/cal/gpmCal.html (accessed June 27, 2001). Morris did visit the Marine Pavilion at Rockaway.

3. Biographical information on Russell is from the web site, "Music of Henry Russell," ibid.

Kings and Suffolk Counties, 1842

John W. Barber and Henry Howe

John W. Barber and Henry Howe wrote "Historical Collections" for a number of states, which they illustrated with their own engravings. This selection is from their volume on New York, whose subtitle concludes, "Geographical Descriptions of Every Township in the State." It is these geographical descriptions rather than the historical information which are the focus of these selections.

John Barber (1798-1885) was an engraver and historian. Born in Connecticut, he moved to New Haven in 1823. He wrote many histories which were illustrated by his wood and copper-plate engravings, including *Historical Scenes in the United States* (1827), *History and Antiquities of New Haven* (1831), *Historical Collections of Connecticut* (1836), *Historical Collections of Massachusetts* (1839), and *Antiquities of New England* (1841). Henry Howe (1816-1893) was born in New Haven where his father was a publisher and bookseller. After writing *Eminent Mechanics* (1839), he collaborated with Barber on *Historical Collections of the State of New York* (1842) and *Historical Collections of New Jersey* (1844). Howe later published similar collections for Virginia and Ohio himself. Barber and Howe followed a similar method for their "Historical Collections," traveling throughout the area, making sketches, collecting materials, and speaking to people.[1]

Barber and Howe divide their work by counties and the towns within. They usually include the original date of settlement, derivation of the name of the town, and the distance from Brooklyn (in Kings County), New York City, or Riverhead (in Suffolk County). Their descriptions encompass the size, topography, soil, names of villages, the number and denominations of churches, principal occupations, and any industries. Their population figures are from the 1840 federal census; for a few communities, they also provide population figures for earlier years. Barber and Howe's engravings provide valuable visual depictions of the larger communities. This selection from their work is limited to Kings and Suffolk Counties because Barber and Howe's chapter on Queens County (including towns which became Nassau County) was reprinted in an appendix of an earlier Long Island Studies Institute publication and hence is easily accessible.[2]

* * *

Kings County

KINGS COUNTY was organized in 1683, by an act of the colonial assembly dividing the province, and abolishing the *ridings* which previously existed. Its greatest length is 12, and greatest breadth 7 miles. The county includes Coney and Barren islands, and all other islands south of the town of

Gravesend, The surface on the NE. for three or four miles back from the river is hilly and ridgy. Upon the SE. a plain of sandy loam and sand extends to the ocean. The soil for the most part is light, warm, and when properly manured, fertile. It is generally well improved, and supplies a large portion of the vegetables sold in New York. . . . Pop. 47,613.

BROOKLYN. This town, the whole of which is now included within the corporation of the city of Brooklyn, lies upon the extreme western part of Long Island, opposite the southern portion of the city of New York, and separated therefrom by the East river, which is here about three quarters of a mile in width. Its length from NE. to SW. is six, and its greatest breadth four miles; giving an area of 9,200 acres, most of which has been apportioned into city lots. "The surface is high, broken, and stony; and the more elevated points afford beautiful and romantic sites, many of which have been built upon, and are not excelled in elegance by any others in the country. . . ."[3]

The most compact part of Brooklyn was incorporated into a village in 1816, which, although much opposed by a portion of the population, gave a new impulse to the spirit of improvement, which has resulted in raising it to be the second city in point of population in the state of New York. In April 1834, the whole territory of the town was incorporated under the name of the "City of Brooklyn." It is divided into 9 wards; the powers of the corporation are vested in a mayor, and a board of aldermen, composed of two elected

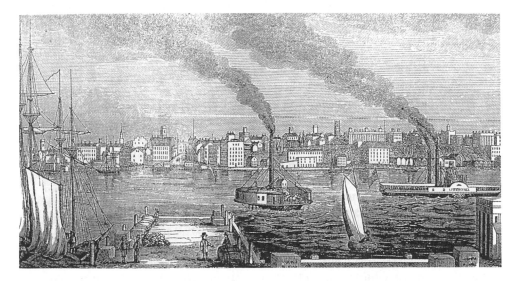

Northwestern view of Brooklyn, N.Y., from near Peck Slip, New York City. The view shows the appearance of the most compact part of Brooklyn, as seen from New York City, opposite Fulton Street, Brooklyn. The Colonnade buildings on Brooklyn Heights, appear on the right.

Northern view of the Navy-yard at Brooklyn.

from each ward. Brooklyn contains 28 churches, viz: 6 Episcopalian, 2 Dutch Reformed, 7 Presbyterian, 2 Baptist, 4 Episcopal Methodist, 1 Centenary Episcopal Methodist, 1 Primitive Methodist, 1 Wesleyan Methodist, 2 Roman Catholic, 1 Unitarian Congregational Church, and 1 Friends Meeting-house. Population in 1820, 7,175; in 1825, 10,790; in 1830, 15,394; in 1835, 25,312; in 1840, 36,233.

The [engraving] shows the appearance of the buildings, shipping, etc., at the navy-yard, at Brooklyn, as seen from Corlear's Hook. The United States possess about forty acres at this spot, including the old mill-pond. Here have been erected a spacious navy-yard, public stores, machine shops, and two immense edifices, in which the largest ships are protected from the weather, while building. On the east side of the *Wallabout* bay, opposite the navy-yard, stands the U.S. Naval Hospital, a magnificent structure. . . .[4]

BUSHWICK is situated in the NE. extremity of Kings county. Population of the town, including Williamsburg, 6,389. The settlement of the town was commenced by the Dutch, who were joined many years after by a number of Huguenot families, whose descendants are numerous and respectable in this and the neighboring towns. The name is of Dutch origin, indicating that the territory was remarkable for the woods which covered its surface in early times. From the organization of the town till 1690, it was for certain civil purposes associated with the other towns in the county, except Gravesend, constituting a separate district under the appellation of the *"Five Dutch Towns,"* and for which a secretary or register was specially commissioned by the governor to take proofs of wills, of marriage settlements, etc. These five towns formed but one ecclesiastical congregation. . . .

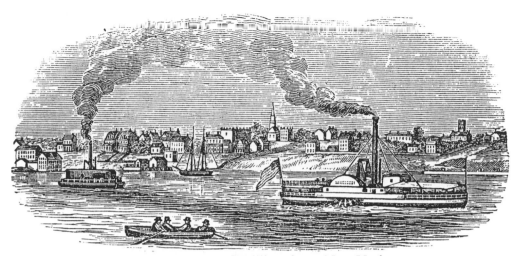

Western view of Williamsburg, New York

The [engraving] shows the appearance of the central part of the village of Williamsburg, as seen from the New York side of the East river.[5] This flourishing village was till within a few years an inconsiderable place, although it was commenced by a few spirited individuals nearly thirty years ago, by erecting a few houses and establishing a ferry between it and the foot of Grand-street. In 1817, a ferry boat, impelled by horse power, gave Williamsburg a new impulse, and in 1827, an act of incorporation was obtained. The village was a bold water front upon the East river, one mile and a half in extent, and a sufficient depth of water for all commercial purposes. Several large and substantial wharves and docks have been constructed, affording safe and convenient moorings for vessels even of the largest class. Its ferry is the nearest approximation to the upper parts of the city of New York from the eastern towns of Long Island, by two lines of steam ferry boats. So great has been the progress of improvement that the ancient village of Bushwick can scarcely be identified, having been amalgamated with Williamsburg. The village has now upwards of 70 streets permanently laid out, about thirty of which have been graded and regulated, some paved, and one macadamized. There are upwards of six hundred dwellings, 5 churches—3 Methodist, 1 Dutch Reformed, and 1 Episcopal—a newspaper printing office, and manufacturing establishments of various kinds. Population of the village 5,094.

FLATBUSH, called by the Dutch Midwout, or *Middle Woods,* was first settled in 1651. . . .

The soil in this township is generally of a good quality, and by careful cultivation is made highly productive. The village of Flatbush is about four miles from the City Hall of New York, and has several splendid private residences finely situated. The courthouse of the county was erected here in 1685, and the courts continued to be held therein till it was destroyed by fire in 1832. *Erasmus Hall,* an academical institution, was incorporated in 1787, and has ever maintained a high reputation.[6] Pop. 2,099.

FLATLANDS was originally called by the Dutch, New Amersfort. The settlement was commenced in 1636; and one of the first grants for land was that for Barren Island, which at that time was much larger than at present, and covered with cedar and other timber which has long since disappeared. Ex-governor [Wouter] Van Twiller had a farm in this town at the time of its first settlement. The village of Flatlands, situated about 8 miles from Brooklyn, is a pleasant spot, in the center of which is the Dutch church, originally erected in 1661, and has been since twice rebuilt. Pop. 810.

"The surface of the town is, as its name indicates, a perfect level; the soil, a light sandy loam, warm and pleasant to till; and from the skill and industry of its farming population, yields a large amount over and above the wants of the inhabitants. The people, generally, are conspicuous for habits of economy; and modern fashions have not yet extinguished their love of simplicity and substantial comfort."[7]

GRAVESEND occupies the most southerly part of Kings county. Much of this town consists of salt marsh, not more than one third being under cultivation; the surface is generally level, but near the seashore there are some ridges of sand hills. Coney Island, which covers the town on the ocean, is about 5 miles long by 1 in breadth. The central part of the town is about 10 miles from the city of New York. Pop. 799. This place was settled by English emigrants from Massachusetts as early as 1640, who gave it the name of Gravesend, they having sailed from a place of that name in England, on their departure for America. They were soon after joined by Lady Deborah Moody, a woman of rank, education, and wealth, who, with her associates, were obliged to leave Lynn, and other places in Massachusetts, on account of their religious sentiments. . . .

"Coney Island, on the seaboard, is a place of great resort for strangers in the summer season, is constantly fanned by cool breezes, and affords an unlimited view of the ocean.

"It is separated from the main of Long Island by a narrow creek or inlet, over which a handsome bridge has been erected. There is a fine spacious hotel here, called the Ocean House, which is conducted in a superior manner; a railroad is attached to the establishment, and cars leave the hotel for the beach a distance of 80 rods, at particular intervals during the day. The bathing at this place is not surpassed by any in the United States. The beach is a beautiful white sand. The island is about 5 miles long and 1 wide, and is entirely an alluvial formation. The destructive effect of ocean storms has long been very visible here, for much of what was once Coney Island has now disappeared. . . . The exposed situation of this island subjects it to great encroachments of the sea, and to the probability that at some future (though perhaps distant) period it will be entirely destroyed. In a terrible gale which occurred upon the coast on the 26th of January 1839, the whole of Coney Island, with the exception of a few sand-hills, was completely inundated by the sea; the basement of the Ocean House was filled with water; the bridge was carried away, several small vessels were cast on shore, and one was driven a considerable distance towards Flatlands."[8]

New UTRECHT is at the west end of Long Island, opposite the Narrows; 9 miles S. from Brooklyn. The soil of the township is mostly a light loam or sand. Pop. 1,283. Bath House and village are upon the margin of the bay, a mile and a half from the Narrows, having a full view of the military works at that place. It is quite a favorite place of resort during the warm season. It was near this delightful spot that the British army, under the command of Sir William Howe, effected a landing, August 22, 1776, a few days previous to the disastrous battle of Long Island. Fort Hamilton, at the Narrows, has become an important military station; several handsome buildings, with an Episcopal church, have been erected at this place, and few situations can boast of a finer prospect.

Suffolk County

Suffolk County, which comprises about two thirds of Long Island, was organized in 1683, at which time the ridings were abolished, and Long Island was divided into three counties, as they have remained ever since. It is about one hundred and ten miles in length, and in some parts twenty in width.[9] On the north side next [to] the sound the land is considerably broken and hilly; in the interior, and on the south side it is mostly a sandy plain, covered for the greater part with forests of pine, in which the wild deer is still an inhabitant. The county is not well watered, the streams being few and small. The chief business of the inhabitants is agriculture and fishing; they also send large quantities of pine wood to market. The original settlers of the county were mostly from New England, and the inhabitants have ever retained to a great degree the habits and manners of the Puritans. The county is divided into 9 towns, all of which, except Riverhead, were organized in 1788.[10] Pop. 32,468.

BROOKHAVEN, the largest town in the county, embraces the whole width of the island. It contains more than 103,000 acres, of which only about 35,000 are improved. The greater part of the inhabitants are distributed along the villages on the south and the ocean. The middle portion is for the most part covered with pine forests, in which deer abound. Pop. 7,050. . . .

Setauket, the oldest and one of the most populous villages in the town, received its name from its being the residence of the Seatalcott [Setauket] tribe of Indians. It is situated on both sides of the harbor, occupying about two square miles. The village of Stonybrook is on the western side of the town adjoining the sound, and has one of the best harbors in this part of the island. There are about 60 dwellings; shipbuilding to a considerable extent is carried on in this place. Port Jefferson and Millers Place are small villages.

Corum [Coram] is near the center of the town, and has been the seat of the town business for more than 60 years. It is a small village containing about 150 inhabitants. . . .[11]

The [engraving] is a view taken at the western entrance into the village of Patchogue; the Congregational and Methodist churches are seen on the left, and the compact part of the village in the distance on the right. The village is named after the Patchogue tribe of Indians, who once possessed the territory in this part of the island. It contains about 75 dwellings, the greater part of which have been erected within a few years. It is 28 miles from Riverhead, and 60 from New York, upon the great thoroughfare from Brooklyn to Sagg Harbor. Four miles east is the recently built village of Bell Port, containing about 30 dwellings, an academy, 2 ship-yards, etc. Five miles east of here is a small settlement called Fire-place [Brookhaven hamlet] known as a

View of Patchogue in Brookhaven, Long Island

rendezvous for sportsmen. Moriches is in the east part of the town, extending east from Mastic river. The groves of Mastic are somewhat celebrated.

EASTHAMPTON, the most easterly town on Long Island, includes the peninsula of Montauk and Gardiner's Island. It is centrally distant from New York 110 miles. Pop. 2,076. . . . The village of Easthampton is confined to a single street, of about a mile in length, having about 100 dwellings, mostly of an antiquated appearance, a church, and the Clinton academy, erected here in 1785, being the first institution of the kind on Long Island. The village of Amagansett, containing about 50 houses, is three miles to the east. Wainscott is a small village in the SW. part.

Gardiner's Island contains about 3,300 acres, with a soil mostly of a good quality; the nearest point of distance to Long Island is three miles. . . .[12]

The peninsula of Montauk contains 9,000 acres. The land is owned by about forty individuals, as tenants in common. The Indians have non-fructuary interest in a portion of the land; but as the race is nearly extinct, this incumbrance must be of short duration.[13] The soil is generally good, and is used as pasture land. The surface is rough, and in some places precipitous. "There is a sublimity and wildness, as well as solitariness here, which leave a powerful impression on the heart. In a storm, the scene which the ocean presents is awfully grand and terrific. On the extreme point stands the tall white column erected by the government for a lighthouse in 1795, at an expense of $22,300. It is constructed of stone, in the most substantial manner. . . ."[14]

HUNTINGTON, the westernmost town in the county, is bounded on the N. by the sound, and S. by the ocean. [The Town of Huntington included Babylon Town until 1872.] The surface in the N. is rough and hilly, in the center a high sandy plain covered with pines and shrub oaks. The South Bay has on its northern shore a strip of salt meadow nearly a mile wide. The soil near the sound, and particularly upon the necks, is the best in the town. Pop. 6,562. . . .

The [engraving] shows the appearance of the village of Huntington as it is entered from the westward. The Presbyterian church and academy are seen in the distance, near the central part of the engraving. The Universalist church is seen near the burying ground on the right. There are about one hundred dwellings in the vicinity of the churches. A newspaper is published in this place. This village is 40 miles W. from Riverhead, and about 45 from New York. The thriving village of Babylon, 40 miles from New York, on the south side of the island, in full view of the bay and ocean, contains about 250 inhabitants. It is situated upon *Sunquams Neck,* and has a fine stream of water on either side, upon which mills have long been erected. The village of

Western View of Huntington Village

Little Cow Harbor is now called Center Port [Centerport], and the name of Great Cow Harbor changed to North Port [Northport]. The steamer *Lexington* was burnt near Eaton's Neck, Jan. 13, 1840.

ISLIP. This town, on the S. side of the island, is centrally distant about 45 miles from New York. It received its name from the first settlers, many of whom came from Islip, in Oxfordshire, England. It has a level surface and a light and sandy soil, rendered productive by manures of sea-weed and fish. The bay on the south is 4 or 5 miles wide, containing an inexhaustible variety of fish, and is visited by a vast number of wildfowl. Pop. 1,909. The extensive domain known as Nicol's Patent, includes more than sixty square miles of land, and has, since its first purchase from the Indians in 1683 by William Nicol, been by successive entailment preserved as one estate.

RIVERHEAD, the shire town, was taken from Southold in 1792. Only a comparatively small portion of the town is under improvement; much of its territory is covered with wood, which has for a long period been a staple article for transportation.

The [engraving] is a southern view of the central part of the village of Riverhead, as seen from the residence of Mr. J.P. Terry, about 50 rods S. from the courthouse. The village is situated upon Peconic creek or river, a mill stream, about 2 miles above Peconic bay, about 90 miles from New York, 24 from Sagg Harbor, and 23 from Greenport. The village contains about 70 dwellings, a large proportion of which are one story in height, 1 Methodist, 1 Congregational, and 1 Swedenbourg or New Jerusalem church,

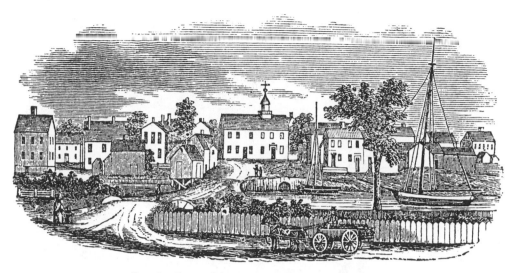

South view of the central part of Riverhead

an academy, and about 500 inhabitants. The courthouse, seen in the central part of the engraving with a small spire, has stood more than a century. James Port is a recent village E. of Riverhead. Old Aquabogue, Upper Aquabogue, Fresh Pond, Baiting Hollow, and Wading River, are small villages.

SHELTER Island is a town comprehending the island of that name in Gardiner's bay. It is about six miles long and four broad, containing about 8,000 acres, divided into several farms. Pop. 379. The surface of the island is generally undulating and covered in part by oak and other timber. The Indian name of this island was *Manhansack-aha-qushu-wamock,* meaning *an island sheltered by other islands.* . . .

SMITHTOWN is centrally distant from New York 47 miles. Pop. 1,932. The town is nearly 10 miles square: the surface on the north is broken and hilly, and on the south a perfectly level plain. The inhabitants are much scattered over the surface. There are several small villages, the most considerable of which are the *Branch* and the settlement called *Head of the River* [now, the Village of the Branch and Smithtown hamlet] . . . .[15]

SOUTHAMPTON, called by the natives Agawam, was settled in 1640, principally by about forty families from Lynn, Mass. Its name was given in remembrance of Southampton, Eng. The surface of the township is generally level, in the W. and N. the soil is light and sandy, in the S. mixed with loam, and when properly manured, produces good crops. Pop. 6,205. . . .

The village of Southampton is built on a single street, 18 miles from Riverhead. Bridgehampton, Westhampton, Good Ground, Flanders,

Northern view of Sag Harbor, Long Island

Speunk, Quogue, Canoe Place, and Beaverdam [Westhampton], are names of localities and villages. Shinnecock, or Southampton bay, is a fine sheet of water, 10 miles long, and from 3 to 4 wide. The territory of Shinnecock, containing some thousands of acres, is little else than a collection of sand hills. A small remnant of the Shinnecock tribe of Indians still linger on the SE. part of this tract, where they have a small church and a few dwellings.[16]

The [engraving] is a northern view of Sagg Harbor, situated in the NE. corner of the town, 100 miles from New York. It has a good harbor, lying on an arm of Gardiner's bay. The village contains 400 dwellings, 1 Presbyterian, 1 Methodist, 1 Catholic, and 1 African church, 2 printing offices, and about 3,000 inhabitants. The wealth and trade of the place may with propriety be said to be founded on the whaling business.

"Sagg Harbor is the most populous, wealthy, and commercial place in the county, and may therefore not improperly be considered the emporium of Suffolk. The capital employed in trade here probably exceeds that of the whole county besides, there being nearly a million of dollars invested in the whale-fishery alone, employing a tonnage of more than six thousand, exclusive of several fine packets and other vessels engaged in the coasting business. . . ."[17]

SOUTHOLD embraces the N. branch of Long Island, and includes Fisher's, Plumb [Plum], Robins, and Gull islands. It is centrally situated 17 miles from Riverhead, and 103 from New York. The surface is generally

Southern View of Greenport in Southold

level, and the soil a sandy loam, and productive under careful cultivation. Pop. 3,907. The inhabitants are principally settled along the great road which passes centrally through the town in a number of thickly settled neighborhoods or villages, as at Mattatuc [Mattituck], Cutchogue, Southold, Oyster Ponds, or Orient, forming almost a continued village.

Greenport, the largest village in the town, is situated at what is called Southold harbor, a part of the great Peconic bay, 23 miles from the courthouse at Riverhead. It is laid out into streets and building lots, and contains about 100 dwellings, 1 Baptist, 1 Methodist, and 1 Presbyterian church, and wharves and railways for the accommodation of vessels. The water is of sufficient depth for large ships and well sheltered from storms. The village was commenced by a few spirited individuals in 1827. The ancient village of Southold contains 1 Presbyterian and 1 Universalist church, and an academy. The peninsula of Oyster Ponds is the eastern extremity of the island; the village, now called Orient, contains two churches, two docks or wharves, and upwards of 500 inhabitants. *Fisher's Island,* belonging to this town, is 9 miles from New London, Conn., and 4 from Stonington. It is about 9 miles long, and has a medial width of one mile, containing about 4,000 acres. This island was purchased by Gov. [John] Winthrop [Jr.] of Connecticut in 1664, and has been in possession of the Winthrop family ever since. The staple articles raised on the island are wool, butter, and cheese. There are about 45 persons of all ages upon the island. *Plumb Island* contains about 800 acres of land, and has a population of about 75 persons. *Great* and *Little Gull islands* are situated in what is called the *Race,* on account of the swiftness of the current. Great Gull contains 15 acres; Little Gull one acre, mostly a solid rock. Upon this last island a lighthouse has been erected, which is of much importance to the navigation of the sound.[18]

Notes

Source: John W. Barber and Henry Howe, *Historical Collections of the State of New York: Containing a General Collection of the Most Interesting Facts, Traditions, Biographical Sketches, Anecdotes, etc. Relating to the History and Antiquities with Geographical Descriptions of Every Township in the State* (New York: S. Tuttle, 1842), pp. 219-22, 233-37, 533-41, 543-46. This volume was reprinted in a facsimile edition by Ira J. Friedman in Port Washington in 1970. Much of Barber and Howe's historical information was taken from secondary sources (including Benjamin F. Thompson's *History of Long Island)*, and most has been omitted here to focus on the geographical descriptions.

Editing changes have been minor and limited to some modernization of punctuation. To facilitate placement of illustrations, where the original text stated "above" or "following," the word "engraving" has been substituted in brackets. Most of their engravings have been included, and the captions are verbatim from the original. Elipses (. . .) indicate omissions in the text; topics of longer sections which are omitted here are identified in the notes, as well as the sources of Barber and Howe's quotations (including page references). All notes for this edition are by the editor except as indicated in no. 3. The initials such as SE., NW. are abbreviations for directions, e.g., southeast, northwest.

1. The biographical information on Barber and Howe is from *The National Cyclopaedia of American Biography*, 3:215-16, 344. Barber and Howe each later wrote many other books in addition to the ones cited in the introduction. See also Richard Hegel, "John Warner Barber," in *American Historians, 1607-1865*, edited by Clyde N. Wilson, vol. 30, *Dictionary of Literary Biography* (Detroit: Gale Research, 1984), pp. 23-30; and Alexander Moore, "Henry Howe," in ibid, 133-40.

2. *The Roots and Heritage of Hempstead Town*, edited by Natalie A. Naylor (Interlaken, NY: Heart of the Lakes Publishing, 1994), pp. 201-4.

3. The quotation is from Benjamin F. Thompson, *History of Long Island* (New York: E. French, 1839), p. 462 (3:196 in the 1918/1962 edition). Barber and Howe also quote Thompson on the early history of Brooklyn and the original Dutch name, Breucklen ("broken land"). In their Preface, Barber and Howe explain, "we have availed ourselves of the labors of those who have preceded us" (p. 3). For geographical information, they acknowledge use of Spafford's and Gordon's Gazetteers and state maps. The 1824 edition of Horatio Gates Spafford's *Gazetteer of the State of New-York* was reprinted by Heart of the Lakes Publishing in Interlaken, NY, in 1981.

Thompson expanded and revised his *History of Long Island* and published it in two volumes in 1842. He continued to expand his *History* and had three volumes ready for publication when he died in 1849. The three volumes were not published until 1918, edited and with additions by Charles J. Werner. Barber and Howe used the original 1839 edition, but since the three-volume edition, which was reprinted by I.J. Friedman in Port Washington in 1962, is the most accessible version, references will also be given to the pertinent pages in that edition (cited as 1918/1962 edition). The quotation from Thompson here and elsewhere in this selection illustrates how Thompson also has descriptions of communities from the late 1830s and 1840s in his well-known *History of Long Island.*

4. Barber and Howe's accounts of the prison ships during the Revolution (from the *Connecticut Journal*, 1771, and an 1838 article by J. Johnson), the explosion of the *Fulton* steam frigate in 1829, and the Battle of Long Island in August 1776 (from Thompson's *History of Long Island*, pp. 515-29; 1:353-63 in the 1918/1962 edition) are omitted here (in *Historical Collections*, pp. 222-33).

5. Williamsburg has recently been erected into a separate town [1840], (footnote in Barber and Howe, *Historical Collections*, p. 234). Later Williamsburg was incorporated as a city (1852) and annexed to Brooklyn (1855).

6. On Erasmus Hall, see Natalie A. Naylor, "The 'Encouragement of Seminaries of Learning': The Origins and Development of Early Long Island Academies," *Long Island Historical Journal* 12 (Fall 1999): 11, 13, 17-19, 23-25.

7. Barber and Howe do not identify the source of the quotation. It is very similar to the editor's addition to Thompson, *History of Long Island*, 3:144 in the 1918/1962 edition; they may have each quoted from the same source.

8. Thompson, *History of Long Island*, 1839, p. 445 (though not totally verbatim); 3:122 (in the 1918/1962 edition).

9. The other two counties were Kings and Queens. Present-day Nassau County was part of Queens County until 1899. The island's length is 118 miles.

10. The Town of Riverhead split off from Southold in 1792. Babylon was part of the Town of Huntington until 1872. Hence, there are now ten towns in Suffolk County.

11. Omitted here is Barber and Howe's account of Colonel Benjamin Talmadge's raid on Coram from Connecticut during the Revolutionary War (*Historical Collections*, p. 535). This is quoted from Thompson, *History*, pp. 289-90; 3:353 in the 1918/1962 edition.

12. A section on "the notorious pirate," Captain William Kidd, is omitted here (*Historical Collections*, pp. 536-37).

13. On the Montaukett Indians, see John A. Strong, *The Montaukett Indians of Eastern Long Island* (Syracuse: Syracuse University Press, 2001); and John A. Strong, *"We Are Still Here!": The Algonquian Peoples of Long Island Today*, 2d ed. (Interlaken, NY: Empire State Books, 1999).

14. The quotation on the lighthouse (although slightly revised) is from Thompson, *History of Long Island*, p. 197; 2:110-11 in the 1918/1962 edition. Omitted here are an account of the capture of the *Amistad* off Culloden Point, Montauk, in 1839 and the trials in 1840-1841 (in *Historical Collections*, pp. 538-39).

15. Omitted here are J.W. Blydenburgh's account of Richard Smith and information quoted from Thompson's *History of Long Island* (2:373) on the "Bull Smiths" (*Historical Collections*, pp. 541-43).

16. On the Shinnecock, see Gaynell Stone, ed., *The Shinnecock Indians: A Cultural History* (Stony Brook: Suffolk County Archaeological Association, 1983); and Strong, *"We Are Still Here!"* pp. 17-20, 36-64, 99-104.

17. The quotation is from Thompson, *History of Long Island*, p. 216 (though not verbatim); 3:176, 191 ff. in 1918/1962 edition. Omitted here is an account of Col. Jonathan Meigs expedition and activities during the War of 1812 from Thompson, *History of Long Island*, pp. 217-29 (1:304-6 in 1918/1962 edition).

18. On the Gull Island Lighthouse, see Jim Crowley, *Lighthouses of New York, The Greater New York Harbor, Hudson River, Long Island* (Saugerties, NY: Hope Farm Press, 2000), pp. 102-3; and note no. 21 in Dwight's "Journey to Long Island" above.

Visiting Long Island Relatives, 1844

Elizabeth Howell Blanchard

Elizabeth Howell was born in Fresh Ponds (now Baiting Hollow) in eastern Suffolk County in 1800 and married Seth Blanchard when she was seventeen. They moved to southwestern Illinois in 1820 where they named their farm near Greenville, "Suffolk Grove." The Blanchards had nine children between 1820 and 1838. Elizabeth Blanchard was in poor health and decided to come back to New York to try to regain her health and visit her old home and relatives.[1] She left home on May 10 and returned five months later, on October 18, 1844. In addition to her ten week visit on Long Island, she spent more than a month in New York City. Her trip from Illinois to Long Island took between three and four weeks each way, traveling mostly by boat. To reach Long Island she took a stagecoach to St. Louis, travelled down the Mississippi River, up the Ohio River to Pittsburgh, on cars and canals to Philadelphia, and a steamboat ("steamer") from Philadelphia to New York City. Her diary records her full trip, but these selections are excerpted from her visit to Long Island.

Blanchard traveled to Islip, Patchogue, Stony Brook, Baiting Hollow, Riverhead, and the North Fork as far as Greenport. She stayed with relatives, one of whom was the keeper of the Fire Island lighthouse. She described the view from the top of the lighthouse in florid language. On Long Island, she traveled by stagecoach, private carriages and wagons, and railroad cars, with excursions on the water. The railroad made its first trip to Greenport during her visit and she saw people gathering to see the train pass. Blanchard briefly describes several of the communities she visited, but her journal focuses on the domestic scene. Blanchard's account provides much information on the common practice of visiting relatives and glimpses of everyday activities of daily life. She attended many church services and temperance meetings. Her descriptions of traveling on Long Island and the food she was served can be compared with Laura Hawkin's visit a half century later (see "A 'Mid-Summer Outing,'" the final selection below).

Blanchard alludes to lines in Shakespeare and is quite familiar with the Bible. Growing up in the years before New York established its school system, Blanchard had learned to read and write, but her spelling is often phonetic. She wrote this account in her personal journal and did not intend it for publication nor indeed for others to read. Her writing is informal and punctuation has been added to make the account more readable (see details on editing in the Notes).

While she was in New York City, a few days after leaving Long Island, Blanchard wrote in her journal, "I think I would like to live on L.I. — but feel quite content with my home in Illinois."[2] Unfortunately, she did not regain her health and died two years after returning from her trip. Her journal remained in the family and it was published in the *Long Island Historical Society Quarterly* in 1941–1942.

* * *

June 17th. Monday came and we left N. York and crossd over to Brooklin, took the stage for Islip. Stopd several times to take in passengers and leave mail at the different towns and postoffices. Was much delighted with the seats and gardens, a great variety of roses and flowers. Specially Mr. Judds country seat was beautiful. Arrivd at our home, that is the home of my cousin, at about five oclock. . . .

June 20. Were all invited to Uncle Henrys and had a most excelant dinner and dessert. Plenty of currants and in the afternoon we went over to another cousins. Had a grand visit, was agreeably entertaind. They are pleasantly situated, have a delightful view of the bay and the vessels. And I felt a great desire that my children should witness this scenry and become acquainted with my relatives on old Long Island. . . .

June 22. Arose early, took breakfast, and set {sat} down to my knitting. Had an excelant dinner. Invited company to dine after which we dressd for an excursion on the water. Mr. [William Wessels] Laws, his wife and daughter, Cousin Chary M., myself, and a Mrs. Strong and a boy went on board the boat with our fishing hooks and lines to catch blue-fish and porgie. We grapled a few clams and a few fish, returnd home again, was ver {very} cold, glad to find a good fire. The tea table set and all things nice and comfortable—after a refreshing rain, for you must know we had quite a squall out to sea during our voyage. Forgot to mention a few nights since of the great fire about a mile off, a large house and store, finely furnishd, burnd to the ground. Islip is quite a large neighborhood, a good society. A church, a school, some manufacturing, boat building, stores, and so forth. I am quite pleased with my visit, tho constantly regreting that neither husband or children are with me to share my pleasures. . . .

June 23. Sabbath morning has come, the great and glorious sun has arisen on a (comparative) unthankful world. Have read a chapter and prayd to the Supreme to bless our endeavrs to do good. Now we prepare to go to the sanctuary and hear the word preachd from the pulpit. Cousin Oliver Smith and his Lady {i.e., wife} calld and invited me to go up to Babilon {Babylon} to Presbyterian meeting. I stepd into the carriage, had a delightful drive; passed a great many fine houses and gardens and millponds and heard a good sermon preachd, work out your salvation. Good singing and praying, returnd home dind at Cousin Hetta's [Hetta Smith] and so on. Sabbath evening—goodnight. . . .

June 26. Today we are going on the beach, quite a large party of us. We had a nice sail. Plenty of company. Arrivd at Capt Smiths, found them finely

situated. Had a fine dinner. Took a walk over to the ocean side of the beach. The sea breaking majesticaly on the shore, then receeding. We rested awhile, then proposed to go up to the top of the {Fire Island} Light-house. It is seven stories high.[3] Quite a curiosity to see the apparatus up there, the large silver reflectors which cost forty dollars apiece. They are splendid. Then to look abroad on the vast ocean and think of the dangers of the great deep and turn and look the other side and see a broad expanse of water calld the bay. With numerous crafts of all sizes almost and pursuing as many occupations, to gain a livelihood or enrich their already well filld coffers. So the world goes. It does indeed seem all the worlds a stage and all the men and women play-acting, but I fear all are too anxious to lay up treasures on earth.

June 27th. Arose, prepard for breakfast, had a very good cup of coffee and trimmings. Set awhile and hemd {hemmed} 1/2 doz towells for Cousin Maria as they were fixing for an immence crowd of company. Building and furnishing their house, they are paid by the government five hundred dollars for lighting and tending the light house and they do live very finely indeed. Catherine and Georgiana are two very handsome girls, and are both of them splendid singers and performers on the acordion, good music. After dinner we dressd accordingly and went down to the salt water and took a bath, the water was not ver cold but grateful. At length we returnd home, dryd {dried}, and dressd, and felt quite refreshd. Set down to sewing and talking and singing and again in the afternoon had a boat load of company. They have left and I have just finished writing an acrostic for Catherine Maria Smith, my cousins daughter. Tis most tea time and I must lay up my pen to resume at a convenient oppty; would be willing to pay a dollar for a letter.[4] [At] 5 m{inutes} to 5, had a beautiful tea. Quince preserves, gooseberries, currants, pound cake, and ginger cake with the very best of wheat bread and butter, chip beef, and so on. After I took a walk, set {sat} up and read the *Family Magazine and Tribune,* went to bed. . . .

June 28. Drank some lemon syrup, very good. Ate some nice bread and butter, an apple, and oisters {oysters} made a good lunch. Took my pen and ink and journal and assended the 7 flights of stairs and am now comfortably seated in the top of the light house on Fire Island, a grand oppty to contemplate the majesty and power of him who can say to the winds and waves, "Peace be still." The sun shines glorious and the wind blows tremendous. The surf and surge, roar and beat upon the shore. A true touch of the sublime is this view of the mighty ocean, constantly pouring and roaring and foaming its white billows against the sandy beach. None but an omnipotent arm could save a frail barque of a ship from the ravages of the great deep. I do not, cannot see how tis possible for man to presume to sail out upon the wonderful expanse of water without imploring divine protection from the dangers of the sea! and heartily resigning all into the hands of Him whom waves and winds obey. None seem to be coasting today. A sloop has just come in through the inlet and saild on through the bay east, probably to Pachougeo {Patchogue} or some of those towns along the coast. Bell-Port, Moriches, Fire Place {Brookhaven hamlet}, Blue Point, etc. The beach is about 1/4 a mile wide and extends almost the length of the Island. The bay was formd a century ago. Some old men knew it when {it was} a forest.

I am calld to dinner and must now descend from this high situation in life. Wish I could describe the prospect from here, from this lofty and commanding view—vast, vast! Eligible and grand and awful, yet sublime to look abroad as far as the eye can possibly reach on the great ocean and think of the trying scenes witnessd and felt by millions, and recollect many circumstances that come within our own knowledge is enough to make us feel our insignificence and entire dependance on Jehovah! for our deliverance from danger by sea or land. Took a walk to a pond, a fish pond, containing a few hundred. They fed them daily with shelfish. It was ver amusing to see their bright eyes and pearly shiny glosy coat, whirling in every direction to catch at their food. We then got in the boat and saild up to the dock a mile or more, a fine ride. Went in bathing, water too cold—like to had an ague {chill}. Took tea and retird to the new parlors they were painting. Was agreeably entertaind by musick on the acordion and Miss Catherines voice. She is a wonderful performer and a splendid singer indeed, a natural musician. . . .

July 3. Arose very early and as it raind hard I feard we could not go, but it cleard away and we got ready. Uncle Henry (who is one of the best men in the world) proferd {proffered} to go with his horses and carriage and take us {to Patchogue}. We said goodby and left Islip at eight or 9 oclock. Traveld on a good road, a ver few fine farms but poor land, a sandy soil—old houses and not able to build. Passd Sayville, a small village and arrivd at John Coreys, another cousin, about noon. Found them ver comfortably situated. Stayd two or three hours, took dinner, then left for Dear Uncle Tuttles [Rev. Ezra Tuttle] or Cousin Wm. Smiths where they board. Went through Pachogue and found our friends happy and contented. Spent an hour or so when Uncle Henry left for home and I remaind to make my visit. Catherine Chary M. left. Had a good supper and retird to rest.

July 4th. Slept well, arose at 6. Beautiful and glorious sun shining on the just and the unjust! Cannons firing to announce that Independence Day is at hand. 10 oclock. Want to go and hear the oration, cant go alone. Farmers too busy; say if 4th of July came in winter they would attend. Find some have to work hard here as well as myself in Illinois. Had a good dinner and now going to ride up in the buggy to town, 1 mile or two with my cousin and her two little sons. Got there too late. The meeting was over and folks gone home. Rode to the church-yard to be admonished by reflection. Great many large white marble tombs bearing inscriptions of my relations and telling passers by {that} they too must die. Returnd home, talkd awhile. Pickd some currants and took tea. Then dressd to go to a temperance lecture, Miss Mary and all of us. We went and found the church near full, a neat and well-finishd edifice, belonging to the Methodist denomination. Brother Osborne officiates as their minister. Is a good man. The temperance address was given by a Mr. {James H.} Thomas a Congregetionist {Congregationalist} who is settld in Pachogue. Gets four hundred dollars a year for preaching! Is a first rate man, gave us a very interesting address indeed! I was delightd with him. Sang an ode and dimisissd [dismissed] the assembly after pressing the subject home to his audience of total abstinence, and renewd efforts against King Alcohol and endeavor to exterminate him from our land, as a base tyrant, and to proclaim ourselves free of such tyrany. Could we as enlightend Americans but avail us of that independence of character we should feel soon the result to be greatly in our favor. Took several ladies home in our carriage and were safe at our residence at ten oclock. Took drink of milk and went to rest.

July 6th. Cool pleasant day. Read an account of President {John} Tylers Marriage with Miss {Julia} Gardner. Concluded she was pleasd with honors of a high situation in life as she was only twenty while he was sixty. Presume he is in favor of anexation {of Texas}.[5]

July 7th. Sabbath has come with all its hallowed associations. The sun shines gloriously, all around is still and, seemingly to me in sollemn reverence of this ever holy day. Cousins have gone to Sunday school. Uncle and aunt are dressd and they do look beautiful in old age. Uncle Tuttle has been a minister of the gospel for above forty years and has been and still is a most devoted Christian, eminent and influential belovd by all, both far and near, He was the same m{inister} that united me to my belovd husband in 1817 and he has married vast numbers in 40 or 50 years past. Is now aged 80 years, is quite active, goes daily to call on some neighbor and talk religion with them. We all rode to their church about 2 or 300 there. Heard a most excelant sermon preachd by Brother Osborne from first Peter, 2nd chapter, 9th verse. Ye are a chosen generation a peculiar people and representing the church. Intermission and I went with Mary Catherine to the old Congregational church to hear Brother Thomas hold forth from the good book and the words, Bring all the lyths {?} in the store house and prove me, etc. etc. A good discourse but all to the church who seem rather in a cold state at pressent. We returnd home ate dinner, read some of Hester Ann Rogers experience.[6] Retird early.

My cousin Mrs. Smith hired a woman to do her washing and mine.[7] After tea we went up to Pachogue to the post office. No letter felt very much grievd, came home tird out. Went right to bed. . . .

July 12th. Am now ready to leave this dear family and test the hospitality of Mr. John Coreys. Got into the pleasure wagon with the old priest, his wife, and daughter and went through the village of Pachogue. Is famous for its manufacturing conveniences being suplied with water from a large pond. A paper mill and 2 cotton factorys which the annual product amounts to about 8 or 10 thousand dollars, mills of various kinds, 2 churchs, Methodist and Congregationalist. Their minister receives 3 to 400 dollars a year sallery. The village is built on the main street, 3 or 400 inhabitants, a post office, and very pretty white houses, fine yds, and gardens! Stage comes and goes 3 times a week to City of New York. Cars, the same railroad depo {depot} 4 miles north of thise, extending through the Middle Island to Oisterpanpoint! {Oysterponds}.[8] The farmers have to work hard and spend from 15 to 20 dollars an acre to manure their land so as to raise grain enough to support their family with all neceraries and save a little for a rainy day or in the decline of life. The friends spent a pleasant day and others were invitd. After tea, uncle, aunt, and cousin bade me adieu with tears and blessings. . . .

July 14. Today is the holy sabbath. We are ready for church. My friends here are all Methodists or nearly so. Good honest farmers and very good livers. I am much pleasd with my visit at Cousin John Coreys. I like his wife ver much, she is a very smart inteligent woman. We went heard a sermon from Mr. Farterx (?) returnd home to dinner. Afternoon it raind very hard. We could not go to class meeting at Blue Point.

July 15. Monday arose early and prepard for a ride up to Westfield [now Selden] to see another cousin. Mrs. Norton, Mr. John Corey, his wife and niece and 2 children, and the school marm all got into the carriage with two beautiful fine horses and set off about 10 miles. Arrivd at 9, after 2 or 3 hours ride on the pine plains and sandy desert. Not a house for 6 or 8 miles, lookd like old times when I have crossd the island 26 or 7 and 8 {i.e., 27 and 28} and 30 years ago, tho under far diferent circumstances. Then I was young and artless and hapy, knew no care, the world went on wheels, and I thought it ever would with me, but now I have a large progeny to be interested for and am full of cares and anxieties. The railroad is laid out through the middle of the island and will be of some benefit to the farmers in its vicinity. The land is too poor to produce enough, hardly to keep a goose alive without puting on the amount of fifteen dollars an acre of manure. Saw plenty of huckleberrys. We all went out with our pails and baskets and pickd near 1/2 bushel of blackberrys. Had a good dinner and super when the pary {party?} left for home. . . .

July 16. Like her {Cousin Norton} much. {She} has made me a present of a nice apron, some pieces like her silk weding and infare {?} dresses, but time, old time has changed the faces of my old friends, from full and fair to old and wrinkled. And now I must acknowledge I far prefer the West to the East and would not exchange our farm out in Illinois for one here except it was near New York and we could have a splendid pasture and garden.

July 17th. Today it rains hard all the time and we are housd up. Pass the time very pleasantly sewing and talking. Have visitd Mr. Nelson Nortons, find them well off too. Large farm, fifty acres in wheat and rye and so forth; large orchards, fine apples, and so on. Good super; staid all night.

July 18th. Slept well, arose, dressd, took leave. Came over to Cousin Sarahs. Had an excelant breakfast and now say good-bye. Got in carriage with Cousin N{orton} and rode ten miles to call on a relative. Passd through old Coram where my old grandparents used to live. Saw the meeting house and grave yard. All lookd old and defacd. Was reminded of the disolution of all things. Recollected the deep pond and many other places, bringing back to my mind my childhood days, and with them my happiest days. Arrive at Mr. Randalls ten oclock at the Ridge! Stopd and found a large and commodious house and barn and outhouses, all of which was built by my dear Uncle but is now passd into other hands as he died without a will. His fine farm and houses were sold for the benefit of heirs and I could have cried heartily to see the change here and alterations in circumstances for the worse, but so it is, some are rich and some are poor. At all events I find the farmers have to work hard too. . . .

July 20. Took breakfast and prepard to set off to Fresh Ponds {Baiting Hollow} to visit dear cousins and their families. Arrivd at Cousin Micah Howells, 8 or 9 oclock, knew his wife the first moment. Was receivd with much kindness, find them handsomely situated. He is a merchant and they have a very pretty house and two very pretty daughters, Maria and Lucetta Pricilla, good girls both of them. I am much pleasd with my visit here, they live very well and Cousin Ann is a most excelant cook and has the most excelant to cook. I am delighted with every thing around, the rooms are kept perfectly neat and clean. They also keep a fine large horse and buggy, which was brot to the door for our pleasure. After tea, which was very refreshing, we got in the carriage and Miss Marie got in and drove us over to Lieutenant Cooks, an old acquaintance. They calld me by name on seeing me and was very glad to see me, talkd and laughd a few minutes and left. Had a delightful ride as the street is level and the sun had set, the air fresh and grateful. Retird to my room, had a first rate bed, and slept all night.

July 21st. Arose, read, and prepard for meeting. We rode in the buggy to our old church. Could hardly command my feelings as I enterd the threshold as it was more than twenty five years since I was there to meeting before! My old friends lookd at me and not one in ten that knew me. A very good discourse preachd from a verse in Isaiah 44 chapt. by Mr. Downs. After meeting, several came and spoke to me, having known my very dear father, he being deacon of this same church about twenty years. First Mrs. Margaret Corwin, a very dear friend, having spent many very happy days with her, when at her dear sisters before either of us was married. She kindly took me home with her and we sociably ate our lunch of pound cake and blackberry pie. I was more pleasd to see her and Mrs. Edwards than all other acquaintances, because their attention to me have been unabating and always the same. I had a hearty cry to look at my dear papas seat in the pew and look back a vista of 25 years, 35, yes 40 years and think of the time I was first awakend and my convictions and I trust conversion and uniting with this same church made me feel ver sollemn indeed. And to see my Cousin Daniel Howell, now deacon, siting in my fathers place, and as he prayd most fervently, my heart responded the Amen. After meeting, I went with Cousin Anna down to the grave yard where my very dear mother and two sisters were buried.[9] I felt as deeply to mourn and grieve as if I had just lost her. I knelt by her head stone which was of white marble and after a most hearty cry, read her dear name, age, death, etc. Went round to read others of my old acquaintances and friends. Felt ver sollemn indeed. Returnd through the gate, rode home, and retird to rest. . . .

July 27th. Next day all rode down a mile and half to see the cars pass, being the first time after the rail-road was finishd.[10] We could see several miles each way. Had been there about 8 minutes when they came in sight as a black boy in the distance, but as they neard us apeard like a grat niger, went past us like a streak, of lightning, on and on out of sight, then a boom on the air was borne along, being the great gun at Riverhead as a token of joy! at the sight of this ponderous machinery and the accomplishment of this great object. A line of steamers intercepting at Greenport to convey passengers to Boston, through Long I. in about half the time of going through the Sound and probably at a cheaper rate. The trains were 20 minutes apart and going 4 miles in 6 minutes. We saw the last and left the railroad to return, five ladies of us (and a boy). On going to the buggy we found none. The horse chose to walk home without us and we had to follow suit. The sun shone in full meridian splendor and I was most exhausted; changd my thick merino dress to a very thin muslin. Felt chilly had a bad hea dach {headache}. . . .

July 29th. {Coming back from beach at "west landing":} We returnd by way of our old location, where we once had a store. Thot of those happy days when I was young and all my life lookd to me like one happy sunshine—oh dear.

Came along, saw not even a board of our old house or store, it being all move away, the meadow in front was overflowd with water so that sail boats can go 1/2 mile or more up the creek. Then we pickd our baskets full of huckleberries! which indeed seemd like old times to wander up the cliffs and over the rocks and precipices and sand hills to the salt shore of old Long Island Sound. We came home, took tea, and retird to rest. . . .

August 6th. Arose early, dressd, and walkd a mile or so up to the cliffs to eat huckleberrys for the last time. . . . Packd my trunk, and wishd 'em well and left them to go over to the manor to visit Mrs. Ann Carter, a cousin. Traveld along on the line of my dear fathers old farm about a mile or more. Brot my young and childhood days back again, when I used to roam in and over and past this, the old orchard, the young orchard, the road lot, the pond lot, the 2nd lot, the west lot, the swamp lot, the gate lot, and so on, round home a circuit of 350 acres of land. I could have cried hard, but I kept up a conversation with Mr. Micah. Passd the railroad several times, crossd over the bridge and the Pecomic {Peconic} river and went along a sandy soil some ten miles through the poorest part of the island. Arrivd at Deacon Carters ten oclock, find them comfortable, with 4 children.

August 7th. Arose, dressd, ate breakfast, took short walk, pasd the church, quite a nice building finishd neatly as I peepd in the windows to see! Set down to write. Going this afternoon to Esq. Wines. Must now go and spin a pair of stockings 1 Oclock have dind and spun my yarn, then rode over to Esq. Wines, calld, and then went to the store where my cousin bot {bought} me 8 yds of calico for a pressent. I was made welcome and pleasd with my visit. They have four fine children. Said goodbye to them as the old jent {gent} was kind enough to take me to another cousins.

Thursday the 8th. . . . Riverhead is a distance about 12 or 14 miles. Got up the horse and carriage, and set off, jogd on about 3 or 4 miles an hour. Was entertaind by the deacon all the way. He thot I had manefestd a great desire to see my friends and said he was much surprisd to know they had not made me any compensation. He thot my own aunts would have least given me a dollar apiece when they are quite able to afford it. We arrivd at Riverhead about noon, and before Deacon Carter left me he handed me a dollar out of his pocket saying "you are quite welcome, Mrs. Blanchard, and if twill do you any good I am glad of it." I thankd him and wishd all my friends were Deacon Carters. Likd the looks of Riverhead. Find it quite a busy lively town, a good seminary, and genteel inhabitants. My old acquaintances here hardly knew me, tho I think they look about as old as myself. . . . Was shewn the grape arbor which was bountifully loaded with grapes about thirty feet, then the shrubery, their names, and qualitys. Sat awhile in their elegant parlor, and curtisied away a good evening. The cars seem to be a great curiosity to the rising generation. The railroad has just been completed through to Greenport and runs a little north of the town. Every day a small colony of men women and children go to see the cars {of the train pass}.

August 9th. Riverhead is the county seat, about six hundred Inhabitants. Suffolk County is very large and all come here to attend court. The Pecomic river runs along past here and emties {empties} into the bay. The sloops and small crafts in sight. And the young jentleman and ladies are to have a picnic on Saturday and go sailing over to the beach. Some fine buildings are nearly finished. 2 churches and the town has a prety appearance. Mills and factories abounding on the river. Think twill be quite a place, in a few years. Still I prefer the far West. 11 Oclock have written a long letter and put it in the letter box at the post office. Returnd, dind, now we dress and walk out to make calls. Returnd, having calld on 1/2 doz families of 2nd cousins and acquaintances. All very glad to see me. Found Mrs. Maria Jagger in good situation, nice home, and nicely furnishd. Her daughter Chary, a lively intelligent girl, just like Mary Elizabeth {her daughter, (JT)}. I like her much. Mrs. J calld to see me, she is an old school mate of mine and was very happy to see me. Pressd me to visit her. I promisd to and she left while we went to tea altho had eaten so many pears I had no appetite for supper. Had many invitations to stay to tea and come again. Calld on Aunt Polly Alberson and her daughter, Mr. and Mrs. Swesey (? {Swezey?}), and Miss Maria Wells and Mr. Wm Griffin and Mr. Daniel Edwards. And then took a walk up to the railroad to see the cars come in about dark. 2 stages were waiting to take the pasengers to the hotels. Very sultry night.

August 10th. Rose early, felt quite unwell, taken cold, got in the stage for Franklinville {now Laurel}, to see Mr. George Tuthill. Bid Cousin Elma a short goodbye intending to return again in a few days and finish my visit. Rode 5 or 6 miles and alighted from the mail stage. Went in and found 'em comfortable, good large house and farm, etc. Plenty of pears, 2 or 3 kinds. Find Mrs. Tuthill very sociable and kind—good dinner and tea. Now start again. Mr. George Tuthill and wife and child got in the buggy and rode down to James Port {Jamesport}, down to the waters edge to visit Uncle David Tuthills, his wife was my dear papas sister. I find them quite handsomely situated, a 2 story brick house, finely furnishd. Aunt Mary cultivating the flowers like any young lady. I am pleasd with {South} James Port, it is directly on the bay. 1 or two hundred people, sloops and packets and boats are daily and hourly in sight. Many are engaged in whaling and fishing and on the railroad and building James Port. . . .

August 13th. Rose early on Tuesday 13 and prepard to leave James Port, for Mathituck {Mattituck}. Aunt Polly had ordered the horse and buggy at

Greenport

the door, and I bid Uncle David goodbye, and we rode along about 8 miles to visit another aunt and cousin. Found them in a very nice house with a plenty to eat drink and wear. Spent the day. Aunt Mary returnd home alone. I felt very homesick. After tea Mr. Maaps took his daughter and me about 3 miles to the town, there to stay till the cars came. They were belated and I did not like to start so late, so I told the landlady I would stop till the stage came. . . .

August 14th. Got in stage and rode through a good road to Cachogue {Cutchogue}, thence to Southold town, then to Miamaug (?)[11] along the Sound oposite to G. Turnd down a lane towards the bay at the beautiful Greenport. About 7 or 800 people, 3 churches, pretty houses, and 7 or 8 ships is ownd here by the inhabitants. Those are mostly whale ships, go a voyage of 2 or 3 years! Many young men from the island go. Tis a few miles to Orient or Oister Ponds and Sagharbor.[12] Steam boats go every day over to Norwich and to New London {in Connecticut}. Stage drove up to Doc'r Fannings. Mrs. F. met me at the door and glad to see me. Handsomely situated, large yard and garden, imence grape arbors, bushels of fruit fine, houses 3 children. Quite accomplishd. 12 or 20 ver genteel boarders, number of ladies. Sat awhile in the parlor then went to dinner. Rested awhile and dressd for tea, after which went to prayer meeting, returnd, went to bed. . . .

August 16th. Rose at 1/2 past 4 oclock, dressd and bade them a formal adieu. Doct. Fanning was at the gate with the buggy to take me to the car {train} depo {depot}. 3 ladies only on board. Left and paid my fare up to Riverhead. 38 cents, whirld along in one hour and 20 minutes. We arrivd, got in stage, and rode to my cousins {in Baiting Hollow (?)}. . . .

August 18. Rose early on Sunday morning, dressd and went to Sabbath school. Teachd a class of young ladies. Found them well informd and genteel girls. Heard a sermon from a Methodist from Corinth, Eng. Im'd {?} after sermon, returnd home, and prepard to leave. Stage drove up and I stepd in. Had my trunk lashd on and left with 3 other ladies, and we traveld on about 25 miles to a cousins, Mrs. Nortons.

August 20. Tuesday felt rather better, tho weak from the pain. Got in the wagon with Mrs. Norton, rode some 8 miles to my Dear Aunts {in Stony Brook} to make them a visit. Find them very nicely and comfortably situated. . . . Mrs. Petta, my cousin, I like ver much, feel that she is a true Christian. Shall prize my visit with her! and all here very much. Stoney Brook is a small town—a harbor for vessels, a church, 6 stores, and about 300 people in it. Rocky and sandy and stoney soil. Mrs. Smith calld for us to go over to Satauket [Setauket], Aunt Chary and me, and we spent the afternoon at Mr. Isaac Brewsters, Mrs. B. being my namesake. After diner we went over to see Aunt Hannah Silas. After tea rode home, realizing that

Peconic Bay

those in Satauket and likewise in many other places did not want to see me half as much as I did them. I came home with a heavy heart. Begd to be excusd and retird to my room and cryd till I went to sleep. Bad dreams and a restless night was the consequence feeling quite unwell, having taken cold. . . .

August 26. Spent the night with Mrs. Davis. . . . had a good dinner, after it Aunt Chary calld and we went over to Mr. Smiths, alias Mr. Howel Howkins and spent the afternoon, had a first rate time. Before tea, Mrs. S and me got in a tiney boat and the little Miss Miami got in, took the oars and rowd us across the pond, the beautiful pond, and around an island an acre or two, a round high surface or rise of grass and barberybushes and large willows drooping their limbs and leaves to drink of the pure and limpid stream. On the island was a flock of wild geese and ducks and a living rabit white as the driven snow with pink eyes and calld an English rabit. Ver beautiful. Pickd some herbs and stepd in the boat again. Returnd found a beautiful supper on the table, of which we all partook very sociably. Said goodby and walkd home. . . .

August 27. Tuesday came and the morning flew by with many promises of regard for those dear members of this family which I have always lovd. The boat was to sail at ten, we hurried and accepted of Uncle Micahs invitation to ride to the wharf. He came and put my trunk in his carriage. Mrs. Petty and Miss Clarissa gallanted me on board. Calld at the store, bot me some crackers, and packed up any amount of cake and pears. Went aboard found the packet crowded with women and children. Got out in the Sound and about 2 oclock came on a squall and hard rain. some were frightened. Some were seasick, some were cross, and some ill behavd. Then at night came a dead calm. Going through Hurlgate {Hell Gate}, the capt. said it was quite dangerous at that time of tide, but no sort of accident and we got to New York about 6 in the morning on Wednesday.

Notes

Source: Elizabeth Howell Blanchard, "Journal of a Trip from Illinois Back to Long Island in 1844," edited by William A. Robbins, *Long Island Historical Society Quarterly* 3 (1941): 48-53, 77-83, 107-15. Reprinted with permission of the Brooklyn Historical Society (formerly the Long Island Historical Society). Blanchard's granddaughter, Jessie Blanchard Allen Tweed, sent the journal to William A. Robbins who was interested in the Howell family history. Robbins published his verbatim transcript in five parts, beginning in January 1941 (3: 3-13) and concluding in the January 1942 issue (4: 3-15). As noted in the introduction, the original articles include Blanchard's trip to Long Island from Illinois and return. She made daily entries; some are omitted here, including many references to other relatives she visited, genealogical information, and the entries on her stay in New York City

Blanchard's writing was informal, with many phrases and run-on sentences. Punctuation has been modernized here to make the account more accessible (e.g., changing most of her dashes to commas or periods as appropriate, dividing some of her long sentences, and standardizing capitalization). The original spellings and abbreviations have been retained, as well as her occasional idiosyncratic use of exclamation points; apostrophes have not been added. However, ampersands (&) have been spelled out. Insertions in the text by William A. Robbins (WAR), who edited the original manuscript, are in brackets [thus]. Where Blanchard's granddaughter, Jessie Tweed, provided information to Robbins, her initials are indicated (JT). Insertions by the editor for this volume are in braces (or wavy brackets), {thus} and she has provided all the notes except no. 9 which is by Robbins. Question marks in parentheses are apparently where Robbins was uncertain of the spelling of a surname or place name; where these could be identified, the question mark has been omitted. Robbins inserted in the text the dates which may have been originally in the margins; the month has been added here. Elipses (three dots . . .) indicate where sections of the previously published original version have been omitted.

1. Biographical information is from the introduction to the journal by William A. Robbins in the *Long Island Historical Society Quarterly* 3 (January 1941): 3-4.

2. Blanchard, "Journal," 4 (January 1942): 9.

3. Blanchard visited the original Fire Island Lighthouse which was built in 1825 and was 74 feet tall. It was replaced by the present 150-foot tall lighthouse in 1858. The lighthouse keeper when she visited in 1844 was Eliphalet Smith. (Smith was the maiden name of Blanchard's mother.) The Fire Island Lighthouse is now a museum with exhibits. It is located east of parking lot 5 in Robert Moses State Park; 631-661-4876.

4. At this time, the recipient of a letter paid the postage.

5. Tyler later signed legislation annexing Texas to the Union. Julia Gardiner, who married the widower president, was from East Hampton. See Natalie A. Naylor, "Long

Island's Mrs. Tippecanoe and Mrs. Tyler Two," *Long Island Historical Journal* 6 (Fall 1993): 2-16.

6. Hester Ann Rogers (1756-1794) was an early leader in Methodism in England and Ireland. Her autobiography and other writings were reprinted widely in England and America in the nineteenth century. See "The Methodist Archives Biographical Index," <rylibweb.man.ac.uk/data1/dg/methodist/bio/bior.html> ; and Leslie F. Church, *The Early Methodist People* (New York: Philosophical Library, 1949).

7. Because washing clothes was the most arduous of household work in the nineteenth century, sometimes it was sent out to be done or someone was hired to do it, as Mrs. Smith had done.

8. Oysterponds today is Orient, but the railroad ended in Greenport, about four miles west of Orient.

9. Inscriptions on the two stones now {1940} remaining: (1) Elizabeth / wife of / Joseph Howell / who died / Sept. 25, 1819 / in the 46 year of / her age. (2) In / Memory of / Huldah, daugh'r of / Joseph and Elizabeth / Howell, who died / Aug. 22, 1815 / Aged 17 years and 7 days (WAR).

10. Blanchard witnessed the first trains to Greenport on July 27, 1844. The railroad was built as a short-cut to Boston (including a ferry trip across Long Island Sound). Her entry for August 8 from Riverhead reports people still going to see the "cars" of the train. See Edwin L. Dunbaugh, "New York to Boston via the Long Island Railroad," in *Evoking a Sense of Place,* edited by Joann P. Krieg (Interlaken, NY: Heart of the Lakes Publishing, 1988), pp. 75-84; Mildred H. Smith, *Early History of the Long Island Railroad, 1834-1900* (Uniondale: Salisbury Printers, 1958); and Sidney C. Schaer, "The Coming of the Iron Horse," in *Long Island: Our Story* (Melville: Newsday, 1998), pp. 178-81.

11. This reference is a bit puzzling. It would seem to be to *Miamog,* which is the Indian name for the area of Jamesport or South Jamesport where there is still Miamogue Point. In 1832, James Tuthill purchased the Miamogue Tract in what is now South Jamesport (originally, James's Port) and began to develop the area. By the time Blanchard was in the area, there were several houses, an inn, store, and school. Later in the century, large hotels, including the Miamogue Hotel were built. See Edna Howell Yeager, *Around the Forks,* edited by Eileen Yeager Carmer (Interlaken, NY: Privately printed, 198?), pp. 137-39. However, Miamogue is west of the area she describes and on the Peconic Bay or south side of the North Fork rather than on Long Island Sound. Contemporary maps do not give a name for any settlements between the hamlets of Southold and Greenport. She may have meant the area north of today's Hashamonack Pond which the 1873 Beers *Atlas* identifies as Ashamomaque.

12. Sag Harbor, of course, is on the South Fork, but vessels sailed between Sag Harbor and Greenport, Southold, or Jamesport. See Dorothy Ingersoll Zaykowski, *Sag Harbor: An American Beauty* (Sag Harbor: Sag Harbor Historical Society, 1991), pp. 222, 349.

Long Island in 1845

Nathaniel S. Prime

Nathaniel S. Prime (1785-1856) was born in Huntington where his father, Benjamin Young Prime (1733-1791), was a doctor, and his paternal grandfather, Ebenezer Prime (1700-1779), had been minister in Huntington's First Presbyterian Church for sixty-two years. His mother, Mary Wheelright Greaton, was the widow of Huntington's Episcopal minister, James Greaton who died in 1773. Although his father died when he was only 6-1/2 years old, he initially planned to follow in his footsteps and become a doctor. Prime attended the Huntington Academy and in 1801 taught at the West Neck School in today's Laurel Hollow. It was during this time that he had a conversion experience, made a public profession of faith, and decided to become a minister.

Prime entered Princeton College that fall as a sophomore and was graduated in 1804. He returned home, began to study theology privately with the Presbyterian minister, the Reverend William Schenck, and took charge of the Huntington Academy. He was licensed to preach the next year, and did supply preaching at various locations on Long Island, including Cutchogue, Sag Harbor, Smithtown, and Fresh Ponds (Baiting Hollow). Ordained as an evangelist in 1809, he was installed as the minister in a church in upstate Cambridge (Washington County) in 1813, where he remained nearly fifteen years. During his pastorate there, he began an academy and subsequently with his daughter founded Mt. Pleasant Female Seminary in Sing Sing (today's Ossining) in Westchester County in 1831. After four years, they moved their school to Newburgh. In 1838, he returned to the ministry and had pastorates in Newburgh, Ballston Spa, Brooklyn, Yorkville, and Huntington.[1]

Prime published his *History of Long Island* in 1845; its subtitle states "With Special Reference to its Ecclesiastical Concerns." Although it has been characterized as "basically an account of each Long Island town's churches and preachers,"[2] there is much contemporary (c. 1845) information and that is the focus of the selections here. In addition to his pastorates in various Long Island churches, Prime would have visited other communities when attending meetings of the Long Island Presbytery (the regional Presbyterian governing agency). No doubt he also corresponded with fellow ministers for historical information.

In the selections here, Prime describes in some detail the natural features of the island, particularly the Hempstead plains, and more briefly, the bushy or scrub oak plains, the great pine plains, and the forests and woods. As appropriate in a rural society, he focuses on the soil and agricultural potential of the various areas and points out also that deer, wild fowl, and birds abound. Prime delineates the condition of roads and difficulties of travel, and explains how turnpikes had overcome initial resentment. The railroad had just been completed to Greenport the year before Prime published his history. He realized that the railroad promised great changes, but it also brought destructive fires. His account of the early days of the railroad has been described as a "minor classic."[3] His description of the Punk's Hole station is particularly amusing.

In his accounts of each of the counties, Prime provides statistics on the size and population, including a calculation of the density of settlement. With the growth of Brooklyn in recent decades, Kings County had the largest population and greatest density. Suffolk's population still surpassed Queens (which included the towns of present-day Nassau), but Queens was more densely settled with less than half the area.

Prime notes that Long Island was "once both the body and soul of the Province of New York," though overshadowed and "almost cast into oblivion" with the growth of the rest of the state. In common with many nineteenth-century writers, Prime characterized the "character" of the residents. As a loyal native son of Suffolk, he is exuberant in extolling the patriotism, puritanism, and toleration of religion of its Yankee residents. Queens County, however, had a "greater diversity of religious views" and despite on-going "effervescence," less "assimilated manners."

Prime is not hesitant to express his strong opinions on subjects as varied as train service on Sunday and box or square pews in churches (see note no. 11). Though it dated from colonial days in Queens County, he condemns horseracing as an "abomination" and "one of the principal means of demoralization." In discussing agriculture in Suffolk, he explains how seaweed and menhaden are used for fertilizer. His descriptions of Hicksville, the county seat, and Roslyn are samples of the information he provides on the various settlements. Interested readers can consult other sections of Prime's *History* for additional information on communities in the mid-nineteenth century.

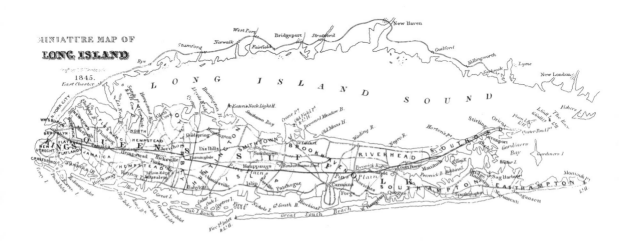

Prime included this 1845 map of Long Island in his *History of Long Island.*

* * *

Surface, Soil and Forests

While the northern half of Long Island is elevated and hilly, and in general presents a stiffer soil, the southern half is remarkably level, and though somewhat diversified, is generally, composed of a light sandy soil. At the water's edge, it is but little elevated above the level of the sea, and as you proceed northward, it rises so gradually as scarcely to be perceptible. This is remarkably the case with the great *Hempstead Plain* which will be more particularly described. This vast tract presents to the eye, from almost every point, the aspect of a horizontal surface, and yet, if we have the correct survey of the Long Island Rail Road, the northeast corner of that remarkable plain must be nearly one hundred and fifty feet above the ocean, and in passing from Jamaica to Hicksville (a distance of only sixteen miles) the assent is one hundred and two feet. The traveller will find it difficult to persuade himself of the fact, as he passes over the ground. Hicksville is the summit of the Rail Road.

The necks on the south side, which are formed by the numerous bays, and frequently large tracts of the adjacent lands, though often mingled with sand, have a strong soil, and abundantly repay the labour of the husbandman. But there are also vast plains of gravel and sand, which are utterly incapable of cultivation, and yield no profit but what arises from their scanty natural productions.

Of these, the most remarkable is the great *Hempstead Plain,* which is a vast tract of level land, commencing about 16 miles from the west end, and extending 12 miles east, with a breadth of 5 or 6 miles. To the eye, this whole tract appears as smooth and unbroken as the surface of the sea in a calm, though as you pass over it, you meet with slight undulations, and the view of the traveller over the whole expanse is unobstructed, by tree, or shrub or any other vegetable production. Within the memory of persons still living, there was scarcely an enclosure in this whole compass. It was cut up with roads or waggon-paths, in almost every direction, so that the stranger, and even the experienced traveller in the night time, or when the ground was covered with snow, was constantly liable to lose his way. Numerous instances of this, sometimes attended with disastrous consequences, occurred in former days. One of the principal country roads led nearly through the middle of the plain, and on it, at intervals of 3 or 4 miles, solitary inns were established to accommodate the lonely way-faring man. Around these, as a matter of necessity, were small enclosures; some efforts were made to cultivate the land, and a few trees planted and nurtured for ornament or use. But the occupants were obliged to transport all their fuel, and the most of their provisions, from beyond the plain. All the wells dug on this extended tract are from 60 to 100 feet, and sometimes more, in depth. The whole plain was formerly held as the common property of the towns in which it lies, and the only use to which it was applied was the pasturage of sheep and cattle during the summer season on the coarse grass, which from time immemorial was its only natural production. Numerous ponds, formed either by natural hollows or excavated by art, and at length made capable of retaining the rain of heaven, offered an abundant supply of water, which is rarely exhausted in the driest season.

Of late years, however, the hand of cultivation, which commenced its operation on the north side of the Plain, has gradually extended its labours, till large portions are now successfully subjected to the implements of husbandry. The soil of this whole tract is a black, rich, vegetable mould, varying in depth from 4 to 12 inches, which needs nothing but warming manure to produce an abundant crop. Large fields of Indian corn, and also of wheat and rye, are readily raised by this mode of treatment. There is no land in any part of the country that presents a more beautiful or promising appearance to the eye than one of these fields when the young blade has just sprung up, and the transient spectator is led to wonder why every rod of ground is not converted into a garden. The main difficulty lies *beneath* the soil. The *substratum* is a coarse, smooth, clean gravel, that appears as if it had been screened and washed from every particle that was capable of retaining moisture, or any other vegetable nourishment, and its depth is unfathomable. The necessary consequence is, that, except in a few places where there is a small admixture of loam, a coat of manure is *leached off* in the course of a year or two, and the work must be done over again. Had nature here deposited a *stratum* of clay or loam beneath the present soil, it is a question whether this tract would be exceeded on this side of the western prairies, and with the present facilities for transporting manure, as the L. I. Rail Road runs nearly through its middle, this vast tract, now so sterile, might be made to furnish sustenance for a population equal in number to the present inhabitants of the whole island. But whether the invention of man, or the spirit of improvement, will ever discover a method by which the expense and labour of applying manure and cultivating the soil on this extended plain may be adequately repaid, is quite problematical. This difficulty once overcome, a few *artesian* wells would afford a supply of water at every man's door. . . .

Adjoining these plains on the east and south of the hills, commences another on nearly the same level and like the other, gradually descending to the South Bay, which has less soil, but the same gravelly substratum, though somewhat more mingled with loam. This is covered principally with a growth of scrub-oak bushes from 4 to 10 feet high, but never attaining the form or stature of trees, they frequently stand so close and interlock their branches as to defy every attempt to pass through them. Hundreds of acres have presented, apparently, the same unvaried aspect, from the first settlement of the country. The *brushy-plains* is as familiar to the ear on Long Island as the great Hempstead Plain, and the contrast is remarkable.

In some places, these wastes are diversified by a larger, though unthrifty growth of oak, or pitch-pine, but in many instances, the trees are scattered and completely encompassed with the *scrub-oak bushes,* which seem to claim title as the original occupants of the ground. These plains, though occasionally interrupted, cover large portions of the *body* of the island. The land which they occupy is sometimes cleared, and a crop or two of some value raised, but there is rarely sufficient soil to render it worthy of permanent cultivation.

As we proceed eastward, the sand increases in fineness, even in some places to *fluidity,* and about 40 miles from the west end, the *Great Pine Plains* commence, which occupy, with little interruption, one-half of the island for 50 miles eastward. This is, in a great measure, one unbroken forest, principally of pitch-pine, occasionally intermingled with oak. Ferns and whortle-berry bushes, woodbine and mosses, with other shrubs and vines in scattered clumps, help to furnish a scanty cover for the sand. The trees, both pine and oak, often attain a larger growth than the nature of the ground (for there is no *soil*) would seem to warrant, being from one to two feet in diameter. In travelling these forests, you will occasionally fall upon a small *oasis,* which cheers the stranger's eye, as it well may the heart of the solitary occupant, but in many places, even at the present day, you may pass through 5, 6 and even 7 miles of unbroken forest, without discerning a human habitation, or the least trace of the hand of man, except the stumps of felled trees.

It is a common opinion, of those who have never travelled through Long Island, that there is very little wood or timber in any part of its lengthened domain. But this is a great mistake, especially in relation to that part of it which was designated as the body of the fish [i.e., from Queens to Riverhead]. There you will find a greater proportion of the land occupied by woods than on either side of the Hudson as far up as it is navigable, or on any of the great roads in the western part of the state. And why should it not be so, since vast portions of the island are of no earthly value but for the wood they produce? Previously to the introduction of anthracite coal into so general use, a large portion of the supply of fuel in the city of New York—thousands of cords, not only of pine from the sandy lands, but of oak and hickory of the finest quality from the more elevated parts, were transported to that market, and singular as the fact may appear in view of the preceding description, there is probably no district of country where a tract of land cut entirely smooth is replaced by natural growth with more rapidity than on the rough and elevated parts of this island. The same ground has often been cut over in 20 or 25 years, and every successive growth is equally productive. Though the flat, sandy lands may require a somewhat longer period, even these are replenished with astonishing rapidity. This circumstance alone renders those tracts, which are utterly incapable of cultivation, a source of profit to their owners, and fully accounts for the fact that so large a portion of the island is still occupied by wood.[4]

It may be worth while to add, in this connexion, that old, worn-out lands, if only defended from the ravages of cattle, in process of time, become covered with wood. This result has, in a few instances, been greatly hastened by ploughing and sowing nuts and acorns. An individual who first tried the experiment with chestnuts, lived to cut the trees for fencing timber, some of which were of sufficient size, to use the words of his labourer, "to split 8 rails out of the but-log."

The forests of Long Island, though long since cleared of wild-cats, wolves, and the like, with which they once abounded, are still occupied by vast numbers of deer, hundreds of which have been killed yearly without destroying the stock. But the Long Island Railroad, which now passes through the heart of their principal resort, may, by frightening these timid animals from their wonted lairs, expose them to the more frequent shot of the huntsman, and thus, ere long, the harmless race may be extirpated from their native forests, which must ever remain undiminished.

The woods as well as the open fields abound also with quails and partridges, the swamps with woodcock, and the plains with grouse and plover, while the surrounding waters, especially the extended south bays, are the common resort of innumerable multitudes of wild-fowl, from the stately goose down to the smallest snipe. Immense numbers of these are killed annually by the inhabitants for their own use, or for market, and the sport or profit of fishing, hunting, and fowling, probably induces more foreigners to visit the island, than all other motives put together, always excepting the abomination of *horse-racing,* which will receive due attention in the proper place. Several kinds of land-birds are protected during the breeding season, by special statutes, and the most of the sea-fowl protect themselves, during the same period, by migration to more unfrequented climes. Upon the return of cold weather, these, with the numerous progeny which they have reared, return and bespeckle the harbours and bays, which constantly resound with their untiring cackle. There is reason, however, to believe that some of these species, particularly the wild-goose, are greatly diminished in number, from what they were formerly. Many persons now living, can distinctly recollect the time when, both spring and fall, the passage of large flocks of geese over the island, at almost any point, was a matter of daily, and sometimes hourly occurrence. But now, it is a sight that is rarely witnessed. The same remark is applicable to a smaller species of fowl, though larger than the duck, commonly distinguished by the name of *brant*. All the larger kinds of wild fowl are evidently scarcer, than they were formerly. The increased population of the country, and the improved skill and implements of gunning, probably account for the fact.

It is a remarkable fact in the natural history of this small territory, that of all the *land-birds* belonging to the United States, either as resident or migratory, *two-thirds* of them are to be found on Long Island; of the *water-birds,* a still larger proportion; and no doubt their number would be increased, if it were not for the reckless amusement of shooting small birds for the mere sport. . . .

The Roads

The roads of Long Island are exceedingly numerous and difficult for strangers. There are three principal avenues running nearly through the whole length of the Island, which are distinguished as the North, Middle, and South Roads.[5] These are not only intersected by others leading from one town and neighbourhood to another, but, in the most uninhabited parts, there are numberless wood-paths, well-worn by constant carting, which vary so little from the course of the main road, and not unfrequently appear the most direct and most used, that the stranger is constantly liable to go astray, and that too, where he might remain a whole day, without meeting a person to set him right. Some of these turn-outs have been guarded by guide-boards, but in general the inhabitants have been too inattentive to this important provision. The only apology is that they are not great travellers themselves, and until of late years, so few from abroad resort thither, either for business or pleasure, that it is scarcely an object to incur the expense, merely for their occasional convenience.

A large portion of the South and Middle roads, after you enter the County of Suffolk, lead through those large sandy plains and forests, which have been previously described. And to one who has never travelled such a region of country, it is impossible to convey an adequate idea of the inconvenience and obstruction to *locomotion* which are here presented.

After a heavy rain, if only a single carriage has preceded you to open the ruts, you may get along with tolerable speed, provided (which is a matter of great doubt) your wheels fit the track. But in a time of drought, the sand in many places is so fine, deep and *fluid,* that you may travel for miles with the lower felloe [rim] of your wheels constantly buried out of sight.

But while the people of Long Island are not to blame for the *natural* condition of their roads, for, unlike many other parts of the country, they have not selected the best lands for themselves, and devoted the hills and hollows and sloughholes to the roads, but have given as good as they had, they are entitled to great credit, in many places, for the efforts which have been made, with vast toil and expense, to improve upon nature. Where a bed of loam has been discovered, they have dug out and hauled thousands and thousands of loads, covering the whole path from six to twelve inches deep, for miles in succession. By this process the road soon becomes compact, and by the gradual admixture with the sand, improves for many years, though like all human works, it does not become everlasting, but its advantage is seen for a long period.

A view of the worst features of Long Island roads has been taken first, that the reader might not be compelled to finish this topic in disgust. Let him not therefore suppose that he has hitherto had a fair specimen of all the roads on this strand of the ocean. The entire counties of King's and Queen's both in their public roads and numerous turnpikes, present as pleasant journeying for man, and as comfortable travelling for beast, in every direction, and at all seasons of the year, as any other equal district in the state. And the north side of the island throughout furnishes a compact *substratum* and excellent materials for roads, though there is too much reason to complain of negligence in their improvement. The most of the labour done in cutting down hills and filling up valleys which are here very frequent, is performed by the direct agency of water, during copious rains. The work thus executed, without the direction of human intelligence, receives a few finishing strokes from the hand of man, when the necessity is imposed by some frightful gully formed, or some huge rock dislodged, by the powerful but senseless agent.

The roads on the two eastern branches of the island, are for the most part excellent. And here, fanned by the balmy sea-breeze, and cheered by the delightful contrast of land and water scenery, you may ride for miles on an unbroken trot. . . .

The introduction of Turnpikes upon the island was an event of some interest in its history, and one which produced not a little excitement in the public mind. The idea of having a public highway fenced up, and of obliging every man to pay for the privilege of riding on the road, was even more obnoxious, as an infringement of natural right, than as a pecuniary tax on the pockets of the people. Hence, the first applications for the incorporation of Turnpike Companies, met with a determined opposition.

The Brooklyn and Jamaica Turnpike Company was first incorporated. The experience of a short period, after the road was completed, soon produced a change of public opinion. Hostility was disarmed. The farmers not only found their rights unimpaired, but they soon discovered that the trifling *toll* they had to pay, was more than compensated by the saving of time, and the wear and tear of their waggons and teams. This soon led to the multiplication of turnpikes. The road was extended from Jamaica to Hempstead on the south side of the Plains, and to Jericho on the north. The Jericho turnpike was still further extended to Smithtown. On the north side there is a turnpike from Williamsburgh, through Newtown and Flushing, to Hempstead Harbour [Roslyn], which has lately been extended to Oysterbay. There is also a turnpike from Williamsburgh to Jamaica, and from Brooklyn to Flatbush. A straight turnpike road from Hempstead to Babylon, passing through Farmingdale, has not been completed. The short turnpike at Sag Harbour [to Bridgehampton] . . . completes the list of these roads on the island. . . .

The Rail Road

If free intercourse with the world is desirable for individuals and communities, and if the interests of both are promoted by facilities for holding such intercourse, then a *rail road* would seem to be as desirable for Long Island as almost any part of the world. Its distance from the main land, excepting at one end, its extreme length, and the unsuitable nature of a great part of its soil for comfortable roads, have necessarily confined a large portion of its population to the spot on which they were born. True, the facilities of travelling by water have been considerable, but this has always been attended with a great expense of time, and with a degree of danger that renders it formidable to many minds. Besides this, during at least one third part of the year, even this mode of intercourse is entirely suspended, or attended with such increased hazard, as nothing but imperious necessity would induce a man to incur. The necessary consequence is that locomotion, at least to any distance from home, is almost unknown on Long Island. The writer has heard men sixty years of age say that they were never 20 miles from the spot on which they were born, and no doubt there are many now living who never breathed the atmosphere of more than two towns in their lives. Seclusion from distant parts, instead of making them restless, seems to have confirmed the habit of staying at home. Even short journeys become irksome to those who seldom or never make long ones.

To people thus situated, in almost entire seclusion from the rest of the world, a rail road must open new and unconceived facilities, which, in its operation, must produce an amazing revolution in the manners and habits of the community.

The Brooklyn and Jamaica Rail Road Company was incorporated April 25th, 1832, but the road was not completed and opened till April 18th, 1836. On that day ground was broken for its continuance through the island by the Long Island Rail Road Company, which had been incorporated April 24th, 1834. It was completed to Hicksville and cars placed thereon in August, 1837. In 1841, it was extended to Suffolk Station [now Central Islip]. In 1843-4 the work was prosecuted to the terminus, and on the 25th of July 1844, the first train of cars passed from Brooklyn to Greenport, 95 miles, where the opening of the road was duly celebrated.

This event forms a new era in the history of the island, and in its results, has virtually altered both its form and location. Even the eastern extremities, are now brought almost into the suburbs of New-York. *Thirty* years ago, it was a tedious journey of *three days,* to travel by stage from Easthampton or Oysterponds [Orient] to Brooklyn. [See Gabriel Furman, "Journey Down the Island, 1835," pp. 127-32 above.] But now the inhabitants of either of those towns may dine at home and take tea in New-York, then breakfast in New-York and dine at home.

This Rail Road is one of the straightest, and most uniform, of its length, in the United States. After proceeding with scarcely a perceptible curvature, from Brooklyn to Jamaica, it passes in a straight course, through the middle of the Great Plain, to Hicksville, sending off by the way, a branch of three miles to Hempstead. At Hicksville, it veers for three or four miles to the south, to avoid the hills. Then resuming its easterly course, it proceeds with little variation to the head of Peconick [Peconic] Bay or Riverhead. Here taking the northern branch it proceeds, with a slight variation to the north, to Greenport, ten miles short of Oysterpond Point, and the whole distance is ordinarily performed by the Boston train, making two short stops merely to replenish fuel and water, *in three and a quarter hours,* and has been accomplished with entire safety in 2 hours and 35 minutes. An accommodation train, making numerous stops, and travelling with less speed, performs the *route* daily, in alternate directions, in five or six hours.

It is so common a thing with other Rail Roads, it is scarcely necessary to say, that the site of this road is through the most sterile and desolate parts of the island. After leaving Jamaica, you scarcely see a village or a farm of good land till you reach the terminus, but barren plains or forests of scrub oak, or stinted pine, environ the traveller on either hand. The principal villages, as well as the best land, are to be found on the sides of the island.

It is impossible to divine the amazing changes, which this improvement will effect on both the intellectual and secular interests of the eastern parts of the island. The inhabitants have scarcely yet recovered from the consternation produced by the actual opening of this Road. Though during its construction, its future facilities were often foretold, multitudes regarded them as the vagaries of a disordered brain, or, more frequently, the wilful misrepresentations of *interested* individuals, who wished to obtain a passage through their stinted pines and sandy plains, for a *mere song.* But, until they beheld with their own eyes, the cumbrous [cumbersome] train of cars, drawn by an iron horse [engine], spouting forth smoke and steam, passing like a steed [stallion] of lightning through their forests and fields, with such velocity that they could not tell whether the countenances of the passengers were human, celestial or infernal, they would not believe that a Rail Road had power almost to annihilate both time and space. But then they cried out with united voice "The one-half was not told."

As a sample of the changes produced by this improved mode of travelling and an earnest of what may yet be effected, even on the most retired parts of the island, the following case is stated. About seven miles east of the actual centre of the island, and in the midst of the great pine forests, about midway between the middle and south roads, is a little scattered settlement of some twenty or thirty families. The spot on which it stands, was originally a part of a great tract patented under the name of "St. George's Manor" [Manorville]. Its ecclesiastical name, bestowed upon it some forty years ago is *Brookfield,* but its vernacular appellation, from time immemorial, has been "Punk's Hole," so called from the name of its first pioneer. The retired and almost isolated situation of the settlement, and the principal part of the inhabitants being constantly occupied in cutting down and transporting the surrounding forests, the place was seldom visited by strangers, or even by the inhabitants of the adjacent towns, unless they happened to get lost in the woods. A more retired solitude, in the midst of an inhabited country, could neither be found nor imagined. And had a man, thirty years ago, ventured to predict that this spot was destined to become a daily stopping place for the refreshment of hundreds of travellers between New-York and Boston, he would have been considered a madman, and possibly might have been bound with cords, for fear he might do injury. The good people would not even have thought it necessary to say, "If the Lord would make windows in heaven, might this thing be?" And yet such is now the sober fact. Punk's Hole under the more *papistical* name of "St. George's

Manor," is one of the two stopping places between Greenport and Brooklyn, and has even become a landing place for passengers of the adjacent towns.

It is to be devoutly wished, that all the advantages of a rail road may be realized by this hitherto secluded island, and that its inhabitants may be preserved from the demoralizing influences which have too often accompanied these modern improvements. Without this, the exchange would prove as unprofitable bargain. For a while the most serious apprehensions were justly entertained. When the road was completed to Hicksville, and gradually extended,into Suffolk, it was made for years a regular *Sabbath-breaking concern.* And in anticipation of its continuance and extension, the good people of the eastern towns, instead of rejoicing in the secular benefits which they were to realize, began to "hang their harps on the willows" and pour out bitter lamentations, in view of the moral desolations that were to set in upon them. But a brighter prospect is presented. The Rail Road has been completed, and throughout its entire length, not a car moves on the Sabbath-day. This important concession to correct sentiment deserves the approbation and support of all good citizens, and it is to be hoped that their patronage will make this arrangement profitable to the Company. . . . [6]

It is a matter to be deeply regretted that an improvement so intimately connected with the interests of Long Island should not have been made to the entire satisfaction, and with the favor of the people. When we recollect that most of the rail roads in the country have met with great opposition from those through whose possessions they pass, it cannot be thought strange that these isolated people, with no experimental knowledge of the advantages of the scheme, should, from the outset, have regarded the road as an undesirable improvement. And then, the extensive and awfully destructive fires, which, in the past season, through alleged carelessness, have swept over immense tracts of land, have vastly increased the irritation of the public mind.

The extent of these disastrous conflagrations can scarcely be conceived of, without ocular [visual] examination. To talk of thousands of acres is scarcely an approximation to the reality. In several places the entire forests for eight or ten miles in length, and from two to four in breadth, have been completely swept over by the devouring element, which, besides destroying every vestige of vegetation, consumed thousands of cords of wood that had been cut and piled. The only value attached to these vast tracts of land is derived from the timber they bear, and when this is destroyed, they become absolutely worthless, at least to the present generation. By these unprecedented calamities, multitudes have suffered great losses, many have been deprived of their entire supply of fuel, while some have absolutely lost their all.[7]

Under these circumstances, the great excitement among the people of Suffolk county is certainly no matter of surprise. And, although the violence which has been threatened to the road would be a most injudicious mode of showing their resentment, and expose the lives of innocent persons without affecting the interests of the Company, it is evident that similar outrages have taken place in other parts of the country from much less provocation. And when it is recollected, that such unjustifiable proceedings are generally transacted by a few reckless individuals, upon whom the discreet and sober have no influence, the people of Suffolk are certainly entitled to great credit that these hasty threats have never, to any considerable extent, been carried into execution. Had there not been a strong moral influence predominating in the community, it is impossible to say what outrages would not have been perpetrated under such powerfully exciting causes.

It is to be hoped that not only measures may speedily be adopted to allay the present excitement, but that such a generous course may hereafter be pursued as shall reconcile the people to the maintenance of the road. The interests of the Company, no less than the benefit of the island, depend upon it.

King's County

Comprehends the smallest, but at the present time [1845] the most populous territory on the island. It occupies the western extremity. . . . It is but 12 miles in length from north to south, and 9 miles in its widest part, containing only 76 square miles, which is much less than the area of several single towns in the other counties.

By the U.S. census of 1840, this county contained 47,613 inhabitants. By the recent State census [1845], its number is 78,691, which gives 1,035 individuals to the square mile, or nearly 2 to the acre.

The face of this county is considerably broken with hills, bays and marshes, but in general the soil is good, and in a high state of cultivation. The southern parts, bordering on the sea, are level and inclining to sand, while the residue is a stiff, strong soil, and in general much incumbered with stone, both lying on the surface and imbedded in the ground. This, however, instead of being a real incumbrance, is becoming more and more valuable for fencing and building material, which, from the scarcity of timber on this part of the island, has been in constant demand.

It may be proper to make a remark here, which will apply to the whole island, that while some parts of it are well supplied with stone, and others are as remarkably destitute, there are no quarries or stone *in situ* throughout its entire extent, except at the narrow strait called Hurl-gate [Hell Gate]. Though there are some rocks of very large dimensions, they all are, in the language of geology, foreigners to the soil.

In regard to the moral character of the people of this county, it is sufficient to say here, that their religious views and feelings took their complexion from the Dutch and French Protestants, who together composed the first settlers, and became entirely amalgamated in all their social, civil, and ecclesiastical relations. . . .[8]

Queen's County

Extends from the eastern boundary of King's, about 25 miles eastward, including the whole breadth of the Island. Its eastern boundary is formed in part by that large arm of the Sound called Oysterbay, running up into the land, and forming Cold Spring Harbour. From the head of tide water, it follows the general course, and nearly the bed of a stream called Cold Spring, about a mile and a half in a south-easterly direction, and then due south across the island, to the Great South Bay and Ocean. Lloyd's Neck, though lying on the east of Oysterbay, and connected with the adjoining county by a sand beach, which is always passable, is attached to this county, and forms a part of the town of Oysterbay. This unnatural and inconvenient arrangement was made at the desire of one of its former proprietors about the year 1734.[9]

The greatest length of this county, from the East River near Blackwell's island to the eastern boundary, is about 27 miles, and its greatest breadth, not far from 18 miles, and is estimated to contain 395-1/2 square miles. Its population by the census of 1840, is 30,324; by that of 1845, 31,849, which gives about 80-2/3 to the square mile, or one to 8 acres.

Much of the land of this county is naturally good, and has been greatly improved by good husbandry. Its contiguity to the city, and its numerous bays and harbours, which are themselves sources of many fertilizing materials, afford peculiar facilities for procuring manures, of which the sagacious inhabitants have long been in the habit of availing themselves. And their fields present to the eye of the traveller as their productions do to the owners, evidence of the wisdom and economy of the practice. The great Hempstead Plain, already described, lies entirely within this county.

The people of this part of the island, are of a more mixed character, both in regard to their origin and religious views, than either of the other counties. In King's, till within a few years, the Dutch character had a decided and obvious preponderance, which is still the case in some towns. This was manifest to the eye of the transient observer in the manners and habits of the people and even in the form and style of their buildings. A Dutch house, or a Dutch barn has been, from time immemorial, a term that conveyed as definite an idea to the mind as the most detailed description could have given.[10] And till after the commencement of the present century, a Dutch church was invariably conceived to bear a strong resemblance to a Light-house, only occupying more ground at its base and not extending to so great a height. And so peculiarly appropriate was this form of church building, in the public estimation, that other denominations sometimes erected their houses of worship on the same plan.

On the other hand, the people of Suffolk County, being almost exclusively of English or New England origin, present to the present day, the constant evidence of *yankee* predilection. Overlooking the physical features of the country, the traveller cannot divest his mind of the idea that he is in the midst of a New England population, living in New England habitations. And had he entered almost any one of their churches some 30 years ago [c. 1815], before "the spirit of improvement" swept over the land, he would have recognised, in the vast pulpit, sufficiently large to hold a dozen ministers, with its deacon's seat beneath and a *sounding board* of corresponding size above, which always attracted the attention of children more than the preacher and filled them with constant apprehension, that it might fall and crush the man of God in the midst of his devotions, in the large square pews too, which obliged one half the congregation (and these were generally the children) to sit with their backs to the minister, and thus, in spite of themselves, and all their efforts, to become listless and sleepy hearers;[11] in all these and many other particulars, the observer, if from New England, would recognise the *facsimile* of his native church.

But in Queen's County there is nothing of this unique, homologous [similar] character, either in the manners of the people, the style of their buildings, or the moral aspect of society. Here Yankees and Dutchmen, presbyterians and quakers, men of every religion and no religion, have for almost two centuries been mingled together with all their various affinities and repulsions, and while the effervescence has been constantly going on, the time is yet future, if it ever is to come, when it is to subside into one homogeneous mass.

It may therefore be readily inferred from the facts of the case, that there is, and always has been, a greater diversity of religious views, and consequently of the moral habits of the people of this county, with far less of fellow-feeling and assimilated manners, than in any other district of the island. Except in a few thickly settled spots, houses of religious worship, till of late years, have been much fewer in number and attended by a less proportion of the population than in the other counties, while in many towns, fishing and hunting, travelling and visiting, and even ordinary secular labour, are indulged in by multitudes on the Sabbath day. Its proximity to the city has doubtless increased these evils, if it has not been their origin, but it is to be apprehended that too many of the inhabitants are voluntary panderers to the votaries of pleasure from the great metropolis.

And here it is proper to notice one of the principal means of demoralization with which this county, as well as the adjacent parts, have been cursed for the space of 180 years. Here has been the permanent arena of "the sports of the turf," as they are denominated in the *jockey* dialect, since the year following the surrender of New-York to the government of Britain.

This regular system of *horse-racing* was established in 1665 by Gov. [Richard] Nicoll. Four years afterwards (1669) his successor Gov. [Francis] Lovelace issued a proclamation, appointing "trials of speed," to take place in the month of May annually, and ordering the justices of Hempstead to receive subscriptions (!) for "a crown of silver, or the value thereof in good wheat," to be the reward of the winner. The ostensible argument for this procedure was "for *the purpose of improving and encouraging a good breed of horses,*" an argument that is most ridiculously retained in our statute book to the present day. Every man of reflection knows that from the first settlement of this country, the breed of *race*-horses is the last species of the animal that the exigencies of the people have demanded. In days gone by, those capable of enduring hardship and of easy support have been sought after, while extraordinary speed has been only a secondary consideration, and of limited demand in the occupations of life. But now, when the *iron horse* [railroad] which travels untired with the speed of a hurricane has entirely superseded the use of the fleetest steeds, it is to be hoped that when the current "15 years" shall have expired, the Act, with its baseless reason, will cease to disgrace the statute book of the State, whose laws forbid every species of *gambling.*

The Hempstead Plain, or its vicinity, has been the permanent theatre of these semi-annual enactments, from their commencement in 1665. The "Newmarket Course," called also "Salisbury Plain," was in the southwest corner of North Hempstead, 5 miles east of Jamaica, and was thus occupied more than 150 years. This was exchanged, some 20 years ago, for the "Union Course," 3 miles west of Jamaica, a circle of a mile's circumference, completely palisaded, for this exclusive purpose. And here are regularly enacted, twice a year, scenes which no imagination, however fertile, can depict without the aid of ocular demonstration. It has been stated, and the statement stands uncontradicted, that at a single course of races, 50,000 persons attended and $200,000 were lost and won, and that during the 5 days that the "sports" continued, the toll of the Fulton Ferry Company averaged $1,000 a day, and it was supposed that the other avenues from the city realised an equal sum. But the gambling, expense and loss of time attending these scenes of dissipation form, only a part of the evils with which they are connected. The drinking, the swearing, the licentiousness, the contentions, and other nameless crimes, which are here periodically committed, with the countenance of *law,* are enough to sicken the soul of every man that fears God and is disposed to reverence his commands, and must induce him to wish most devoutly for the time to come, and that speedily, when this crying abomination, with all its accompaniments, shall be banished from this once sacred soil of Puritans and Huguenots. There is no reason to doubt that the passion for horse racing, so long and so assiduously cultivated, has had a powerful influence in stamping the character of the people of this county with traits so diverse from either of those with which it stands in juxtaposition. . . .

Suffolk County

Embraces the whole of the remaining part of Long Island (proper) with its adjacent islands. Its greatest length is about 90 miles, and its greatest breadth from the extremity of Eaton's Neck on the Sound to the margin of the Great South Bay, 20 miles. Its medium breadth is estimated at 10 or 11 miles. From the general description of the Island previously given, it will be borne in mind that the Eastern part is so cut up by the indentation of bays, harbours, and coves, that through half the length of the county, it is divided into two separate branches, which are from 6 or 8, down to 1 mile wide. The whole county contains 976 square miles and its population in 1840 was 32,469; in 1845, 34,579; which is 36 to the mile, or 18 to the acre.

Much of the land as already described is a barren waste. In travelling through it, the stranger finds it difficult to imagine how even the wandering deer can find sustenance, much more, how human beings can procure an adequate support. And yet it is astonishing to see, in a propitious season, how large crops are raised from these sterile plains. Good Indian corn may frequently be seen growing in the fine white sea-sand, which has evidently been drifted by the waves and the winds to the distance of miles. This, slightly mingled with sea-mud and vegetable mould conveyed by the same agency, forms a substratum, if not a soil, in which in a wet season (for on Long Island, *water* is pre-eminently a main supporter of vegetation), corn and other grain will grow with astonishing rapidity and luxuriance.

But while these remarks apply, with strict propriety, to large portions of this county, there are extensive tracts of excellent land, which amply repay the labor of cultivation. This is true, not only of the numerous necks of land which jut out into the surrounding waters, and the margins of the numberless bays, coves, and harbours, but also of large bodies of land situated in almost every part of the island. But the writer would gladly whisper in the ear of many large land holders in this his native county, if they could be persuaded to believe it, that there is a great deal more profit in cultivating *one acre of land well, than ten acres badly.* The fact is, many on Long Island, as in other parts of the country, own and work *too much* land. The writer has in his mind's eye a farm of nearly a thousand acres, which half a century ago was owned and cultivated under the direction of a single individual, who was called a great farmer. But when he had ruined himself by the operation and had surrendered *the whole* to pay his debts (as honest, but unfortunate men were in the habit of doing in old times), it was cut up and sold to six or eight persons, who have since supported as many families from its productions. And if it could undergo another and even another subdivision, it might afford sustenance to double or quadruple the present number, besides materially improving the aspect of the town in which it is situated. The same remarks apply to scores of farms in this county, which in their present condition are to their owners what self-righteousness is to the sinner, "the more they have, the worse they are off." We have seen that in this county, there is an average of 18 acres to every inhabitant, while there is many an acre in King's County that furnishes support to a whole family. And though the proximity of a great market makes a vast difference in the value of vegetable productions, the disparity in the two cases would be exceedingly reduced by applying more manure and more labor to less ground. There is no knowing, till the experiment is fairly made, how much an acre of land may be made to produce by good husbandry.

But it is not intended by these remarks to convey the idea that all the farmers of old Suffolk are regardless [unmindful] of the improvements made in agriculture, or that they are in the habit of taxing their fields without furnishing them the means of answering the demand. More or less attention has long been paid to the importance of manuring, and they would be singularly culpable if this were not the case, since Nature has furnished them with peculiar facilities for the accomplishment of the work. The waters with which they are surrounded not only furnish a large supply of provisions for immediate use, but they are the unfailing sources of enriching the land. The *sea-weed,* which is cast up in immense quantities on the whole extent of shore, and various other productions of the bays and marshes, are daily yielding vast supplies of fertilizing materials.

But more than all, the countless multitudes of one peculiar species of fish, which crowd the bays and press upon the ocean's shore, of which millions are annually taken for the sole purpose of manure, are the principal source of fertility to the land. In several of the eastern towns, this business is as regularly pursued during a part of the summer as ploughing and sowing, or mowing and reaping in their appropriate seasons. For this purpose, the farmers of a neighbourhood form themselves into a company sufficiently large to afford a relief of hands every week and having provided themselves with a large seine, boats, a fish-house on the shore, and every necessary convenience, the party on duty take up their residence on the water-side, and it is impossible to convey to a stranger's mind the immense produce of a week's labour. A single haul of a seine has been calculated at 1,000,000 of fish.

These [menhaden] fish are called by various names as *skip-hog, moss bonker, shad,* and *bony-fish,* the last of which is most descriptive. Though of a good flavour and generally very fat, they are so perfectly filled with fine bones, that it is hazardous to eat a particle of them. It would seem as if the God of nature had formed and annually sent them in such immense quantities to these shores for the sole purpose of fertilizing the land. By this means alone, the value of much of the land on the east end of the island has been doubled, and by the same means its present value is maintained. For many years, Suffolk county did not raise sufficient grain for its domestic supply, while of late it has exported a large annual surplus. It may be added here that in taking these fish, other kinds of an excellent quality for the table are caught in sufficient quantities to supply the fishermen and the whole vicinity with fresh fish every day, while those which are not wanted for food are cast into the common receptacle. So that on the whole, though this country from the nature of the land may never be able to sustain a population proportioned to its superficial extent in comparison with other portions of the state, it is really questionable whether there is any part of the world in which the means of supporting life can be more readily obtained. And one thing is believed to be certain, that in no part of this republican country is there so great an equality, and such a strong sympathy and perfect fellow feeling, among the whole mass of population as in Suffolk county, especially in the eastern towns. . . .[12]

There was a period and that of some considerable duration, when Long Island constituted the great body of the province of New York. It was the first occupied by actual immigrants for the purpose of a permanent settlement and agricultural pursuits. Here the *first churches* were organized and the first towns formed. . . .

Though now regarded as the mere *"fag-end,"* Long Island was once both the body and soul of the Province of New-York. Nor has she deteriorated in her intrinsic worth, though she has been completely lost sight of and almost cast into oblivion in the extending glory of a great commonwealth which has arrogated to itself the proud title of the "Empire State."

But patriotic views and love of rational liberty do not constitute the chief glory of old Suffolk. It is her primitive *puritanism* which, it is believed, has been illustrated here in piety towards God and love to men for two hundred years, and now exists in more of its original purity than can be found on any spot of equal extent on the American continent. Let it be proclaimed in trumpet-tongued accents, that here no man was ever persecuted and disfranchised for his religious opinions, nor man or woman executed for heresy or *witchcraft.* On the contrary, from the first organization of their civil institutions, they ordained the widest toleration of religious opinions, so long as it was not exercised for the seduction of others and the injury of the community and that too, while as yet such an article had not been enacted, if it had been conceived, on the continent of America.

From the natural reserve of a people brought up in seclusion from the rest of the world, which still, in a measure, distinguishes them, these traits of character may not be readily recognised by the casual observer. But if the present generation have not greatly degenerated from the sentiments and practices of their immediate predecessors, among whom the writer spent some of the happiest years of his early life, a residence of a few months or even weeks among these primitive people on the east end, will afford complete conviction of the correctness of these remarks. . . .

[Hicksville, North Hempstead, and Roslyn]

Hicksville, although unknown in the ecclesiastical annals of the island [i.e., it had no churches], ought probably to receive some notice as we pass by it. It is a "village" of recent origin, situated on the western line of the town, about midway of the great plain. It owes its existence to the temporary termination of the Long Island rail-road at this point. It originally consisted of a large depot and work-shops, a hotel with its out-houses, and 5 or 6 small private dwellings. The rail-road having been extended to Greenport in 1844, the depot being burned down about the same time, and no addition whatever being made to the private dwellings, the "village" bids fair to remain in *statu quo.* Its business, however, is undiminished, as it is a point at which several stages and private conveyances arrive daily, with passengers from the adjacent villages, and after remaining an hour or two, depart with their return cargoes. Of course, its principal trade consists of hay and oats for horses, and cakes and pies, and coffee or *whiskey,* for men—all of which are articles of foreign production, as there is no land under cultivation. Indeed, all the houses stand "out of doors," without any enclosure, except a small garden attached to the hotel. And although the whole territory is as level as a barnfloor, and building-lots can be purchased far cheaper than in New York, the public seem determined not to buy them. It has been said that "by spirit and enterprise, it would become a very desirable and eligible spot for such mechanical branches as do not require the aid of steam or water power," but as all mechanics stand in need of a little water to drink and for culinary purposes, and as Hicksville is the most elevated point on the whole line of the rail-road, being, according to the statement of the engineer, 142 feet above tide-water, it does not seem likely to be selected as a place of residence by any man in his senses. On the whole, Long Island does not furnish, in all its length and breadth, a stronger instance of the folly of attempting to rear cities and villages on the hot-bed principle. East New York and Jamesport are privileged spots compared with Hicksville. The name may live, but the "village" is a miserable abortion. . . .[13]

[North Hempstead] is nominally the capital of Queen's county, the Courthouse having been erected in 1786, within its limits, about one mile from its southern boundary on the verge of the Great Plain [in today's Garden City Park]. But from the time of its erection, it has remained a solitary building, there being not more than 5 or 6 small dwellings within a half a mile or more. It is difficult to image where or how the good people find

The Queens County Courthouse (1787-1895) was located on what is now Jericho Turnpike in Garden City Park. Photograph, c. 1900.

accommodations, when necessarily attending on the courts. They might, indeed, carry their provisions with them, as in primitive times, but the difficulty of obtaining lodging would still remain. Riverhead, in Suffolk, is now a capacious city, compared with this solitary spot. . . .

The principal village in this town [of North Hempstead] is at the head of *Hempstead Harbour,* and bears that name [now Roslyn]. It is environed on three sides by lofty hills—one of which, about half a mile to the east, called *Harbour Hill,* rises to the height of 319 feet and affords a most extended view of both land and water scenery. Hempstead Harbour extends up into the land about 6 miles. At its mouth it is about 3 miles wide and gradually contracts as it proceeds inland, at the head of which the village is situated, with an unobstructed view of the Sound and Connecticut shore. Copious springs and large streams constantly pouring from the surrounding hills afford a greater amount of waterpower than is to be found probably in any other part of the island. The lofty hills that surround this harbour seem to contain vast reservoirs of water, which are constantly gushing out in numberless springs and copious streams. . . .

The harbour is accessible to within one mile of its head at all times of the tide, and greater quantities of lumber and manure are transported thither, and more produce is conveyed away than from almost any other landing. Numerous mills and factories already exist, and there is abundant power and room for more. The village contains about 300 inhabitants.

Notes

Source: Nathaniel S. Prime, *A History of Long Island from its First Settlement by Europeans to the Year 1845, with Special Reference to its Ecclesiastical Concerns* (New York: Robert Carter, 1845), pp. 16-21, 52-60, 67-76, 264, 276-77, 292-93.

Editing changes have been minimal and limited to modernization of punctuation and combining some short paragraphs. Prime's spellings, capitalization, and italics have been retained. The editor's insertions in the text are in brackets [thus]. Prime's notes are identified by his initials (NSP); all others are by the editor for this volume.

1. Biographical information is from "The Recollections of the Reverend Nathaniel S. Prime," edited by Richard P. Harmond, *Long Island Historical Journal* 13 (Fall 2000): 23-43; reprinted from *Journal of Long Island History* 17 (Winter 1981): 30-47.

2. Richard P. Harmond, "Doing and Not Doing Long Island History: The Long Island Historians from Wood to Weeks," *Long Island Historical Journal* 13 (Spring 2001): 175; reprinted from *Journal of Long Island History* 15 (Fall 1978): 16-24.

3. Harmond, "Doing and Not Doing Long Island History," 13: 175.

4. As one out of the many facts in confirmation of this statement, it may be remarked that, in the time of the Revolutionary War, Lloyd's Neck, which contains less than 3,000 acres, was almost entirely divested of wood by the British. And the growth of wood since the peace of 1783 on this small tract, of which several hundred acres have been under

cultivation, has been estimated at 1,000 cords a year, and more than 50,000 have been actually cut since that time (NSP).

5. Today's Route 25A is approximately the route of the North Road; Route 25 (Jericho Turnpike and, in Suffolk County, Middle Country Road), the Middle Road; and Montauk Highway, Route 27, the South Road. See Sylvia Adcock, "Historic Highways and Byways," in *Long Island: Our Story,* by Newsday (Melville: Newsday, 1998), p. 84.

6. The railroad resumed Sunday service during the Civil War. Omitted here is Prime's table with the distances and elevation above sea level of sixteen stations from the Brooklyn terminus to Greenport (p. 59).

7. The actual loss sustained by these fires has not been confined to appropriated property; the brute tribes have been extensive sufferers. Hundreds of deer and rabbits and other game perished in these fires. Many of them were seen while the flames were raging running to and fro in wild dismay, and frequently rushing headlong into the midst of the fire. Others were seen, after the burning subsided, bearing extensive marks of fire on their bodies. The huntsman will have reason to regret these disasters for many years to come (NSP).

8. Omitted here is Prime's table with the seven towns in Kings County (Bushwick, Williamsburgh, Brooklyn, Flatbush, Flatlands, New Utrecht, and Gravesend). He lists for each, its greatest length and breadth, area in square miles, and population in 1840 and 1845 (p. 68). He has similar tables for Queens County's six towns (Newtown, Flushing, Jamaica, Hempstead, North Hempstead, and Oyster Bay), and the towns in Suffolk County (pp. 72, 80).

9. Queens included present-day Nassau County until 1899. Lloyd's Neck was rejoined to Huntington and Suffolk in 1886.

10. On Dutch houses and barns, see John Stevens, "Dutch Buildings on Long Island," in *Long Island Architecture,* edited by Joann P. Krieg (Interlaken, NY: Heart of the Lakes Publishing, 1991), pp. 69-79; and David Stevens Cohen, *The Dutch-American Farm* (New York: New York University Press, 1992).

11. The writer has always been of the opinion that the devil had as much of a hand in the invention of *sounding boards* and *square pews,* as he had in the Salem witchcraft, and that the scheme has been vastly more successful, in its pernicious influences, on the rising generation (NSP).

12. Prime's extensive excerpt from "Observations on Manures," by Ezra L'Hommedieu, Esq., read in March 1795 at the New York State Society for the Promotion of Agriculture, Arts and Manufactures, is omitted here (pp. 75-77).

13. In the year 2000, Hicksville was the fourth largest community in Nassau County with a population of 34,891.

Paumanok in Poetry and Prose, 1850s-1880s

Walt Whitman

The renowned poet, Walt Whitman (1819-1892), had deep roots on Long Island. He was born in West Hills (now South Huntington), and his birthplace is preserved as an historic site.[1] He was only four years old when his family moved to Brooklyn, but he often visited his grandparents in Cold Spring Harbor. When his family later moved to Hempstead, he boarded in Brooklyn and was an apprentice printer in Manhattan. In his late teens, Whitman taught in district schools in Norwich, Woodbury, West Babylon, West Hempstead, and Smithtown.

Whitman began his own newspaper in Huntington in 1838, the *Long Islander,* which is still being published. He returned to Brooklyn where he was editor of the *Brooklyn Daily Eagle* (1846-1848) and wrote for other newspapers. His magnum opus is *Leaves of Grass* which was first published in 1855. Whitman revised and added to this collection of poetry for the rest of his life.[2]

Whitman often visited the seashore and other areas of his beloved Paumanok. Long Island influenced his poetry and some poems specifically describe a Long Island setting, as the selections below illustrate. Since he is describing the land and seascape that he knew so well, Whitman's descriptions in poetry and prose are an excellent primary source of information on mid-nineteenth century Long Island.

* * *

A Song of Joys

O to go back to the place where I was born!
To hear the birds sing once more!
To ramble about the house and barn and over the fields, once
    more
And through the orchard and along the old lanes once more.

O to have been brought up on the bays, lagoons, creeks, or
    along the coast!
O to continue and be employ'd there all my life!
O the briny and damp smell—the shore—the salt weeds
    exposed at low water,
The work of fishermen—the work of the eel-fisher and
    clam-fisher;
I come with my clam-rake and spade, I come with my
    eel-spear,

Is the tide out? I join the group of clam-diggers on the flats
I laugh and work with them, I joke at my work like a
   mettlesome young man.

My Life on Paumanok as Child and Young Man [written 1882]

Worth fully and particularly investigating indeed this Paumanok (to give the spot its aboriginal name),[3] stretching east through Kings, Queens and Suffolk counties, 120 miles altogether—on the north Long Island sound, a beautiful, varied and picturesque series of inlets, "necks" and sea-like expansions, for a hundred miles to Orient point. On the ocean side the great south bay dotted with countless hummocks, mostly small, some quite large, occasionally long bars of sand out two hundred rods to a mile-and-a-half from the shore. While now and then, as at Rockaway and far east along the Hamptons, the beach makes right on the island, the sea dashing up without intervention. Several light-houses on the shores east; a long history of wrecks tragedies, some even of late years. As a youngster, I was in the atmosphere and traditions of many of these wrecks—of one or two almost an observer. Off Hempstead beach for example, was the loss of the ship *Mexico* in 1840 (alluded to in "the Sleepers" in L. of G. [*Leaves of Grass*]).[4] And at Hampton [off Fire Island], some years later, the destruction of the brig *Elizabeth*, a fearful affair, in one of the worst winter gales, where Margaret Fuller went down, with her husband and child.[5]

Inside the outer bars or beach this south bay is everywhere comparatively shallow; of cold winters all thick ice on the surface. As a boy I often went forth with a chum or two, on those frozen fields, with hand-sled, axe and eel-spear, after messes of eels. We would cut holes in the ice, sometimes striking quite an eel-bonanza, and filling our baskets with great, fat, sweet, white-meated fellows. The scenes, the ice, drawing the hand-sled, cutting holes, spearing the eels, etc., were of course just such fun as is dearest to boyhood. The shores of this bay, winter and summer, and my doings there in early life, are woven all through L. of G. One sport I was very fond of was to go on a bay-party in summer to gather sea-gull's eggs. (The gulls lay two or three eggs, more than half the size of hen's eggs, right on the sand, and leave the sun's heat to hatch them.)

Walt Whitman, 1855

The eastern end of Long Island, the Peconic bay region, I knew quite well too—sail'd more than once around Shelter Island, and down to Montauk—spent many an hour on Turtle hill by the old [Montauk] light-house, on the extreme point, looking out over the ceaseless roll of the Atlantic. I used to like to go down there and fraternize with the blue-fishers, or the annual squads of sea-bass takers. Sometimes along Montauk peninsula (it is some 15 miles long, and good grazing), met the strange, unkempt, half-barbarous herdsmen, at that time living there entirely aloof from society or civilization, in charge, on those rich pasturages, of vast droves of horses, kine [cows] or sheep, own'd by farmers of the eastern towns. Sometimes, too, the few remaining Indians, or half-breeds, at that period left on Montauk peninsula, but now I believe altogether extinct.[6]

More in the middle of the island were the spreading Hempstead plains, then (1830-'40) quite prairie-like, open, uninhabited, rather sterile, cover'd with kill-calf and huckleberry bushes, yet plenty of fair pasture for the cattle, mostly milch-cows, who fed there by hundreds, even thousands, and at evening (the plains too were owned by the towns, and this was the use of them in common), might be seen taking their way home, branching off regularly in the right places. I have often been out on the edges of these plains toward sundown, and can yet recall in fancy the interminable cow-processions, and hear the music of the tin or copper bells clanking far or near, and breathe the cool of the sweet and slightly aromatic evening air, and note the sunset.

Through the same region of the island, but further east, extended wide central tracts of pine and scrub-oak (charcoal was largely made here), monotonous and sterile. But many a good day or half-day did I have, wandering through those solitary cross-roads, inhaling the peculiar and wild aroma. Here, and all along the island and its shores, I spent intervals many years, all seasons, sometimes riding, sometimes boating, but generally afoot (I was always then a good walker), absorbing fields, shores, marine incidents, characters, the bay-men, farmers, pilots—always had a plentiful acquaintance with the latter, and with fishermen—went every summer on sailing trips—always liked the bare sea-beach, south side, and have some of my happiest hours on it to this day.

As I write, the whole experience comes back to me after the lapse of forty and more years—the soothing rustle of the waves, and the saline smell—boyhood's times, the clam-digging, barefoot, and with trowsers roll'd up—hauling down the creek—the perfume of the sege [sedge]-meadows—the hay-boat, and the chowder and fishing excursions;—or, of later years, little voyages down and out New York bay, in the pilot boats.

Those same later years also, while living in Brooklyn (1836-'50), I went regularly every week in the mild seasons down to Coney island, at that time a long, bare unfrequented shore, which I had all to myself, and where I loved, after bathing, to race up and down the hard sand, and declaim Homer or Shakespeare to the surf and sea-gulls by the hour.

A Paumanok Picture

Two boats with nets lying off the sea-beach, quite still,
Ten fishermen waiting—they discover a thick school of
      mossbonkers—they drop the join'd seine-ends in the water,
The boats separate and row off, each on its rounding course to
      the beach, enclosing the mossbonkers,
The net is drawn in by a windlass by those who stop ashore,
Some of the fishermen lounge in their boats, others stand
      ankle-deep in the water, pois'd on strong legs,
The boats partly drawn up, the water slapping against them,
Strew'd on the sand in heaps and windows, well out from the
      water, the green-back'd spotted mossbonkers.[7]

Good Old Long Island, 1862

We now come to an extensive and most interesting section of Long Island, and one which might have more reference to Brooklyn and its inhabitants than has hitherto been supposed. It is astonishing that immense quantities of good land lie yet untilled, within two hours' reach of this great city [Brooklyn] and New York. For after leaving Jamaica and Brushville [Queens Village] which is three miles east, we stretch out pretty soon upon "the Plains," that prairie-like and comparatively profitless expanse of land. The character of the country now becomes flat, and bare of trees; the houses are far from each other, and there is an uncomfortably naked and shrubless look about them. As the locomotive whisks us along, we see to a great distance on both sides, north and south—and see, mostly, large square fields, a great portion of which is devoted to pasturage.

The "Branch" {Mineola}, or turning off place for Hempstead, is about eighteen miles from Brooklyn. A cluster of houses has been built up here, in the midst of the wide expanse, and a tolerable degree of traffic is carried on; of course nearly all derives its life-blood from the railroad—Hempstead, otherwise "Clamtown," otherwise "Old Blue," is some two miles to the south; which two miles you pass over on a railway, in cars drawn by horses that the crows, as they fly overhead, must feel astonished at not having got some time before. The village is rather a pleasant one, of perhaps 1400 inhabitants. It hath a Presbyterian tinge, of the deepest cerulean. . . . Branching out from Hempstead, in a southeasterly direction is the fine south turnpike, that leads along through (among other places), Merrick, Babylon, Patchogue, Speonk, Good-Ground, away east to the Hamptons.

For some miles east of "the Branch" there is little but a mighty stretch of these uncultivated plains. True, there are some patches inclosed, alongside of the railroad, here and there. Around Hicksville, there is quite a group of these settlings. Hicksville! that place of vanished greatness! O, what a cutting up of lots and selling them off at high prices there was here in "the time of the great speculation," years ago! An immense city *was sure* to be that same Hicksville; *now* its sovereign sway enfolds a large unoccupied tavern, a few pig-pens, a very few scattered houses, and the aforesaid little enclosures. But joking not, we shouldn't wonder to see Hicksville gradually pick up and be a tidy little hamlet in the course of a few years. . . .

At Farmingdale, anciently known under the appelation of "Hardscrabble," you begin to come among the more popular specimens of humanity which good old Long Island produces. (Though we ought not to have overlooked the goodly Village of Jericho, two miles north of Hicksville—a Quaker place, with stiff old farmers, and the native spot of Elias Hicks.) Farmingdale rears its towers in the midst of "the brush," and is one of the numerous offspring of the railroad, depriving no considerable portion of its importance from the fact that the train stops here for the passengers to get pie, coffee and sandwiches.

We are now in the midst of the aforementioned "brush," a growth of pine and scrub-oak, mostly, though interspersed with birch, sumac, and other modest-sized trees. But at this time (late in the autumn) it is beautiful exceedingly! We can sit and gaze admiringly for miles and miles, at those colors that the chemistry of autumn has profusely dyed every leaf with. Deep and pale red, the green of the pines, the bright yellow of the hickory, are the prevailing hues, in numberless lovely combinations. We have often thought that those who make designs for carpets could get most excellent hints from these autumn garnishings. How pleasing and grateful would be a carpet pattern, richly covered with figures and colors, closely imitated from what one sees here—how much better than the tasteless, meaningless, and every way unartistical diagrams that we walk over now, in the most fashionably carpeted parlors.

After leaving Farmingdale the railroad runs for about forty miles through a comparatively barren region, with stations every few miles, for the passengers for Babylon, Islip, Patchogue, etc., on the south side, and for Comac [Commack], Smithtown and diverse other villages, toward the north.

We arrive at Riverhead, which is the county seat of Suffolk, and quite a handsome village—and pass on through Southold, and one or two other settlements, and whisk into Greenport, looking out upon Peconic Bay.

Montauk Light and the two forms of cliff

From Montauk Point [written 1888]
I stand as on some mighty eagle's beak,
Eastward the sea absorbing, viewing (nothing but sea and sky),
The tossing waves, the foam, the ships in the distance,
The wild unrest, the snowy, curling caps—that inbound urge
    and urge of waves,
Seeking the shores forever.

Montauk, 1862
    The peninsula is nearly altogether used for pasturage, in shares, and is thus occupied by thousands of horses, sheep, etc., turned out to graze and grow fat. There is quite a peculiar race of fellows here, who live in huts by themselves, at large distances from each other, and act as horse-herds. You may be surprised, perhaps, to hear that occasionally these horses have a regular stampede, forming in solid bodies, charging along the open grounds at a tremendous rate, shaking the earth like thunder. The horse-herds have curious instruments, exactly on the principle of the toys vulgarly called "horse-fiddles"—and when these stampedes get under way, they rush out, and try to break the integrity of the enemy by whirling said instruments in a manner fast and furious. . . .

Montauk Point! how few Americans there are who have not heard of thee—although there are equally few who have seen thee with their bodily eyes, or trodden on thy greensward. Most people possess an idea (if they think at all about the matter), that Montauk Point is a low stretch of land, poking its barren nose out toward the east, and hailing the sea-wearied mariner, as he approaches our republican shores, with a sort of dry and sterile countenance. Not so is the fact. To its very extreme verge, Montauk is fertile and verdant. The soil is rich, the grass is green and plentiful; the best patches of Indian corn and vegetables I saw last autumn are within gun shot of the salt waves of the Atlantic, being just five degrees east longitude from Washington, and the very extremest terra firma of the good State of New York.

Nor is the land low in the situation. It binds the shore generally in bluffs and elevations. The point where the lighthouse stands—and it is the extreme point—is quite a high hill; it was called by the Indians *Wamponomon*—by modern folks Turtlehill. The light-house here is a very substantial one of an old-fashioned sort, built in 1795; the lights are two hundred feet above the level of the sea. Sheltered in a little vale near by is the dwelling of the keeper and his family, the only comfortable residence for many miles. It is a tolerably roomy cottage—a sort of public house; and some inveterate sportsmen and lovers of nature in her wild aspects come here during the summer and fall, and board awhile and have fun.

As every man was master of his time between our arrival and the period of dinner, I, with the rest of the party, took a good long ramble for several miles to and fro. To a mineralogist, I fancy Montauk Point must be a perpetual feast. Even to my unscientific eyes there were innumerable wonders and beauties all along the shore, and edges of the cliffs. There were earths of all colors, and stones of every conceivable shape, hue, and destiny, with shells, large boulders of a pure white substance, and layers of those smooth round pebbles called "milk-stones" by the country children. There were some of them tinged with pale green, blue or yellow—some streaked with various colors and so on.

We rambled up the hills to the top of the highest, we ran races down, we scampered along the shore, jumping from rock to rock we declaimed all the violent appeals and defiances we could remember, commencing with "Celestial states, immortal powers, give ear!" away on to the ending which announced that Richard had almost lost his wind by dint of calling Richmond to arms. I doubt whether these astonished echoes ever before vibrated with such terrible ado. Then we pranced forth again, like mad kine [cows], we threw our hats in the air, aimed stones at the shrieking sea-gulls, mocked the wind, and imitated the cries of various animals in a style that beat nature all out! . . .

In conclusion, it must be confessed that the east end of Long Island, for a summer journey, affords better sport, greater economy, and a relief from the trammels of fashion, beyond any of the fashionable resorts or watering places and is emphatically a good spot to go to, as many of our Brooklynites have long since discovered.

Paumanok [written 1888]

Sea-Beauty! stretch'd and basking!

One side thy inland ocean laving, broad, with copious
          commerce, steamers, sails,

And one the Atlantic's wind caressing, fierce or
          gentle—mighty hulls dark-gliding in the distance.

Isle of sweet brooks of drinking-water—healthy air and soil!

Isle of the salty shore and breeze and brine!

Walt Whitman's Birthplace. Photograph c. 1905.

Notes

Sources: There are many editions of Whitman's *Leaves of Grass.* Whitman's poetry is from the Oxford World's Classics edition, edited by Jerome Loving (New York: Oxford University Press, 1998), pp. 143, 351, 385. The first prose selection ("My Life on Paumanok as Child and Young Man") is from *Specimen Days & Collect* (Philadelphia: David McKay, 1882-1883), pp. 12-14. The balance of the prose is selected from Whitman's "Brooklyniana" in the *Brooklyn Standard,* 1861-1862, which also includes articles on other parts of Long Island. It is reprinted in *Walt Whitman's New York: From Manhattan to Montauk,* edited by Henry M. Christman (New York: Macmillan, 1963), pp. 164-67, 175, 179-81, 188 (headings have been added). Herbert Bergman has edited Walt Whitman's newspaper articles in *The Journalism* (New York: Peter Lang, 1998); the first volume includes articles from 1834-1846. The second volume has not been published to date.

Editing changes have been limited to modernizing some of the punctuation in the prose selections; insertions are in brackets. All notes are by the editor except for the first paragraph in no. 3 by John Burroughs which was in the original edition of *Specimen Days.*

1. The Walt Whitman Birthplace State Historic Site and Interpretive Center is located at 246 Old Walt Whitman Road (west of the Walt Whitman Mall), Huntington Station, NY 11476; (631) 427-5240.

2. Biographical information is from Joann P. Krieg, *Long Island and Literature* (Interlaken, NY: Heart of the Lakes Publishing, 1989), pp. 27-38. See also Bertha H. Funnell, *Walt Whitman on Long Island* (Port Washington: Kennikat Press, 1971); and George DeWan, "The Paumanok Poet," in *Long Island: Our Story,* by Newsday (Melville: Newsday, 1998), pp. 188-92. There are many biographies of Whitman; see Gay Wilson Allen, *The Solitary Singer: A Critical Biography of Walt Whitman* (New York: New York University Press, 1955); Justin Kaplan, *Walt Whitman, A Life* (New York: Simon and Shuster, 1980); and Jerome Loving, *Walt Whitman: The Song of Himself* (Berkeley: University of California Press, 1999).

3. "Paumanok (or Paumanake, or Paumanack, the Indian name of Long Island), over a hundred miles long; shaped like a fish—plenty of sea shore, sandy, stormy, uninviting, the horizon boundless, the air too strong for invalids, the bays a wonderful resort for aquatic birds, the south-side meadows coverd with salt hay, the soil of the island generally tough, but good for the locust-tree, the apple orchard, and the blackberry, and with numberless springs of the sweetest water in the world. Years ago, among the bay-men—a strong, wild race, now extinct, or rather entirely changed—a native of Long Island was called a *Paumanacker,* or *Creole-Paumanacker."* —John Burroughs. (Footnote in original.)

Paumanok (also spelled Pommanock) means "land of tribute," and was the name of Eastern Long Island, according to William Wallace Tooker, *The Indian Place-Names of Long Island,* 1911 (Reprint; Port Washington: Ira J. Friedman, 1962), p. 183. Seawanhacky (or Sewanhaka, "island of shells" or the "seawan [wampum] country") was another Algonquian name for Long Island (ibid., pp. 232-33).

4. On the sinking of the *Mexico,* see Harold E. Tumey, "The Bristol and Mexico Tragedies," *Long Island Forum* 6 (November 1943): 215-17; and Lou Pearsall, "The 'Mexico Wreck,'" *Long Island Forum* 26 (August 1963): 175.

5. On Margaret Fuller's shipwreck, see George DeWan, "A Life Cut Short by the Sea," *Newsday,* September 19, 2000; and George DeWan, "A Woman's Fate Rewritten," *Newsday,* February 6, 2001 (also available on website: <lihistory.com>; Meadle C. Dobson, "Fire Island's Historic Shipwreck," *Long Island Forum* 4 (August 1941): 185-86; and Douglas Tuomey, "The Death of Margaret Fuller," *Long Island Forum* 23 (December 1960): 277-78, 285.

6. The Montaukett Indians still survive in the twenty-first century and are seeking federal recognition. See John A. Strong, *"We Are Still Here!" The Algonquian Peoples of Long Island Today,* 2d rev. ed. (Interlaken, NY: Hofstra University and Empire State Books, 1998), pp. 19-21. 88-94; on their history, see John A. Strong, *The Montauket Indians of Eastern Long Island* (Syracuse: Syracuse University Press, 2001).

7. Mossbunkers ("bunkers") or menhaden are used for bait and processed for their oil and fertilizer. See Jeffrey Kassner, "Long Island and the Menhaden," *Long Island Forum* 47 (November 1984): 212-17.

This "Island of the Sea" in 1873

Richard M. Bayles

Richard M. Bayles (1846-1930) grew up in Coram and Middle Island. His father died shortly before he was born, his mother when he was thirteen, and his two older brothers in the Civil War. Bayles attended the district school and the Northville Academy. He lived with an uncle in Middle Island and operated a store there for a few years.

Bayles devoted much of his adult life to teaching school and writing history. He wrote *Historical and Descriptive Sketches of Suffolk County* (1874), the chapters on Brookhaven Town and Riverhead Town for W.W. Munsell's *History of Suffolk County* (1882), *Handbook of Long Island* (1885), and many historical articles for local newspapers and the Brooklyn *Daily Eagle Almanac.* Publishers sought him to write histories of other areas as well, and he wrote chapters or books on other New York, Connecticut, and Rhode Island counties.[1] He taught at various times from 1877 to 1893 in the common schools in Coram, Eastport, Center Moriches, Manorville, and Middle Island. He was a surveyor, insurance agent, realtor, and printer. Bayles was a trustee of the Middle Island school district for twenty-five years and in his later years was the Brookhaven Town Historian.[2]

These selections are from his *Historical and Descriptive Sketches of Suffolk County* which established his reputation as an historian. Bayles indicated in his preface that he wanted to "bring forward the record of history" from the time that Benjamin Thompson and Nathaniel Prime had written in the 1840s. But of most interest today is that he included "a more complete effort in the matter of description" and selections from those parts are excerpted here. In earlier chapters, he sketched the discovery, Dutch and English settlements, Indian tribes, and early customs of the settlers. Here he describes the geography, soil, natural resources, shipwrecks, the railroad, and the growing attraction of the "island of the sea" for "summer rustication." He believed that the important institutions of Suffolk County in his day were the Agricultural Society, Temperance Convention, Sabbath School Association, and the common school system. He has chapters on each of the towns of Suffolk. Included here is his information from the chapters on Huntington and Brookhaven and they provide a sample of the type of information on each Suffolk community. Ten years later in his *Handbook of Long Island,* Bayles includes a gazetteer with briefer information on neighborhoods and settlements throughout the island, including Kings and Queens Counties. Some of his accounts, particularly for areas of Brookhaven, were reprinted in the last decades of the twentieth century. As these selections indicate, Bayles was a careful observer and his writings are now primary sources on Long Island in the 1870s and 1880s.

* * *

General Description of Long Island

Long Island Sound, which separates the island from Connecticut, on the north, extends the length of the island, from west to east, its greatest width being about twenty miles, from which it tapers off each way. The greatest width of the island, is at a point about forty miles from the west end. Its general shape has been likened to that of a huge fish, the west end of which is the head, and the peninsulas of the east end the flukes of its tail.

The southern shore is protected from the Atlantic Ocean by a narrow sand beach, which extends its entire length, for most of the distance enclosing a bay, from one to three miles wide, between it and the island proper. Outside the beach, at an average distance of a quarter to half a mile from it, lies a shoal or bar of sand, which is frequently shifted about by the action of the waves. At different points along the shore, the beach is connected with the main island, dividing the inside waters into distinct bays, some of which are entirely land-locked. A few inlets or openings through this beach, connect the inside bays with the ocean, and admit navigation.

The water in these bays is generally shoal, and the bottom muddy, affording favorable conditions for the propagation and growth of oysters, and other shell-fish, eels, fish, and the like, with which they abound. The business of securing and marketing these products affords an important industrial and commercial interest to the inhabitants of the vicinity, thousands of whom are dependent upon this source for their support. Bordering these waters are extensive salt meadows, producing different kinds of grasses peculiar to such situations.

The harbors and bays on the north side of the island, are generally deeper water, and better adapted to purposes of navigation. There, ship-building is carried on to a greater extent than on the south side. The inlets from the Sound are more frequent, and less dangerous of approach.

The shores of Long Island abound in running streams and brooks, many of which are large enough to furnish considerable power for driving machinery. These are mainly applied to running saw and grist mills, with now and then a paper mill, or a cotton or woolen factory. Many of the smaller streams have of late years been occupied and improved as trout ponds, and immense numbers of these fish have thus been propagated at great expense, for sporting purposes.

Lakes and ponds of fresh water are quite frequent in some parts. Many of these are looked upon as natural curiosities, from the remarkable positions which they occupy. Some are found on the summit of high hills, others in the bottom of deep valleys, surrounded by steep sand hills, others again resting quietly upon the bosom of sandy plains, in close proximity to bodies of salt water, yet elevated many feet above the sea level.

Extensive deposits of peat are found in many parts of the island, mostly in the interior. These have attracted some attention, and the article is used to some extent, principally in composting manures for agricultural purposes. Some attempts have been made to utilize it for fuel.

The north shore of the island is for the most, considerably elevated, and broken into rugged hills and bluffs. The rocks which are more abundant in this section than any other, though nowhere as frequent as on the hills of Connecticut, across the Sound, are of such irregular shapes that they are of little use for building purposes, or even for laying up stone walls for fences, though they are used to a small extent for that purpose. The stones and rocks found on Long Island, from the huge boulder of a hundred tons weight down to the smallest pebble, whether found on the sea-shore, below high water mark, or far inland upon the top of the highest hill, or in the bowels of the earth at the bottom of the deepest well, are almost without exception devoid of angles, having to all appearances been worn smooth by the long continued washing of water. . . .

Inexhaustible beds of clay, of a quality suitable for brick making, and pottery, are found in the hills of the north side, and on the plains of the interior. These are worked to some extent, but the supply of material is a hundred fold in excess of the present facilities for working it.

The surface of Long Island may be set down as an average slope, from the elevated plains and cliffs which extend along the Sound shore, to the ocean and bays that wash the level shores of the south side. An irregular range of hills extends most of the length of the island, nearly through its centre, and south of this range the surface is comparatively smooth and to appearances level. Between this range and the rugged elevation along the north shore, the surface is frequently broken into a confusion of hills and valleys; then again extensive tracts of beautiful level plain intervene between the ridges, which are from two to five miles apart. In this central ridge we find the highest elevated points on the island. The average elevation of the land along the north side, within three or four miles of the Sound, would be about 100 feet. The hills in the immediate vicinity would range much higher. The hills adjoining the Sound are broken abruptly off, presenting on the north side a bare wall of earth, rising as nearly perpendicular as it could be made with the loose materials of which it is composed.

Soil and Resources

The soil of Long Island like its surface presents a great variety. To "lump" the thing, and express as near the truth as it is possible to do in as few words, we will say the soil is a sandy loam, which on the north side is heavy, while through the middle and on the south side it is a grade lighter, and interspersed by an occasional tract of comparatively sterile sand. We are aware that it is customary for a certain class of sages, who are fond of parading their stores of wisdom before the world through the medium of the New York Farmers' Club or the city press, to insinuate heavily or indulge in the plain assertion, that Long Island is a desert of sand, with only here and there an oasis of even tolerably fair soil. Such insinuations and assertions are false and contemptible. They are no doubt based upon actual observations (?), made by occasional glances from the car windows while passing over the island by rail, in the meanwhile intently absorbed in the perusal of "to-day's paper." The only apology we need offer for venturing assertions differing from those promulgated by such luminaries, is that having improved more extended opportunities for observation of the nature and qualities of Long Island soil, a reverential regard for the truth stimulates us to do so.

In support of the claim that Long Island is not, as many suppose it to be, a barren tract of unproductive waste, incapable of profitable cultivation, we might, if necessary, bring a cloud of witnesses—men whose words carry power and influence with them—but we do not consider that the necessity exists, and space will not permit. We however, take pleasure in presenting the following extract from the address of Hon. (now Gov.) John A. Dix, before the N. Y. State Agricultural Society, delivered October 7, 1859.

> The surface soil of this whole region, with some inconsiderable exceptions, consists of a rich loam, from twenty to thirty inches in depth, easily cultivated, and made highly productive without immoderate manuring. Some of the best farms in the southern part of the State have, during the last five years, been made in this condemned region [of the "barren plains"]; and it is shown by the agricultural survey of the State that the Island produces fourteen bushels of wheat to the acre, considerably beyond the average of the State, and very little less than that of the western district. . . .

> Of all the districts of the State, this has the finest summer climate, and the winters are mitigated and made temperate by the surrounding waters. Closer observation and experiment have dissipated misapprehension in regard to its fertility; they have shown that its soil is warm, genial and productive; and there is little hazard in predicting that it will, at no distant time, become the garden of the city of New York.

The land along the south side is usually kept in a better state of productiveness than that in the interior. This is owing to the greater convenience enjoyed by the cultivators there, for obtaining the fertilizing products of the adjoining bays and creeks. These products are fish, mussels, oyster-shells, sea-weed, eel-grass, meadow-muck, drift, and the like, which are used to good advantage on the farming lands of the vicinity. They are valuable manures and easily obtained, but their bulkiness forbids their being hauled many miles with profit. Fish, of that species known by the different names menhaden, white fish, shad, bunkers, bony fish, etc., are considered the most valuable of these manures. They are taken in large quantities in the bays and ocean, by companies of men and fleets of vessels armed with large nets. During late years a business of considerable importance has sprung up in the manufacture of oil from these fish, the refuse matter being used as a fertilizer.

In extracting the oil, the fish are first put into huge caldrons, where they are steamed over a great brick furnace. After this they are turned into strong boxes made of heavy planks with openings for the juice to escape, and placed under powerful presses which squeeze out the oil. A great number of these factories have been established on the shores of the bays along the south side and about the east end of the island. The mania for "oil" in this direction has raged to such an extent that the former lucrativeness of the business is impaired, and its dimensions on the decrease. The "scrap" or refuse of the fish, after the oil has been forced out is in convenient shape to be applied to the soil, and it is claimed by many that it contains all the fertilizing elements of the original fish. This has been sold during the past ten years at prices ranging from twelve to twenty-five dollars a ton, at the factories, in bulk.

The agricultural products of Long Island include a great variety. In the eastern and central portions grass and grain raising receives most attention. The western part which lies in convenient proximity to New York and Brooklyn markets, is devoted mainly to the raising of root crops and market garden produce. In Queens county and the western part of Suffolk, considerable quantities of milk are produced and sent daily to the New York market by special trains run for the accommodation of the business. Corn, wheat, hay, potatoes, and dressed hogs are shipped in considerable quantities from the east end.

Some attention is paid to the cultivation of small fruits, principally strawberries, blackberries, and cranberries. All these are found growing spontaneous in some parts. In the central part of the island and its vicinity, blackberries grow wild in great profusion. A few years since, the gathering and marketing of these berries was a business of some importance, which during the picking season engaged the attention of a greater part of the agricultural inhabitants. The growth and productiveness of the briars is greatly augmented by an occasional plowing of the ground, immediately after which, in many instances, the crop of berries produced without further cultivation or care, will return much better profits than any ordinary field crop with all its necessary labor and expense. The supply of cultivated and improved varieties, which has since been thrown upon the markets of New York and other cities, has nearly silenced the demand for the wild fruit of Long Island.

Apples, pears, peaches, plums, cherries, currants, raspberries, and grapes, are cultivated to some extent. Several extensive nurseries and seed gardens are among the important enterprises of the island. The atmosphere in the immediate vicinity of the ocean is less favorable to the healthy and vigorous growth, and the productiveness of fruit trees, than that of the interior and north side.

The principal forest trees of Long Island are the oak, pitch-pine, hickory, maple, chestnut, and cedar. Of these, the oak and hickory are found chiefly on the loamy or clay bottom soils, the pine on the sandy plains, the chestnut on the elevated northern parts, the maple in swampy localities, and the cedar here and there on the cliffs and sea shores, as well as on the sandy plains of the interior. The pine plains are covered with a thick under growth of snagged bushes familiarly known as scrub oaks or grubs. These have the appearance of the oak family, but seldom attain a greater height than four to eight feet. In some localities the ground is covered with an evergreen trailing plant called "deer feed," which grows in such a mass as to form a complete carpeting for the "nakedness of the land."

Here and there, especially on the south side, extensive patches of wintergreen plants are found. In some seasons the crop of berries produced by them is so large, that a great many people, mostly women and children, find profitable employment in gathering them for market. At such times wagon loads of them are collected and shipped to market by amateur speculators.

Huckleberries in the oak forests, blue-berries in the pines, bill-berries in the swamps, and beach-plums on the sand, are also among the wild fruits of Long Island, which grow in spontaneous abundance.

Industrial Enterprises

A very important industrial enterprise, especially of Suffolk county, is the cutting and transporting to market of cordwood, from the extensive oak and pine forests which occupy a great portion of this region. This business gives employment through the winter months, to a large number of the inhabitants, and is to some a regular business through all seasons of the year. A great many vessels, mostly of small size, are constantly engaged in transporting wood from the harbors and bays on both sides of the island, as well as from landings along the Sound shore, to New York and other places.

May 9th, 1862, a very destructive fire originated in the town of Smithtown, and swept over a large part of the timber land of that town, and through Brookhaven into the towns of Southampton and Riverhead. This fire charred the standing timber so that it was unfit for cordwood, and to make their losses good as possible, the owners of the black wood resorted to the experiment of converting it into charcoal. This proved to many, unexperienced in the business, an unprofitable speculation which was soon abandoned.

The conflagration of 1862, though perhaps of greater magnitude and more destructive in its effect than any other which has ever swept over any part of the forests of the island, was a specimen of what transpires every season in some or other part of the island. Oftentimes the same spot of ground will be burned over every year or two. These annual fires which usually occur in the spring time, when everything is dry, and just before the trees and bushes are clothed with their summer foliage, are most frequently originated by fire from passing trains on the railroads, or by the intentional act of vicious persons. Occasionally a "new ground" burning gets beyond the control of its guard, and scours over a large tract before it can be subdued. The timber growth on many large tracts has become so stunted and sickly, from the effect of these repeated fires, that it is almost valueless, and in a fair way to become annihilated.

Shipwrecks are of frequent occurrence along the ocean shore of Long Island. Stretching away from the entrance to New York Bay, as this beach does, for a distance of one hundred and twenty miles, it presents an inhospitable front to vessels approaching that harbor. By a slight variation from their course, or the influence of heavy winds blowing landward, after having weathered the storms of mid-ocean and arrived almost within sight of their anchorage, ship and cargo is often washed upon this strand, frequently resulting in a total loss of property, to which is sometimes added that of human lives. Not a year passes but more or less shipping is wrecked on some part of this beach. If the story of all the wrecks that have been thrown upon the Long Island shore could be gathered into a volume, what a series of destructive events, of distressing circumstances, and terrible scenes that book would contain! . . .[3]

In order to alleviate to some extent, the sufferings of shipwrecked mariners, the government has erected life saving stations along the beach, at a distance of four or five miles apart, from one end of the island to the other. These houses are supplied with cordage, ropes, and hawsers, powder, balls, mortars, life boats, and provisions. Each "station" is in charge of a keeper who resides in the vicinity. By a new arrangement, recently instituted, the number of these stations has been increased, and a crew of seven men is maintained at each house, during the winter months, while the danger and frequency of disaster is greatest. By this means the efficiency of the provision is increased.[4]

Improvements and Important Institutions

In olden times, before the advent of railroads here, the mails, and the traveling public, were carried and accommodated by stage lines, running through the length of the island. There were three routes,—one along the north side, another on the south side, and the other through the middle. By authority of an act of the general assembly, passed in 1724, commissioners were appointed, who laid out these three roads, about the year 1733, and gave them the names, North, Middle, and South, Country Roads. These three roads are at the present day the principal thoroughfares of wagon travel up and down the island, and most of the villages and settlements are located on or near them.

In the matter of railroads, Long Island at the present day is not behind the times. True, we have here no great thoroughfare opening into an expanseless region beyond, yet we think no suburb of New York or other great city, containing the same number of inhabitants scattered over a like extent of territory, is better served by railroad facilities supported merely by local patronage than Long Island.

The first of these enterprises was the Brooklyn Central and Jamaica railroad. This was opened for travel April 18th, 1836. The western terminus was South Ferry, Brooklyn, and the distance from that point to Jamaica eleven miles. The Long Island Railroad Company commenced the extension of this road from Jamaica eastward in 1836. In August of the following year the road was completed and put in operation as far as Hicksville, 26 miles. In 1841 the extension reached Suffolk Station [Central Islip]. In the summer of 1844 the road was completed to Greenport, its final terminus, and the first train of cars passed over it on the 25th of July, of that year. The length of this road, from Brooklyn to Greenport is ninety-five miles. This is the longest and principal road on the island. In 1860 a branch was constructed from

Jamaica to Hunter's Point, and the main western terminus and depot of the road established at that place. . . .[5]

Thus it will be seen, Long Island has about 300 miles of railroad; more than enough to put a belt around its entire limits, without counting any of the street car lines of Brooklyn or other places. And yet, railroad projects too numerous to mention are constantly exciting gossip in all parts of the island, and though in this matter as in many others, there is always more or less "talk" without any "cider," yet as "straws show which way the wind blows," it is safe to predict that a few years' time will bring much greater improvements in this direction, than a similar period of the past can show. Some of these projects, and many others yet untalked of, will ere-long be carried into effect. . . .

Through the instrumentality of these increased facilities for communication between New York and all parts of the island, it is asserting its legitimate claim as a proper suburb and tributary to the great American Metropolis. The public are beginning to realize and admit the weight of that claim, and the tide of immigration is setting hitherward. Capitalists and real estate dealers are giving their attention to Long Island lands, and improvements, to a greater extent than ever before. Professional men, business men, and nabobs, men of wealth and means, are buying and fitting up places for summer rustication, while other thousands are becoming permanent residents; building up and improving the waste of places of this beautiful "island of the sea."

As a watering place, and a popular resort for the overtaxed, over-heated, and over-stimulated people of New York and other cities during the heat of summer, Long Island, particularly the south side, is assuming a position of increasing importance. All along the south side, from Coney Island to Montauk, commodious hotels have been fitted up, for the accommodation of the thousands who flock hither during the summer months. New ones are being opened every season, but still the facilities are inadequate to the demand. Clubhouses, villas and cottages, for the summer retreat of city residents and men of wealth and prominence in political, judicial, literary or commercial circles, are scattered all through the villages of the south side, and other parts of the island as well.

That Long Island should become such a popular resort is not wonderful. It is more a wonder that it should have remained so long in comparative obscurity. But the fact that the Long Island Railroad, which until a few years ago monopolized the land travel over the island, runs most of its way through the least inviting and most monotonous route that could have been selected, affords a pretty good explanation of the mystery.[6] It would be hard to find a more beautiful combination, or greater variety of scenery—of valley and plain, hill-side and bluff, sea-shore and high-land, river and lake, harbor and cove, forest and clearing, meadow and wild, village and hamlet—within so short a distance of the great city than Long Island presents. Nearly all this beauty and variety however is hidden from the traveler as he passes over the railroad, nor has it been conveniently accessible from the city by way of the railroad. Pleasurists and settlers in search of desirable locations have therefore passed Long Island by, and bestowed their patronage upon other places. The new railroad facilities which have been opened upon the sides of the island, have developed its attractions very rapidly within a few years past, and doubtless will continue to do so for many years to come. . . .

Suffolk County

Suffolk county occupies about two thirds of the whole territory of Long Island. Its western boundary is the east line of Queens county. On the north and east it is washed by the Sound, and its tributary bays and harbors, and the Atlantic Ocean, which also washes the south shore. It contains four hundred and twenty-four thousand, three hundred and eighty-eight acres, about two fifths of which is under cultivation. The east end is divided by several large bays, which contain a number of islands. The Great South Bay, and East Bay extend along the south side, half the length of the county, from the west end. These bays in connection with South Oyster and Hempstead Bays at the west end, form a continuous opening inside the beach, from Rockaway to Ketchaboneck [Westhampton Beach], a distance of sixty miles. The entire length of the county, from east to west, is about ninety miles, and its greatest width, which is at the west end, about twenty miles. . . .

Montauk Lighthouse, 1877

On the beach which extends along the south side of this county, three tall light-houses have been placed: one at Fire

Exhibition Hall, Suffolk County Fairgrounds, Riverhead.

Island, another at Ponquogue [Shinnecock Lighthouse] forty miles east, and the third on Montauk Point, the easternmost extremity. The shore is almost literally strewn with fragments of wrecks. Some idea of the frequency of these casualties may be obtained from the fact, that between the first of November 1854, and the 28th of June, 1857, less than three years, sixty-four vessels, mostly of large size, were either wrecked or in distress upon this shore. . . .[7]

Institutions

The Suffolk County Agricultural Society, or at least the society from which it grew, whatever its name might have been, was originally formed in 1841. Its first record is lost. In 1843 it was re-organized, and that year, and each year following until 1853, including the latter, fairs were held under its auspices. These were held at different places in the towns of Huntington, Islip, and Smithtown, with the single exception that the fair for 1849 was held at Greenport. From 1853 to 1865 the matter rested, and no fairs were held. February 1st of the latter year, a meeting was held at Thompson Station [Brentwood] to revive the subject, and re-organize the society on a more permanent and liberal basis. A fair was held that year, and in 1866, at Riverhead. In 1867 the annual fair was held at Greenport. In 1868 a permanent ground had been secured and enclosed at Riverhead, and the fair was held in that place, which arrangement has continued till the present time. The Society now numbers about 255 life members.[8]

In the matter of temperance, Suffolk County has long retained a high rank. The County Temperance Convention, a society which has given expression to the temperance sentiment of the people for nearly a quarter of a century has been the means of accomplishing much good in this direction. It holds monthly meetings, changing about from one place to another whenever the temperance element is strong enough to furnish accommodation. Its sessions usually last two days. Besides this, local societies are or have been maintained in most of the villages. The various orders of Temperance whose meetings are open only to their own pledged members are also represented here, that of the "Sons of Temperance" to the greatest extent. The last report of the Grand Division of Eastern New York gives twenty-nine Divisions in Suffolk county, located at the following places: Yaphank, Babylon, Riverhead, Cold Spring Harbor, Bay Shore, Sag Harbor, Port Jefferson, Hauppauge, Patchogue, Sayville, Blue Point, Stony Brook, Southold, Mattituck, Jamesport, Mount Sinai, Smithtown, Northport, Ronkonkoma, Holbrook, Cutchogue, Bellport, Huntington, East Marion, Orient, Islip, Setauket, Atlanticville [East Quogue], Southampton.

The Suffolk County Sabbath School Association a union designed for the advancement of the cause, and promotion of the interest in Sunday School work, was organized about fifteen years ago and has been in operation ever since. . . . Though the number of schools which have taken an active interest in this institution is not as large as might be desired to make it a complete success, the encouragement afforded by the interest which has been taken in it has been sufficient to insure it a prosperous existence. It holds conventions four times a year, and its meetings are generally well attended. There are one hundred and twelve Sunday Schools in the county, and the thirty-four schools from which the officers of this Association have received returns, report in the aggregate five hundred and fifty-one teachers and officers, and three thousand and fifty-five scholars.

During the great national commotion, which less than ten years ago was shaking the foundations of the American Republic, and trying by the fiery test of war, the power of the people to sustain their own government, the towns of Suffolk County responded nobly and promptly to the frequent calls for men and money with which to carry on the war for the preservation of the Union. . . .[9]

There are at present about twenty cigar and tobacco factories in operation in the county, yielding a revenue of about fifteen hundred dollars a month, and three or four banks and about five hundred license tax payers. The former system has been abolished and the taxes are now assessed and collected by collectors and their deputies. . . .

The common school system is of course the same in general features in this county as in other rural counties throughout the state. In a few of the large villages, well regulated, graded schools, accommodated in spacious and magnificent buildings, are maintained with able management. These landmarks of civilization are the pride of our villages and a credit and honor to the county. A great part of our rising population is however, accommodated in the small, old-fashioned district school buildings, which are scattered at intervals of a mile or two all through the lesser villages and thinly settled portions. These buildings are in the main nearly all of the same model. They are usually sixteen to twenty feet wide, by thirty to forty feet long; a single low story in height; plainly built, and upon both exterior and interior, bear countless evidences of the early developments of that seething propensity which Americans have, for making their *mark* in the world. . . . [10]

Town of Huntington

The town of Huntington as it now is [i.e., after 1872 when the town of Babylon was formed from the southern part], occupies the northwest corner of the county. It contains about forty-six thousand acres, more than one half of which is improved and divided into beautiful farms. The northern part and some of the interior is hilly, and the surface generally is elevated, but large tracts of rich level plain stretch "far and wide" in different parts. Farming is the chief industry of the people. The inhabitants are thinly scattered over nearly the whole surface of the town. The population would probably vary but little from seven thousand. [11]

The northern part of the town is thrown into irregular necks and projections of land by counter irregularities of water, which form a labyrinth of bays, harbors and coves upon the north shore. . . .

Northport

Keeping the road eastward from this village [Centerport] as it winds among the hills across the head of Little Neck, about a mile brings us within sight of the village of Northport with its romantic surroundings. The road from which we gain this delightful prospect of water, hills and village, passes over the mounds which skirt the southwestern extremity of Northport Harbor which in olden times was burdened with the uncouth name of Great Cow Harbor. Another mile brings us round to the village, which lies upon the eastern shore. Among the first indications that we are approaching an inhabited centre we pass a Christian burying-ground occupying a hill on our right. Half a mile south, or southeast from here, but not within sight of this road is another—the village cemetery. A little further on we pass a small grist-mill standing on the left which is something of a curiosity in its way.

The driving wheel of this mill is an overshot, about five feet wide and twenty-five feet in diameter. It receives water by a wooden tube about a foot in diameter, which runs over the highway from a pond upon the top of a hill several rods to the right. The supply of water being limited the mill can only be run six or seven hours a day.

From here the road leads along a steep side hill thirty to fifty feet about the base which skirts high water mark, and along the outside of this road there is nothing to protect a person or animal from stepping, stumbling, plunging, or in any other way being precipitated down the wild precipice. Here and there the face of the declivity is covered with trees and brambles. To us it seems remarkable that in the time of some freshet this narrow step is not washed away and torn by running water so as to be made impassable. On the harbor below us are numberless fleets of small boats, some intended for business and others for pleasure. On the rising ground above us pleasant sited dwellings are thinly scattered along the roadside till we come into the heart of the village. The Northport House, is to the traveler at the close of day one of the most interesting features of the place. The road by which we have entered leads directly up in front of it. Here is the focal point of the village. Wharves, shipyards, lumber-yards, stores and mechanic shops are huddled in lively confusion about this point. Main Street starts here and runs up a moderately inclined plane, eastward, and upon the first half mile of it most of the business concerns of the village are located. Bay View Avenue runs north from the central point mentioned above, and its course lies from ten to twenty rods from the shore, and elevated fifty feet more or less above the level of the water. On both sides it is lined with neat looking dwellings for a distance of three-fourths of a mile. It is appropriately named. It is like a grand balcony from almost any point of which we can look over the whole harbor with its shipping and its scores of little pleasure boats skimming hither and thither upon the face of the smooth water. The bluffs of Eaton's Neck in the northern distance, and the hills and valleys of Little Neck across to the west add variety and beauty to the scene.

Northport is without question the most flourishing village in this town. In fact it is hardly surpassed in its rapid growth by any other village on the north side of the county. Forty years ago the place only contained eight dwellings. Now it has three shipyards, two hotels, six or eight general stores, dealers in specialties of dry goods, drugs and medicines, millinery, boots and shoes, saddlery, paints and oils, lumber, etc., a good representation of the professions and trades, and a population by the last census of one thousand and sixty. It has a district school, numbering one hundred and forty pupils, and employing two teachers. The present building stands on Main

Street and though of apparently comfortable size is considered too small for the purpose, and the question of supplying its place with a new one is being discussed. The enterprise of this village has quite recently been directed to the matter of church building. Within the year past a new Methodist Episcopal church has been completed. This is a large handsome building, standing on the Main Street near the school, and on the same lot on which stands the old church of the same denomination. The walls of the old church are of brick, and the structure was erected about the year 1833. A short distance further up the street stands a small church erected a few years ago and occupied by a society of New School Presbyterians.[12] A much larger edifice is now in process of erection by the united Presbyterian society. Its location is on the same lot.

Northport has a flourishing Lodge of Free Masons, numbering about forty members. It has only been instituted a few years, its original members having withdrawn from the Lodge at Huntington. A Division of the Sons of Temperance meets every week. They number one hundred and thirty-two members.

Shipbuilding is carried on to a considerable extent here. There are five sets of marine railways, and three shipyards and from these, barks [ships] as large as six or seven hundred tons capacity are launched.

Great quantities of manure are brought from New York and landed at the docks for the farmers of the back region. A packet sloop plies between here and New York.

Large quantities of clams, oysters and eels are taken from the flats and beds of this harbor. These bivalve fisheries give employment to a great many people, and no doubt they have had a large influence in building up the place. The oysters of this harbor are among the finest in the world. . . .[13]

Vernon Valley is a pleasant little farming district containing perhaps one hundred and fifty inhabitants located about two miles east of Northport, to which it is a sort of tributary. It was formerly called Red Hook. It contains a Presbyterian church and a school. The church was built here in 1829, having been removed from Fresh Pond its former site.

One and a half miles northeast of this is the hamlet of Fresh Pond, lying on the sound shore, in the northeast corner of this town and extending partly into Smithtown. It takes its name from a body of water which puts in from the sound on the line between the towns. It has a store and a post office. Two extensive brick yards are located upon the sound shore at this place. These are the Long Island Brick Yards, and the works of Provost Brothers. The latter use steam power for tempering the clay and moulding the brick.

Just west of here Crab Meadow is a marshy region drained by a creek which empties into the sound [now Crab Meadow Park]. In this vicinity are about a dozen farm houses. . . .

Green Lawn is a railroad station on the Northport Branch two miles and a half east of Huntington Station. It is a pleasant locality, on the elevated plain, and consists of a hotel, two stores, a "Real Estate Exchange," a blacksmith shop, and about a dozen houses, with several hundred acres of rich farming land. From this neighborhood the hills of the interior present a fine landscape view.

About a mile south from here is a little rural vicinity called Cuba, and a mile and a half further still and bearing a little eastward is a scattered settlement of farmers lately named Elwood.

The population and dwellings are so scattered over a greater part of this town (Huntington) that it is a difficult matter to decide just where one village or hamlet leaves off and the next one commences. To the best of our knowledge and ability, however, we will fix the territorial dimensions of Elwood at two miles square. This is occupied by thirty dwellings and inhabitants in proportion. Within its limits are a school and a Methodist church. A steam grist-mill was started here a few years ago, but has been removed for want of support.

Adjoining Elwood on the northeast is another district of similar characteristics and proportions, and the description of one will answer very well in a general way for the other. This is known by the name of Clay Pitts or the modernized synonyms of Genola and Fair View. Which of the two names will be the accepted one is to be decided by time. We think the latter is perfectly appropriate but the former looks more like a *name*.[14]

Town of Brookhaven

Lake Ronkonkoma, in this neighborhood, on the line of Brookhaven, Islip and Smithtown, is one of the largest and most beautiful sheets of fresh water on the island. The lake is about three miles in circumference, and lies some twenty feet below the average surface of the neighboring land. It is surrounded by a beach of *white sand* from which peculiarity it is said the Indian name it bears was derived. The water is remarkably clear, of great depth, and abounds with fish of different varieties. In the olden time the neighborhood of this lake was a favorite resort of the huntsman, frequented as it was by great numbers of deer. It is now a popular retreat for pleasure-seekers and pic-nic parties from the neighboring villages. Thousands annually visit its shores, for recreation and to enjoy the delights of its scenery. Its banks are shaded by a belt of sturdy oaks, which grew "from little acorns" many long years ago. Several fine groves in the vicinity are used for camp-meetings, mass-meetings, celebrations and other public gatherings of a religious, political, or social character. . . .

Adjoining Bellport on the east lies the village of Brookhaven, until recently called Fire Place. It contains two churches, two district schools, two stores and a population of about four hundred. Immense tracts of salt meadows skirt the shore of the bay at this point. A great part of this meadowland is owned by farmers of the interior, many of whom come from eight to sixteen miles to gather the hay product and haul it home. The people of this village are mostly farmers and fishermen. Gunning for wild-fowl in the neighborhood is followed as a source of profit by some and as pastime by others. Trout-ponds have been established on a small stream called Beaver Dam River which runs through the midst of the settlement. The eastern part, sometimes called the "Neck," borders on the Connecticut [now Carmans] River, and a dock has been constructed here, at a point which bears the Indian name Squassucks. . . . A line of mail and express stages connects this village and Bellport with the South Side Railroad at Patchogue.

Notes

Source: Richard M. Bayles, *Historical and Descriptive Sketches of Suffolk County and its Towns, Villages, Hamlets, Scenery, Institutions and Important Enterprises; with an Historical Outline of Long Island; From its First Settlement by Europeans* (Port Jefferson: The author, 1873), pp. 74-87, 89-91, 109-14, 117-18, 137-38, 160-66, 266, 274-75. (This book was reprinted by Ira J. Friedman in 1962.) Editing changes have been minimal. A few typos in the original have been corrected. The subheads are taken from Bayles' topics at the beginning of chapters. All notes are by the editor for this edition and her insertions in the text are in brackets.

1. His other histories include Green County, New York (1884); City of Yonkers (1885); Richmond County, Staten Island (1886); Newport County, Rhode Island (1887); Windham County, Connecticut (1889); and Providence County, Rhode Island (2 vols. 1890-1891). Selections from his *Handbook of Long Island* are reprinted in "Glimpses of Local Communities in the Late Nineteenth Century," edited by Natalie A. Naylor, *Nassau County Historical Society Journal* 56 (2001): 28-38.

2. Biographical information is from Donald Bayles, "Richard M. Bayles," typescript 1990, in the Bayles Collection, Longwood Public Library, Middle Island; Osborn Shaw, "Richard M. Bayles, Island Historian," *Long Island Forum* 9 (March 1946): 43-44. (Osborn's article includes much of the information from the obituary of Bayles which he wrote for the *Patchogue Advance,* November 7, 1930.)

3. Bayles briefly mentions three wrecks which each claimed more than one hundred lives: the *Sylph* in 1815; the *Bristol* in 1836; and the *Mexico* in 1837 (p. 85).

4. See Van R. Field, *Wrecks and Rescues on Long Island: The Story of the U.S. Life Saving Service* (Privately printed, 1997); and Ellice B. Gonzales, *Storms, Ships & Surfmen: The Life-Savers of Fire Island* (Patchogue, NY: Eastern National Park and Monument

Association, 1982). The Long Island Maritime Museum in West Sayville (86 West Avenue; 631-854-4974) has exhibits on shipwrecks off Long Island and the U.S. Life Saving Service.

5. Omitted here are descriptions of other branches of the railroad. In a table, Bayles includes for each the cost per mile, capital stock, and debt (pp. 87-89).

6. Because the Long Island Railroad was originally designed as a shortcut from New York City to Boston rather than to serve Long Island, it was built through the middle of the island which was less expensive. Most of Long Island's population, however, was along the north and south shores.

7. Omitted here is Bayles' brief description and condemnation of those who plunder shipwrecks (p. 112).

8. The Queens County Agricultural Society was also organized in 1841 and held fairs at different sites in the county. It established a permanent fairgrounds in Mineola in 1866 where annual fairs were held for more than eight decades. The new Nassau County Court complex began transforming the fairgrounds area beginning in 1938, and the fair moved to Roosevelt Raceway in 1953. Now under the Agricultural Society of Queens, Nassau and Suffolk Counties, the Long Island Fair has been held at Old Bethpage Village Restoration since 1970, where some of the original Mineola Fair buildings have been recreated. See Gary R. Hammond, "The Mineola Fair: Mirror of a County's Growth," *Nassau County Historical Society Journal* 54 (1999): 23-30.

9. In a section omitted here (pp. 114-17), Bayles lists for each town, the number of men liable to the draft, those who served in the army, and the number of deaths from the state census of 1865. He also discusses the taxes imposed during the Civil War and the names of the assessors.

10. Bayles includes 1872 statistics on Suffolk schools from reports to the School Commissioner including the number of students, teachers' wages, value of school, and assessed value of property for each district (pp. 118-25). See also Natalie A. Naylor, "'Diligent in Study and Respectful in Deportment': Early Long Island Schooling," *Nassau County Historical Society Journal* 43 (1988): 1-13.

11. The population of Huntington in 1870 was 10,704 (including what became the town of Babylon). Bayles' estimate of about 7,000 is probably reasonable since in 1880, Huntington's population was 8,783 and Babylon's 4,739. See Long Island Regional Planning Board, *Historical Population of Long Island Communities, 1790-1980* (Hauppauge: Long Island Regional Planning Board, 1982), p. 16.

12. The Presbyterian Church split nationally in 1837-1838, primarily over theological and polity issues, including the role of voluntary benevolent societies. Schisms over slavery occurred in both the Old School and New School denominations on the eve of the Civil War. There were some reunions after the war, but geographical differences remained in the main groups until the United Presbyterian Church was formed in 1958.

13. Omitted here are Bayles' descriptions of two clay and sand companies and their products (pp. 163-64).

14. The area today is known as East Northport. Clay Pitts Road is a vestige of the earlier place name.

"Out on the Island," 1890

Long Island Railroad

The Long Island Railroad (LIRR) was a major promoter of Long Island.[1] In 1877, the railroad issued the first of its promotional books, *Long Island and Where to Go: A Descriptive Work Compiled for the Long Island Railroad Company for the Benefit and Use of its Patrons.* The 262-page paperback featured attractive wood engravings and advertisements. Obviously the railroad publicized the attractions of the island to increase its own business from summer visitors and year-round residents. The LIRR continued to promote Long Island and issued numerous free or inexpensive booklets in the last decades of the nineteenth century and early decades of the twentieth century including such titles as: *Long Island by the Sound (or, The Beauties of Long Island); Long Island Illustrated; Summer Homes on Long Island; Suburban Long Island; Unique Long Island;* and *Long Island and Real Life.* Over the years, photographs replaced engravings and some of the booklets listed information on train service for each community.[2]

These selections are from the railroad's 1890 promotional booklet, *Out on Long Island.* After a general introduction and overview, sections on Nearby Seaside Resorts, the South Shore, Central Section, and North Shore provide descriptions of seaside resorts and suburban towns. Communities are discussed from west to east as passengers might travel on the various lines of the railroad. Long Island's attractions are described effusively and almost every community has its own particular attraction.

* * *

Long Island has held in waiting every variety of beauty, scenery of entrancing loveliness, air fresh with the salt breezes of the sea and sweetened with the balsams of its pines and spruces. The fish have fattened in its ponds, and the breakers have thundered on its beaches. . . .

The world's vision is always far-sighted and sees the distant, while it is blind to the beauty that is near at hand. . . . Long Island has hills as fair as the Scottish Highlands, cliffs that well-nigh rival those of Dover, quaint towns as curious as those of Normandy, gable-roofed cottages and windmills as antique as those of Holland, while in its summer cities by the sea Vanity Fair as curious masquerades of pleasure seekers as any in the old world. . . .

New York has become one of the great cities of the world, because it is the gateway of a continent. The sea has dowried it with riches. And yet Long Island is its only seaboard. There are states not larger than Long Island. One hundred and twenty miles in length, from eight to twenty broad; within this

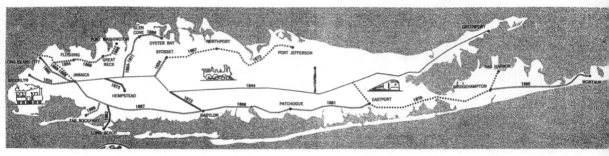

Growth of the Long Island Railroad

area there is all that heart can wish and industry desire. Through the wise enterprise of the Long Island Railroad Company, with its several hundred trains a day, this wonderland, so long unknown, is taking its rightful place as one of the fairest portions of the Empire State. Great resorts grow populous. The tide of emigration is setting eastward from the metropolis, industry is tickling the swift island with the plough, and it responds with laughing harvests. Wealth is lining the shores with villas, and the great middle classes are finding homes in the pleasant island village contiguous to the cities. While there has been none of the artificial excitement of "Western booms," there has been a phenomenal growth in the towns and villages of the island, so that "out on the Island" now is a familiar phrase to the dwellers in the great cities of New York and Brooklyn.[3]

Long Island may be conveniently divided into three divisions. From the same starting-points in Long Island City and Brooklyn, the trains leave for the central portion, the south and north shores.[4]

The central part is a great plain. In places, for miles one passes over great prairie-like reaches, dotted with forests of fir and pine, with soil clean and easily worked. John Randolph said that the soil of Virginia was poor by nature and ruined by cultivation, and so to the casual tourist the soil of Long Island seems unfertile; but turn it with the plough, and throw the seed into it, and it rewards toil with plenty. It seems as if Nature, knowing how tired human brains would get in the great hurryings of the city, had set this great central belt midway here between the sea and the Sound, as a sanitarium for the healing of sick nerves and spent brains; for here are "the murmuring pines and the hemlocks," and in this porous soil there is no feeding-place of malaria, and the air, washed clean with the sweet baptisms of the sea, brings invigoration in every breeze, while there is room enough for the tired thousands, who at night would escape the cities' heats, to touch old Mother Nature and rise up strong for the new day's work.

The south side is the sea side of the island; but as if, in her great kindness to this "snug little, tight little island," Nature desired to guard it from the raw, untempered sea, she has made a breakwater between the island and the ocean, and behind this outer rampart she has for sixty miles placed the Great South Bay, which is a kind of inner lake, with waters smooth and sunny on summer days, but having in it a touch of the old fury of the sea when occasion calls. Along the shores of this bay there are inlets, bays, and coves; into it the streams run, and along it there are villages which once were filled with those who tilled the land and spread their nets within the waters, who made the towns quaint with curious streets and lanes, and kept alive the old customs of the good old days. In recent years the summer throngs have filled these villages. The dog-cart and the tally-ho are seen within the streets; the old clocks and heirlooms have been bought and are now "hung up for ornament;" the village pastures are cut up into villa lots; great hotels are in the places where the fishers dried their nets, and land that was once given away by the acre is now sold by the foot. But Nature has been very prodigal of her charms here upon this old island.

The Great South Bay is a splendid institution; but even that would have been overdone if it had bounded the island along its entire length. And so, at either end of it the sea comes up and has direct dealings with the island, and without a foot of intervening sand or island it pours the whole torrent of three thousand miles of sea upon the beaches. And what superb things these beaches are! As smooth as ivory and almost as white. No quicksands here, nor treacherous undertow of backward sweeping currents, but good, honest, hearty, noisy breakers, pounding on beaches hard as adamant! Nowhere on the Atlantic coast are there greater reaches of white sand, and along these magnificent shores there are great hotels, and small hotels, every wonderment of summer merriment and pleasure, bands of world-wide fame, a great phantasmagoria, to which half the multitudes of the great cities go, and to whose dazzling brilliancy of scene the tourists of the world come to be amazed. And at the other end Nature gives another turn to her kaleidoscope, and here she has built behind the beaches high hills of sand, as though she knew that the ocean was a treacherous thing, and needed some mighty rampart to keep her back from the great continent. From these one looks down and out upon the sea. Had he but vision strong enough he could look straight across to the old world without one intervening thing. The sea is flecked with sails, and tired watchers on the deck see these white cliffs as the first token of their voyage's end, and on and on these beaches go, eastward and northward, the cliffs broken here and there, until at last the end is reached in Montauk Point, where the island culminates in a great cliff of grandeur.

These things are on the seaward side. Backward the cliffs slope with gentle declivity into fertile fields. There are winding roads leading to pleasant towns, not spoiled by art or fashion, but having a simple life and simple ways, taking just pride in the relics of an honorable past, not anxious for rapid growth, but having the oldtime virtues of hospitality and friendliness.

The north side of the island faces Long Island Sound. It is a noted place, and not even the far-famed St. George's Channel [between Ireland and Wales] is such a waterway as this. The traffic of New England and not a little of the ocean commerce passes here; for many years the Sound steamers, at early morn and eve, have passed up and down with their stately beauty. There have been many tragedies on this watercourse, and it is famous not only for its exceeding beauty, but for the memorable events that have happened here. Long Island along the north shore is bold and precipitous. The Sound makes many indentations of deep bays or harbors, and on either side of this the land is high and wooded with the finest growth of timber. There are villages and farms, pleasant villas and homes embowered with trees, winding roads skirting the bays with little vessels in the harbors and along the shore, shipyards where once great ships were built. The grandeur here is not of the sea, as it is upon the island's other side, but it is of mingled land and water. Beyond, northward, are the shores of Connecticut, just far enough away to have the misty glamour which Nature loves, with her artless coquetry, to spread before her face. There is the glimmer of city spires, the white gleam of town and village, the upward rising land, which stands like lesser mountains against the sky. And near at hand are the blue waters of the Sound, not always smooth, but having wayward moods of passion when the storm is on.

For the lover of beauty the north side is rich. There is grandeur in these high ramparts of land which separate the harbors. The shores are irregular, iron-bound with rock and boulder, on which the sea weeds have hung their draperies, while there are pleasant surprises of woodland nooks, winding paths and roads, with fertile farms such as one sees on New England hills, with soil as warm and rich as Nature ever made. There are staid and prosperous towns here, having all the comforts that years of prosperous industry and enterprise can bring. The invasion of the city is already felt. At morning and night the depots are surrounded with the carriages of those who go daily to the city to their business, and year by year the summer homes increase, the tide of travel swells, as the incomparable beauties and delights of the island are discovered. At the farther end of the island Shelter Island stands to "Sentinel enchanted land." Beyond is still another island

[Gardiner's Island], and both of these have their own legends and traditions. There is no need that citizens of New York and Brooklyn should live within crowded tenements, or waste half their living on expensive rents, when for a small sum a home can be bought or built in some one of the many towns of Long Island. Summer boarding places can be found within easy distance of the cities at moderate cost, and men can go to and fro at small expense of time and money.

The Woodruff parlor coaches are attached to all the principal trains of the Long Island Railroad. They are handsomely appointed, and offer the traveler every convenience and comfort. The island from one end to the other is well supplied with the daily newspapers and periodicals by the Long Island News Company. New York morning papers are delivered at early hours every day and are sold on all the trains. During the season special Sunday trains are run to insure early distribution of newspapers.

Long Island offers every variety of scenery, an unrivaled climate and easy accessibility to the great cities. The time is not far distant when the entire island will be a suburban New York and Brooklyn, and if one is missed from his accustomed place in the great city the answer to the question, "Where is he?" will bring the response, "Out on Long Island."

Near-by Seaside Resorts

For years after the New Jersey ocean resorts were in the full tide of prosperity, the broad, inviting beaches of Southern Long Island were unpopulated, and, with few exceptions, almost unvisited. But in the seventies it dawned on the minds of certain capitalists that right here, within a half-hour's ride of New York, was a series of the finest beaches in America—yes, in the world—and they resolved to develop them into watering-places, with what result of success the world knows. It spoils a day to go to Long Branch and home again, but the tired man of business can run down to Manhattan Beach with his family in thirty minutes after office hours, take a bath in the surf, get an excellent dinner, listen to the music and see the fireworks, and be home and in bed an hour earlier than he would be if he spent the evening at the theatre. Coney Island is the most cosmopolitan of places. There is a sliding social scale extending from the West End to the elegant and exclusive Oriental Hotel at the East End with its adjacent miles of protected beach. Nowhere in America is there so famous a seaside resort as Manhattan Beach. It is the metropolis among summer cities of the country as New York is among the commercial cities. It is no unusual sight on a pleasant summer's day to witness over 100,000 people at this magnificent

Manhattan Beach Hotel, Coney Island, c. 1890

resort, and yet so large are the two hotels and so extensive the grounds about them that every one can have full measure of the enjoyment which he seeks.

The Manhattan and Oriental are two of the largest and best hotels on Long Island, the former accommodating five hundred people and the latter seven hundred. These houses are equipped with every modern improvement, and the grounds they stand in are beautified with lawns and gardens. The cuisine is excellent, and both variety and abundance are assured. A broad promenade extends before them, furnished with seats that young people like to occupy when the moon rises, and it often takes a surprisingly long time for the moon to come up. The ride from the city is in itself a pleasant thing on a warm day, the temperature seeming to fall as the open cars—you can ride in the parlor car if you prefer—speed over the green fields and through the cool and rustling forests. Arrived at Manhattan, many pleasures offer, chief among which is the bathing. The whole coast of Long Island is washed by a branch of the Gulf Stream, so the water has never the icy chill that shrivels the person who takes his sea baths north of Cape Cod. There is a good surf, too; not so heavy as to make an undertow, or to render it unsafe for ladies and children, but a good, bracing roll to the water that puts every one in a glow. Bathers at Manhattan have the advantage of a detached structure that screens them from promiscuous observation. The dresses and towels are absolutely clean, a matter of no small account, and valuables may be safely entrusted to the care of the clerks.

Excellent music is to be heard at the spacious music pavilion, which is splendidly arranged with reference to acoustic properties, and [Patrick S.] Gilmore's famous band is frequently supplemented during the season by choral societies and distinguished soloists, and on Sundays clergymen of celebrity conduct divine worship. The amphitheatre is one of the best-constructed in the world, finely decorated within and without. As for Gilmore, everybody knows him. He is to the brass band what Theodore Thomas is to the orchestra, and the rich tone and grand sonority of his music have never been equaled by any other band in the country. From the time of his connection with the great jubilees in Boston, Mr. Gilmore has been the best-known musician in America, and his name has never been associated with a failure. So great an attraction are his concerts that thousands of people visit Manhattan Beach during the summer just to hear the music.[5] Fire Dramas, under supervision of Pain of London, are enacted on nearly every summer night in the great inclosure east of the hotel, hundreds of people assisting in the performance, boats navigating the lake between stage and audience, the show concluding with a dazzling exhibition of pyrotechnic devices.

Back of Manhattan Beach is the narrow Sheepshead Bay, thus named because of the fish known as sheepshead that abound there. It is a rendezvous for yachtsmen, and now that the cottagers who dwell on its shores have solved the drainage problem and have begun to beautify their streets and holdings, the village of Sheepshead Bay has sprung into prominence. The local population is greatly increased through the hot season by a summer colony of city folks, and on racing days thousands visit the Coney Island Jockey Club track, which is one of the amplest and best managed in the country. . . .[6]

Before Long Branch [New Jersey] could claim any social consequence, Far Rockaway was the most famous watering-place in this country, Newport alone excepted. The Marine Hotel that stood there forty years ago was a great hotel for its time, and its register bore the names of presidents, governors, mayors, authors, soldiers, and so on, down to common little European princes, who were not above eating clams and struggling with other articles of the traditional diet of the Long Islander. With the burning of this hotel, Far Rockaway lapsed into a state of innocuous desuetude, and slept a Rip Van Winkle sleep, forgotten by its neighbors; but with the development of watering places around it, a spark of enthusiasm woke this little village, too, and it is taking on new importance as a resort, and increasing as a place of permanent homes. It is but thirty-five minutes from Hunter's Point, and although the sea winds are strong in cold weather, and the ocean storms are magnificent to witness, the temperature is not only cooler than that of the cities in summer, but the thermometer never falls quite so low in winter as it does in the interior. For this fact the Gulf Stream is responsible. Far Rockaway Bay extends before the village, offering safe water for bathers and boaters; even children may be trusted to row about this inlet, and just across the sands that separate it from the sea roars and seethes the ocean. The sheltered waters of Jamaica Bay are less than half a mile distant on the west. All kinds of hotels and restaurants are found there, and for the benefit of the local populace there are shops, markets, schools, churches, telegraph offices, telephones, and a court-house. The site is on ground of moderate elevation, supporting a natural growth of sweet-scented bay and larger bushes and trees. Cottages are multiplying rapidly, and the value of real estate is rising. . . .

Lawrence, a mile back from Far Rockaway, is a handsome village with telegraphic and telephonic touch with the city, boating, bathing, fishing and sleeping—the latter an item worth considering by the fagged and brain-sick business man; for cool, pure air, the lull of a distant surf and the plash of wind through the cedars will do a [great] deal toward the cure of insomnia. Most of the Lawrentians own elegant houses and live in them through the year. They are wealthy, well-bred and well-situated; therefore they should be happy. The village is one great garden, blazing with flowers and ornamental shrubbery, while broad avenues lead to Ocean Point [Cedarhurst], Isle of Wight [Lawrence Beach], Westville [Inwood] and Far Rockaway. With its advantages and its society, Lawrence may justly claim to be one of the most stylish resorts on Long Island. Few places of its size contain so many costly residences.[7]

At Cedarhurst, between Lawrence and Woodsburgh, the country is undulating and fertile, and, although the name hints at cedars only, there is abundance of oak, maple, willow, acacia and pine. The sea views and bay views are fine, and are enhanced by the rustic beauty of the foreground. An equable climate and plenty of ozone are likewise assured to its residents, and sixty handsome villas attest the appreciation with which certain influential families regard this delightful place, many of the villas being occupied the year through. The headquarters of the Rockaway Hunt Club is an imposing clubhouse in Queen Anne style, and it contains everything needed by the members from a kitchen to a postoffice. There are polo grounds, tennis courts, gymnasium, hunting-stables, game and fish preserves and kennels.

The "meets" of the hunters are picturesque affairs, and bring out large numbers of people.

Returning from Lawrence to the main line of the railroad, Hewletts, Woodsburgh and Ocean Point [Cedarhurst] are rapidly traversed, and the tourist has glimpses of quiet streets, country shops, modest little churches and cozy cottages. Woodsburgh is so named from the late Samuel Wood, of Brooklyn, a rich and philanthropic gentleman who aimed to establish there a town that should excel Garden City in size and beauty; but the estates are in litigation, and when, years hence, the courts render their decisions and perfect titles to land may be secured, this town will rank among the most desirable places of residence on Southern Long Island. Boulevard Avenue is one hundred feet wide and lined with shade trees all the way to the shore.

The last of these near-by seaside resorts is Long Beach, a narrow island seven miles long, that guards Hempstead Bay, with its grassy islands, from the direct assaults of the sea. It is twenty-four miles from New York, and "one of the brightest in the string of ocean pearls" that adorn the Long Island coast. The beach has a barely perceptible slope, and is so hard and smooth that driving, horseback exercise and walking are attended with no fatigue, while the sea that tumbles on the shore in magnificent breakers is as clear and bright as crystal. Long Beach is popular with the better class of people, and even on days when there is a crowd from town there is no noise or

Long Beach Hotel, c. 1890

roughness. The big hotel, in Queen Anne style, is one of the best-built and best-kept of the many hostelries between Brooklyn and Montauk, and among its guests are and have been statesmen, men of the professions and notables of all kinds from different parts of the country. It is nine hundred feet long by one hundred and fifty wide, its verandas are broad enough to dance upon, the conveniences and comforts are such as are found in the best city hotels. Heating, ventilation and lighting have been scientifically adjusted. Through the season an orchestra furnishes music. A number of pretty and roomy cottages are for rent there to those who prefer a degree of privacy that the hotel cannot insure, or who have large families. They can dine at the hotel or they may keep house, as suits their convenience and pleasure. The Marine Railway runs to the east end of the island, where on breezy Point Lookout that is thrust into the blue Atlantic, there is another hotel and group of cottages. Many of the cottagers own their yachts, and the season there is enlivened with sailing, fishing, bathing, games and dances.[8]

The South Shore

The south side of Long Island is the seaward side. The great South Bay, and at either end of that the great Atlantic, have made it attractive to tourists. Its facilities for boating and fishing have no doubt added much to its charms. The Montauk division of the Long Island Railroad skirts the shore, and in most cases passes through or near the business centres of the towns, giving such excellent railroad accommodations that for fifty miles at least the island is a veritable suburb of the metropolis. At Valley Stream the railroad branches to Rockaway, and at Pearsalls [Lynbrook] to Long Beach, and then, without divergences, continues for one hundred miles to Sag Harbor, the terminus. To stop and particularize about every place along this delightful route is unnecessary, and would only weary the reader. Naturally many of the south side villages are much alike in general characteristics. All are noted for healthfulness, a feature already dwelt upon. All have access to the water. And as to the attractiveness of each, such as the location of streets, the architecture of the houses, and the nearness to the depots, etc., these are matters which appeal with varying force to different individuals. For a distance of some twenty miles, from Valley Stream to Amityville and beyond, the geographical features are similar, and all the villages in that section are especially favored by being within easy reach of the cities [of Brooklyn and New York City].

It is true that the ocean waves do not roll in upon the mainland, nor is there broad sweep of bay, but there is compensation in the hundred inlets and coves and numerous islands, making not only a paradise for the amateur sportsman, but an El Dorado for the honest fishermen of the towns who derive their sustenance from these productive waters. From Freeport come the luscious Rockaway oysters, and in these waters are caught the finest blue-fish that are sent to market, while all the region is dotted with ponds and trout-streams famous for what they offer. In July the summer flight of bay birds commences, and then the gunners come in for their share of the sport, and as the fall approaches the ducks and geese appear. It is indeed a charming country. The farmers thereabouts are a well-to-do class, the villages are wide awake and are growing with a rapidity that is simply marvelous. At Freeport a tract of land of thirty acres, north of the railroad, called Randall Park, has been handsomely laid out, and already thirty modern cottages have been erected, while at Rockville Centre extensive real estate transfers have been made this year which promise large results in the way of local improvements. Many attractive cottages have already been erected and several good boarding-houses. Oceanville [Oceanside] a contiguous settlement, contains a cluster of houses, over twenty of which are occupied by retired "Down-East" shipmasters. The Brooklyn Water Works have a large pumping station in the vicinity.[9] Pearsalls, Baldwins, Bellmore, Ridgewood [Seaford/Wantagh], Merrick, are all desirable summer villages with many attractive features. At Merrick are the famous camp-meeting grounds.[10]

On Long Island, with its superior Indian nomenclature, there is no excuse for giving "North" and "South" prefixes and the commonplace names of individuals. "Massapequa" is the pleasant-sounding name which has replaced "South Oyster Bay," and the place is not less delightful than its attractive name. That portion of the village which is about the station is not imposing, but a few minutes' walk will take one to the great South Side highway [Merrick Road], along which on either side are stately summer residences, many of them owned by New York millionaires and families whose names are historic in the annals of the State. Here is Massapequa Lake, and to the south of it the new Massapequa Hotel, a recent applicant for public favor, and one of the most commodious and best-arranged hotels on the island. It overlooks the Great South Bay, which is reached by a natural canal with a stone's throw of the hotel. On the spacious grounds fronting the hotel handsome villas will be erected. The drives in the vicinity are superb, and near by are several large trout-ponds.

Three miles to the east is Amityville, a thriving town, which has come to the front within a year past as a very popular resort, and already the Amityville Land Improvement Company, composed of local capitalists, have purchased 165 acres of land lying on the east side of Amityville Creek and have divided it into building plots with broad avenues extending to the bay. Just west of the village over 150 acres have been purchased, which will be developed in a similar manner. On the bay front has been built a large pavilion with ample docks and bathing-houses. Amityville does not cater to the wealthy and exclusive class, her citizens preferring to give greeting to people of moderate circumstances, who demand comfort rather than style, and who enjoy summer life there because they are free to seek pleasure without bowing to the mandates of fashion. The Dominican Convent is located there, also the Brunswick Home for nervous invalids. The Long Island Railroad Company, appreciating the importance of the place, has erected a handsome depot modeled after the new station at Patchogue. The new steamer *Massapequa* will make daily excursions to prominent points on the Great South Bay.

The Great South Bay Resorts

Following the highway which leads to Sag Harbor, and over which the stages ran before the railroad, we pass Breslau [Lindenhurst], a thrifty German village, and come to Babylon, and thence on for another twenty miles through probably the wealthiest and most aristocratic, and to many the most attractive, section on all Long Island. Nature did much for this region, but man, with large prodigality, has worked wonderful transformation scenes. These wide-awake modern villages hug close the shores of the Great South Bay, a body of water which for sailing and fishing cannot be surpassed in all this country. Gaze upon it any summer's day and a hundred cat-boats meet the eye. They are the safest and fastest boats made, and the most useful too, for when not in commission to pleasure-seekers they are decked in fisherman's garb and go into actual service, with no international fishery question to interfere.

In the season, the Great South Bay abounds in geese, brant, canvas-back, broad-bills, red-heads, black-heads, and mallards. In June the bluefish, the gamest of our salt-water fish, come into the bay and remain all summer, and in the fall and winter the oyster beds yield large harvests. But why dwell upon the attractions of the Great South Bay which are known to people the world over? But where could there be a more desirable shore upon which to spend a vacation or to make a permanent residence? 'Tis not alone the bay that makes attractive these island villages. This part of the island is rich with trees and foliage. Poplars, oaks, pines and breezy maples, with now and then a sad-hued cedar in their midst, abound. Trees line the drives and lanes and make them beautiful, and wealthy land-owners have macadamized the main thoroughfares, so that no city park offers such superb driveways as along

Argyle Hotel, Babylon, c. 1890

this twenty-mile stretch through a summer city of cottages in a never-ending, picturesque chain.

Babylon is forty miles from New York. It is aristocratic in outward appearance, and has been compared to Newport and other fashionable seaside resorts, but no comparisons can do it justice. It is a Long Island town which gives generous hospitality to all who come within its limits. It is fashionable, but not exclusive. There is gaiety, healthy recreation, and pleasures of every kind. Its location for summer enjoyment is perfect; for, under all circumstances, there are cool breezes from the bay and ocean, and yet it is far enough back from the Atlantic to escape the sea mists. In the village proper, which numbers nearly three thousand inhabitants, are large stores and numerous cottages, handsome, but unpretentious, while nearby are palatial homes, amid extensive parks, owned by wealthy New Yorkers. North of the depot a half hour's ride is the Westminster Kennel Club Preserve, where are to be found some of the best pointers and retrievers in the country, and further on are the princely mansions of August Belmont, Austin Corbin, and many other gentlemen prominent in financial circles. Trout-ponds are to be found on many of the estates. Much can be said of the superior hotel accommodations at Babylon. The Argyle is one of the most unique and picturesque hotels in the country. It will accommodate two hundred and fifty guests. Thirteen elegant cottages are in the Argyle Park. This park consists of seventy acres of land. It is intersected with winding paths and drives, shaded with numerous trees, having in its midst a beautiful lake of twenty-five acres. A large Casino, containing a billiard-hall, gymnasium, and reading-room was built last year for the exclusive use of the guests. The hotel is run in first-class style, and is always well patronized.[11]

Babylon is the harbor for embarkation to one of the most unique summer resorts on the Atlantic coast—Fire Island. One of the first writers to bring this place into prominence was James Gordon Bennett.[12] He was enthusiastic over his visit, and the verdict which he pronounced through the columns of his paper has been accepted by thousands of delighted tourists. Way back in 1855, David Sturgiss Sprague Sammis opened a chowder-house near the lighthouse, on the strip of sand which makes the ocean border of the Great South Bay, and from that day to this the genial boniface [innkeeper] has kept open house in summer. From the small chowder-house has been evolved by gradual development the present commodious Surf Hotel.[13] The processes of annually adding to the house were not calculated to give beauty or architectural display, but it did give abundance of room and all the conveniences found in the more pretentious hotels. Board covered walks connect the hotel on one side with the bay, and on the other with the ocean. There are miles of these shady walks, some of them leading to the cottages which are in close proximity to the hotel, and as the soil is sandy and unattractive, there is no desire to leave Mr. Sammis's plank-walks, except at the beach, where the well-fed boarder spends most of his time when not sailing and fishing on the bay. There is a fine surf, and the bathing cannot be excelled.

One of the points of interest on this weather-beaten coast is the Fire Island Signal Station, from which ocean steamers are sighted and the announcement made in New York four hours before the vessel reaches her dock. Mr. Patrick Keegan is the operator in charge. He has never been on board one of the large steamers, and says if he should see one passing through the "Narrows" he could not identify it, so accustomed has he become to distinguishing ocean steamers at long distances. The tracks of the ocean-flyers on an average are thirteen miles from the observatory, and Mr. Keegan can only identify a vessel by a most careful observation of minute details, such as the position of the smoke-stack, the rigging, manner of carrying sails, and general outline of the steamer. From one port-hole in the lookout-room at a certain angle he watches for a steamer of the Cunard Line, and from another the Inman, and so on. The place is well worth a visit.[14] A staunch boat makes regular trips from Mr. Sammis's dock to Babylon, connecting with trains east and west. A few miles to the west of Fire Island is Jesse Smith's famous chowder-house, the "Armory," on Oak Island Beach, and near by are the headquarters of the Wawayanda and Short Beach Clubs, and on Oak Island proper is a settlement of cottagers.

Returning to the main land and continuing the journey eastward, it is easy to see that Bay Shore and Islip are conspicuously attractive villages, practically joining each other, and within only a few miles of Babylon. If anything, the scenery round about is more entrancing than at Babylon. The villages have many ponds, while running brooks and long inlets cut their way through the green marshes up to the higher lands. Pretty villas and pretentious summer homes dot the landscape, agreeably distant from each other, and many of them amid forest trees. There, also, wealth has been lavish in beautifying houses and lawns, so that even the villagers have built their stores with an eye to the aesthetic. There are three hotels at Bay Shore, the largest being the Prospect House, located near the water, with cottages and a billiard-hall. The Olympic Club House, one of the finest establishments of the kind on the island, is located at Bay Shore. At Islip, the Pavilion and the Lake House are the principal hotels. Islip is an old town, and the Long Island map has borne its name for more than two hundred years, or ever since Richard Nicolls came from England to drive out old Peter Stuyvesant and take by force the rule of New Amsterdam from the sturdy Dutchman. The South Side Sportsman's Club [now Connetquot State Park] has commodious quarters and extensive preserves at Islip. Babylon, Bay Shore, and Islip are supplied with gas, electric lights, telephones, and all the appliances of modern life.

Oakdale, a charming woodland place, containing the palatial home of W.K. Vanderbilt, is just beyond Islip.[15] A tract of four hundred acres of land, the title of which is one of the oldest on Long Island, having come directly from the Indians, and confirmed by a patent from the Duke of York in 1664, has recently been transferred for the first time, and will be improved and beautified. Opposite this property is St. John's [Episcopal] Church, which was built ten years before the Revolutionary War.[16] Sayville, a thriving town next in order, emerges from the forest, and permits free sweep to the ocean breezes. It, too, contains many handsome homes, and several fine hotels and numerous boarding-houses. It has been very popular in recent years and gives record of large growth. The village is joined by Bayport, and then comes Patchogue, one of the largest villages on Long Island. It is a wide-awake town, summer or winter. In the former season it swarms with young, rollicking, and fun-making city folks. Patchogue is less expensive and more democratic than some of its neighbors, and for many years has been one of the most popular places on the coast. It has two beautiful lakes, one at each end of the village, and superb dock facilities at the bay. It is the chief harbor for the South Bay boats. There are several excellent hotels in the place, and numerous boarding-houses, and summer guests are always well provided for. Just beyond Patchogue is Bellport, another place that has been inviting attention in recent years. For beauty of situation and water facilities few towns on the island can excel it. A portion of the village occupies a high bluff overlooking the bay, which at this point is three miles wide. The Bellport hotels and boarding-houses have the reputation of taking excellent care of their visitors. Many costly mansions have been erected. . . .

Suburban Towns

Garden City is well named, for it is an *urbs in rure* [city in the countryside], with all the charm of rural belongings pervading its streets—a place of green shades and sweet odors, of tinkling fountains and balmy fields. It was laid out on a scale of generous proportion by the late A.T. Stewart, who bought for the purpose an immense reach of plain then called the Hempstead Barrens, and thought by farmers to be worth nothing except as pasture land. On this plain one of the most exquisite little towns in the country has developed, charming in appearance, with unusual advantages, and inhabited by people of refinement. Its thirty miles of streets and roads offer a delightful series of walks and drives, and in the surrounding "barrens," which are vocal through the summer with birds' songs, and which are freely swept by refreshing breezes, are wide and satisfying views of field, wood, and distant village. There is here a large and well-directed school [St. Paul's], a casino, a park, and a cathedral; for Garden City is the ecclesiastical centre of the Long Island [Episcopal] diocese, and the bishop lives here in a house that is furnished with every luxury that taste and riches can suggest. The cathedral is a landmark that is visible for miles, and is a beautiful specimen of the Gothic, designed primarily as a mausoleum for the Stewart family. It is richly decorated within and without, contains fine organs, and its musical services draw visitors by the score from other places on every Sunday.[17]

Hempstead is a good old town, not unlike a new England village, with its shaded trees, its big white houses and green blinds, its old churches, and its fat farms on the outlying plains. The people are well to do, and are noted for kindliness and sense. Gas has been brought into the houses, a fire-department has been organized, there are large halls for meetings, fairs, and entertainments, good schools, fine churches, and three hotels. . . . Near Hempstead are fresh and salt water rowing, fishing, and shooting, while the "barrens" are full of delightful walks and drives.

The Central Section

From Garden City the main line of the railroad continues through the central portion of Long Island, and then along the northern shore to Greenport. This region has not until recent years received that attention which it deserved, so little has it been known to Long Island tourists. From the car-windows a very poor idea of the country can be obtained, and even residents on the island have been accustomed to depreciate the value of the land. It has already been demonstrated by practical experiment, as in the case of Garden City, Central Islip, and other points, that the land is extremely fertile, and can with small labor be brought to the highest state of productiveness. The section throughout is rich in natural scenery, and because of its peculiar situation, with the soil perfect for drainage, the hills to the north offering shelter from harsh winds, and the pine trees giving forth health, it is a region unsurpassed for salubrity. To thoroughly appreciate this section, one must visit the towns, scramble over the hills and green fields and through the forest groves, and mingle with the unostentatious and hospitable inhabitants.

Nearest to Garden City is Mineola, where the Queens County Fair grounds are located. It is the centre of a good farming country, and is a growing place. East Williston, Jericho, Westbury, Hicksville, are included in this section. At a short distance from Westbury is located the famous Meadow Brook Club, an organization of well-known New York gentlemen. Central Park [Bethpage] and Farmingdale are thriving villages, where much of the produce is raised that finds its way to the city markets. A large portion of the farm products that are supplied to Brooklyn come from Long Island, and a still larger quantity finds its way to New York. These villages all offer quiet retreats for the summer vacationist.

Passing through Wyandance [Wyandanch] and Deer Park, Brentwood is reached, where a new phase of Long Island is presented. During the past year the attention of the public has been directed to a complete health resort on Long Island, distance only forty-one miles from New York. Brentwood has that health resort, and is destined to become as popular as Lakewood, New Jersey. It has long been known that the atmosphere of pine forests is most favorable to invalids suffering from pulmonary affection, and physicians, in recent years, have been sending patients to the pine groves with satisfactory results. At Brentwood there is such a forest, in the midst of which is an excellent hotel that meets all requirements, keeping open summer and winter. The property was originally owned by a wealthy gentleman, Mr. R.W. Pearsall, who had twelve acres of the land made into a park, planting over twelve varieties of trees, the pines predominating, and the natural growth being entirely of pines. Some of these trees are nearly fifty feet in height, which speaks well for the fertility of the soil. The designer of Central Park, New York, and Prospect Park, Brooklyn [Frederick Law Olmsted], laid out the grounds. Mr. Pearsall erected a handsome house, modeled after a château in France, and richly furnished it throughout, the floors being inlaid with hardwood panels, and the decorations being artistic and costly. This house, now called "The Austral," was purchased by some wealthy New York gentlemen who had experienced beneficial results from the New Jersey pine groves. These parties have opened it to the public, and their venture has met with a large degree of success. There are pine trees on all sides, extending for twelve miles to the west, and on the east almost to Peconic Bay. The sands from the north are broken by the ridge of hills along the north shore of the island, and from the east are wafted over sixty miles of pine forests, while from the south they come in the summer, bringing cooling breezes from the ocean. The sanitary arrangements are pronounced by experts as perfect. A glass-inclosed solarium on the south permits invalids to get the full benefit of all sunshine. The hotel will accommodate about two hundred boarders, having been recently extensively enlarged. A competent physician lives in the hotel.[18]

An observing physician of national repute once remarked that the two counties in the United States most remarkable for health were Suffolk, Long Island, and Berkshire, Mass[achusetts]. As to Suffolk County, no one who has lived there will doubt the truth of this statement. The temperature of this portion of the island is several degrees warmer in winter and cooler in summer than that of the mainland. The reason for this is that the prevailing winds are from the south and southwest, blowing directly over the water from the Gulf Stream, which is only ninety miles' distant.

Several very handsome houses have been built in Brentwood and are occupied by gentlemen of wealth and culture, and during the past year many eligible building sites have been sold. There is an Episcopal church in the village, and near the depot is a large nursery. Three miles to the east is Central Islip, a cheerful village with pleasant surroundings. New York City, in 1884, through its Commissioners of Charities and Corrections, purchased one thousand acres on the line of the railroad at Central Islip station, and extending for two miles and a half to Islip proper. The land cost $25,000, and at the present time $257,200 have been expended on buildings, water supply, etc. The farm is meant to accommodate quiet chronic male patients, and especially those who are able to perform outdoor work. There are already three hundred patients on the premises.[19]

Midway in the island, Ronkonkoma, the most charming of lakes, is set. The station nearest it bears the same name, and is less than a mile away. The road leading to this peerless lake approaches by gentle descent, with trees on either side, many of them of great size. The lake is about three miles in circumference. It is fed by springs, and is of remarkable clearness and purity. A white-sand beach borders it, and its shores are delightful in their varied contour. The banks rise in pleasant ascent, and are bordered with every variety of vegetation. Large trees hang their graceful branches downward, while vines and shrubbery grow with rich luxuriance. The road follows the shore, and winds in and out, following every indentation, while beside it is the little footpath, in which lovers can walk and tell the pleasant tales that lovers have ever whispered. From whatever point one looks at this incomparable lake it is a thing of beauty, for its waters are of brightest color, easily susceptible to every breeze, while the shores are picturesque in their happy mingling of forest, farm, and homestead. There are many attractive houses about the lake, where summer boarders are accommodated. The drives in the vicinity are interesting, the walks are inviting, the air is tempered by the breezes of the lake; and nowhere on the island is there a more attractive spot than this lake, with its pleasant name and its old traditions of Indian days.

Beyond Ronkonkoma are Waverly [Holtsville], Medford, Yaphank, Manor [Manorville], and Baiting Hollow, all healthy places, surrounded by a good farming section with fish and game in abundance. At Yaphank is a model [poor] farm connected with the county institution. The shire town of Suffolk County is Riverhead. It is centrally located, and an active village of two thousand inhabitants. It takes its name from the Peconic River, which empties into a bay of that name a short distance away. Riverhead has many advantages as a summer resort. A half-hour's drive will take one to Peconic Bay, and a ride of eight miles to the ocean, and it is less than that distance to the Sound. The village is handsomely laid out and has many fine residences. It is a bustling town, and during Fair week and Court time is crowded with strangers. It has one newspaper, a savings bank, one of the best in the State, six churches, and numerous local institutions. The court-house, jail, and county clerk's office are substantial buildings, with well-kept lawns in front. The county fair grounds cover twenty acres of land upon which are well-appointed buildings. A mile from the village is a beautiful body of water, called Great Pond.[20] The water is as clear as crystal, with a fine sand bottom, and on the south are high bluffs from which can be seen the ocean. Cauliflower and sweet potatoes are raised in large quantities, and in the spring carloads of strawberries are sent to market daily. Even peanuts have been successfully raised in this fertile soil, and several cranberry bogs are profitably cultivated. Two miles from Riverhead is Flanders, a modest resort, where sailing, fishing, and bathing are among the many attractions.

Peconic Bay Resorts

At Jamesport is a resort which has been so popular in recent years that the hotels and boarding-houses have been unable to accommodate the rush of summer guests. The popularity of the place is easily understood. It stands at the head of Peconic Bay, the yachtsman's favorite domain and the tourist's delight, while pleasant roads offer delightful drives through a charming rural region. The boating in Peconic Bay is regarded by some as even superior to that in the Great South Bay. There is direct communication with the Sound; the fishing is excellent. The slope from the shores is so gradual that children can go in bathing and paddle about in boats with comparative safety. There is much life and gaiety at Jamesport, and those who go there once are apt to become permanent visitors.

Mattituck is a quiet country village and never wants for boarders. The epicure can be especially favored by the number and quality of crabs that are caught in the lake-like inlet or creek which forms so pleasant a feature of the view to the north of the village. The inhabitants are a thrifty class of people, judging by the commodious and well-kept houses and by the harvests which the land annually gives forth. For those who are seeking rural homes near New York no more desirable locations can possibly be found than in this section of Long Island. Not only is the land excellent, but the scenery and climate are not surpassed in the State. Franklinville [Laurel] is near by. Cutchogue, another of these north side villages, is famous for its fine horses as well as its attractive homes. It is a place frequented by artists in the summer. A mile and a half toward the bay is New Suffolk, which has been an old and popular resort for forty years or more. Opposite this point, and distant a few minute's sail, is Robins Island, a famous hunting preserve, owned by the Robins Island Gun Club, an organization composed of prominent Brooklyn gentlemen. The island contains four hundred and sixty-nine acres of land. It is diversified with hills, cliffs, forests, fertile fields, and sand beaches.[21]

Continuing eastward by the railroad is Southold . . . an attractive village with clean streets, houses newly painted, and lawns well kept. A homelike atmosphere pervades the place. It is but a short walk to Peconic Bay and only a mile distant to the Sound. There are five churches, a newspaper, a hotel, and numerous boarding-houses. There are several handsome residences in the place. On Horton's Point, north of the village, is an important light-house.[22] The next station beyond is Greenport, the terminus of the railroad. It was formerly a famous port for whaling vessels, but now the inhabitants devote themselves principally to ship-building, railroading, menhaden fishing, and caring for the wants of summer visitors. It has an excellent harbor, one of the finest on the Atlantic coast, which has recently been much improved by the building of a breakwater. It has nearly three thousand inhabitants, with a bank, fire department, two newspapers, and seven churches. There is a steamboat running between Greenport and New London, and hourly communication with Shelter Island by a ferry. It has been a popular summer resort for many years. . . .[23]

The North Shore

Long Island on its north shore is entirely different in physical aspect from the south side. The latter has plains and beaches, besides its remarkable outlying sand-spits, while the former is high ground, a pile of glacial drift, corrugated by hillocks and valleys, and cut into by a series of a dozen harbors, narrow, somewhat too shallow for vessels of deep draught, but safe anchorage for yachts, of which a fleet will generally be found off Flushing, Great Neck, Roslyn, Glen Cove, Oyster Bay, Huntington, Northport, and Port Jefferson. The southern face of the hills is a gradual slope, advantageous for crops requiring quick drainage and sunny exposure, while the northern face has been eroded by the waves of the Sound until it falls away in steep and often precipitous bluffs of gravel that occasionally rise one hundred feet above the water. At the foot of these bluffs are beaches, dissimilar to the broad, hard sands of Fire Island and Rockaway, for they are narrow and strewn with boulders, though bathing is always feasible from them, and one may more readily wade into deeper water. There is but little surf, as breakers gain small sea-room in the Sound.

The hills of the north side constitute "the backbone of the island," and while they are not bold, they are agreeable and sometimes picturesque, much of their surface being clothed with forest and dotted with new and substantial villas and summer homes. The highest point is Harbor Hill, near Roslyn, about three hundred and fifty feet in altitude. Like all the heights in this range, it commands a splendid view of the green fields and forests to east and south, the shining Sound below, and the cultivated shores of Westchester and Connecticut to the northwest and north. The air is pure, the drainage is facilitated by light soil and by valleys with a seaward trend; wild flowers and fruits flourish, vegetation is rich and beautiful; little brooks babble through the forest dells, and the forest aisles resound with songs of birds. In the pine and oak regions the hunter or the traveler might easily imagine himself in the fastnesses [remoteness] of an Adirondack [Mountain] wilderness, were it not for the lack of peaks in the field of vision. These hills will undoubtedly be taken up in time as homesteads by people of taste and means, since the attractions, both of the country and seaside, are accessible from the cities, and are "handy" to safe harbors. The little towns that nestle between the headlands have obvious comfort, and may be resorted to for their shops, factories, schools, and churches, while summer board is to be secured in all of them.

A little chain of towns, extending from Brooklyn to Great Neck, is served by branches of the Long Island railroad, over which forty to fifty trains a day are dispatched. These towns may be regarded as centering about

Flushing, and are cozy places that are furnished with numerous modern conveniences. Woodside and Winfield, respectively three and four miles from Long Island City, occupy rising ground, and many pretty villas stand there.[24] In Newtown there are not a few fine old places, though the township is occupied mainly by market-gardens, from which New York and Brooklyn are supplied with tons of vegetables during the season. Corona is a hopeful little suburb that is built on a good plan, and a couple of miles beyond it the passenger may alight at either of the two stations in Flushing.

It would be difficult to say which town on Long Island is the more attractive, but if a decision of the public were taken on this subject it is certain that Flushing would not fare ill in general verdict, for it is a charming town, with an individuality of its own. Its long business street has the look of a city thoroughfare in spite of the trees that almost arch it, for there are stores, banks, hotels, restaurants, agencies, and newspaper offices, and on the clean and shaded side streets and avenues are churches and schools, and many homes that bespeak the possession of comfortable bank accounts, as well as of taste and moderate leisure. Some of the houses are sufficiently quaint and ancient to take on an old-world aspect. There is a park in the business centre, and famous nurseries on the skirts of the town. Flushing has a gas and water service, and is protected by firemen and police. Its schools, among them St. Joseph's Academy, Fairchild's Institute, St. Michael's, the Young Ladies' Seminary, and the High School, are attended by many pupils from other places, and are noted for efficiency.

College Point occupies the stubby cape between Flushing Bay and the Sound, and is devoted to manufactures. Its streets are well paved; it has gas, water, sewerage, and fire-engines, and it is better cared for than most factory settlements, for it has a free technological institute, library, kindergarten, reading-room, several good schools, a bank, a newspaper, shops, and churches. Whitestone, on a well-drained slope where the East River debouches into the Sound, is gathering a considerable population of city workers, and stands near the fort and Government reservation at Willett's Point [Fort Totten], to which visitors are often attracted by engineer practice, drill, gunnery experiments, and band concerts.

Bay Side, Douglaston, and Little Neck are small and quiet places on Little Neck Bay, where the famous Little Neck clam is found on its "native heath." These are places of savory suggestion to many a New Yorker, and the seat of many fine residences and substantial farm-houses. The roads, hedged by noble old trees, wind along close to the bluff, disclosing rare views of land and water. Great Neck, fourteen miles from the western terminus of the road, is of limited importance as a village, but is the summer seat of many rich New Yorkers, and contains many elegant mansions and rich estates. This promontory, or great neck of land, juts out into the Sound for a distance of about two miles, and has a superb water front on two sides. The ground is high, the roads are sheltered by trees and edged with wild flowers and berry-bushes, and the salt breezes sweeping in from the Sound keep the thermometer several degrees lower than it is in New York during the August heats. The drives are enjoyable, the views superb, and the tables of the community are furnished from scores of well-managed gardens, farms, and dairies. Bathing and boating are common enjoyments through the summer. A little beyond Great Neck is the secluded village of Manhasset.

Another promontory to the east of Great Neck juts out into the Sound a still greater distance, and has every vantage point that heart could desire. Here, too, have been erected costly residences, surrounded by foliage and evergreen hedges. Sands Point is where the steamers stop, and where the fleet of pleasure-boats are anchored.

Roslyn to Oyster Bay

The Glen Cove branch of the railroad diverges from the main line at Mineola, and passes through one of the most beautiful portions of the island. The terminus is at Oyster Bay, the road having been extended the past year from Locust Valley. To fully appreciate the beauties of this region one must leave the railroad and travel along the woodland roads, and from the hills and high bluffs view the numerous bays, inlets, and delightful vistas of blue waters, with sails of vessels going up and down the Sound. Wherever one wanders among these wooded hills, if he is a lover of beauty, "He cannot err in this delicious land," for there is forest and bay, with distant hills and valleys, while all around him are surprises of pleasant dells, "With spots of sunny openings, and with nooks / To lie and nod [read] in, sloping into brooks."[25]

Were these places unknown it would be fit to describe in detail their many advantages, but for years Roslyn, Glen Cove, Sea Cliff, and Oyster Bay have been written about in prose and verse, and their beauties delineated by the artist's pencil. Men of means have built palatial homes, and poets and authors have sought rest and quiet there. Who has not heard of Roslyn? At the old tollhouse at the summit of the hill, at the foot of which is Roslyn, one gets the first glimpse of the little town, which is memorable as containing the home where the poet [William Cullen] Bryant lived and the grave where his ashes rest. The village is in the valley, divided by an inlet from Hempstead Harbor, which runs backward to the hills, and across which is a narrow causeway, over which the railroad winds. Northward is a little stretch of marsh, which the tides keep sweet and clean, and beyond is the harbor, white with the sails of oystermen, and in the distance, across the Sound, are the hills of Connecticut, and bounding the harbor on either side are great hills, thick with foliage, in which great estates and castles rise among the branches, and look off upon the waters of the bay.

Half a mile or more on the road which lies eastward of the harbor is Cedarmere, the home of Bryant.[26] Here he wrote some of his best songs, and here he came when in mood of inspiration. The house is large and rambling, the frame being at least a century old. There are broad piazzas, quiet nooks and coverts, extensions and subextensions, and the house is high enough above the waters to get the effect of intervening lawns, yet not too far to hear the music of the waves. There is a great variety of trees about the place, with ivy and clambering vines, truly a poet's home, where in spring it learns to, "Wear the green coronal of leaves, / And a thousand suns could not add aught / Of splendor in the grass."

The grave of Bryant is in the village cemetery, about a mile away.[27] Mr. Parke Goodwin owns one of the many fine estates about Roslyn. The highest elevation on Long Island is the summit back of the village [Harbor Hill], and from the observatory which surmounts it can be seen the surrounding country for miles about. Roslyn has a paper-mill, the oldest in the State, a flouring-mill, a good hotel, and a very popular place in summer.[28] Beyond are Glen Head, a picturesque and growing resort, and Sea Cliff, possessing one of the most superb locations on all Long Island. The ground rises abruptly from the shore for several hundred feet, and upon the bluff which skirts the village can be had views of the Sound that for beauty cannot be rivaled. Cottages stud the banks, which rise tier upon tier after the manner of seats in an amphitheatre. Shade trees abound and make pleasant music to the touch of the winds that play among their branches. Well-constructed roads in every direction, shaded by large trees, afford opportunities for driving and riding. Knolls and hills, studded with many varieties of wild flowers, invite ascent. Sea Cliff is a very lively place in the summer season, and several hotels and numerous boarding-houses are taxed to their utmost to accommodate all the guests who seek admission, the largest hotel being the Sea Cliff House, first-class in appointment, with accommodations for three hundred guests, while every year witnesses a large increase in the number of cottages owned by city people. The village was originally owned by the Sea Cliff Grove and Metropolitan Camp-Meeting Association, and after several years of vicissitudes the land passed out of the control of the Association, and the only camp-meetings now held are by the German Methodists. It is needless to add that the boating and bathing are excellent.

To the east, by pleasant roads, is Glen Cove, where a different condition of affairs is noted. The same beautiful scenery and bracing air is seen and felt, but the village presents the appearance of a busy and prosperous town, one that is not dependent in any way upon the influx of city folks in vacation time. The Duryea Starch Factory is located there, giving employment to seven hundred people, and upon the business streets are other factories and many well-kept stores. The village is itself attractive, while the drives in every direction are surpassingly beautiful. Two miles away is the famous Island of Dosoris, where the Hon. Charles A. Dana has a park and a fine residence, which are constant sources of attraction to visitors. Boarding-houses and hotels are plentiful, but no more than sufficient to meet the demands of summer travel. At Glen Cove, as well as at all these north-side towns, there is always a cool breeze from the Sound at night, making a blanket an acceptable article. Excellent facilities are offered for boating and bathing. The fishing at all times is good, and from the middle of July to December many a pleasant day may be spent in hunting plover or bay snipe. At Locust Valley, a quiet village between the hills and along the shores of the Sound, one may find a pleasant abiding-place. Among the curious old landmarks is the Friends' Academy, erected one hundred and twenty years ago, and endowed as a school for higher education by Gideon Frost.[29] The main street is lined with wooden houses of oldtime pattern, and big locust-trees which give abundant shade, while in every direction are pleasant walks and drives, and to those who seek a quiet retreat none more desirable can be found.

Until this year Locust Valley has been the terminus of the Glen Cove branch, but now Oyster Bay has that distinction. Notwithstanding the fact that the permanent inhabitants of Oyster Bay desired and were entitled to this extension of the railroad, there were many among the summer visitors who opposed it, fearing that with the coming of the [railroad] cars the quiet town would lose much of the exclusiveness for which it has been noted. Such fears will doubtless prove to be groundless, for the class of people who bring discredit upon a place and make it common prefer to seek resorts nearer the cities. Oyster Bay will remain just as exclusive and just as charming as in years past, when it was reached by a long and wearisome stage-ride. It is indeed a pretty village, and it is not strange that property owners zealously guard its interests. Situated directly on a beautiful bay, the boating facilities are unsurpassed, a fact easily seen on a summer's day by counting the yachts and pleasure-boats which harbor there. It is the headquarters for several prominent yacht-clubs, and regattas and rowing-races are frequently held during the season. The drives are numerous and delightful. The place is noted for its many fine residences. There are several old homesteads which played important parts in the early history of the country, and many relics of colonial times are to be found. At one time the Quakers had a footing there.

Cold Spring Harbor

Cold Spring to Port Jefferson

Beyond Oyster Bay is Cold Spring, reached by the railroad of the Port Jefferson branch. No better evidence of the popularity of this place need be mentioned than the fact that the rush of summer travel is so great that many visitors are turned away because of lack of accommodation, notwithstanding the large number of excellent hotels and boarding-houses. Every year an attempt is made to meet this demand, but it has never yet been fully accomplished. The ride from the depot to the village and to the harbor is picturesque at every point, and each turn of the road reveals some new surprise: it may be a trout-pond hidden in the woods, or a bit of pastoral scenery, or a glimpse of the bay through an opening in the trees, or perhaps a handsome residence. And then the harbor itself is more than a surprise, it is a revelation. Whether seen from the surrounding hills or from the sandy beaches, it is an inspiring sight, more beautiful than words can describe. Crafts of every kind find safe harbor there. The fishing must be good, for there is located a fish hatchery under the supervision of the New York Fish Commission, where each year are hatched thousands of brook trout, rainbow trout, land-locked salmon, lake trout, shad, whitefish, smelts, tomcods, lobsters, and Penobscot salmon. Since 1883, 17,892,772 fish have been distributed on Long Island from this hatchery.[30]

On the terraced and wood-covered hills which bound the bay are large hotels which are provided with all modern conveniences. The Glenada, Laurelton Hall, and Forest Lawn are among the best known. In the past Cold Spring has been a manufacturing village of no small importance, and ruins of once extensive factories are visible. Up the valley are a series of lakes, and near them are several mineral springs which have medicinal qualities of merit. The drives in every direction are beautiful, but none more so than the one that winds around Lloyd's Neck, having the Bay and Sound always in view. The land must be fertile, for all the farmers appear to be prosperous, and live in fine residences not inferior to those occupied by gentlemen who reside for a portion of the year in New York. This neck, which geographically belongs to Suffolk, was recently [1881] cut off from Queens County by an act of the Legislature and made a part of the town of Huntington. At the extreme end of the neck are the remains of an old fort [Fort Franklin], which in revolutionary times was occupied by the British troops.

Huntington deserves notice apart from any claim it may have as a desirable place for summer homes. It has an activity of its own which is not materially increased or diminished by the tide of summer travel. Many local enterprises have contributed to its growth, and its prosperity to-day is greater than it has been at any time in the past. The academy of the village ranks high among the educational institutions of the State, and a public library has been established. The location of Huntington has been likened to the Roman Coliseum, and the comparison is proper. The surrounding hills recede with fine gradations, and from their summits are views of Huntington Bay, Eaton's Neck, Lloyd's Neck, and Long Island Sound, and from one or two points Babylon, Islip, and Fire Island. The harbor is about a mile from the village, beautifully situated amid encircling hills, its windings concealed from view, so that it resembles a mountain lake much more than an arm of the sea. It is usually dotted with yachts and boats that are kept in frequent use by the lovers of the waves.

After the battle of Long Island, Huntington was selected by the English as a place for a garrison and permanent occupancy, and many relics in the place recall those memorable times. In the burying-ground is a gravestone marked by a cannon ball, and on Gallows Hill are remains of a fort. Huntington is growing rapidly as a resort. A large tract of land on the bay has been purchased by capitalists, who are making it a village of handsome residences clustered in a magnificent part. There are many large estates with fine houses and extensive gardens and lawns. West Neck is one of the charming points along the shore, and is already occupied by many wealthy New Yorkers. Mr. J.R. Maxwell is the owner of one hundred acres, where he has erected an elegant house. The grounds are laid out with great taste, and the estate ranks among the most notable of its class. Near the village is the Suffolk Driving Park, one of the best on the island, and every year becoming more popular.

The scenery about Greenlawn and Centreport is much the same. They nestle among the hills and have a long stretch of the Sound penetrating far inland, and offer as good a vantage ground for an economical vacation as can be desired. And then comes Northport, charmingly set around a harbor that makes in from Huntington Bay, which has often been likened to the Bay of Naples. It is as beautiful as any harbor in the land. So completely is it landlocked, that from the village it seems more like a great lake. The long semicircle of Eaton's Neck, a spit of land shaped like a fishhook, guards it from the Sound and makes it the safest of havens. Its entrance is narrow, but deep and easy of access. On either side of the harbor rise the hills, thickly crowned with forests, and at its head lies a green meadow. Northport once flourished with shipbuilding, and owned a fine fleet of vessels. Some part of the industry lingers, and until very recently vessels of eight hundred or one thousand tons have been launched from the stocks. The fleet now consists of a score or more of coasting schooners, and a swarm of oyster and fishing-smacks [boats] and pleasure-boats. Three ship-yards are kept busy repairing and building. There is a large printing establishment, enterprising stores, two hotels, and several boardinghouses. As a place of summer resort Northport is very popular among the north-side villages. Eaton's Neck, which scans both Sound and harbor, is a high peninsula and headland, where is located the famous Bacon farm and the palatial residence of the late Mr. C.H. Delamater. Duck Island is within easy distance, where extensive improvements are now in progress. . . .[31]

This whole region in the vicinity of St. Johnland, Smithtown, St. James, and Stony Brook is covered with excellent farms, and, while it is a quiet rural district with small and unpretentious villages, it offers great attraction to a large class of city people who are seeking just such retreats. The shores are fronted with precipitous cliffs, and the bays and inlets furnish superior boating, fishing, and bathing. The drives are among woods of tall and shapely trees and through green fields, while fresh-water lakes here and there make summer pilgrimage a thing of great delight. A few hotels and many hospitable farm-houses provide the visitors with pleasant temporary homes. At Comac [Commack] is a farm famous for its fine horses.

Stony Brook is an especially attractive village, stretching along the sloping side of a valley and near a large pond emptying into the Great Bay, with stores and churches and well-kept farms and many pleasant villas for summer use. There is a large hotel in the place. Beyond is Setauket, beautiful for situation, having a large freshwater lake on one side and Setauket Bay and the Sound on the other. The fishing and hunting are something to tempt the most exacting sportsman. A large rubber goods manufactory gives

Port Jefferson

employment to many people. To those who delight in ante-revolutionary relics, two quaint old shingled churches with burying-grounds containing moss-covered gravestones, will prove of interest.[32] It is said that when Washington visited this portion of Long Island he spent a night at Setauket, stopping at an inn kept by a zealous Tory. The General did not make himself known until he was taking his departure, when he kissed the landlord's little daughter, saying to her that after he had gone she might tell her parents that George Washington had kissed her.[33]

Two miles to the east is Port Jefferson, the terminus of the railroad. The main portion of the village is in a valley. The streets are irregular, and houses and stores have been built with slight regard to street lines and architectural grace. It is a curious and odd town, but strikingly interesting. The greatest charm is the harbor, one of the finest on the north shore. It is well protected by natural and artificial breakwaters, and serves the purpose of pleasure boats and large ships as well. Upon both sides are lofty hills covered with trees with a commanding view of the Sound and the Connecticut shore. It is as a ship-building port that Port Jefferson is especially noted. A few old hulls, the frame of a half-completed vessel, and numerous ship-yards give evidence of the activity that once existed and made Port Jefferson known the world over. The sailing ship has gradually given way to the steamer, and America has lost its hold on that once important industry of vessel-building. Port Jefferson has suffered with other places, but no town between New York and Boston, even now, both in building and repairing vessels, excels this quaint and enterprising village. Many associated industries exist. A steamer ferry crosses the Sound to Bridgeport. There are fine views from its

Centerport Harbor

overlooking hills, while there are many quaint nooks and walks of great attractiveness to the visitor. The place has great charms for its residents, and a delightful social life exists. It has long been popular as a summer home, and its popularity has not been eclipsed by the attraction of newer resorts.

Northwest of Port Jefferson Harbor is Oldfield Point, a quiet place, known to many pleasure seekers, and to the east, beyond the railroad, are Mount Sinai, Miller's Place, Rocky Point, and Middle Island, retired country settlements, where visitors can find many charming summer homes. The scenery is beautiful, and sport with rod and gun always at hand.

We have taken our gentle readers with hasty flight through all the sections of the island that is dowered with so many charms. Only a touch of the foot here and there could be permitted by limitations of time and space. If the friends who have followed us in our hasty rambles will make their summer homes in some one of the many places of rest and beauty we have pictured, we are certain they will find that each day will reveal new graces; for in this fair island "He who lingers longest is the happiest."

Notes

Source: *Out on Long Island* (New York: Long Island Railroad, 1890), pp. 3-11, 15, 17-27, 40-47, 51-65. Editing changes have been minimal. Punctuation has been modernized and some long paragraphs divided.

1. Today, the name is Long Island Rail Road, but in 1890 the LIRR spelled Railroad as one word and that usage is followed in this article.

2. In 1897, the LIRR hired Hal B. Fullerton as a special agent to promote the railroad. He was a talented amateur photographer and in the *Unique Long Island* series, photographs replaced the engravings in the earlier works and the text was limited to captions identifying the location of the photographs (the first had 165 photographs on 96 pages). The railroad later tried to increased its freight traffic by promoting Long Island agriculture and had Fullerton start a demonstration farm at Wading River in 1905 and at Medford in 1907. The productivity of the land was publicized in Edith Loring Fullerton's *The Lure of the Land, The History of a Market-Garden and Dairy Plot Developed within Eight Months upon Long Island's Idle Territory, Long Designated as "Scrub Oak Waste," and "Pine Barrens,"* published by the Long Island Railroad in 1906. On the work of the Fullertons promoting Long Island for the railroad, see Charles L. Sachs, *The Blessed Isle: Hal B. Fullerton and His Image of Long Island, 1897-1927* (Interlaken, NY: Heart of the Lakes Publishing, 1991). Fullerton's photographs of Long Island in the early twentieth century are one of the important legacies of the railroad's promotional activities.

3. Brooklyn was incorporated as a city in 1834; it did not become part of New York City until 1898. For nearly a half century it was the third or fourth largest city in the United States. Today Brooklyn has the largest population of the five boroughs of New York City (nearly 2.3 million in 2000).

4. The Long Island Railroad did not terminate in Pennsylvania Station until its tunnels under the East River were completed in 1910. Until that time, those going to Manhattan had to take ferries from Long Island City.

5. Patrick S. Gilmore (1829-1892) was bandmaster of the 22nd Regiment Band and, beginning in 1875, conducted concerts at the Hippodrome (known as "Gilmore's Concert Garden"). See Marc Gerris, "Gilmore, Patrick S(carsfield)," in *Encyclopedia of New York City,* edited by Kenneth T. Jackson (New Haven: Yale University Press, 1995), p. 467.

6. Descriptions of the Rockaway peninsula and Ocean Park, Averne-by-the-Sea, Nameoke, Wave Crest, and Bayswater are omitted here. On Rockaway, see also Charles Brockden Brown's "Jaunt to Rockaway" and "Rockaway on 'Old Long Island's Sea Girt Shore,'" above, as well as Vincent Seyfried and William Assadorian, *Old Rockaway, New York in Early Photographs* (Mineola: Dover Publications, 2000).

7. The population of Lawrence in 1890 was 626; it incorporated as a village in 1897. Long Island Regional Planning Board, *Historical Population of Long Island Communities, 1790-1980: Decennial Census Data* (Hauppauge: Long Island Regional Planning Board, 1982), p. 24.

8. The Long Beach Hotel advertised itself as the "largest hotel in the world." However, its business declined and it burned in 1907. William H. Reynolds then developed a residential resort with privately owned homes, the "Estates of Long Beach." Long Beach incorporated as a village in 1912 and as a city in 1922. See Roberta Fiore and Elizabeth Coffin Allerhand, "Sandbar to City: William H. Reynolds and the Planned Community of Long Beach, 1906-1922," in *Nassau County: From Rural Hinterland to Suburban Metropolis,* edited by Joann P. Krieg and Natalie A. Naylor (Interlaken, NY: Empire State Books, 2000), p. 265-72. On the western end of Long Beach island today is Atlantic Beach and the communities of Lido Beach and Point Lookout are east of the city of Long Beach.

9. The Milburn Pumping Station was located on North Brookside Avenue, Freeport. See Richard A. Winsche, "When Nassau Supplied Brooklyn's Water," in *Nassau County,* p. 153.

10.   The camp meeting grounds were located east of Merrick Avenue and north of Camp Avenue in today's North Merrick. The area is easily identifiable on a street map by the circular and spoke pattern of streets. The Town of Hempstead's Landmarks Preservation Commission designated the Chapel and Minister's House as Historic Landmarks in 1994. They were built c. 1870 and are now private residences on Peck and Wesley Avenues respectively. See James B. York, "Landmarks Preservation in the Town of Hempstead," in *Roots and Heritage of Hempstead Town,* edited by Natalie A. Naylor (Interlaken, NY: Heart of the Lakes Publishing, 1994), pp. 168-71.

For a description of camp meetings in 1830, see James Stuart, "Camp Meetings in Musquito Cove and Flushing," above.

11.   On the South Bay resorts, see also Harry W. Havemeyer, *Along the Great South Bay: From Oakdale to Babylon, The Story of a Summer Spa, 1840 to 1940* (Mattituck: Amereon House, 1996), and the sequel, *East on the Great South Bay: Sayville and Bayport, 1860-1960* (Mattituck: Amereon House, 2001).

12.   James Gordon Bennett, Jr. (1841-1918) published the *New York Herald* beginning in 1867. See Steven H. Jaffe, "Bennett, James Gordon, Jr." in *Encyclopedia of New York City,* p. 101.

13.   Sammis also built a dock in Babylon and operated a steamship ferry to his hotel on Fire Island. New York State purchased the Surf Hotel and 120 acres on Fire Island from Sammis to quarantine transatlantic passengers during a cholera epidemic in 1892-1893. After leasing the hotel for several years, the land was designated as Fire Island State Park in 1908—the first on Long Island. (It was renamed Robert Moses State Park in 1964.) See Chester R. Blakelock, "History of Long Island State Parks," in *Long Island: A History of Two Great Counties, Nassau and Suffolk,* edited by Paul Bailey, 2 vols. (New York: Lewis Historical Publishing, 1949), 2:248-51.

14.   The ship spotting tower was operated by Western Union and Postal Telegraph. See Van R. Field, *Wrecks and Rescues on Long Island: The Story of the U.S. Life Saving Service* (Privately printed, 1977), p. 129. The Fire Island Lighthouse is now part of Fire Island National Seashore. It is open from April through December and has museum exhibits on the lighthouse and U.S. Life Saving Service (631-661-4876).

15.   Vanderbilt's home, "Idle Hour" was destroyed by fire in 1899. Dowling College occupies the second Vanderbilt home on the estate, although the mansion was damaged by fire in 1974.

16.   St. John's Episcopal Church was built in 1765. It was rebuilt and enlarged in 1842 and renovated in 1916. The surrounding cemetery has gravestones dating from the early years of the church. St. John's is located on the north side of Montauk Highway (Route 27A).

17.   The Cathedral of the Incarnation in Garden City, designed by Henry G. Richardson, was completed in 1883. Preceding the entry on Garden City but omitted here are descriptions of the suburban communities of Richmond Hill, Morris Park, Jamaica, Hollis, Queens Village, Hinsdale, and East Hinsdale (now Floral Park).

18.   The Austral Hotel, a large new building, was built on the Pearsall estate grounds and opened in 1888; before it was completed, Pearsall's house was used for borders and designated the "Brentwood Hotel." The LIRR account is mistaken in referring to Pearsall's house as the "Austral." The hotel soon encountered financial difficulties and the Sisters of St. Joseph bought the property in 1896 which included the 125-room Austral Hotel, Pearsall's French chateau, and three cottages. The Sisters used their property of nearly 300 acres for their motherhouse, novitiate, and academy. (The Austral House was demolished in

1960 in order to build a new residence hall, Our Lady of Grace Juniorate, which was dedicated in 1961. The Sisters renamed Pearsall's house, first the Bishop's Cottage and later St. Charles Cottage. It was razed in 1960.) Dr. William H. Ross who had been the resident physician at the Austral Hotel in 1890 established a private practice and opened a sanitarium at a different location in Brentwood in 1898 which he operated until 1945. See Vernon Dyson, *A Century of Brentwood* (Brentwood: Privately printed, 1950), pp. 154, 161-65, 177-79, 197-99 (photographs of Pearsall's house and the Austral Hotel are on pp. 154 and 162); Sr. Mary Ignatius Meany, C.S.J., *By Railway or Rainbow: A History of the Sisters of St. Joseph of Brentwood* (Brentwood: Pine Press, 1964); and letter from Sr. Edna McKeever, C.S.J., Archivist, Sisters of St. Joseph, Brentwood, October 12, 2001.

19. New York State took over the Central Islip farm in 1895. The New York Institute of Technology now occupies some of the buildings of the former mental institution. See Bill Blyer, "Caring for the Mentally Ill," in *Long Island: Our Story,* by Newsday (Melville: Newsday, 1998), p. 249.

20. This is today's Wildwood Lake and is south of the junction of Routes 51 and 63.

21. Robins Island, which has been undeveloped, continued to be used by different owners as a hunting preserve. Suffolk County had sought unsuccessfully to acquire the island in the early 1990s. Louis Bacon, who purchased the island in 1997, donated a conservation easement on most of the land on Robins Island to the Nature Conservancy.

22. Horton Point Lighthouse was built in 1857 and is now a museum with exhibits; Lighthouse Road, Southold; 631-765-2101.

23. Omitted here are the sections on Shelter Island and Gardiner's Island.

24. Winfield was east of Woodside and named for General Winfield Scott. It had a railroad station from 1861-1929. See Vincent Seyfried, "Winfield," in *Encyclopedia of New York City,* p. 1,267.

25. The quotation ("With spots of sunny openings . . .") is from a poem by Leigh Hunt (1759-1859), "The Story of Rimini," first published in 1816. It can be found in *Poetical Works of Leigh Hunt,* ed. H.S. Milford, 1923 (Reprint; New York: AUS Press, 1978), p. 22 (canto 3, lines 418-19). Efforts to identify the source of other quotations in these excerpts have not been successful.

26. Cedarmere is now owned by Nassau County and has exhibits on Bryant. Open from May through October, it is located on Bryant Avenue in Roslyn Harbor (516-571-8130). See also Diane Bennett Tarleton and Linda Tarleton, *W.C. Bryant in Roslyn* (Roslyn: Bryant Library, 1978).

27. The Roslyn Cemetery is just east of the village on Northern Boulevard in Greenvale. Two later authors are also buried there, Frances Hodgson Burnett and Christopher Morley.

28. Jaynes Hill in West Hills County Park in South Huntington is actually higher than Harbor Hill. The grist ("flouring") mill on Old Northern Boulevard in Roslyn is under restoration by Nassau County. A replica of the paper mill, built near the original site on Paper Mill Road in 1915, is in the Gerry Pond Park in Roslyn.

29. In the nineteenth century, the term "higher education" could refer to any school beyond the elementary level. Friends Academy opened in 1877 in a new structure built for the school. The "curious old landmark" may refer to the Matinecock (Quaker) Meeting House, across the road from the academy, which dated from c. 1725. The Friends Academy and Meeting House are located at the intersection of Piping Rock and Duck Pond Roads in Locust Valley. Friends Academy now enrolls students from pre-kindergarten through twelfth grade. On its history, see Harold A. Nomer, "The Beginnings of Friend's

Academy," *Nassau County Historical Journal* 6 (Spring 1943): 23-26; and William M. Masland, "The Story of Friends Academy," *Nassau County Historical Society Journal* 38 (1983): 19-35. The Matinecock Meeting House was destroyed by fire in 1985, but was rebuilt in a careful reconstruction. It is regularly used by the Academy and the Society of Friends.

30. The Cold Spring Harbor Fish Hatchery and Aquarium has been a private non-profit educational facility since 1982. Located on Route 25A, it is open year-round; 516-692- 6768.

31. Cornelius Henry DeLamater (1821-1889) owned the DeLamater Iron works foundry in New York City which constructed much of the machinery for the *Monitor* during the Civil War. He bought Walnut Neck on East Asharoken in 1862 and built a home, "Vermland," named after the native village in Sweden of his collaborator, John Ericsson. His eldest daughter, Laura Bevin, inherited the house which still stands at 76 Bevin Road. Beacon Farm was established by DeLamater in 1863 and was a stock farm which developed Beacon Downs sheep and Beacon Comet bulls. The superintendent's farmhouse, built in 1804, survives on Lighthouse Road. Duck Island was owned by Richard W. Rowland who had a picnic area and hotel ("Rowland's Grove"), from c. 1875-1887. It is uncertain what the "extensive improvements" refer to since Duck Island remained in the ownership of one or two families and was not developed until the 1970s. See Edward A.T. Carr, *Faded Laurels: The History of Eaton's Neck and Asharoken* (Interlaken, NY: Privately printed, 1994), pp. 12-17, 101, 110, 114-19, 159-60.

32. The two churches are adjacent to the Village Green (formerly the commons). The Caroline (Episcopal) Church in Setauket dates from 1729. The Setauket Presbyterian Church was organized c. 1660; their current sanctuary, the third on the site, was built in 1812. See engravings in Timothy Dwight's "Journey to Long Island," above; and Howard Klein, *Three Village Guidebook: The Setaukets, Poquott, Old Field, and Stony Brook,* 2d ed. (East Setauket: Three Village Historical Society, 1986), pp. 29-35.

33. Austin Roe was not a "zealous Tory"; he had been involved in the American spy ring. It is difficult to believe the adults did not know Washington. See George Washington's "Tour of Long Island, 1790," above.

A "Mid-Summer Outing," 1893

Laura L. Hawkins

Laura L. Hammond was born in New York City in 1824, but she spent the formative years of her childhood and young adulthood in New Village, which is now Centereach, Long Island. A few weeks before her seventeenth birthday in 1841, Laura married a neighbor, Samuel Livingston Hawkins (called Livingston).[1] In 1850, they moved to Connecticut where Livingston was a silver plater in New Haven. They had four children, only two of whom survived to adulthood.[2] Livingston served in the 1st Connecticut Battery in the Civil War. Later, he petitioned for and received a divorce in 1868; he soon remarried and moved back to Long Island.[3] Laura continued to live in New Haven with her two daughters; she is listed in the city directories as a dressmaker. In July 1893, Laura Hawkins came back to Long Island with her widowed sister, Mary Lampson, to visit friends and relatives in New Village, Lake Grove, and Patchogue. A few months later, she wrote a journal about their trip for her sister, Mary.[4]

Laura Hawkins was sixty-nine years old and her sister Mary seventy-three at the time of their excursion. They traveled by steamboat, ferry, railroad, stagecoach, and private carriage to reach their destination and often walked from house to house in the country. They had not written in advance that they were planning to come, but they received a warm welcome from their relatives and old friends. News of their arrival spread by word of mouth. One of their cousins, who owned a seaside hotel in Patchogue, invited the sisters to dinner and to join an excursion to Fire Island. Thus they enjoyed a brief glimpse of one of Long Island's summer resorts. Most of the journal, however, focuses on the daily life of rural families. Laura describes in detail the furnishings in the farmhouses they visited, the meals they ate, and their activities during their two-week visit. Many general histories indicate that women often visited relatives and friends in the nineteenth century, whether for a day or weeks at a time. This account relates what such visits might involve: exchanging recollections from earlier years and news of friends and family, looking at photograph albums, playing the piano and singing, revisiting familiar places, and attending church services.

Laura wrote the book for her sister, Mary, and she felt that "no one else" would be "interested in it." However, she added, "still someone in time might have the curiosity to read it." Laura hoped that her story of their visit "may give pleasure to the reader." Indeed, Laura's charming journal, with its many humorous comments, provides a fitting conclusion to this collection of journeys to old Long Island. In addition to her reminiscences of earlier years, it is an interesting and revealing account of life on rural Long Island at the end of the nineteenth century. More than a century later, we can walk in our imagination with her along country roads and cow paths and glimpse life of a by-gone time on Long Island's sea-girt shore.

Laura Hawkins' journal was the impetus for this collection of travel accounts. Hofstra University acquired the small handwritten book in 1998 and selections from it appeared in the *Long Island Forum*.[5] Several people suggested publishing the entire account, and it was decided to include it in a larger collection of descriptions of Long Island in the eighteenth and nineteenth centuries, beginning with Dr. Alexander Hamilton's visit in 1744 and ending nearly 150 years later with this journal from 1893.

* * *

My sister and I at last take a start on our visit to Long Island and the home of our childhood. The writing of this little book is my first attempt and will be my last. I hope the reader will overlook all errors.

Preface

I have heard the remark that a book without a preface was not worth reading. I should not like to have my little story thrown away on that account. So in presenting this little story, a word or two may not be out of place in explanation.

The tour which forms its subject was taken by my sister and myself and was delightfully spent. I have described things as they appeared to me. It may be rather overdrawn. So I leave my story with you. That it may give pleasure to the reader is the wish of the author.

L.L.H.

New Haven, Oct. 1893

O dear, I never wanted to go so bad in my life as I do this summer. Seems to me, so said my sister as I called on her one day. My sister and myself had often talked about our friends on Long Island and the old places we used to be in so much when we were young, but not being able to go we had to take it out in talking. We spent many hours together and when the work was done and my sister had sat down in her easy chair in the cosy sitting room, she would want me to play and sing some old fashion tunes on the melodeon. Then we would talk about Long Island, of this cousin and that cousin, aunts, and uncles, and in immagination we would visit many places and travel over the never to be forgotten roads and cow paths that we used to walk in so much when we were young. On this day she had been thinking no doubt about Long Island which led her to say what she did. That she never wanted to go so bad in her life as now. I felt that way myself, but we had not gone yet.

At last we made up our minds to take a trip to Long Island. Mary has many cares and now she must have a new dress and a fashionable mantle [cloak] and sundry other things. We do not take a trunk, only a small leather bag, as we shall have to walk a great deal and the weather is hot (for it is July) and it would be tiresome for us. I of course must get a new dress and a pair of gloves for I would not like to look shabby. It was a beautiful day the 21st of July that we were ready to start and as we were to go on the night boat we did not hurry. At nine oclock the carriage was at my door. My sister was inside, it having called for her at no. 15 Park Street on the way over to 156 Spring Street where I live. I was all ready and waiting and after receiveing many charges from my family, we left amid cheers of goodby, good luck, hope you'l have a good time and so forth. Ah, here we are on the splendid steamer *Richard Peck.*

Traveling to Long Island

We take a state room together. Soon we hear the bell ring, then the steam wants to give vent. It is tired of waiting. The machinary moves. The paddles are in motion, now we move. We are going out of the harbor to the Sound. We do not feel like retireing. So after carefully locking our state room, we go out on deck. It was a beautiful moonlight night and so calm. How invigorating the smell of the sea breeze. We could still see the lights in our City of Elms [New Haven], but they soon grew dim so we heaved a little sigh and said good by to our homes that we were fast leaving behind us and turned our faces seaward. The light house looked down upon us as we sailed by. We saw lights in West Haven where some of our loved ones live, then on to Milford, Stratford, and Bridgeport. We saw several vessels. Some came quite near us. The captains spoke to each other.

My sister says we must go to bed, we shant feel like seeing anything tomorrow if we don't get some sleep. So leaving the captain in charge of the boat, we went in. As I passed along, I saw a very plain looking woman coming to meet me. I did not quite like her looks, so I turned one side to let her pass by, but she turned one side also. I thought I had seen her before somewhere. As I drew nearer, I saw it was myself in the looking glass. I felt cheap to say the least. We found our state room but I was so flustered I could not go to bed but I knew I must. So after we had asked our heavenly father to take care of us we retired, but not to sleep. The clanking of machinery, the walking to and fro over head by the officers of the boat, the shoveling of coal in the furnace, all prevented us from going to sleep. We had at last almost gone to the land of dreams when our ears was saluted with the cry of a child in the next room, loudly calling for a drink of water. I wantez drink of wahter. Some one moved about, you could hear the glass jingle, then all was quiet, only now and then the softly step of some one passing through the hall. Perhaps some one going outside for a little fresh air as it was very warm.

We must have slept quite awhile for the next noise we heard was the whistle. I jumped out of the berth and tried to see out. It was morning. We were soon on deck and found we were in the Narrows [actually, the East River]. How delightful it was to see the shore on both sides and the beautiful residences with sloped lawns. The vessels and the small boats, the busy tugs towing out the large brigs to the sea. We soon were in the dock, the rattle of carts, the busy throng on their way to cross the ferry. The shout of the milkman and marketmen. Ho here beans, peas, tatoes [potatoes]. Here is your hot buns, all hots. It made us hungry. It being still early, we waited awhile on deck.

About half past seven we took our little bags and went out to get some break fast and to see the city before going on the cars [railroad] which left Brooklyn about ten o clock for Lake Land. We soon found a nice looking place, refreshments for ladies and gents. We went in. Such nice looking cakes and pies, and many fine things to eat that we did not know their names. I had had some experience before this, that the looks was better than the taste. So we got a cup of coffee, four warm buns with butter, and a fine omelet. Mary had just the same for her breakfast. Coffee 5 cts., buns and butter 2 cts., omelet 5 cts., 12 cts apeice, and it was worth it. We went up on Broadway. We saw the elevated road, but we did not want to be elevated. We saw many fine things. We would like to have gone to Central Park, but we should not have time. The sun was hot. We had our sun umberells, but they did not keep us cool. We were thirsty.

We soon came to a beautiful place, it said Delmonicoes.[6] I had heard of that place as a very nice one to get refreshments and so we went in. It was so grand inside and so many fine looking ladies and gentlemen that I felt quite out of place and was a good mind to go out, but want [weren't] we from the city? We want no country green'y. We stept in one of the little reception places and sat on the elegant divan, and tried to look as though we were used to such fine things everyday. Soon a dandy waiter with white apron stood beside us. I asked for two glasses of lemon cream. I felt red in the face but I didn't suppose they would use plates so I said glasses for I wanted to let them see I was posted [?], but in came blackey [the black waiter] with a silver tray and two beautiful cups of cream. I did not tell him I felt flat but I did just the same. O such a lot of cream and it was delicious. Supposing the price was 10 cts each, we were about to hand out two dimes when blackey hands us a silver tray and says four shillings if you plaze. Now a [New] York shilling is

12-1/2 cts, [so it was] 50 cents. Whew, 25 cts each We did not go in the great Delmonicoes again.

From Brooklyn to New Village[7]

Being near the time we wanted to leave for Brooklyn, we turned about and found a boat just leaving. I like the ferry boat, the little tug is my favorite. It is so plucky, a little spitfire. We landed near the train, then came the hurry of buying our tickets. Soon we were on our way, we had a whole seat to ourselves, and was being whirled along at a rapid rate when all of a sudden the bell rang. The steam wheezed and we came to a stop. I had not noticed it before. We were on the accomodation train all right.[8] I like this stopping, to see folks coming and going. But I did not like it so well when they crowded in our car. A giant of a man with a gold headed cane and a very small leather bag sat right down in our seat. Of course it was all right, but we thought of pick pockets. But we had taken the precaution before leaving the boat of placing our money where we could feel it everytime we breathed and had but little in our pocket book. So we sat quite easy. We were soon on our way again. How grand the fields looked. Such quantities of vegetables growing for the city markets. It was interesting to watch the many faces. Some were sad, some very jolly.

A young man came in our car with a tray of sandwiches. The goldheaded cane man was hungry, I guess, for he bought several, and taking a sheet of white paper from the tray, laid four or five on it and offered them to us, saying would we help him eat them. We thanked him and said we had just been having something to eat (didn't we eat at Delmonicoes?). So he wrapt them up and before long he saw a little boy in the next seat who was uneasy, jumping up and down and making quite a noise with his mouth. So out came the paper of sandwiches. Here soney, have a cake? Soney took two, one in each hand. His mouth was soon full, and his noise was stopped.

We stopped at many places as we drew near a fine large station. Many got off, among them was our gold headed cane man. We saw a fine coach with a pair of high headed prancing bays drive up to the station. The driver dismounted, opened the door. We saw a fine looking lady inside. Our gold headed cane man got in and we saw him no more. My sister says, how do we know but it was the president of the United States who offered us sandwiches. I said it was to bad. I wish now I had taken them, for they did look so good. They made me feel hungry, but it is to late now. Mary says I wonder if we aint most to Lake Land for we dont stop as often and it is all woods. How we did go. The trees and fences seemed to fly by us. We soon saw a farm house and barns, fields of corn and many cattle. Some nice houses, a school house, and a church. We wondered what place this was. The door opened and Lake Land was shouted out.[9] We felt all in a fluster, we caught up our bags and made our way out to the platform. A gentleman [was] standing near. Mary asked him how we could get to Lake Grove. He said a stage goes from here to Stonybrook and stops at the public house in Lake Grove and they have teams and we could get them to take us where we wanted to go.

We were beginning to feel the need of something to eat. We found a nicely fetted [fitted] up refreshment room. As the stage left in a few moments we had to hurry. We saw some rye bread on the table, so we called for rye bread and butter, a cup of tea, a piece of molasses cake, and cheese, 15 cts each. We felt better. We went out, saw the stage driver. He was ready to go. It was now near two o'clock and he was in a hurry. Had a good team and two passengers beside us, a young lady, and a gentleman. The man sat outside with the driver. The lady was very quiet, no one spoke a word for some time. I felt like going to sleep. Mary says does it seem to you as though we are really near New Village? Laura, do you remember this place? I guess I did. It was where I used to live. We built the house. There is Grandfather Yalingtons [Yarrington's] old home, but it had been made over.

I ventured to speak to the young lady. I says do you have to go far? She said she stopped at Lake Grove. I said we stop there too, then we go on east about two miles to Mr. Horace Rulands. Why, says she, I live near them. The stage drove up to the hotel. It was the New Village Inn when I lived there, kept by Mr. Reves. We paid 50 cts each to the stage driver. He took in two or three passengers, then left for Stony Brook. Just then a team drove up. A large red faced man sung out, well Sarah, you've got back home again. Jump in. Your mother wants to see you the worst way. Say father, here is two ladies that want to go to Horace Rulands, can't they go with us? Beshure they can. Ladies? Will you accept a ride with us? You are very welcome if you will. I live near where you are a going. We thanked him, and said we would be pleased to go with them. So we got in.

We saw many things that reminded us of years gone by, the church, and the grave yard where many dear ones lie. Here is Edgar Goulds, and here is Cousins Mobrays old place, and Uncle Sammy Hammonds, the old pump is still standing. Now we pass Ambrose Gould house. We see a man out to the wood pile cutting wood. He looks at us and says to our big man, How do you fa'r [fare]. I wave my handkerchief, but he dont know us. I says to the old man, I am well acquainted with Mr. Gould. Is that so? Why do tell. We ride along and cannot realize that we are on the old country road. Now here we are by Uncle Isaac place, a dear we say. Here is the path and here a blackberry vine. The bushes, old rail fence, now we near the old place, we like most of all. O how natureal we exclaim. Here is the barn, the granery [granary], the big tree still standing, the old well, the cows troth [trough], and why where is the old man a going, for he has turned his horses up near the gate. Here is where I live. Do you live here, say I? Why we think more of this old place than any other place in this world. Why here is where our grandfather and grandmother used to live and we have spent many happy days here when we were young.

Grandfather's Old Place

Was old Uncle Isaac Hammond your grandfather, says the old man. Well now pray tell what may be your name. My name was Hammond before I was married. My name is Hawkins now and this is my sister, Mrs. Lampson. We are from New Haven, Conn. Our fathers name was Joseph Caulkins [Calkins] Hammond.[10] (The old man still sat in the wagon. Sarah had gone in to see her mother.) Well, well, says the old man, then this is Livingstons wife. Well, well. Your uncle Isaac Hammond married my mother's sister for pity sake. Says I, who in the world are you. My name is Smith, Jason Smith. I think you can remember him now. I said I did.

Now come in wont you? And have some dinner with us. It is most four o'clock. You can go over to your cousins after you have had somthing to eat and taken a look about the old place. You have over three hours yet before dark. Well Mary, says I, what shall we do. Mary told Mr. Smith she did not want to put him and his wife to so much trouble. No trouble at all, says Mr. Smith. I used to know Laura Hammond. We went to school together. I give her a pewter ring once, I remember. Come, come, let me help you out. Whoa Charley, you shall have your oats soon. Sam? Here drive to the barn. Walk in. This is my wife, says he, leading up a nice looking middle-aged woman, and wife these ladies are from New Haven, Conn., old friends of mine an [and] this one (putting his hand on my shoulder), I used to know well. I think I went a courting her once, but she would not be courted. Ha, ha, ha, laughed Mr. Smith. Less [let's] have some dinner, wife now.

We were invited into the old middle room. We could remember the green venetian blinds. The little cupboard over the mantle where grandmother kept her nice dishes, her slate sugar bowl and milk pitcher. We could almost see the sand on the floor.[11] And to know that we were in that room now. Mrs. Smith looked in upon us and says, now look around any where in the house you please and enjoy yourselves. We will have supper soon. So we went in the old kitchen. There was the old fireplace, the crane, the tea kettle, and cook pot was hanging on the hooks. We took a look out the back door and went in the milk room—pans of milk and a pot of cream, several pies and a large dish of pot cheese balls [large curd cottage cheese]. We could almost see the pewter basins that used to be on the shelves.

We went in the sitting room. Grandmother used to have a bed in there with a blue and white spread on it. We could almost see grandmother sitting on one corner of the bed near the window doing some mending. She would stop now and then, take out her snuff box, give it a little rap or two, then take a pinch. There used to be asparagrass and sweet fern upon the nails for the flies to light on. And while standing there we could imagine the old wagon seat in the fireplace with green bushes behind it. And the little box with a glass door that grandmother said Uncle Ezra made for grandfather to hang his watch in. It was up high in the corner near the mantle. I could almost see grandfather get up out of his big arm chair and take it down an [and] wind it. Once when I was young I was over to grandmothers one day. I told her I would sweep up her room for her after dinner while she went out. So I went at it. I was in a hurry.

Grandfather got up out of his armchair [and] took down his watch to wind it. He was a going to sit down with it in his hand. The first thing I saw was grandfather going down on the floor. I had taken his chair away to sweep, not thinking he was a going to sit down. I was so careless. Oh how I did holler, why grandfather, grandfather. I didn't mean too, I never thought, I didn't know, and oh and oh. Grandfather got up slowly. He saw I was scare'd most to death so [he] didn't say annything to me. Well grandfather is gone. So is the watch case. And to think, after twenty five years has gone, we now stand in that same room. We cant begin to realize it.

We went out doors over in the orchard behind the barn. How sweet the green apples did smell. The very ground we stood on seemed sweet. We felt like Columbus when he landed in America. We wanted to kiss the ground. We wanted to take some of the old ground home with us almost. We could see over the lot to Uncle Isaac's. Was it true? Was we on grandfather's old place? We saw the potatoe hole where grandfather used to bury his sauce [liquor]. We went around to the east end of the house. The same yellow lillies were still growing under the east window. We took a piece off from them to keep as a momento. O how we did enjoy it all. We looked as far as we could to see the old lots and the strip of woods. How delightful it all was. Here we stood on the pikel. So grandmother used to call it.

Sarah came out and said supper was ready. It was near six oclock. The sun was still over an hour high, and we felt just like eating. The table was sett in the east-room. How nice the table looked. We had ham and eggs, wheat and rye bread, potatoes, cucumbers, blackberry pie, pot cheese, and gingerbread and tea. The rye bread, the delicious new butter. O my, how I

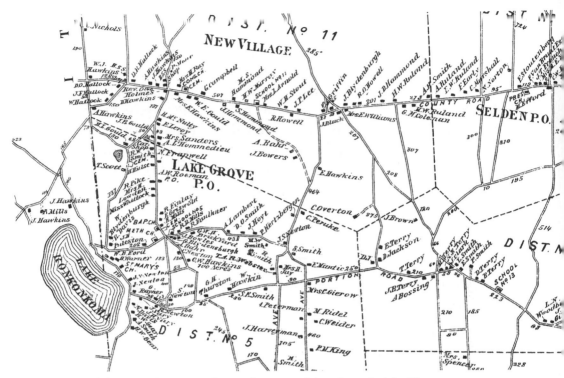

This detail from a 1873 map shows the area of the sisters' visit. The names of property owners are indicated; there are many Hammonds and other names mentioned in their journal.

did eat. Mary said to Mrs. Smith, you would not like to board us long, I guess, but your supper is so good and we have a good appetite you see and evrything is so good. Mrs. Smith said she was glad to see us enjoy her supper.[12] I pointed overhead to a shelf and told them grandfather used to keep his chicken pie upon it, so Sam Roe and Havens could not get it, for they both worked for grandfather. Our Grandfather Hammond had some curious notions. He wanted Cousin Havens to marry my sister here and Cousin Samuel Roe to marry me. How they all did laugh. After thanking our friends over and over for their kindness to us, we put on our wraps, was about to leave them. When Mr. Smith and his wife both said they should like to hear from us after we got home, Mary said she was not much of a hand to write, but here is Laura. She is a great hand to write and dont seem to mind it. I told them I would with pleasure write to them as soon after we got home as I could. I told them we would be pleased to hear from them at anytime.

Visiting Cousin Eliza Ruland

The walk over to Cousin Eliza Rulands was pleasant. We saw the little old house where I lived when I was about thirteen years old. We soon got to Liza's. Mary knocked at the door. An old thin lady came to the door. She caught hold of Mary's hand and says, Why Cousin Mary, and Cousin Laura, how do you do, come right in. We told her we were surprised to find that she knew us. She said, Sarah came over and told her she was agoing to have company, that two ladies from New Haven were coming to see her, that they were to her house now. Pop [Jason] brought them from the hotel this afternoon and they was agoing to stay to supper and their names was Lampson and Hawkins. So you see I was looking for you, but I should not have known either of you. Let me take your things. I am so glad to see you once more. Come in this room, it is cooler. Why Mary, how many years is it since we have seen each other. So Mary and Liza talked until most dark. They could think of many things to talk about. I heard some one come in the back room. Liza went out and came in with a dark looking old man and said this is my husband. We shook hands. He said he remembered me very well, but he did not know Mary. Cousin Liza and Horace had their tea [supper] out in the kitchen. Then they came in to the front room and we spent a very pleasant evening. We went to bed early for we were tired. We slept on a huge feather bed and we did not even have the nightmare as I was afraid I should, for I had eaten such a hearty supper.

We got up very early as we wanted to take a walk before breakfast. We went east as far as Wickham Ruland's, his son Edmund lives on the place now. His wife was Emeline Lee.[13] I remember that I sent Edmund a valentine once and got a nice pair of brown kid gloves in return. It is a beautiful morning, the robins are singing, the blue jay is screaming, squaw, squaw, wheetle, wheetle. We find now and then a blackbird near the fence.

We return and find breakfast ready, and we are ready also, for our walk had given us an appetite. Cousin Eliza is hard of hearing and we find it tiresome to talk long at a time. We did intend to take the stage about eleven oclock for Lake Land, then the cars [train] for Medford Station, then the stage for Patchogue. But it is cloudy now and we are afraid it will rain before we can get there and Cousin Liza wants us to stay the day with them. She says we have not made her any visit at all, so we thought if any one wanted us so bad we would stay with them. Liza brought her [photograph] album for us to to look in. We saw her family. Some are dead. We saw many others that we knew. We would like to have taken some of them home with us, but of course we would not ask for them. Cousin Eliza does not have very good health. They have a small farm and Horace does some shoemaking.

We had pens and beans for dinner, rye bread and butter, bread pudding, and tea. After we had got the work done up (for we both helped her), we went in the sitting room. It was raining some. I was looking out of the window and saw some one come in the gate with an umberella. Why, says I, here comes Cousin Davis [Hammond]. He was at home and having heard we were in the place (Jason Smith told him), he came to see us and wanted us to go home with him. He said it didn't rain now. So we told Cousin Liza we guessed we had better go, for we would like to see Cousin Davis family and we had made her quite a visit. We were soon ready and said good by to Cousin Liza and Horace with promises to write soon. We took a farewell look at grandfathers old, old place as we passed by, heaved a sigh. We turned to take one more look [and] saw two or three standing in the door waveing their hands to us. We out with our handkerchiefs and returned their salute. Davis introduced us to his married daughter and her husband. They said they was glad we had made up our minds to stay and make them a visit. They are both very nice and we know Cousin Davis is nice.

It was all clear in the west. Mary said she could not realize that we was in Uncle Isaac's house. We could almost see Uncle Isaac as he came in, his eye twitching. He would say, well how do you do, and quiet Aunt Sally would wipe her hands on her apron and say, your well? Sit down, rest yourselves. The sun sett clear. We went out to take a look around. The house had been built over some and many improvements made since we saw it. The land was there, we could see down the road as we did in old times. We felt as though we must walk in that little cowpath once more, so out we went, walked through and around it, stood and looked at it, found two or three green whortleberry. We broke off a sprig or two off the bushes to take home. I must say it was hard work to leave the spot, but we could not take it with us. We retraced our steps, found them waiting tea for us. Such a tea table, warm biscuit and butter, two kinds of preserves, pot cheese, and dried beef, three kinds of cake and tea. We all enjoyed the evening verry much, we retired early for we wanted to start early in the morning. Only think, Thursday night now.

Friday morning fine, a little cooler, but as we had a long walk before us, it was splendid. Soon after breakfast we bid them good by and started on our way. We found walking in the country very different than the city. We were tired before we had gone half a mile. We passed by Samuel Hawkins place, then we came to old Uncle Azry's place. The house Livingston was brought up in.[14] O what a shanty it seemed to us. Here is Mr. Lees, it is a good looking place yet. I said to Mary, would you stop here and rest? We can tell them who we are. Maybe some one may know us or remember me, for I used to work for Mrs. Lee. Then the house was full, had three sons, two daughters. The front door was open, we stood on the portico. Seeing no bell, Mary knocked on the door. A large middleaged woman came to the door. I said does Mr. Lee live here? She said yes. I said my name is Laura Hawkins, you remember her, dont you? (for I saw it was Nancy Lee, Jeremiah wife). I do, she said. This is my sister, Mrs. Lampson. We have walked from Cousin Davis Hammonds. Being tired we have stopped here to see if we could come in and rest a few moments. We are on our way to the hotel to take the stage: Why certainly, walk in, take a seat, have a fan, you look warm. Wont you take off your bonnets? O no thank you, we said. We would rest awhile and then hurry on for it was getting warm. Mrs. Lee stepped in the pantry. Soon came out with a glass of lemonade for each of us. It was very refreshing. She says I should never have known you. Mary thought she was rested. So we left Mrs. Lee and started on our way.

Saw Uncle Jerry Wheelers old house. Mary thinks she was born in that old house. Here is the little red school house. We saw several faces to the window. I suppose it was an unusual thing for two females with traveling bags to be out in that place. Here is Uncle Tommy Tuckers old house and close by is where Ambrose Gould lives. Of course we must call, but we are not acquainted with his wife, and we dont care to meet strangers, but we had heard she was very social. Just then we saw a man come out of a barn someways from the house. He saw us and came down to the house. We stopped in front, he came out to the gate (it was Ambrose). I says does Ambrose Gould live here?[15] Bless me if here aint Mary and Laura, well, well, come right in.

Visiting Ambrose Gould

We were taken into a nicely furnished parlor. Ambrose flew out of the room, but soon returned with a fleshy, good looking old lady. This is my wife, and wife, these are our friends, Mary Lampson and Laura Hawkins from New Haven. She shook hands and said she was delighted to see us. I have heard Ambrose say so much about you both that I feel as though we were old friends. Mrs. Hawkins in particular. I have read her letters and papers and have wanted very much to see her, and now take of [off] your bonnets, let me take your things. We told her we did not think it worth while as we were going to take the stage at eleven oclock for Lake Land. Take the what? says Ambrose who had just come in from the kitchen in time to hear us say we were agoing to take the stage. Now look here Laura, do you mean to say that this is all the visit you intended to make us? And are you

Ambrose Gould Farm, c. 1890s. His property was located on the north side of Middle Country Road, opposite Rustic Road in present-day Centereach.

positively oblidged to take that stage? I said no. Now we want you both, if you feel like it, to stay and make us a good visit. Come now can't you?

Well Mary, I said, what do you say? Mary said I am shure it is very pleasant here, and if we wont be to much trouble for your wife, I should be pleased to stay with you a while. Dont talk about making us trouble, said Mrs. Gould. If we did not want you, we would not have asked you to stay. Thats so, said Ambrose. Now, says Ambrose (slaping me on my shoulder), make yourselves at home. I am glad you have come to see us at last. Then he turned me around and says, you have grown old as well as myself. Mrs. Gould laughed and said, why Ambrose you are not very polite. Ah Laura knows me. Mrs. Gould excused herself, said she had a pie in the oven.

Ambrose sat down by us, wanted to know about our girls and how we had been since he saw us. He said it does seem so good to look at you once more. Well I must go out to the barn and finish up my work. I shall be in soon, now do make yourselves at home. You must go out and see my wife. I think you will like her for she is real jolly for an old lady. When we were left alone, we took a survey of the parlor, a handsome brussles [Brussels] carpet with border, a fine upright piano, plush chairs, splendid lace curtains, pictures, and many fancy things. We could hear Mrs. Gould troting around. We did not like to venture out in her kitchen for fear we should be in the way. We could hear dishes and kettles rattle and we heard a great commotion in the chicken pen. I said to Mary, kinder [kind of] softly, see if we don't have chicken for dinner. We each sat in a nice rocker and took it easy. We could hear laughing and talking, pots and pans hit each other. The stove oven door shut with a bang, but not until we had a smell of something good. Chairs seemed moveing about, and castors squeaked as though a table was being drawn out from its usual place. It did seem as though we had created quite a sensation. I was glad of it, for it was a treat to us to have anyone make such a fuss on our account.

Ambrose came in with two ladies, introduced them as Mr. Arnold's daughters. Mrs. Gould had been married before to a widower named Arnold. They lived up stairs. I think one was married, her name was Kellogg. They seemed glad to see us. They had heard Mr. Gould speak of his New Haven friends. Mrs. Gould came in and we had a social time. We could not help feeling at home, all were so pleasant. Some one knocked at the back door. Mr. Gould went out to the door and came back with a real old man. Ambrose says to me, Laura I think you used to know this gentleman. The man laughed, then I knew it was Samuel Hallock. I introduced him to Mary. How old he looked. Yes, I said, I remember you well, and I guess you do me also. Yes, I have great reason to, says he. Mr. Hallock used to board with my father. I was young, he was an old batch [bachelor] and a real Samhill and a pester. I used to wish he was out of the house. He was such a teaze, but I think he got paid off. He is a widower now and a pleasant old man. He said he was glad to see me and my sister. Ambrose told him that we were agoing to make our home with them as long as we staid in the place, and if any one wished to see us, they could come to his house. Mr. Hallock said he thought he should call again.

We heard the clock striking twelve. I was so glad for I was hungry and I guess Mary was also for we had our breakfast early. Mrs. Gould said dinner was ready. Mr. Hallock, wont you stay and have some dinner? So out we all went into the dining room. That dinner table groaned fairly with the good things that was on it, roasted chickens with dressing, mashed turnips and mashed potatoes, cowcumbers [cucumbers], boiled onions, a cottage pudding with sauce, custard pie, wheat and rye bread and butter, tea and coffee, and fruit. Well now, didnt I do justice to that dinner. Echo says yes. Many things were said that sett us all to laughing. O what a dinner party that was. Mr. and Mrs. Gould, the two ladies from up stairs, Mr. Hallock, Mary, and myself, and we had plenty of time to eat. Things staid on the table until we could eat what we wanted, no darkey behind your chair to hurry you up. [This is an allusion to the meal they had later at the Ocean Avenue Hotel in Patchogue.]

Mrs. Gould is fleshy. Mr. Gould is lean. They are a happy couple as ever I have seen. We females all helped do up the work, then we sat down in the sitting room for a chat Mrs. Gould brought out some sewing she was doing. I asked her if she did not have some for me. Yes, Mary said, give us something to do. Mrs. Gould, I said, I want you to sit still and rest. I said if she wanted us to stay contented, we must have some work. Well, she said, what will you have. I said, well I will put on the faceing and braid in this skirt. Mary said she would face the basque [i.e., put a lining in a bodice]. Mrs. Gould took the sleaves and the ruffles. Now dont hurry, for I do not need the dress, but as I do not get much time to sew, I begin in season. The hired man came to the door and wanted to see her. So off she went. We sat there talking and sewing.

When she beckoned for us to come out, we put our handkerchiefs on our heads and went out. She wanted us to see her flowers. She had some beautiful ones, her beds were laid out very pretty. She beat us at home for she had a greater variety. We then went in the kitchen garden. O what beans and peas, beets, cowcumbers, and other things. Next she took us to the orchard, the trees were loaded with apples. Some were early, some sweet. Mary had a feast. I like tart apples best, early pears, now and then a peach tree. How nice, and beautiful they looked to us. Mrs. Gould said, here are our cows come in the lot. Dont be afraid, they are very gentle. I had to tell them how afraid I was of cows when I was a very small child and went to school. I had to go through a lot where was some cows. Often some one of our folks would go with me, but some times I had to go alone. Some of the big girls told me if I would make a kerchu [sneeze] when I went by them, they would not hurt me. So I did. The cows were standing under a tree in the shade. They looked at me but still kept on chewing their cud.

Mrs. Gould said she must go in for she had got to churn [cream into butter]. So we returned to the house. As we sat sewing, we could hear the churning going on. I said to Mary, I am going to ask her if we cannot have some buttermilk. I went out and asked her. She said we could have all we wanted as they gave it to the pigs. We heard her spatting the butter [i.e., using a butter paddle to press out the buttermilk]. Ambrose came in and says, put on your things, and we will take a drive before tea. I says, is your horse gentle? O yes, a lazy old fellow. Mrs. Gould did not go. Mrs. Kellog went. We went up west by the church out where Aunt Sophonia used to live and where Uncle Isaac Gould lived once. We did not stop anywhere. We shall never forget that ride. Mrs. Gould said she was real glad we enjoyed our ride.

We found on going in, Mr. Edgar Gould waiting to see us. How he did shake hands. He said he was surprised and glad to see us as he never expected to see us again. His health is not very good but he can joke yet. He said, if he was younger now he thought perhaps he could get a wife as we

The New Village School was built in 1860 on Middle Country Road, across from today's Rustic Road, and was in use until 1914.

both were widows.[16] He stayed to tea, a pitcher of buttermilk was near our plates. We had warm biscuit and new butter. Very nice cake, pot cheese and preserves, and tea. We fixed some buttermilk as we wanted it. How good it was, to good to eat. I wanted some cake and cheese, but if I eat all the buttermilk I wanted, I should not have room for any. So I said to Mrs. Gould, if I do not eat all the buttermilk I want, can I have it tomorrow? They all laughed. She said, yes, I will keep you on buttermilk, if you say so. So I eat some cake and cheese and felt as though I should not need anything to eat tomorrow. Edgar soon went home. We helped do up the dishes. The lamps were lighted. Sewing was put away. The parlor was all lighted up. The portieres [curtains or drapes in the doorway] were tied back and we all went in. The young lady from up stairs came down and played on the piano. Old femeliar tunes were sung and we made the welkin [heavens] ring. It was grand, o so grand. Ambrose showed us the pictures of his father and mother, sister, and brothers, and many others that I had seen.

The evening soon was gone and we had been happy. Ambrose took the Bible, read a chapter, then he had prayer. I have heard him sing and pray many times before when I was young. Now after so many years have gone, I have heard him again. We retired soon. We had a high feather bed. We took it off as a nice mattrass was under it, but we could not sleep. It was so very warm in that room. It was awful quiet in that country home, at last we slept.

Ambrose was up early as he had got to go to Stony Brook. He said, dont sit and sew all the time, but walk out, get the fresh air. It being Saturday, Mrs. Gould had many things to do. So Mary and I done up the work, brushed up the crumbs, shelled some peas, then went out for a stroll. We had heard that Mary Foster and Eliza had gone to make a visit to one of Eliza's daughters. Samuel Hallock was keeping house for them. As there was no school that day, we went over to the school house. How many times I have been in it, so many prayer meetings and singing schools and old Captain Wheeler was the teacher and then the boys used to go home with us and that was better than singing, I thought.

The First Congregational Church of New Village was built in 1818.

We did not stay out long but went back and had some buttermilk. Did we ever have such a nice time before, no never, but time was fast passing. We must leave soon. We returned to the sitting room and took our sewing. Mary had the basque nearly done, and so was my skirt. When we got through, we went in the parlor. Mary says cant you play on the piano? I said not very good. I can play on the organ better but I will try, but the ladies up stairs will laugh at my performance. So I gave them some of our New Haven music, first one thing and than annother, a few dances and I was playing a full blown jig. When Ambrose came in the room he stopped and looked at me as though he was surprised and exclaimed, Why Laura Hawkins, if you dont beat the dutch. I did not think it was you that was making such a noise. I was about to leave the instrument when he said go on, go on, I like it. So I played away my fashion until I was tired. Well, well, he says, I wish my wife could play like that. She understands music and used to be quite a performer when young, but it is many years since she has tried to play and I suppose she has forgotten how.

Dinner being ready we went out and sat down to peas and beans, potatoes, bread and butter, a nice pudding with cream and sugar on it. Ambrose saw Cousin Davis over to Stoney Brook. He was surprised to hear that we still was in the place. I told him that I intended to keep you as long as you would stay. Mary said she thought we had made them a big visit allready. She thought it best for us to go next Monday morning. Mrs. Gould said, of course you know best. We shall have to let you go, I suppose, but shall have you one day more anyhow.

Sunday morning was cloudy but Ambrose said it would not prevent us from going to church.[17] The folks up stairs did not go, his wife seldom went, as it was hard work for her to get in and out of the wagon. So Mary and I went. The same old church painted up, quite a good many out. The minister was good, the singing with a small organ was fine. They had a large choir. The contribution box was passed. I declare I had'nt a cent, but Mary is a Methodist and always goes prepared. Now the folks looked at us. Ambrose introduced us to several. His brother Lewis was one. One man who was hard of hearing, I guess, for the other man had to whisper in his ear so loud that I heard, Hawkin? yes Hawkins. Livingstons wife. I pretended not to hear them but I saw them looking at us. One stepped up to Ambrose, said something softly to him, after we had got out. They could not understand how it was that Ambrose Gould should be so interested as to fetch us up to church and to think we were staying to his house. We saw Ambrose motion to them. He must have invited them to be introduced to us, for they came up with him and Ambrose said, this is Walter Smith, and this is Whitmans Smith. They smiled and said I think we can claim relationship for your mother and our mother were sisters. Why, Mary says, these are Aunt Desires sons. I asked them about their sister Elvina. They invited us to go home with them. We thanked them and said as we were going to Patchogue in the morning we did not think it best. We shook hands, said good by, and they left us. Then came Edgar Gould and Cousin Davis, Jason Smith and family. Edmund Ruland came and introduced himself and Emeline. All appeared glad to see us and Edmund thought we ought to go home with them. Ambrose said he could not spare us. How the folks stood around, they did not want to leave until we did. It was something new to them. Some looked at us as though they would not speak to us if they could, a disdainful look was on their face. But they were young and did'nt know any better. We forgave them. Edgar rode home with us and stayed to dinner. The news had spread that Laura Hawkins and her sister Mary Lampson from New Haven, Conn. were visiting in the place. No wonder the country folks turned out to church, for they knew that Ambrose would go and thought we would also.[18] So we had annother *fuss* made over us.

In the evening after tea, Samuel Hallock came in. The ladies from up stairs came down and played on the piano. Some old tunes were played and we *all* joined in singing. So we spent the *last* Sunday and evening that in all probability we should ever spend together in this world. When Mr. Hallock went out to go home, he said it rained. He bid us good by. We shall never see him again, I said to myself. We sat up quite late talking over old times, about many who are now dead. We told our friends we should never forget our delightful visit with them, and we would be glad to have them come and see us. We would try and make them as happy as they had us.

Ambrose said Laura: dont you remember that I wrote to you once that if you would come and make us a visit, that when you got tired of staying with us, I would take you to any of your friends you wish to go too. So tomorrow, if it is a plasant day, I will take you to your cousins in Patchogue. I said, we are not tired of staying here at all and as it was on that condition your promis was made, you wont have to take us. Well, we will see tomorrow, Ambrose said. After family worship we said good night to our kind friends. We slept good for the rain had cooled the air. The morning was bright and clear. It had cleared off during the night. Ambrose said he had some business to do in Patchogue, so we would start early after breakfast when the shakeing of hands and good bye's were said and do come again and see us. We left Ambrose Goulds home. The ride was delightful. Only think after so many years we are riding over the plains to Patchogue. We came out in the same old road by the red meeting house, just the same road grandfather used to take when he went to mill with his wagon load of grain. O dear me, that feeling came over us again, such as Columbus had when he first landed. Ambrose found out where Cousin Phebeann lived and took us to the house. It was about ten oclock. We had drove pretty fast. Well, says Ambrose, I cannot say goodby but bid you good morning. We thanked him, shook hands, and he drove away.

Visiting Cousin Phebeann Weeks

As we went into the gate, a woman came around from the back of the house and says, who do you wish to see? I almost laughed for it was Cousin Phebeann Weeks and she did not know us. Mary says, could we get board here? We are from the city and we would like to stay in the country a while near the water. We have heard this place spoken off as a healthy one. We were directed to Mr. Weeks. They said you kept boarders and we were directed to this house. I think you mean my son. He has a hotel near the water and has a good many boarders. We told her we did not care to go to a hotel, we prefered a private place. I said, could you keep us a few days until we can find a good place? If not could you give us a cup of tea? It would rest us. O she says I can give you a cup of tea. Step in. So in we went. She put on the tea kettle.

What to say next was my trouble. She eyed us sharply (thought of burglars I expect) and said, was you ever in Patchogue before? We said yes. Somehow it seems as though I had seen you before. Where did you stay when you was here before. I said to my Uncles. What was your Uncles name. Joshua Smith. Why, why, O is it Cousin Mary and Cousin Laura? O dear me, no wonder I thought I had seen you before, but I did not know you. How you both have changed. I never expected to see you again. I am so glad, and she shook our hands [and] then sat down quite overcome. How we did laugh at her. How you did fool me. Yes, you felt the need of a cup of tea and to think I did not dream of it being you. Well you shall have that cup of tea. I told her she need not get it, for I did not want it. I said I had to say something, for we see she did not know us.

We went into her sitting room and had a real nice time. Now she says, you have come to make me a good visit, hav'nt you? You can stay as well as not, cant you? Mary said her daughter would get tired keeping house if she stayed to long, as we had been away from home now nearly a week. Why, where have you been all that time. So we told her. She was glad to hear from the friends in that place. We told Cousin Phebeann not to put herself out of the way for us as she was going too and fro, we thought she would get tired. She says I am going to the market. I want you to keep house while I am gone. We did not let it trouble us if she did spend some money for our dinner, for we knew she had a plenty to do with. The market was not far off. She soon came back with her basket filled. We thought we were a going to have a tip top visit with her, no man around to hurry up things. We could do as we were a mind too. We had a fine dinner of fried chicken, potatoes, bread and butter, apple pie and cheese, tea of course. How good it was, we were hungry and I guess she thought so too. When she cleared off the table it looked some like a shower, so we did not walk out but had a pleasant talk with our cousin. She has four or five rooms, the house is nice and situated on a busy street. Our tea was plain and nice.

We did not sit up long, we found on retireing a mountain feather bed. We needed a step ladder. We found she had two [feather] beds on. We took off one. We thought we could stand that, but o my, how hot and close it was. I got up and drew up the curtain, just then a flash of lightning lit up the room. Soon a peal of thunder, we were agoing to have a thunder shower. Soon the lightning was so blinding that we put down the curtains and lit the lamp. Cousin Phebeann did the same. How it did rain and the wind blew a gale. We could hear the blinds slam, the gates banging, clothes poles fall down. A carraige went by in a hurry. Some docter perhaps, *he must* go if it did rain. The worst was over. We could hear the distant thunder, the wind had ceased its violence and we got to sleep.

When we awoke in the morning we could see it was bright out doors. We could hear Cousin Phebeann moveing about in her room. Mary says let us take a little walk before breakfast, So we did, but all was strange to us. The ground was wet, we had no rubbers [overshoes] on. We did not go far. When we got back, cousin had breakfast nearly ready. After we got through I said many hands make light work, so we was soon ready to sit down and talk. So the fore noon passed away. We helped cousin shell peas and string and cut the beans. She had quite a good garden. She kept some chickens. She had fresh eggs every day. She wanted us to feel at home and we did. Good fresh beans and peas with a small peice of country pork, a streak of lean now and then in it, I think is just nice. How sweet they tasted.

Cousin showed us many pretty things she had and was making. She had beautiful paintings and such a lot of beautiful rugs. She said if we could carry one home, she would give us one. I told her to give us one and see if we could'nt. So she gave us our choice. We done them up telling her we should always keep them very careful to remember her by. It was near tea time, her son Sanford came in. He is a fine looking man. He invited us to his house and said he would send a carriage for us if we would come tomorrow and spend the day. Cousin Phebeann was to go too. We said yes, that we would be ready by ten oclock.

A c. 1898 postcard view of the Ocean Avenue Hotel in Patchogue, "Where the Cool Breezes Blow Continually From Old Ocean."

At the Ocean Avenue Hotel

So bright was the morning and happy were we as we rode in the carriage to our friends by the sea. We drove up to the hotel.[19] Many ladies were sitting on the verandah, enjoying the breeze from the bay. We were shown into one of the parlors. Before long Cousin Sanford Weeks came in with his wife.[20] She was stately looking and much older than her husband. Cousin Phebeann introduced us, Mrs. Lampson and her sister Mrs. Hawkins, our cousins from New Haven, Conn. Mrs. Sanford Weeks said she had heard of New Haven spoken of as a beautiful city. Some of her boarders had passed through the place on their way from New York to Boston. They spoke very highly of the city and the fine buildings and the grand institutions of learning. The beautiful elm trees meeting overhead in some streets completely shading the street and they had the appearence of a tunnel while passing through them. Yes we said, that was so and we were proud of our City of Elms. Mrs. Sanford Weeks excused herself, a waiting maid wanted her.

Cousin Phebeann said this is the way it is here, all summer. So much coming and going all the time. I dont like it. I had rather live alone. Mary said she never could stand it. I thought I could awhile if I did not have anything to do. We enjoyed looking out of the window. We could see the [Great] South Bay and the beach beyond it. It was interesting to watch the boarders as they started for the beach. They did not feel very particular about their looks. One lady had her poodle leading it by a string. She took it evry day to the shore and gave it a bath. How clean it looked when she came back.

We had a real hotel dinner. We sat down feeling rather bashful at first to see the ladies look so fine in their dinner dresses, and the waiters thick as hops, and the different courses we had. Why we would no more than begin to eat and if we stopped a moment to look at some one, our plate was gone, and a new course was given us, and so it kept going, but we got a taste of them all. I wished I could take my plate of roast turkey and go out in the kitchen and eat it all up but no, it was gone. I was in the act of eating a nice piece, had stopped to use my napkin and turned to speak to Mary. When lo, on faceing my plate, it was gone. I felt like hollering to the waiter as I saw him going out, to fetch back my turkey, but I did'nt. I did not want to appear or let them know but that I was used to such things.

My plate was brought back with two kinds of pie on it. Fearing I should not have time to eat both peices, I took the one that looked best. It was mince, for I am very fond of mince pie. I had eaten about half of it when I could not seem to get off a peice. At last I made out, took it up on my fork was about to transfer it to my mouth when I saw the rest of the piece dangling in mid *air*. I quickly laid it down, found it hung by a *hair*. As no one had yet appeared to take my plate, I commenced on the other piece. That was apple, and real good. I had eaten the most of it when I discovered that most of the boarders was done and ready to have their plates taken. So I put down my fork, just in time, for the darkey [black waiter] was on hand and took away our plates and put on clean plates, clean napkins and fruit knifes. Then came the fruit. I had rather have my turkey [that] they took away, but it was gone. I should never see it more, so I took an orange. I had had no time to see how Mary and Cousin Phebeann got along, for they hurried me so that I was all in a perspireation and should be glad when dinner was over. But I tried to take it easy and to look as though I was often in such places. Evrything has an end, so did our hotel dinner. How we did laugh when we got a chance. I shall never forget our hotel dinner.

About five oclock, Sanford came in the sitting room and says, well Mother, have you and these cousins enjoyed yourselves? We said, o yes very much (I thought of my turkey). Cousin Phebean said to Sanford and his wife, cant you both come over some evening while Mary and Laura are here? Well I must go home early and see to my chickens, so the carriage came for us and we left quite early. I found out that Mary and Cousin Phebeann did'nt eat scarcely anything. I had done better than they had [even] if I did find a hair in my pie. We laughed until our sides ached while we were having our tea (we were all hungry), talking about our hotel dinner. We slept well that night. I supposed I should dream of roast turkey, but I did not.

Visiting Havens Hammond

Wednesday morning was clear, So we thought we would call on Cousin Havens Hammond. That forenoon cousin Phebeann went out to feed her chickens. I says, have they got a plenty of water? O she said, I should have had to come away back after some if you had not thought if it. I said you must make your head, save your heels. You know well, she says, I never did. She said she would not go with us to Cousin Havens as his wife didnt come to see her very often, and she had some work she wanted to do that forenoon. So we started alone. We told Cousin Phebeann we should be back early without [unless] we were invited to dinner. We took it very easy, found Cousins Havens house with out any trouble. I said to Mary, I wonder if Havens will shake hands with me now. So I told her how I made him mad once.

I used to be over to grandmother often and Cousin Amy Roe lived with grandmother. Havens lived there too, worked for grandfather. Havens was sly and tricky, and some of his tricks he played on us young girls. He was much older than either of us. I was agoing to stay all night and sleep with Cousin Amy Roe. Havens was tricky as usual. I said to Amy, let us pay him off. So early, about daylight, Amy got up, lit her candle, then I got up. We slept in the west end of the old house. It had a pantry and a fire place. Father and mother lived in that room once. Amy says to me, we have some bean porrige. I am agoing to make a fire and heat up some and we will take some to Havens while he is in bed. Amy put on some wood and we soon had a blaze. She put on the porrige pot, it was soon hot. I took a small dish, put some bean broth in it, took a spoon. Amy took the candle, I took the porrige. We went in Havens room (it was next to ours), and I said we have brought you some bean porrige, it is warm. So open your mouth and I will feed you. He said, he should'nt. I told him he must. So he took a spoonful and said, O it is hot. I said open your mouth again and take some more. He made me spill some and I guess it was to hot for he got mad. So we left. We had to be very still for grandfather used to call Havens early and we heard him coming and we had no time to loose. I see at breakfast that Havens looked as though he could bite. So I went home. It was many months after that I met Havens on the road. I did not think anything, so I says, Why how do you do Cousin Havens and held out my hand to him when he said, *Let evry dog shake his own tail* and passed on. Well, I said to myself, he aint got over that yet. I have not seen him much since and now after 25 years or more I am agoing to see him.

We went in the gate. Mary rang the bell, a spare old lady came to the door. Mary said does Mr. Havens Hammond live here? He does, would you like to see him? Mary said, yes. Walk in then, my husband will soon be in, he is out to the barn. We could see she did not know us. Havens came in (o how old *he* was). Mary says (stepping up to him), how do you do Cousin Havens? I am sure I dont know who you are. My name is Lampson. Is this cousin Mary Lampson? Yes, I guess it is and this is (turning to me), my sister Laura. Why, I want to know, and he shook hands with us both (I thought of the dog), and cousin Elizebeth was so surprised. No, we should not have known them, or they us, they said.

They were glad to see us. Their children had grown up and gone from home. They asked about our family's and we told them we had seen Davis and Liza. They was glad to hear from them, although only living ten miles apart they seldom see each other. How old and changed evrybody looked. I suppose they thought the same of us. They asked where we were staying and how long we were going to stay. Said they would like to have us come and spend a day with them. We did not promis, so we said good by without we see you again before we leave. We told Cousin Phebeann that we had to come back, as we did not get invited to dinner. I said perhaps they was not prepared to have company. We had dinner and we spent the rest of the day with Cousin Phebeann. She had several calls in the afternoon. Two or three of her children came in. They each brought her something nice. Sanford came over to see if we would not like to take a sail over to the beach, then walk over to the beach to the surf, as a party from the hotel was going, tomorrow afternoon. We asked what they were going in. He said a small sloop, and would start about one oclock.

A Sail to Fire Island

It was a pleasant calm day, and we thought it would be a fine sail. So we had an early dinner, picked up dinner [probably leftovers], Cousin Phebeann said it was. The work was done up and we [were] ready in time. A very long open wagon with four horses drove up to the door. We got in and was taken back to the hotel, about twenty five got in, the driver cracked his whip, and away we went. A little wharf led out to the sloop and we soon was on our way. A gentle breeze wafted us along and we could see that we were nearing the South beach [Fire Island]. The company were in great glee. They sung "Life on the Ocean Wave," and it sounded nice on the water. "Land ho," shouted the captain. We landed and went across the beach. The young people got over first, but we got there and once more in my life I stood on the broad Atlantic shore. Water, water, as far as the eye could reach. We could see many ships in the distance. The surf was not heavy, it was not rough enough for that. We found many curious shells to take home with us. O what a grand sight. We sat down and gaze'ed upon this large body of water. What was beyond it we longed to see. Good by you grand old ocean, to some you give joy, to some you give sorrow. We are living to day, we die on the morrow.

We returned in safety, rode home, and had a nice supper, our sail had made us hungry as bears. We had some cold chicken, warm biscuit and butter (pot cheese one of the neighbors sent in), fruit cake and tea. We had much to talk about all the evening. It was a great treat for us. We shall never forget our visit to the ocean. We were permitted to enjoy all these things. Our visit thus far had been delightful. We must soon leave these familiar places. Time was fast passing away and we should have to say good bye.

Visiting More Cousins

Saturday morning we took a walk and after breakfast we went over to where Uncle Joshua Smith used to live. The old house was all fixed over, it did not look natural. We found Cousin Nichols place, made a call, was invited to stay to dinner. We told him that Cousin Phebeann expected us back, so we must go but would come in again. His wife is nice and said she would like to have us come and stay all day. So we told them we would come if we could. We found Cousin Edmund, he was not very well. His wife was a stranger to us. I knew his first wife well and she was a handsome woman. We did not stay long. We found on our return that Cousin Bartlett Hammond had been there and left word for us to come and see them. We spent the rest of the day and night with Cousin Phebeann. Sunday morning we all went to church. It was not far to go, many attended, the sermon was good. The text was in Matthew 12, chap 30.

We are having beautiful weather. I hope it will last until we get home. We have sent two or three letters home, but we move about so much that they cannot send us letters very often. We had a letter, both of us, soon after getting to Patchogue. They want us to stay as long as we want to. That is just what we are agoing to do. We told Cousin Phebeann we did not wish to make her twice glad.

On Monday about ten oclock we went to Cousin Bartletts in Uncle Joshua Hammonds old place. Bartlett was away, his wife was very nice indeed. She rather expected us, she said. So we had no trouble in making ourselves known. She wanted us to stay as Bartlett would not be home until night. We had told Phebeann not to look for us until she saw us. Bartletts wife sent one of her boys over to tell Phebeann that we was agoing to stay and make them a visit. We thought that was kind for her to do. It was most dinner time, our cousin sett a splendid table. We had some old fashioned sucotash, two kinds of bread, potatoes, beets, cold boiled ham sliced, and cold boiled eggs sliced and laid on with a little mustard, rasberry pie, and tea. We praised her dinner, the sucotash just touched the spot. We had to much to eat.

After dinner as we sat in the parlor, we saw some of Cousin Sanfords city boarders go by riding out for pleasure. Bartletts wife joined us very soon. She is a real worker. She showed us a beautiful knit bed spread and curtains, a table cover all knit with thread. She spoke of Aunt Liza and the cousins. We enjoyed the afternoon and it seemed short. Cousin Bartlett came home about tea time. We spent a very pleasant evening. I did not feel much acquainted with Bartlett as I have never seen much of him. He wanted to hear about all the friends in Lake Grove and our family's. We retired about nine, for they had to get up early. Mary and I got used to sleeping together, and we have not had the nightmare yet. The last time we took a trip together we both had it the same night. We were up in season, had breakfast. Cousin Bartlett left home for all day to work. I do not remember what his business is.

As we were near Cousin Nickols, we thought we would go there from here. It was a hot morning, we did not care to go out, but thought we must. We left our cousin about nine oclock and started for Nickols. We saw two or three cows eating the grass by the roadside. What to do we did not know (I knew a kerchy [sneeze] was out of date). We could go back and get one of the boys to go along with us. Just then we saw two famelish [familiar] looking men coming. We waited for them. I said we feel afraid to pass by those cows. O they wont tetch [touch] you, come right along. So we did and they did not tetch us, the cows nor the men either. We saw Cousin Nickols out leading a wagon with cord wood near his house. He met us and waited on us in his house [which] is small and he has a small farm. His children are grown up, but still help their father and mother some. Mrs. Smith was glad to see us again, she said. She is very pleasant indeed. I think that they are very frugal or close in their living, but have enough. But it is very plain to be seen that they mean to get rich or to save what they have got and to get what they can. For dinner we had peas and beans, potatoes, bread and butter, pie and tea. Cousin Nickols had to go up town and said if we must go he would take us along. He took us to Cousin Phebeann's. He did not go in. Said good by and left.

I tell you we was glad to get back. Only think it will be Wednesday tomorrow. We thought it time to think of going home, but Cousin Phebeann said she would like to have us stay one day with her as we had been going evry day somewhere. We told her we was afraid it would storm, but it did not trouble us much for we was in a good place. Mary and Phebeann had so much to talk about that we might stay a week and still have a plenty to talk about. We all hands got the dinner and when it was ready we had got sucotash, bread and butter, blackberry pie, and tea. Time went fast and before night it rained fast. We was glad we had not started for home in the morning. How it did rain and who should drive up but Sanford right in the midst of it. He came in and said if it was a good day tomorrow, a party were going to Fire Island and we were invited by the ladies to go with them. I told Mary that it was because we was from New Haven that we got invited so much to join their party's. We told Sanford that if it cleared off we expected to start for home tomorrow morning. He said good by, jumped in his covered carriage, and rode away. We told him to thank the ladies for us. Mary says how kind of them to think of us, and how kind evryone has been to us all through our visit. We feel paid over and over, for our time and money. Cousin Phebeann gave each of us a painting that she made of forget me nots and red pinks. I got up in the night to see if it rained, it was clear as a bell. I heard a clock strike three. I said to Mary, it has cleared off but we could not sleep much after that.

Patchogue Railroad Station

Leaving Long Island

We wanted to take the early train, so we should have a plenty of time. The train goes at six oclock. At half past four we was up and put what money we had to spare in its old safe place again. At half past five we was ready. Shook hands and left on the South Long Island Rail Road for New York. Well, we left our Cousin Phebeann never expecting to see her again, but we did not say so. Here we are on the through lightning express train. We got in Brooklyn half past eight. As the boat leaves for New Haven at three, we thought we could go to Central Park. After crossing the ferry we went to the New Haven boat, left our bags in the waiting maid's care, then left for Central Park.

We stept [stepped] in a nice place where we saw some fine looking cakes and buns, bought a few, then took the car to Central Park.[21] What a long ride, we rode and rode. We began to think we was there almost, when we saw a great crowd of people scampering, men, women, and children. Why: what can be the matter. Soon we saw quite an army of men with guns. I said to Mary, aint you glad we are in the car, if we are most suffocated, but they still crowded in. We heard a woman say that one of [P.T.] Barnum's big lions was loose, and she said it had gone up towards Central Park. Mary said, let us get out and take a car back. I was perfectly willing and saw a car coming that was right for us to take, and we changed cars in a hurry. We breathed easier and as we had been bothered with the crowd; we had lost much time. So may be it was the best thing to do, to turn back. We thought we would get out and walk the rest of the way and get some dinner. When, here, here, they come, here comes the lion. There he goes in that big yard. See folks run. There he is. They'v got him, I guess. This is the way the people hollered; the horses was frightened and went to forty [?]. We staid in, didn't stop for dinner. We

was down town before noon. So we stopped in the market and got all we
wanted, ice cream and all, but we still felt kinder weak in the knees. We over
heard some one say the lion was caught. He was most tired out.

We still had some time so we went over the ferry to Brooklyn, [and] took
a car out to Greenwood Cemetary.[22] How beautiful. We staid awhile, but
time goes so fast that we felt uneasy. So we turned about, got to the ferry all
right, went over to New York, got to the steamboat, went on board just as the
first bell was ringing. We found the waiting maid, payed her ten cents each
for our bags, then went out on deck. How bright and clear, not a cloud to be
seen. I told Mary that we should have a storm soon as it cleared off in the
night. Soon after three oclock we gave good by to New York, and I was sorry
to leave it if we did not go to Central Park.

We met annother boat just coming in, the crews hailed each other and
they made for the land. And *we* made for the sea. They *were* nearing their
home and *homeward bound* were we. It was Thursday. We had been gone
over two weeks. We saw Blackwels Island. We did not mind Hellgate at all
but was soon through it. Here we are on the open [Long Island] Sound,
schools of porposes were playing around us, once in a while one would jump
clear out of the water. We saw many boats on the Sound, one vessel came
quite near us. We saw a woman on board and a child. She was sewing and
had been washing, for we saw a line of clothes. Mary said, she must put her
clothes pins on tight. I said perhaps she uses safety pins. The captain no
doubt was her husband.

We were fast nearing our home. We strain'd our eyes with all our might
to see if New Haven was yet in sight. I saw a gentleman pointing out the
different places as we passed by them. It was nearly dark and we could see
some lights off on shore, though far off. I thought I would go and stand near
this gentleman and hear what he said. This place off here, pointing, is
Bridgeport. I went and told Mary that was Bridgeport off there. Why how
can you tell, she said. So I had to tell her how I knew so much. We went in to
take a look in the glass to see if our bonnet was on straight and our faces
clean, then out we went again to see how far we had gone. O my, we were
going in the harbor. The whistle blew three times, and (did our folks hear
that whistle? for they knew we was coming), soon it was ding, ding. We had
got to the wharf [but] it was sometime before the plank was out. Have a
carriage? express? carriage? Ladies? New Haven house? We picked out a
good looking man and I asked him what he would charge to take me to 156
Spring Street and Mary to 15 Park St.[23] 50 cents each. I said no sir, I will go
on the cars first. Annother hackman saw us. So he came up. I asked *him.* 25

cents apiece he said, two other ladies were inside. We got home safe. Thus ended our trip to Long Island.[24]

1898

Nearly five years have gone by since we took our Outing. Many of our friends whom we saw then have left this world, among them was Cousin Eliza Ruland, Cousin Havens Hammond and his wife, Cousin Nickols Smith and his wife, Samuel Hallock, and Edgar Gould. We are left and we enjoy thinking over the many pleasant days we spent with them five years ago. We shall never forget them, we feel like going again, but no doubt but that was our last visit to Long Islands sea girt shore that we shall ever make.[25]

Homeward Bound

In conclusion, I will say that this book was written on purpose for my sister, Mary. No one else would feel interested in it. She knew all about the people and places. Still some one in time might have the curiosity to read it. I will say that most all were our relatives that are in my story.

I will mention our neighbors sons. Ambrose Gould was a fine young man who lived near us, we went to the same church and singing schools. I knew his first wife well. Edgar Gould was his brother. Ambrose wrote to me after we moved to Conn. and kept me posted about that part of Long Island, my relations would not take the trouble. He is a fine old man, still living in Lake Grove, L.I. Jason Smith went to the same school I did. A big fat boy and lazy, I thought. Samuel Hallock boarded with father and mother and put many jokes on me, but I paid him off *well.* I was about 14 years old.

I was about 28, I think, when I moved to New Haven, Ct. I had had three children then, Saphronia, Hattie, and Emma; Saphronia died on Long Island. I was married 20th of June, and on the 16th of July I was 17 years old. I was born in New York City. I was quite young when father moved to Long Island, then soon he moved to Conn. He lived in Derby. And then he moved to Bridgeport. I was about ten years old, I think, when father moved back to Long Island from Bridgeport. I got married and we moved to New Haven Ct. Then in about two years, I had a son. He lived to be one year old.[26]

Notes

Source: Laura Hawkins entitled her account, "Our Mid-Summer Outing." The journal is in the Hofstra University Axinn Library, Long Island Studies Institute collection in the Rare Books and Manuscripts Department. The handwritten 5"x8" booklet has 112 pages of text with some pictures and a poem pasted in. As noted at the end of the account, it was written in October 1893, probably drawing on a diary kept during the trip. Some penciled corrections were added, perhaps in 1898 when the final sections were written.

we still had some time so
we went over the ferry to Brooklyn
took a car out to greenwood
cemetary. how beautiful. we
staid awhile. but time goes
so fast that we felt uneasy. so
we turned about, got to the
ferry all right. went over to new-
york, got to the steamboat.
went on board just as the
first bell was ringing. we
found the waitingsmaid.
payed ten cents each
for our bags. then went
out on deck. how bright &
clear. not a cloud to be seen.
I told Mary that we should have
a storm soon as it cleared
off in the night. soon after
three o'clock we gave good
bye to newyork. and I was sorry
to leave it. if we did not
go to central park.

A reduced page from Laura Hawkins'
journal; see p. 317 above

Laura Hawkins' handwriting is usually clear, but it is difficult to distinguish between her commas and periods. Her sentences often run on, particularly because her capitalization and punctuation are idiosyncratic. To facilitate readability, capitalization and much of the punctuation have been standardized in editing and her long paragraphs divided. Hawkins did not use quotation marks when recording dialogue and used apostrophes infrequently (usually inserting them in the wrong place); they have not been added or changed. Her misspellings and colloquialisms (e.g., "a going") have been retained to give the flavor of her writing; they may also give clues to local pronunciations of the time. Underlined words have been italicized. The sub-headings have been added except for two at the end which are in the original, "1898" and "Homeward Bound." Other insertions and explanations in the text are in brackets.

Victoria Aspinwall, the Long Island Studies Institute secretary transcribed the handwriting and entered the diary on the computer. I also appreciate assistance in identifying individuals from Luise Weiss at the Middle Country Public Library, Mark Rothenberg at the Patchogue-Medford Library, Martha H. Smart at the Connecticut Historical Society, Susan Carmiencke, Genealogist for the Hawkins Association, and David A. Overton and Mallory Leoniak in the Town of Brookhaven's Historian's Office.

1. Laura's parents were Sarah (Sally) Maria Yarrington (1795-1878) and Joseph Calkins Hammond (1795-1868). Joseph Hammond's father, Isaac (1763-1844), had been one of the first settlers in the "wilderness" of New Village, where he moved his family in 1790. His wife (Laura's grandmother) was Phebe Overton (born 1763). Laura's parents had four children: John N., born c. 1818, Mary, born c. 1820, Laura (1824-1916), and Joseph W. (1830-1907). (The Hammond *Genealogies* lists the four children, but gives a birth date only for Joseph. Other dates are from internment records in the Evergreen Cemetery in New Haven where several of the Hammonds and Hawkins are buried or based on ages in the manuscript census records.) The New Haven city directories list Joseph C. Hammond (Laura's father) as a joiner or cooper; in the 1850 Census (Brookhaven, NY), his occupation is carpenter. Laura and Livingston Hawkins lived next door to her parents on Chatham Street in New Haven. See Frederick S. Hammond, *History and Genealogies of the Hammond Families,* 2 vols. (Oneida, NY: Bulkhard and Ryan, 1904), 2:329; Alvin R.L. Smith, *The Overton Genealogy: The Overton Family of Long Island, New York* (N.p.: Privately printed, 1965), p. 35; Ralph Clymer Hawkins, *A Hawkins Genealogy, 1635-1939* (Reprint; Baltimore, Cateway Press, 1987), pp. 109-10; and Susan H. Carmiencke and

Bayard C. Carmiencke, *A Hawkins Genealogy Supplement,* vol. 2 (Baltimore, MD: Gateway Press, 2001), 2:66; see also Laura's final entry in the journal for additional information on the family and where they lived in Connecticut and on Long Island.

2. Their children were: Sarah Saphronia (1843-1849); Harriet (Hattie, c. 1847-1939); Emma (1849-1898); and Franklin (1853-1854). Laura and her daughter Hattie are listed in the New Haven city directories as dressmakers by the 1870s. Neither of the two daughters who reached adulthood married, so there are no descendants of Laura Hawkins. Unfortunately, no photograph of Laura or her sister Mary could be located.

3. Although Connecticut had liberalized its divorce laws in 1849, divorce was not common in the nineteenth century. Two-thirds of the divorces granted in the United States in the period 1867-1881 were initiated by women (desertion was the usual grounds). In the case of the Hawkins, however, the divorce was initiated by the husband. Livingston's petition, on a pre-printed form claimed "desertion with total neglect of all the duties of the marriage covenant on *her* part to be performed" and that she "for a period of more than *five* years last past has been guilty of such misconduct as permanently destroys the happiness of the petitioner, and defeats the purposes of the marriage relation." (The italicized words indicate the handwritten insertions on the form. Three years was the minimum period required by law. The sections crossed out on the form as not applicable were the other possible reasons for divorce: adultery, habitually intemperate, and intolerable cruelty.) Livingston had served in the Civil War during some of those five years and, according to city directories, they apparently lived in the same house until a few months before he filed for divorce. Laura did not contest the divorce petition. See Glenda Riley, *Divorce: An American Tradition* (New York: Oxford University Press, 1991), pp. 46, 79, 87; and "Samuel L. Hawkins v. Laura L. Hawkins," March 3, 1868, New Haven Divorce Records, microfilm, Connecticut State Library, Hartford.

After the divorce, Livingston (1822-1882) married Eliza Ann Poynts Hammond (1842-1903), widow of Austin R. Hammond (1833-1865); they had a daughter, Eliza Hammond Hawkins (1871-1947). Livingston's second wife was undoubtedly "Eliza A. Points Hammond," listed in the 1860 census as a twenty-one-year-old seamstress and living next door to the Hawkins in New Haven with Laura's parents. (Eliza Points was also living with the Hammonds on Long Island in 1850 when she was listed as eleven years old.) She was probably a relative. (The Hammonds and Hawkins intermarried over the generations. In fact, Hammond was the maiden name of Livingston's mother, who was also named Eliza.) Livingston and Eliza Hawkins (his second wife) are buried in the cemetery of the First Congregational Church of New Village. See note no. 17 below on the church.

4. Mary Hammond married Henry Lampson who was a silver plater in New Haven. The 1860 census lists four children in the household: Edwin, 19 years old; Carrie, 8; Laura E., 6; and Elbert, 2. In the 1870 census, Edwin is no longer living at home, the occupation of 18 year old Clara (Carrie in 1860) is dressmaker, and the 12 year old son is listed as Elliot. In the 1875 city directory, Laura E. Lampson is a teacher, and by 1885, Mary Lampson is a widow living with her daughter, Laura E., who is still teaching. Additional information about Mary Lampson's children and possible descendants could not be located.

5. Natalie A. Naylor, ed., "A 'Mid-Summer Outing': Visiting Long Island in 1893," parts 1 and 2, *Long Island Forum* 62 (Summer 1999): 8-23, 62 (Fall 1999): 4-15. Space limitations in the *Forum* meant that some of the parts of Laura's account were summarized; the full journal is in this book. Some inadvertent errors in the *Forum's* notes have been corrected here.

6. The famous (and expensive) Delmonico's Restaurant had opened in 1827 and was the best-known restaurant in the United States in the nineteenth century." It was in different locations over the years and in 1893 was on Fifth Avenue at 26th Street. It is currently located in an 1891 building at 56 Beaver Street. See Betty Gilbert Gubert, "Delmonico's," *The Encyclopedia of New York City,* edited by Kenneth T. Jackson (New Haven: Yale University Press, 1995), p. 325.

7. New Village was the early name for Centereach. Richard Bayles described it in 1885 as "an old settlement of farmers, lying on the Middle Country Road in the western part of Brookhaven town one mile north of Lake Grove. It has a population of 200, and a Congregational church. It extends along the main road three or four miles." *Long Island Handbook* (Babylon: Budget Steam Print, 1885), p. 41.

8. The accommodation train stopped at whatever station passengers wanted to board or disembark.

9. Lake Land or Lakeland was the name for the area south of Lake Ronkonkoma and was the name of the Ronkonkoma railroad station. The name survives today in Lakeland Avenue (Route 93).

10. See note no. 1 above on Joseph and Isaac Hammond, Laura's father and grandfather.

11. It was common on Long Island to put wet sand on wooden floors and sweep it up to clean the floor. Sand also might be left on the floor and swept into different designs. See Gabriel Furman, *Antiquities of Long Island,* 1874 (Reprint; Port Washington: Ira J. Friedman, 1968), p. 229.

12. The noontime dinner was the main meal of the day and supper or tea was usually a lighter meal. Mrs. Smith probably prepared a more extensive spread for her guests than the family usually ate.

13. Edmund Ruland (1825-1905) and Emeline Lee Ruland (1827-1894) are buried in the graveyard of the First Congregational Church of New Village. See note no. 17 below on the church.

14. Livingston was Laura's former husband who had divorced her in 1868 and died in 1882; see note no. 3 above. With the stigma attached to divorce in the nineteenth century, Laura may have felt uncomfortable returning to the neighborhood where her husband's second wife was still living.

15. Ambrose Barnaby Gould (1820-1905) had five children by his first wife, Charlotte, who died in 1872. He is listed in the 1850 census as a ship carpenter. The genealogical information does not list his second wife. See typescript of Gould genealogy by Kenneth Lawrence Gould, c. 1991 in Gould Vertical File, Brookhaven Town Historian's Office, Patchogue, NY.

16. As indicated earlier, Laura had been divorced (see note no. 3 above) and her former husband had died a decade before her visit. Popular usage sometimes distinguished grass and sod widows. Mary Lampson was a "sod widow" since her husband had died; when her former husband was still living, Laura Hawkins might have been called a "grass widow." The New Haven city directories sometimes list her as a widow after Livingston died. "Widow" was clearly a more acceptable designation than divorcée.

17. Gould was a member of the First Congregational Church of New Village. The church, located on the north side of Middle Country Road, east of Stony Brook Road in Lake Grove, is now preserved by the Town of Brookhaven. It is open during the summer; contact the Town Historian's office for information (631-654-7897).

18. Laura Hawkins does not mention that her former husband, Livingston Hawkins, was buried in the cemetery behind this church. Livingston's second wife was still alive (see note no. 3 above), but she attended the Methodist Church.

19. Sanford Weeks was proprietor of the Ocean Avenue Hotel, which was at the foot of Ocean Avenue in Patchogue and less than a hundred feet from the "sandy shore of the Great South Bay." The hotel advertised in 1898 that "the Ocean Avenue Hotel, throughout its interior, is one of the best appointed hotels in the United States. It is finished in hard wood: the rooms are large and airy; furniture durable, easy and cheerful in appearance; beds, bedding, springs and mattresses the very best; parlors spacious; large dining room 32-75 feet; and the cuisine first class." The rates in 1898 were $2.50 and $3.00 a day with special rates by the week. See *Argus,* 1898, no. 43, copy in Local History Collection, vertical file (hotels), Patchogue-Medford Library.

20 Sanford Weeks' wife, Augusta J. Smith Weeks, was born in Patchogue in 1831. At the age of sixteen she went to New York City and, with her sister Charlotte, manufactured furs and cloaks for twenty years. She returned to Patchogue in 1869 and married Sanford Weeks. Augusta Weeks donated a plot in the Lake View Cemetery for sailors who drowned in the wreck of the schooner *Nahum Chapin* in 1897. She died in 1901 and left property to the village for Four Sisters Park. See *Patchogue Advance,* February 25, 1930, clipping in Local History Collection, vertical files (biography), Patchogue-Medford Library .

21. A cable street railway from Bowling Green to Central Park had opened in May 1893. There were many horse-drawn streetcars or street railways in Manhattan at this time, as well as the elevated railway lines (the sisters had declined to ride the "elevated" when they first arrived in New York City). Electric streetcars (trolleys) and subways were not available in New York City until the next decade. See entries on "cable cars," "elevated railways," and "streetcars," in Jackson, *Encyclopedia of New York City,* pp. 174, 368, 1127-28.

22. Cemeteries often functioned as parks in the nineteenth century. Green-Wood Cemetery was designed to be a rural retreat and it became a tourist destination.

23. The 1893 New Haven City Directory lists Laura L. Hawkins, and her daughters Emma and Hattie living at 156 Spring Street. Mary Lampson and her daughter Laura E. lived at 15 Park Street. They had lived at different locations in earlier years.

24. A printed poem, "From a Buck board" is pasted in at this point which is about a drive in a horse-drawn carriage. It concludes, "I've had a lovely ride."

25. The phrase "Long Islands sea girt shore" may be from the song, *Rockaway,* which is reprinted in an earlier selection in this collection.

26. Laura Hawkins lived for two more decades. She died in New Haven in 1916 at the age of 92, having outlived three of her four children. Her sister, Mary Lampson, last appears in the New Haven City Directory in 1900. She may have moved out of state since she is not listed in Connecticut burial records ("Hale Index to Headstones in the State of Connecticut," typescript; copies in New Haven Historical Society and the Connecticut Historical Society in Hartford).

Laura Hawkins is buried in the Evergreen Cemetery in New Haven. Her gravestone also bears the name of two of her children who are buried in the family plot. The inscriptions on the four-and one-half-foot-high monument are: "Emma F. Hawkins [daughter, born 1849], Died 1898 / Aged 49 years; Frankie A. Hawkins [son], died March 4, 1854 / Aged 1 year; [and] Laura L. Hawkins, 1824-1916." Her older daughter, Harriet (Hattie, c. 1847-1939) is also interred in the family plot. The first child, Sarah Saphronia (1843-1849) had died on Long Island.

Scenic Long Island

Engravings by the American Bank Note Company for the *Hand-book of Long Island* (1888). *Upper left*: Sag Harbor; *upper right*, Hempstead; and *lower*, Birdseye View of Long Island, 1888.

Yacht Rendezvous, Gowanus Bay, Brooklyn:
Preparing for the Yachting Season, 1877

Central part of Jamaica Village, 1842

Holiday Excursions:
Steamers in Rockaway Inlet, 1878

Montauk Lighthouse, 1910 Photograph

Lake House, Islip, 1885

Babylon Railroad Station, c. 1880

The Beach at Fire Island, 1888

Toll Gate at Jamaica, c. 1890

The Vechte-Cortelyou House was built in Gowanus in 1699. Site of important fighting during the Battle of Long Island, it was destroyed in military demonstrations in the 1890s. The Old Stone House was rebuilt in the 1930s and is now an historic interpretive center located in J.J. Byrne Park (5th Avenue and Third Street). Engraving, c. 1867.

Rockaway Beach, 1905

Surf Hotel, Fire Island, 1885

Index

Page numbers in *italics* refer to illustrations. Most localities are indexed only under their modern names, without variant spellings. When a variant spelling is given, it follows a slash (/). Where a community and town have the same name (e.g., Huntington), following nineteenth century usage, the community is identified as "(village)," though it may not have been incorporated as a village. Surnames are indexed under their standard spelling. Notes are indexed only for names and localities not in the text; the page and number (n.) of the note is indicated.

Illustration Credits

Frontispiece, Nathaniel S. Prime, *A History of Long Island* (New York, 1845); p. viii, courtesy of the Nassau County Museum Collection, Long Island Studies Institute at Hofstra University (hereafter cited as Nassau County Museum/LISI); p. 10, W.W. Munsell, *History of Queens County* (New York, 1882); p. 15, Long Island Railroad (hereafter LIRR), *Long Island and Where to Go* (New York, 1877); p. 20, *Flatbush: Past and Present* (Brooklyn, 1901); pp. 29 and 35, Nassau County Museum/LISI; p. 43, Ettie Hedges Pennybacker, "Francisco de Miranda's Visit to Long Island in 1784," *Nassau County Historical [Society] Journal* 1 (Summer 1937): 4; p. 44, Peter Ross, *A History of Long Island* (New York, 1903); p. 45, Henry R. Stiles, *A History of the City of Brooklyn,* vol. 1 (Brooklyn, 1867); pp. 55 and 57, Nassau County Museum/LISI; p. 75, Richard M. Bayles, *Long Island Handbook* (Babylon, 1885); p. 87, LIRR, *Long Island and Where to Go* (1877); pp. 89 and 98, William S. Pelletreau, *History of Long Island* (New York, 1903); p. 99, W.W. Munsell, *History of Queens County* (New York, 1882); p. 101, Stiles, *History of Brooklyn* (1867); p. 103, William S. Pelletreau, *History of Long Island* (1903); p. 125, postcard from H.O. Korten photograph, courtesy of Gary Hammond; p. 128, John W. Barber and Henry Howe, *Historical Collections of the State of New York* (New York, 1842); p. 132, undated *Harper's,* editor's collection; p. 137, courtesy Nassau County Museum/LISI; pp. 141, 148, 167, Daniel M. Tredwell, *Personal Reminiscences of Men and Things on Long Island,* 2 vols. (Brooklyn, 1912, 1917); p. 174, Munsell, *History of Queens County* (1882); pp. 177, 178, 179, 182, 184, 185, 186, and 187, Barber and Howe, *Historical Collections* (1842); p. 192, 200 LIRR, *Hand-book of Long Island* (New York, 1888); p. 202, LIRR, *Long Island Illustrated* (1882); p. 206, Prime, *History of Long Island* (1845); p. 225 courtesy Nassau County Museum/LISI; p. 231, Walt Whitman, *Leaves of Grass* (Brooklyn, 1855); p. 233, Raymond H. Torrey, Frank Place, and Robert C. Dickinson, *New York Walk Book* (New York: American Geographical Society, 1923); p. 235, courtesy of Nassau County Museum/LISI; pp. 246, LIRR, *Long Island and Where to Go* (1877); p. 247, Bayles, *Long Island Handbook* (1885); p. 256, LIRR, *For 125 Years . . . Long Island's Main Line to the Mainland, 1834-1959* (New York: LIRR, 1959); pp. 260, 263, 267, 280, 284, LIRR, *Out on Long Island* (New York, 1890); p. 283, Bayles, *Long Island Hand-book* (1885); p. 297, F.W. Beers, *Atlas of Long Island, New York* (New York, 1873); pp. 301 and 305, courtesy, Middle Country Public Library; p. 304, drawing by Ed McManus in *The Chronicle of Centereach,* by Luise Weiss and Doris Halowitch (Centereach: Middle Country Public Library, 1989), courtesy of the Middle Country Public Library; p. 309, courtesy of Local History Room, Patchogue-Medford Library; p. 316, LIRR, *Out on Long Island* (1890); p. 319, Hofstra University Rare Books and Manuscripts, Long Island Studies Institute collection, Hofstra University Library, (hereafter cited as HU/LISI); p. 323, LIRR, *Hand-book of Long Island* (1888); p. 324, Steamers, *Harper's Weekly,* September 28, 1878, HU/LISI; p. 324, Yachts, *Harper's Weekly,* June 9, 1877, HU/LISI; p. 324, Lighthouse, courtesy of Nassau County Museum/LISI; p. 324, Jamaica, Barber and Howe, *Historical Collections* (1842); p. 325, Fire Island, LIRR, *Hand-book of Long Island* (1888); p. 325, Lake House, Bayles, *Long Island Handbook* (1885); p. 325, Toll Gate, courtesy of Nassau County Museum/LISI; p. 325, Babylon RR Station, George Brainerd photograph, courtesy of Nassau County Museum/LISI; p. 326, Vechte-Corelyou House, Stiles, *History of Brooklyn* (1867); p. 326, Rockaway, postcard, courtesy of Nassau County Museum/LISI; p. 326, Surf Hotel, Bayles, *Long Island Handbook* (1885); p. 342, HU/LISI; endpapers, editor's collection. All of the books cited are in the Long Island Studies Institute collections at Hofstra University's West Campus Library (see p. 342).

The Long Island Studies Institute

The Long Island Studies Institute is a cooperative endeavor of Hofstra University and Nassau County. This major center for the study of local and regional history was established in 1985 to foster the study of Long Island history and heritage. Two major research collections on the study of Nassau County, Long Island, and New York State are located on the second floor of the University's West Campus Library, 619 Fulton Avenue, Hempstead, New York, 11549. These collections—the Nassau County Museum collection and Hofstra University's James N. MacLean American Legion Memorial collection—are available to historians, librarians, teachers, and the general public, as well as to Hofstra students and faculty. Together they offer a rich repository of books, photographs, newspapers, maps, census records, genealogies, government documents, manuscripts, and audiovisual materials.

In addition to its research collections, the Institute sponsors publications, meetings, and conferences pertaining to Long Island and its heritage. Through its programs, the Institute complements various Long Island Studies courses offered by the University through the History Department, New College, and University College for Continuing Education. The Institute also houses the central historical research facility for the Nassau County Division of Museum Services, (516) 463-6417.

The Long Island Studies Institute is open Monday-Friday (except major holidays and between Christmas and New Years Day), 9-5 (Fridays to 4 in the summer). For further information, contact the Institute, (516) 463-6411; fax (516) 463-6441; e-mail, LISI@ Hofstra.edu; (www.hofstra.edu/LISI).

The Institute collections and reading room are on the second floor of the West Campus Library, which is located at 619 Fulton Avenue, Hempstead, New York.

Long Island Studies Institute Publications

Heart of the Lakes Publishing/Empire State Books:

Aerospace Heritage of Long Island, by Joshua Stoff (1989).

Algonquian Peoples of Long Island from Earliest Times to 1700, by John A. Strong (1997; paperback edition, 2000).

Blessed Isle: Hal B. Fullerton and His Image of Long Island, 1897-1927, by Charles L. Sachs (1991).

Evoking a Sense of Place, edited by Joann P. Krieg (1988).

From Airship to Spaceship: Long Island in Aviation and Spaceflight, by Joshua Stoff (1991). For younger readers.

From Canoes to Cruisers: The Maritime Heritage of Long Island, by Joshua Stoff (1994). For younger readers.

History of Nassau County Community Place-Names, by Richard Winsche (1999).

Journeys on Old Long Island: Travelers' Accounts, Contemporary Descriptions, and Residents' Reminiscences, 1744-1893, edited by Natalie A. Naylor (2002).

Long Island and Literature, by Joann P. Krieg (1989).

Long Island Architecture, edited by Joann P. Krieg (1991).

Long Island: The Suburban Experience, edited by Barbara M. Kelly (1990).

Long Island Women: Activists and Innovators, edited by Natalie A. Naylor and Maureen O. Murphy (1998).

Making a Way to Freedom: A History of African Americans on Long Island, by Lynda R. Day (1997).

Nassau County: From Rural Hinterland to Suburban Metropolis, edited by Joann P. Krieg and Natalie A. Naylor (2000).

Robert Moses: Single-Minded Genius, edited by Joann P. Krieg (1989; reprinted 2000).

Roots and Heritage of Hempstead Town, edited by Natalie A. Naylor (1994).

Theodore Roosevelt: Many-Sided American, edited by Natalie A. Naylor, Douglas Brinkley, and John Allen Gable (1992).

"The People Called Quakers": Records of Long Island Friends, 1671-1703, edited by Natalie A. Naylor (2001).

To Know the Place: Exploring Local History, edited by Joann P. Krieg and Natalie A. Naylor (rev. edition, 1995).

"We Are Still Here!" The Algonquian Peoples of Long Island Today, by John A. Strong (1996; 2d edition, 1998).

Long Island Studies Institute:

Bibliography of Dissertations and Theses on Long Island Studies, by
    Natalie A. Naylor (1999).
*Calderone Theatres on Long Island: An Introductory Essay and
    Description of the Calderone Theatre Collection at Hofstra University,*
    by Miriam Tulin (1991).
Cumulative Index, Nassau County Historical Society Journal, 1958-1988,
    by Jeanne M. Burke (1989; reprinted with Addendum, 1990-2000,
    2000).
Exploring African-American History, edited by Natalie A. Naylor (1991;
    reprinted 1995).
*Index of Articles on Long Island Studies in Journals and Conference
    Volumes,* by Natalie A. Naylor (2001).
Long Island Quaker Minutes, 1671-1703, edited by Natalie A. Naylor
    (2001). A line-by-line literal transcription; see also *"The People
    Called Quakers"* published by Empire State Books.
To Know the Place: Teaching Local History, edited by Joann P. Krieg
    (1986). See also rev. 2d. edition, *To Know the Place: Exploring Local
    History*, published by Heart of the Lakes.
Nassau County at 100: The Past and Present in Photographs, by Linda B.
    Martin (1999).

Greenwood Press:

Contested Terrain: Power, Politics, and Participation in Suburbia, edited
    by Marc L. Silver and Martin Melkonian (1995).
Suburbia Re-examined, edited by Barbara M. Kelly (1989).

About the Editor

Natalie A. Naylor is Professor Emerita from Hofstra University where
she taught American and Long Island history. As director of the Long Island
Studies Institute (1985-2000), she organized many conferences on various
aspects of Long Island's history and heritage and oversaw the publication of
thirty-one titles. Among the Institute books Dr. Naylor edited or co-edited
are: *Theodore Roosevelt: Many-Sided American* (1992); *Roots and Heritage of
Hempstead Town* (1994); *To Know the Place: Exploring Long Island History*
(1995); *Long Island Women: Activists and Innovators* (1998); and *Nassau County:
From Rural Hinterland to Suburban Metropolis* (2000). She has published many
articles on Long Island and educational history and has been editor of the *Nassau
County Historical Society Journal* since 1991.